Adven ...

Northern
California

Lee Foster & Mary Lou Janson

HUNTER

Hunter Publishing, Inc.
130 Campus Drive, Edison NJ 08818
(732) 225 1900, (800) 255 0343, Fax (732) 417 0482
e-mail: hunterpub@emi.net

In Canada
1220 Nicholson Rd., Newmarket, Ontario
Canada L3Y 7V1, (800) 399 6858

In the UK
Windsor Books International
The Boundary, Wheatley Road
Garsington, Oxford 0X44 9EJ
England, 01865 361122, Fax 01865 361133

ISBN 1-55650-821-2

© 1998 Lee Foster & Mary Lou Janson

Maps by Kim André & Lissa K. Dailey
(© 1998 Hunter Publishing, Inc.)

Photos: *El Capitan* (front cover); *Lady Bird Johnson Grove,
Redwood National Park* (back cover)
All photos by Lee Foster

For complete information about the hundreds of other travel
guides offered by Hunter Publishing, visit our Web site at:

www.hunterpublishing.com

Dedication

We dedicate this book to the immediate family members with whom we have shared the adventure of travel in Northern California. For Mary Lou, that's Russ and Barbara. For Lee, that's Sheila, Nancy, Mary Jane, Colleen, Bart, Karin, and Paul.

About the Authors

Since teaming up personally and professionally in 1996, Lee Foster and Mary Lou Janson have crisscrossed Northern California to research this book. For Lee, this quest has been a pleasant re-discovery of a terrain he has watched for the past 25 years. Mary Lou, new to California, has brought an outsider's inquisitiveness and fresh perspective to the task. Foster and Janson also publish travel writing/photography widely in magazines, newspapers, and on the Internet. Both are members of the Society of American Travel Writers.

Please send your comments and tips for future editions of this book to the authors at Foster Travel Publishing, PO Box 5715, Berkeley, CA 94705, 510/549-2202, email lee@fostertravel.com.

Acknowledgments

We wish to thank the knowledgeable people from various parts of Northern California who have helped us with information and insight during our research. We salute all the talented and dedicated people in tourism who make the travel experience in Northern California so extraordinary for everyone. Unfortunately, space does not permit us to list the hundreds of people who helped us. But let the following represent all the good tourism folks in their regions. Considering Northern California as a whole, we thank Fred Sater (California Division of Tourism). Looking at the individual areas, we thank Helen Chang (San Francisco), Megan Smith (San Jose), Harry Hamilton (Oakland), Gerry Coles (Marin), Cammie Conlon and Sharon Rooney (Mendocino), Heather Parker (Redwood Country), Gail Spangler (Sonoma), Jan Austerman and Catherine Boire (Napa), Bonnie Sharp (Shasta-Cascade), Lucy Steffens (Sacramento), Phil Weidinger (Lake Tahoe), Keith Walklet (Yosemite), Diane Mandeville (Monterey), and Katrina Paz (Santa Cruz).

Contents

Introduction

Northern California is one of the world's great places for adventure travel.

The terrain is stunningly beautiful and relatively well protected. The coastlines of Big Sur and Monterey, the views of Yosemite and Lake Tahoe, and the cultivated beauty of the Wine Country are just a few of this vast region's enticing elements. Citizens of Northern California have made a huge commitment to purchase choice lands for the public and restrict development.

The weather is a major reason adventure travel flourishes here year round. While other areas are oppressed by extreme heat, cold, or annoying insects for much of the year, Northern California provides a congenial environment for some outdoor activities at all times. Dependable waves lure surfers to Santa Cruz and a heavy snowfall attracts skiers to Lake Tahoe. Temperature, precipitation, wind, and water currents contribute to the right conditions for doing some kind of adventure on land, in the water, or even in the air.

Just about any type of outdoor adventure is possible here. Scuba divers relish Monterey Bay while, a few miles away, skydivers are leaping from planes at Marina Airport. Horseback riders can explore the back country at Mammoth Lakes and kayakers can enjoy the placid beauty of Tomales Bay. One wonders if there is any adventure travel activity you can't do in Northern California.

Moreover, the people of Northern California are a congenial group. They are generally progressive and innovative, a racially, religiously, and ethnically diversified group. Their innovations range from contributing to the development of modern mountain biking, a movement that owes part of its existence to the bikers of Marin County, to the development of the modern microchip in Silicon Valley, a phenomenon that can be enjoyed at the Intel Museum north of San Jose.

Standard touring opportunities of interest to all travelers also abound here, from art and history museums to amusement parks. San Francisco, a wonderful place to base your Northern California exploration, is a perennial favorite of worldwide travelers. Add to that such desirable amenities as interesting lodgings and exceptional dining, and you have the ultimate in adventure destinations.

■ History

Northern California has always been an adventure. California first existed, for the European mind, as an image in a 15th-century Spanish novel. The fantasy involved Amazons, voluptuous and self-reliant women, in a terrestrial paradise.

To the Miwok and other Native Americans, Northern California was indeed such a paradise. Food was abundant and it is said that the Miwoks had no word for war. Salmon choked the streams in the spawning season. Fairly tame herds of deer and tule elk awaited the bow-and-arrow harvester. Oak trees invariably yielded copious amounts of acorns, a reliable element in the daily diet.

When Europeans first encountered Northern California, the element of adventure was strong. Sir Francis Drake landed at Point Reyes, north of San Francisco, to repair his ships in 1579. Ironically, he never saw San Francisco Bay because Angel Island obscured the entrance.

The Russians eyed California from their base in Sitka, Alaska. California meant sea otter furs, which could be sold in the fashion markets of the day. California also appeared to be far enough south to grow grain and vegetables that would sustain the Russian colony in Alaska.

The Spanish reacted to the Russians with some alarm. To control the territory, the Spanish crown enlisted the Franciscans, led by Junipero Serra, to set up a chain of 21 missions in California from 1769-1832. The missions would subdue and Christianize the Indians. A parallel pueblo settlement, near each mission, would establish a Spanish secular presence.

Whaling and trading ships intruded into this Spanish realm, as recorded by Henry Dana and other observers. Dana talked of California cattle hides, known as "California banknotes," that were sailed off the cliffs to the waiting boats below. New England shoe manufacturers were a ready market for the skins.

But, as in all adventure, there were elements of the unexpected. California's modern founding was indeed a total accident. The event occurred on the American River, east of Sacramento, in January of 1848. At Coloma, James Marshall, who was working for the Swiss entrepreneur of Sacramento, John Sutter, discovered some shiny nuggets at a sawmill he was building along the river. The substance proved to be gold and the news could not be suppressed. Within two years, over 300,000 miners stampeded to California from all around the globe in one of the most frenzied voluntary migrations in human history.

Yet the true wealth of California proved to be, not in gold, but in agriculture. The Central Valley of California became one of the most productive agricultural areas on Earth. The coastal valleys, such as Napa and Sonoma, became prime wine-producing regions.

As California developed, with industries from agriculture to high tech, there was a strong ethic of protecting the environment and setting land aside for future generations to enjoy. Possibly the most important historical story in California is that so much public land has been saved and held in public trust.

If you have seen desecrated coastlines around the US and abroad, you will appreciate that the Northern California coast, such as Mendocino or Big Sur, has a relative absence of billboards. Even the few homes allowed for the elite, such as those at Sea Ranch in Mendocino, require coastal access through the property for the public.

Northern California's modern history has been highly entrepreneurial. Businesses born in garages have become giants in the high-growth, high-tech world of computers and computer software. These innovators, and their impact on our day-to-day lives, are celebrated at The Tech Museum in Silicon Valley's San Jose. The area has also become a mecca for artists, athletes, entertainers, writers, and scholars who choose to make their homes here.

The modern adventure traveler epitomizes this spirit of discovery. One quest may be a hike to see the spring wildflowers in Point Reyes at Chimney Rock in May and, perhaps, to view a few linger-

ing whales slowly make their way up the coast. Another realizable
dream might be a backpacking trip into the Yosemite High Country to commune with oneself. California has the exterior landscape to stimulate a whole range of interior adventures.

■ Geography

Northern California is a geographic entity of wondrous elements.
The delightful complexity of the area's geography allows an unusually wide range of adventure travel activities.

Geologically, of course, the **San Andreas Fault** remains restlessly
below everything. There was the Great Earthquake of 1906 and
the more recent Quake of 1989, which wiped out Santa Cruz, a
special tourism area now reborn. On the earthquake walk at Point
Reyes National Seashore you can see a fence that ripped 16 feet
apart as the earth slid sideways in 1906.

The coast is a defining geographic element of Northern California. Simply stated, the **Big Sur** and **Mendocino** coasts are two of
the most stunning automotive drives on earth. The joy of hiking,
kayaking, and camping along this coast could absorb a lifetime.

Behind the coast is a low range of coastal mountains, stretching
up and down northern California. In this narrow belt live the redwood trees, the world's tallest trees, which thrive on coastal moisture and condensation from fog. There are many special places to
study these trees like Redwood National Park at Orick, site of the
world's tallest tree.

Beyond the coastal mountains are the favored valleys, such as
Napa, **Sonoma**, and **Monterey**, which are sunny but relatively
cool. Here the choicest grapes of California are grown. In these ar
eas, bicyclists can savor some of the loveliest backcountry available anywhere, such as Pope Valley east of Napa.

Beyond the coastal valleys is the **Great Valley**, one of the most fecund agricultural areas on earth for everything from rice to cotton,
beef to almonds. In the Great Valley, along the Pacific flyway refuges north of Sacramento, you can still watch the sky darken as
the mass migrations of ducks and geese get underway in autumn.

On a clear day you can see beyond this valley, even from the coastal mountain tops, such as Mt. Diablo in the East Bay. What you see is the **Sierra Nevada**, the "snowy mountain" as named by the first Spanish explorers. This is where the wintersports of Northern California are celebrated, especially downhill and cross-country skiing around Lake Tahoe.

■ Climate

The climate of Northern California is relatively benign, compared to other parts of the country. Adventure travel activities can be enjoyed year round, but a knowledge of the climate is critical.

San Francisco has a cool summer. In fact, Mark Twain said that the "coldest winter I ever spent was my first summer in San Francisco."

The rains of Northern California may last from October through April, pelting the coast, especially the north coast from Eureka to Crescent City. Further inland, the rains are blocked, creating more arid environments, except in the high mountains. This causes the precipitation to fall as snow on the west faces of the Sierra.

From April through October there is little rain, except for summer thunderstorms in the mountains. In this sunny and dry period, many adventure travel enthusiasts venture forth, secure in the knowledge that weather will not impede their bike, hike, or rafting trips.

Because of the semi-arid climate, the summer traveler is relatively free from insect attacks.

Temperatures in the summer sizzle in the Central Valley, but the heat remains manageable in the coastal valleys.

In winter, the ski areas around Lake Tahoe seldom get devastatingly cold, as do ski areas in other states. Typically, the afternoon sun and clear sky around Tahoe will warm the skier. Snow conditions are often good from November to April.

■ Flora & Fauna

The flora of greatest interest to the traveler might well be the lavish displays of spring wildflowers, especially the California poppy, which blooms ubiquitously. **Chimney Rock** in Point Reyes and the **Mendocino Headlands** are some of the choicest places to experience this wildflower outburst in April and May.

The special redwood environment along the coast is a world-class experience in itself, primarily from **Muir Woods** in Marin County, immediately north of San Francisco, to **Redwood National Park**, along the north coast at Orick. *(Primarily* is used advisedly here because, while the Redwood Country is usually considered to be north of San Francisco, there are also some impressive groves and parks to the south, such as at **Big Basin Redwoods State Park** near Santa Cruz.)

Oak trees in a sere brown grassland might be said to be the most classic landscape of northern California. It is amazing to think that grizzly bears, now extinct in California, were the dominant residents of these grasslands only 200 years ago.

Much fauna of great interest to adventure travelers in Northern California tends to be in the sea. The largest animals are the whales. **Gray whales** migrate south along the California coast, December-February, moving from their summer homes in the Arctic to the warm birthing and mating lagoons in Baja, Mexico, such as Scammon's Lagoon. The whales return north along the coast March-May. Whale watching is popular from both shore and boat.

Another treasured animal in the region is the California **sea otter**, which can be seen in abundance if you choose to kayak on Monterey Bay. It could be said that the sea otter was the animal that provoked the settlement of California. Russians came to hunt the sea otter because of the European demand for the furs. The Spanish became nervous about the Russian presence, so they set up missions and pueblos to counter the incursion.

Northern California is also a major migration flyway for birds, both in the Central Valley refuges mentioned earlier and at estuarine places along the coast, such as Elkhorn Slough near Monterey.

A special insect, the **Monarch butterfly**, is another celebrated fauna of California. Monarchs congregate at **Natural Bridges State Park**, north of Santa Cruz, and on trees in **Pacific Grove** on the Monterey Peninsula. What is wondrous about the Monarch is that they make a long-term migration, taking them into the valleys around Mexico City and back on a grand circle migration. Individuals in the species perish along the route, but somehow the collective knowledge of where and when to fly persists in the genetic heritage of the Monarchs.

■ Government/Economy

California has been governed by individuals rather than parties. The electorate will zigzag back and forth between a Jerry Brown and a Ronald Reagan, voting for the person who articulates the passionate ideas of the times.

There is relatively strong bi-partisan support for the main issues that affect the adventure traveler. The electorate has invested heavily in national parks, state parks, and special regional parks, like the East Bay Regional Parks in the Alameda/Contra Costa county area east of San Francisco.

The conservation and heritage ethic is widespread, from recycling to regulating toxic dumping. John Muir started his Sierra club, an organization dedicated to protecting and preserving the natural environment, in Northern California. You can make a pilgrimage to Muir's house in Martinez.

If you were a bird flying over or a fish swimming in San Francisco Bay, chances are your life would be happier in the 1990s than in the 1970s. While the struggles against further environmental degradation continue, Northern California is a world leader in environmental awareness and protection. Humboldt State University at Arcata recently set before its students the question of determining whether the school mascot, the Lumberjack, should be replaced by the name of an endangered species, the marble murrelet. The murrelet is a bird that lives in the tallest branches of the redwoods. The murrelet partisans lost, but the notable event was that the vote was taken. If the murrelets had won,

Humboldt State would have been the first college in the country with an endangered species for a mascot.

Northern California's economy is fairly resilient and diversified. Much of the US technology revolution, including hardware and software, comes out of the **Silicon Valley**, home of the Intel chip makers and Apple Computers, to name just two luminaries. The Bay Area is a major center for bio-technology research. The agricultural economy of Northern California remains strong as long as abundant water and relatively cheap energy make production and distribution easy. San Francisco and Oakland rank as major world trading ports, particularly in light of the potential economic boom in and around the Pacific Rim.

■ People/Culture

The arrival of many types of people during the Gold Rush had a profound effect on Northern California. No single group or creed became dominant.

A *carpe diem* aspect of the Northern California sensibility was inspired by the Great Earthquake of 1907. If the basis of life is geologic instability, some savoring of the present might be considered.

While California has at times shown its ugly prejudice against many groups, such as the Chinese, African Americans, and Japanese, the truth is that California also has been a land of tolerance and opportunity. The most recent wave of migration to Northern California from countries in Asia has resulted in a substantial intellectual source for the San Francisco Bay Area. In fact, Asian American students have been so successful at the state's most prestigious university, the University of California Berkeley, that their numbers have been curtailed, at times, in the interest of greater student body diversity.

Northern Californians are an energetic and inquisitive folk. They want to get out and explore the landscape, and they know that they live in one of the world's more favored environments.

■ How to Use This Book

Areas of Northern California

For this book we have divided Northern California into six regions, the San Francisco Bay Area and five outlying areas, sweeping clockwise around the region.

Chapter 2 considers the **San Francisco Bay Area**, where a traveler entering the region is likely to arrive. This is also where the main local population base of adventure travelers lives. The San Francisco Bay Area offers substantial touring prospects and many enticing adventures, from bicycling along the Golden Gate Promenade and across the Golden Gate Bridge to hiking the East Bay Parks, such as Briones.

Chapter 3 portrays the **North Coast and Redwood Country**, the area north of San Francisco. The adventures here range from whale watching along the Mendocino bluffs in January to meditative hikes in the quiet of the redwoods, such as at Lady Bird Johnson Grove in Redwood National Park.

Chapter 4 covers the **Napa-Sonoma Wine Country**, where some culinary and wine tasting adventures await you. But that's not all. The area has **Calistoga**, the busiest soaring port in Northern California. Glider guides are ready to take you for a ride – pilot in front, you in back. At dawn you can also float over the vineyards in a balloon.

Chapter 5 outlines the **Shasta Cascade Region**, a vast and lesser known wilderness and lake area of California. Shasta Cascade is the main houseboating place in Northern California and the West, primarily on Shasta Lake. If you are a hiker or backpacker, you will also enjoy one of our lesser-known national parks, **Lassen**.

Chapter 6 takes you east from San Francisco into the mountains, **The Sierra and Gold Country: Lake Tahoe and Yosemite**. This is the great downhill and cross-country ski area of California, especially around Lake Tahoe. The Gold Country, celebrating the 150th Anniversary of the discovery of gold from 1998-2000, also hosts some special adventure travel opportunities, such as raft-

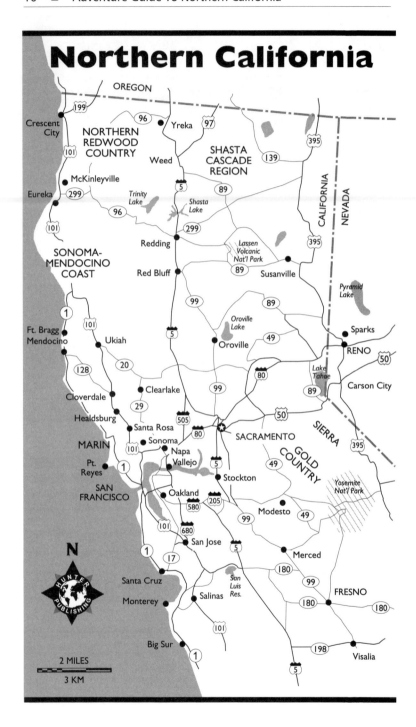

Northern California

OREGON

Crescent City

199

96 · Yreka 97

NORTHERN
REDWOOD
COUNTRY

101

Weed

SHASTA
CASCADE
REGION

395

139

McKinleyville

Eureka 299

Trinity
Lake

Shasta
Lake

89

96

299

CALIFORNIA

NEVADA

Redding

SONOMA-
MENDOCINO
COAST

Red Bluff

Lassen
Volcanic
Nat'l Park

89

Susanville

395

Pyramid
Lake

1

99

89

Ft. Bragg
Mendocino

101

Ukiah

Oroville
Lake

Sparks

5

49

Oroville

RENO

50

128

20

80

Lake
Tahoe

Carson City

Cloverdale

Clearlake

99

89

29

Healdsburg

50

Santa Rosa

505

MARIN

80

SACRAMENTO

SIERRA

395

Sonoma

101

Napa

GOLD
COUNTRY

Pt.
Reyes

1

Vallejo

5

49

SAN
FRANCISCO

Stockton

Yosemite
Nat'l Park

Oakland

580

205

99

Modesto

49

101

680

San Jose

5

N

1

17

Merced

180

Santa Cruz

San
Luis
Res.

99

HUNTER
PUBLISHING

Monterey

Salinas

180

FRESNO

101

180

2 MILES

Big Sur

1

198

Visalia

3 KM

5

ing. The South Fork of the American River is the busiest rafting river in the West.

Chapter 7 covers the area south from San Francisco, **Monterey/Santa Cruz** and **The Big Sur Coast**. The coastal mountains of this region boast some of the loveliest state parks in California, outstanding for hiking and backpacking. The Big Sur Coast is one of America's most scenic drives, with backpacking access into the Ventana Wilderness.

How Chapters are Organized

Touring

Each chapter begins with **touring** information, which will orient you to the area, regardless of the type of adventure travel activity that interests you. We'll cover the principal sights in the area. The chapter is then divided into the various **travel adventures** you can find. Finally, the five chapters covering the area beyond San Francisco Bay close with a brief **personal essay** on some aspect of adventure travel in that region.

Adventures On Wheels

Chances are part of your adventure will be on wheels, so we're putting that first.

Scenic Drives are a favorite Northern California adventure, especially on the coast roads, such as in Mendocino and Big Sur, or on the back-country roads, such as Highway 49 in the **Gold Country**.

Bicycling and inline skating are popular in all the California regions. We'll share with you some of our favorite bike trips in each area and recommend a local bike shop for rentals and repairs.

Railroading is an interesting part of Northern California travel, whether one considers special scenic rail trips (**Roaring Camp** in Santa Cruz, the **Skunk Train** in Mendocino, or the **Wine Train** in Napa, or **Amtrak**, the workhorse of railroading. Amtrak offers a comfortable, viable way to get from San Francisco to Yosemite.

On Foot

 Hiking and backpacking can be enjoyed in every region. We'll share with you some favorite, moderate hikes for each territory. There are also some surprising backpacking opportunities, such as staying overnight on Angel Island in San Francisco Bay.

Spelunking (cave exploring) opportunities in the Shasta Cascade area at Shasta Caverns and other sites will take you into the scenic underground.

Rock climbing is popular at sites such as Pinnacles National Monument, near Monterey. The numerous indoor and outdoor "rock gyms", found throughout Northern California, are a new and safe way to experience this sport. Major mountains, such as Lassen and Shasta, can sometimes be climbed alone, and at other times, only with expert guidance, depending on weather conditions.

On Horseback

 Horseback riding may be short excursions, such as the Chanslor Ranch rides on the beach at Bodega Bay, or more ambitious back country trips, such as Mammoth Lakes trips into the eastern Sierras.

On Water

 Rafting is a big part of the Northern California adventure experience, especially on the South Fork of the American River in the Gold Country. The South Fork of the American River is the busiest rafting river in the West. Other rivers to raft include the Klamath and the Trinity.

Kayaking is popular at coastal locations, such as Monterey Bay and San Francisco Bay. Canoeing takes place on the Russian River and the Big River in Mendocino.

Boating and houseboating occur on the major reservoirs and lakes. Sailing and windsurfing are popular especially on San Francisco Bay. We'll indicate some sailing excursions and windsurfing spots you might enjoy.

Scuba is popular at Monterey, where there is an unusual walk-in beach park, complete with showers, allowing you to venture eas-

Introduction

ily into the kelp beds. Monterey is a favorite place for people to get their dive certification. At the North Coast parks, such as Van Damme, you'll find skin divers searching for abalone on the rocks. Waters in California are definitely cold, so this is wetsuit country.

Fishing enthusiasts seek trout in the mountain streams and salmon or halibut from charter boats all along the coast. During the winter gray whale migration, charter boats sometimes become whale watching platforms.

On Snow

The Sierra is the primary snow adventure area, though some **cross-country** and **alpine skiing** also occurs in the Shasta Cascade. At Yosemite you can cross-country ski out to a remote but elegant hut at Glacier Point, spend the night, and wake up to see pristine views of Half Dome. The great downhill ski areas are around Lake Tahoe. You could spend a week there and enjoy a different major downhill venue each day.

Snowmobiling and **snowboarding** also are popular at Lake Tahoe. A few dogsledding providers are listed as well.

Snowshoe hiking is making a comeback with lighter, smaller showshoes. Some cross-country ski resorts, such as Kirkwood, now rent snowshoes.

In The Air

Scenic Flights, including some unusual variations, are favored ways to enjoy the views throughout Northern California. In Sonoma you can fly aloft in a vintage biplane with an open air cockpit. At Marina Beach north of Monterey you can be the passenger in an ultralight skimming over the dunes.

Balloonists are plentiful in the scenic Wine Country region encompassing Napa and Sonoma counties.

Soaring takes place at Calistoga, where the warm thermals rising off the Napa Valley hills carry the gliders aloft.

Hang gliding is popular especially at Marina Beach north of Monterey or at Fort Funston in San Francisco.

Parasailing can be enjoyed in the Santa Cruz harbor and on Shasta Lake.

Where To Stay & Eat

 Northern California has an outstanding selection of lodgings. One special category is the bed-and-breakfast in an interesting historic structure, probably a Victorian house, managed by professional and sociable innkeepers. Murphy's Inn in Grass Valley would be an example.

Lodgings are rated as follows:	
$	up to $60/night
$$	from $60-$130
$$$	$130 and higher.

Northern California is not an inexpensive place to travel. But almost every lodging has some special deal or discount, and most people don't pay the rack rate. Don't hesitate to ask for a discount if you are part of a qualifying group. A $$$ lodging may in fact sell for $$, but prudence requires us to list their highest published rate for the purposes of this book. Also, don't hesitate to bargain if you have the temperament to do so. Hoteliers know that there are few things more perishable than an unsold hotel room. There are budget lodgings, but we are recommending them only when they show you something special about Northern California, which is our goal here. Some $ lodgings in our selections are true originals, such as a night in the Pigeon Point Lighthouse, now a hostel, covered in the Santa Cruz section. Many of the lodgings recommended are places at which we have stayed.

When making travel decisions based on budget, keep in mind that California's sales and use tax is 8¼%. There may be local taxes as well as lodging taxes that vary from area-to-area as well.

Dining in Northern California is a major travel pleasure. A huge amount of creative energy now goes into food production and preparation. This starts with the boutique farmer, probably an organic farmer who pioneered techniques that are now mainstream. The produce may be sold in a local farmer's market, where celebrity chefs select the best from each seasonal harvest.

In Northern California, the chef is a status figure, an artist, on par with the visual or literary artist. Ingredients, preparation, and presentation are all part of the drama. Culinary schools abound. A new generation of chefs stands ready to take over whenever an icon stumbles. In this guide, $ will represent lunches less than $10 and dinners under $15. Sometimes the most interesting places are relatively economical, such as the fabled Samoa Cookhouse, near Eureka, where you'll never leave hungry. For midrange meals, $$ means lunch under $15 and dinner under $25. Higher-priced meals are identified with the $$$ symbol. Of course, the total price varies according to what and how much you order. If you choose any of the restaurants we recommend, you will discover culinary delights. Evans in South Lake Tahoe and Chez Panisse in Berkeley are fine-dining experiences that you will long remember. Many of the restaurants recommended are places where we have dined recently.

Camping & RV

Northern California presents an outstanding range of camping and RV opportunities.

Most of the **camping sites** are part of the extensive state and national park system and can be reserved with a call to a reservation system. The number for national parks is ☎ 800-436-7275; for state parks reservations, ☎ 800-444-7275. Besides parks, there are national forests in California with campgrounds, some of which are reservable (☎ 800-280-2267). Regional park systems provide further options. For each of our six areas of California, we'll suggest some good camping and RV options. For more popular areas, you may need to reserve space several months in advance.

The **RV options** include dependable KOAs and a cluster of independent RV parks. Many of the independents are part of an organization called the California Travel Park Association. Their California *RV and Camping Guide* is available from ESG Mail Services, ☎ 916-823-1076; PO Box 5578, Auburn, CA 95604; Web site www.campgrounds.com.

■ Travel Information

When to Go

Every month of the year offers outstanding adventure travel options in Northern California, but you need to be conscious of the season.

For example, whale watching is good from late December to early May, with December and January the peak viewing months. At that time the whales are moving south; March-May they proceed north.

Ski season runs from late November to early March in the Sierra.

The rainy season lasts roughly October-April, but when it isn't raining the days can be brilliantly blue and the skies unusually clear, swept free by wind of any fog, haze, or pollution.

Summers in the Central Valley can be so warm that air-conditioning is a survival requirement in your car and your accommodations. Summers can be foggy along the coast, something that disappoints many summer travelers.

The spring wildflower season, March-April at sea level, can be inspiring, especially at places such as Point Reyes. The wildflowers will peak in July at Lassen Park or Yosemite, due to the altitude.

Clothing & Gear

- Protection from wind and rain can be important for the Northern California traveler. Wind can cause hypothermia even in relatively warm periods if you happen to get wet and chilled. Rain in the mountains in summer, in the form of thunderstorms, catches many travelers by surprise. Always carry a full-body poncho to protect yourself.

- Dress in layers, so you can add and subtract clothing as needed. A daypack to store your emergency protective gear is invaluable.

- Sturdy hiking boots or shoes that enclose the foot and support the ankle are very important. Make sure that you have broken in any new boots before a trip.

■ Good maps are essential. AAA maps of California are indispensable for the roads. Topographical maps, obtainable at outdoor gear stores, such as REI, are useful if you are hiking or backpacking. Be sure to carry a compass and a whistle if you are hiking in remote areas.

■ Packing water is critical. It's amazing how much you can sweat doing adventure travel activities, and drinking from lakes, streams, and rivers without purifying the water is generally unwise.

■ Sunscreen is important at sea level, but even more so in the mountains, where elevation allows greater penetration of UV rays.

When considering dress, be aware that San Francisco is comparatively formal. For San Francisco, women will be comfortable in suits or pants and dresses with a jacket or light coat. Men should wear light-to medium-weight suits and sports clothes. An all-weather coat is advisable for cool evenings. The dress code for restaurants in Northern California outside of San Francisco tends to be more casual. San Francisco's brisk, windy climate calls for warmer clothing. Comfortable walking shoes are advised because the city can best be explored on foot.

Transportation & Driving

A car is useful for most of Northern California travel. For the San Francisco area, BART (Bay Area Rapid Transit) is good if you want to stay within the urban area.

A few other destinations have well-organized public transportation. For example, the ski shuttles in South Lake Tahoe can get you to the slopes from your lodging without the hassle of a car.

Keep your car in good condition. Consider buying an emergency towing service resource, such as AAA, in case you get stranded. A cellular phone should be considered as an added safety device, in case you need to summon help in a remote area.

The major airports for Northern California are in the San Francisco Bay area. They are at San Francisco, Oakland, and San Jose. Smaller airports in outlying areas can save you substantial time if your adventure time-budget is short. For example, it takes about five hours to drive from the San Francisco Bay Area to either Eureka or Redding. Eureka, Redding, South Lake Tahoe, Sacramento, and Monterey all have regional airports served by the commuter partners of main air carriers. Sacramento, the state capital, is the biggest of the small airports.

Major rental car agencies are available at all these major and minor airports, as well as in the main cities.

All-Weather Driving Tips

■ Always carry chains when driving in the mountains from November-April. Snow can fall in huge amounts and immobilize travel. Even vehicles with four-wheel drive may be forced to turn back.

■ Watch for slippery wet roads along the coast, even in summer when there is no rain. Condensation from fog can make roads slick.

■ For weather and road information for Northern California, call the Caltrans 24-hour service and information numbers, ☎ 916-445-7623 for the region and 800-427-7623 for statewide information.

Sustainable Adventure Travel

Maintaining the quality of the travel experience is the joint goal of providers and users in adventure travel. Several prudent trends have been on the rise resulting in more environmental responsibility.

Watching wildlife and observing plantlife, rather than destroying them, is one of the most obvious examples. Viewing has replaced hunting and collecting as a non-consumptive pastime. Observing tidepools, rather than gathering samples from them, and leaving all the wildflowers for others to see is commendable, and is the law. The "leave only footprints, take only memories" ethic has taken hold. In the wilderness, take out everything that you backpacked in.

Lower impact consumption, such as seeing Northern California from two-wheeled bikes rather than from four-wheeled cars, is on the rise. The kayak, rather than the outboard, is a parallel expression of these trends.

Northern California is in better shape than most tourism areas on this sustainability issue. Vocal supporters of the conservation effort are watching over the scene to make sure that public areas are well maintained and preserved.

Information Sources

One of the exciting information changes in recent years is the emergence of the world wide web on the **Internet** that allows travelers to access an amazing amount of highly specific information. We are includng the website for all the major tourism entities in this introduction. In the individual chapters, we repeat the website for the major tourism sources, but can't put in websites for every minor entity, due to space limitations.

The following is a list of Northern California's major tourism information sources. Please note that some organizations may charge a slight fee for publications or to cover mailing costs.

California Office of Tourism, ☎ 916-322-2881 or 800-862-2543, 1121 L Street, Suite 103, Sacramento, CA 95814; Web site www.gocalif.ca.gov.

The state has three Welcome Centers in Northern California dispensing tourism information. The first is at **Pier 39** in San Francisco, corner of Beach and Embarcadero streets. The second is on **Highway 101**, north of San Francisco, in **Rohnert Park** at ☎ 707-586-3795; 5000 Roberts Lake Road. The third is along **Interstate 5** in the Shasta Cascade area at the Deschutes Exit in Anderson.

If the weather outlook causes some concern for your adventure travel activities, contact the people with the most accurate predictive technology. **The National Weather Service** offers a taped message about Bay Area and Northern California weather at ☎ 415-936-1212.

San Francisco

San Francisco Convention and Visitors Bureau, Visitor Information Center, ☎ 415-391-2000; PO Box 429097, San Francisco, CA 94142-9097; Web site: www.sfvisitor.org.

Information Hotline: ☎ 415-391-2001.

The Visitor Center for drop-in traffic is at **Hallidie Plaza,** Powell and Market streets.

For recreational information on the national parks around San Francisco, contact the **Golden Gate National Recreation Area, Marin Headlands Visitor Center,** ☎ 415-331-1540; Building 948, Fort Barry, Sausalito, CA 94965.

Marin County

Marin County Convention & Visitors Bureau, ☎ 415-472-7470, Avenue of the Flags, San Rafael, CA 94903; Web site www.marin.org.

West Marin Chamber of Commerce, ☎ 415-663-9232; PO Box 1045, Point Reyes Station, CA 94956; Web site www.nbn.com/home/wmw/chamber.

East Bay

Oakland Convention and Visitors Authority, ☎ 510-839-9000 or 800-262-5526; 550 10th Street, Suite 214, Oakland, CA 94607; Web site www.ocva.com.

Silicon Valley Region

San Jose Convention & Visitors Bureau, ☎ 408-295-9600, 888-726-5673; 333 West San Carlos Street, Suite 1000, San Jose, CA 95110-2720; Web site www.sanjose.org.

Between San Francisco and San Jose, the San Mateo County area has its own visitor information resource: **San Mateo County Convention and Visitors Bureau,** ☎ 650-348-7600, 111 Anza Boulevard, Burlingame, CA, 94010; Web site www.sanmateo-countycvb.com.

Coast North of San Francisco

Redwood Empire Association, ☎ 415-394-5994, or 888-678-8502; 2801 Leavenworth, 2nd Floor, San Francisco, CA 94133-1117; Web site www.redwoodempire.com.

Fort Bragg-Mendocino Coast Chamber of Commerce, ☎ 707-961-6300 or 800-726-2780; 332 N. Main Street, Fort Bragg, CA 95437.

Mendocino County Tourism Board, ☎ 707-459-7910; 239 S. Main Street, Willits, CA 95490.

Sonoma-Mendocino Coast

Department of Parks and Recreation Mendocino Area State Parks, ☎ 707-937-5804; PO Box 440, Mendocino, CA 95460.

Far Northern Redwood Region

Eureka/Humboldt County Convention & Visitors Bureau, ☎ 707-443-5097 or 800-346-3482; 1034 Second Street, Eureka, CA 95501; Web site www.northcoast.com/~redwoods.

Wine Country of Napa-Sonoma

Napa Valley Conference & Visitors Bureau, ☎ 707-226-7459; 1310 Napa Town Center, Napa, CA 94559; Web site www.napanet.net.

St. Helena Chamber of Commerce, ☎ 707-799-6456; 1010 Main Street, St. Helena, CA 94574.

Calistoga Chamber of Commerce, ☎ 707-942-6333; 1458 Lincoln Avenue, Calistoga, CA 94515; Web site www.napanet.net.

Sonoma County Convention and Visitors Bureau, ☎ 707-586-8100; 5000 Roberts Lake Road, Suite A, Rohnert Park, CA 94928; Web site www.visitsonoma.com.

The area around the historic town of Sonoma is represented by the **Sonoma Valley Visitors Bureau**, ☎ 707-996-1090; 453 First Street East, Sonoma, CA 95476; Web site www.sonomavalley.com.

The wineries of Sonoma have joined together as the **Sonoma County Wineries Association/California Welcome Center**;

☎ 707-586-3795; 5000 Roberts Lake Road, Rohnert Park, CA 94928; Web site www.sonomawine.com.

Shasta Cascade Area

Redding Convention & Visitors Bureau, ☎ 916-225-4100 or 800-874-7562; 777 Auditorium Drive, Redding, CA 96001.

Shasta-Cascade Wonderland Association, ☎ 916-275-5555 or 800-474-2782, 14250 Holiday Road, Redding, CA 96003; Web site www.shastacascade.org.

Sierra and Gold Country

North Lake Tahoe Resort Association, ☎ 800-824-6348; PO Box 5459, Tahoe City, CA 96145; Web site www.tahoeguide.com.

Lake Tahoe

Lake Tahoe Visitors Authority, ☎ 800-288-2463; 1156 Ski Run Boulevard, South Lake Tahoe, CA 96150; Web site www.virtualtahoe.com.

For hiking and wilderness backpacking in the Lake Tahoe area, especially in Desolation Wilderness, contact **Forest Supervisor, US Forest Service, Lake Tahoe Basin Management Unit**, ☎ 916-573-2600; 870 Emerald Bay Road, Suite 1, South Lake Tahoe, CA 96150.

Yosemite

Yosemite Concession Services-Reservation; ☎ 209-252-4848, or 209-253-5654; 5410 East Home Avenue, Fresno, CA 93727; Web site www.yosemitepark.com and www.nps.gov/yose.

East Side of the Sierra

Mammoth Lakes Visitor Bureau; ☎ 800-367-6572; PO Box 48, Mammoth Lakes, CA 93546; Web site www.visitmammoth.com.

On the Way to Gold Country and Sierra:

Sacramento Convention and Visitors Bureau, ☎ (916-264-7777; 1421 K Street, Sacramento, CA 95814; Web site www.sacto.org/cvb.

California Gold Country Visitors Association, ☎ 800-225-3764; PO Box 637, Angels Camp, CA 95222.

Monterey & Santa Cruz

Monterey Peninsula Visitors and Convention Bureau, ☎ 408-649-1770; 380 Alvarado Street, Monterey, CA 93942-1770; Web site www.mpcc.com.

Santa Cruz County Conference and Visitors Council; ☎ 408-425-1234 or 800-833-3494; 701 Front Street, Santa Cruz, CA 95060; Web site www.scccvc.org.

Major Attractions

For San Francisco Harbor Tours:

Blue and Gold Fleet, ☎ 415-705-5444; Pier 39, Fisherman's Wharf, San Francisco.

Red and White Fleet, ☎ 800-229-2784; Pier 43, Fisherman's Wharf, San Francisco.

Destinations in Themselves:

Marine World/Africa USA, Marine World Parkway, ☎ 707-644-4000; Vallejo, CA 94589-4006.

Paramount's Great America, ☎ 408-988-1776; 2401 Agnew Road, Santa Clara, CA 95054; Web site www.pgathrills.com.

Monterey Bay Aquarium, ☎ 408-375-3333; 886 Cannery Row, Monterey, CA 93940; Web site www.mbayaq.org.

Public Lands

National Park Service Western Region Information Center, ☎ 415-556-0560; Fort Mason, Bldg. 201, Bay and Franklin Streets, San Francisco, CA 94123.

The extensive state parks system, with 264 units and 250 miles of coastal beaches in California, is administered by:

California State Park System Department of Parks and Recreation, ☎ 916-653-6995, or 916-445-6477; PO Box 942896, Sacramento, CA 94296-0001; Web site www.ceres.ca.gov/parks/travel.html.

For camping reservations at state parks, call ☎ 800-444-7275; for national parks, the reservation number is ☎ 800-365-2267; Web site www.destinet.com.

National Forests Information:

US Forest Service Pacific Southwest Region, ☎ 415-705-2874 or 800-280-2267; 630 Sansome Street, Room 807, San Francisco, CA 94111.

Some national forest service campgrounds can be reserved by calling the NFS Reservation Center at ☎ 800-280-2267.

The Bureau of Land Management controls some lands of special interest to mountain bikers and hikers/backpackers. The contact is Bureau of Land Management, ☎ 916-979-2800; 2800 Cottage Way, Sacramento, CA 95825.

Chapter 2

San Francisco & the Bay Area

The San Francisco Bay Area can be conveniently considered to have four parts – San Francisco, Marin County to the North, the East Bay of Oakland/Berkeley, and the South Bay of San Jose and the San Francisco Peninsula.

■ San Francisco

No other American city evokes such images of romance, including sweeping hills studded with pastel Victorians, the clanking of Cable Cars, the wail of the foghorns, the glow of the Golden Gate Bridge at sunset, the way-stop to the Gold Rush, and the meeting of sea, fog, and hill.

San Francisco, sitting on the edge of a peninsula separating the Pacific Ocean from San Francisco Bay, is a city of neighborhoods where diverse cultures and lifestyles comfortably co-exist. You can immerse yourself in worlds as different as Chinatown, Italian North Beach, and the Mexican-American Mission District.

This setting, with its abundance of creature comforts, is where adventures can take many forms, from sailing on tall ships, such as the **Hawaiian Chieftain**, to tucking in at a backpacking camp for the night on **Angel Island**, just off the San Francisco shore.

In 1776, Juan Bautista de Anza established the **Presidio**, a Spanish fort and settlement. Soon after, Junipero Serra founded Mission San Francisco de Asis, his sixth in California. Popularly known as **Mission Dolores**, the restored structure at 16th and Dolores streets still stands, the oldest building in San Francisco.

The **Gold Rush** of 1848 transformed the face of San Francisco. Within a few years, the pastoral scattering of Spanish-Mexican dwellings with a population of 100 became a restless prospecting region of 250,000. Statehood came in 1850. By 1852 an esti-

San Francisco & The Bay Area

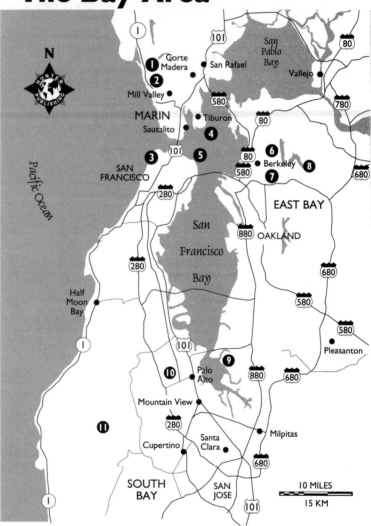

1. Mt. Tamalpais State Park
2. Muir Woods Nat'l Monument
3. Golden Gate Park
4. Angel Island State Park
5. Alcatraz Island
6. Tilden Park
7. Univ. of California
8. Briones Park
9. San Francisco Bay
   Nat'l Wildlife Refuge Visitor Ctr
10. Stanford University
11. Pescadero Creek County Park

mated $200 million in gold had been mined in California and shipped to the treasure houses in San Francisco.

To witness this early American era in San Francisco's history you can visit the brick fortification called **Fort Point**, located immediately below the south anchor of the Golden Gate Bridge. This was where Juan Bautista de Anza first planted a cross in 1776 and the Spaniards erected a crude stockade by 1794. Today the Civil War-era fort remains as a prime example of 19th-century military architecture.

The Great Earthquake shook San Francisco on April 18, 1906, but the Great Fire that followed caused the most damage. Fed by broken natural gas lines and unchecked because the city's water mains were destroyed, the fire raged for three days, destroying 28,000 buildings. Thereafter, San Francisco developed a certain fondness for firemen, most noticeably expressed in Lillie Hitchcock Coit's fire-nozzle-shaped **Coit Tower** on Telegraph Hill. (A fireboat in the Bay made a substantial contribution to dousing the fire in the Marina district after the Quake of 1989.)

San Francisco's Victorian houses that survived the 1906 earthquake have become a symbol of the city as much as the cable cars or the Golden Gate Bridge.

■ Marin County

Starting just across the Golden Gate and stretching north along the coast, west of the Wine Country of Napa/Sonoma, is **Marin County**. One of California's loveliest and most diverse areas, Marin celebrates the natural environment.

Immediately north of the Golden Gate Bridge, the **Marin Headlands** is a choice outdoor area, administered by the Golden Gate National Recreation Area and laced with trails. Here you can get views of the Bridge and the City itself. After enjoying the views, push on to discover some of the best hiking and biking spots available in Northern California.

The towns of **Sausalito** and **Tiburon**, across the Bay, offer a clear view of San Francisco. They epitomize the artsy and trendy environs of yuppies. Travelers revel in the outdoor cafés along their waterfronts.

Muir Woods, a 560-acre sanctuary north and west from Sausalito along Highway 1, is home to California's signature coastal redwood trees, dating back over a thousand years and reaching heights of over 200 feet. Specimens of the same tree, in the state's far northern region, are the tallest trees on earth.

Dominating Marin is 2,571-foot **Mt. Tamalpais**, one of the most agreeable hiking areas in the state, and also one of the places where the modern sport of mountain biking was born. Trails range from shady paths deep within the forest, to wide open sunny strips running to the top of the mountain.

Further up the west Marin coast is **Point Reyes**, designated as a National Seashore, where you can immerse yourself in Miwok Indian culture, witness the force of the 1906 Earthquake, and savor many miles of excellent hiking and biking trails. Point Reyes, famous for wildflower viewing in spring and whale-watching in winter, has pristine beaches, rocky coastlines, rolling dairy ranch terrain, and an historic lighthouse.

Marin County is also prime bed-and-breakfast country along the Point Reyes coast.

Marin County was one of the first areas of Northern California to be explored. At Point Reyes, pause for a stop at **Drake's Bay**. Historians continue to write their Ph.D. dissertations arguing Drake's exact landing spot near what is now Drake's Bay. However, there is little doubt that somewhere near here the English swashbuckler, Sir Francis Drake, put in his ship, the *Golden Hind*, for repairs in 1579. Drake was the first English explorer to land on the North American continent. Though he claimed the land for England, the English never invested the manpower necessary to hold California, as the Spanish did.

■ East Bay

Stretching east from San Francisco are **Oakland**, **Berkeley**, and the **East Bay**, dominated along the shore by the long cultural shadow of San Francisco and inland by the dark mountain called Mt. Diablo.

Oakland is a brawny port city, one of the large, containerized freight ports on the west coast. It is the third largest city in Northern California and an industrial center.

Neighboring **Berkeley** is the intellectual and liberal political mecca of Northern California, home of the University of California, the state's most prestigious public university. Berkeley is Oakland's cerebral counterpart, whether the revolution is 1960s politics or 1990s croissants.

An observer might think of Berkeley as the whiz kid scholar and trendy culinary explorer and Oakland as the salt-of-the-earth, rapping and streetwise urban dweller. The analogy falters, however, because Oakland probably has more resident artists than any place except Greenwich Village. The reason is economic. Oakland is one of the few places in the Bay Area where creative writers and artists can survive financially and live affordably.

The East Bay includes one of the largest American concentrations of immigrants from Asian and Pacific Island regions, including Viet Nam. The cultural diversity of the area is immediately apparent and includes many benefits for the traveler, such as the charming Burmese restaurant Nan Yang (6048 College Avenue, Oakland; ☎ 510-655-3298).

Rising above Oakland and Berkeley are the East Bay hills, which include 53,000 acres set aside for recreational use as part of the **East Bay Regional Parks** system.

Stretching beyond the hills is the affluent suburban world of Walnut Creek-Concord in Contra Costa County, a great place to live except during the choking rush hours. Central to the view from all perspectives is 3,849-foot-tall **Mt. Diablo**, whose crown is a state park. In the town of Martinez you can visit the home of the patron saint of the environmental movement, John Muir.

■ South Bay

The computer revolution, affecting all of America, has changed the face of San Jose, Silicon Valley, and the rest of the world. Located 50 miles south of San Francisco, Silicon Valley was originally an 18th-century bucolic ranching region, nurtured by a small pueblo and Spanish mission. It developed in the late 19th

San Francisco & the Bay Area

and early 20th century as one of America's most important fruit-growing areas. Prunes, plums, apricots, peaches, and cherries were shipped all over the country from here.

At the end of World War II a new direction emerged – electronics and other high technology industries. San Jose began to grow, expanding to become the 11th largest metropolitan region in the country. The county has one of the highest per capita incomes in the US. Computers, computer components, and other high-tech efforts, both civilian and military, are the main manufacturing enterprises.

Few American cities have experienced as extensive a renaissance as California's **San Jose**. The process of transformation, in the heart of the city, is so complete that a current traveler gets the feeling of a work in progress. The canvas for this artistry is the urban landscape. About a billion dollars in public and private money has gone into redevelopment in recent years.

A visitor sees a great city emerging, rising to share the spotlight with its glamorous sister to the north, San Francisco. The languid Guadeloupe River, for example, which now meanders through San Jose, is becoming a landscaped urban stream, whose banks are known as **River Park**.

■ Getting to & Around the Bay Area

Two major airports serve San Francisco, both an easy half-hour drive to downtown, traffic permitting. **San Francisco International Airport** lies 14 miles south of San Francisco off Freeway 101. Take the SFO Airporter bus that departs from the lower level baggage area for a low cost ride to Union Square or the Financial District (☎ 415-495-8404). Across the bay, the **Oakland Airport** offers easy access by frequent bus and BART service. Travel into and within the city is easy without a car. One nuance of driving here is that cable cars, as well as pedestrians, have the right-of-way.

The world famous **cable cars** are a major part of the San Francisco experience for many travelers. They were entirely restored in the

1980s and the line newly opened. Cars on the three branches of the line are now painted in the original 1870s colors, maroon with cream and blue trim. Board at any place along the routes: Powell Street to Fisherman's Wharf, Powell to Hyde streets, and California Street from Market to Van Ness streets. Waiting lines to ride the cable cars are sometimes long, especially at Powell and Market streets. Drivers will collect fares after you have boarded.

Leave some time in your schedule for a visit to the **Cable Car Barn and Museum** (☎ 415-474-1887; 1201 Mason Street) where you can see historic paraphernalia about the system and glimpse the innards at work. At the barn, you can watch the huge wheels that pull the cable cars slowly up the street. Large 750 horsepower engines turn a massive steel wheel, pulling the thick cable, capable of carrying 31 cars, six tons apiece, at a speed of 9½ miles per hour, up a 21% grade. The 127 miles of track in the 1880s have been reduced to a mere 10½ miles today.

Origin of the Cable Cars

Originally, the impulse to build the cable car system came from the sickening but familiar sight of horses slipping on the steep hills in wet weather and breaking their legs. This legacy of cable cars began with the offended sensibility of a manufacturer of iron cable, **Andrew S. Hallidie**, in the 1870s. While climbing the steep Jackson Street hill, he saw a horse-drawn car, loaded with passengers, proceed slowly up the hill, then falter as the lead horse lost its footing. The car slid quickly down hill, fortunately without loss of human life. However, the fallen lead horse pulled down the other horses. The horses endured broken legs and mutilated muscles and had to be shot.

Hallidie went home shaking his head, thinking there must be a better way. Working alone and at his own expense, Hallidie devised a cable car system, finally putting it into operation in August 1873. When he took the first ride downhill, the San Franciscans in attendance were as skeptical as the modern traveler, who wonders what would happen if the car lets loose. Hallidie made the first trip alone.

San Francisco & the Bay Area

Among more mundane and more substantial transit systems in the city, the two most important to a traveler are the **BART** and the **MUNI**. The BART, ☎ 415-992-2278, is the underground system that travels through downtown and links San Francisco with the East Bay, providing easy access to Oakland and Berkeley. The MUNI, Metro Street Cars and Municipal Railway, ☎ 415-673-6864, offers an elaborate system of trolleys and buses in San Francisco that can get you close to anywhere. However, San Francisco is relatively compact. If you like to walk, you can get around to see most of the sites on foot. MUNI also operates bus #76 to the Marin Headlands and the Golden Gate Recreation Area.

Transportation Tips

- Several door-to-door **shuttles** operate from the San Francisco airport. The best plan is usually to walk out to the front of the airport at the designated shuttle stops and wait for one headed your direction. One provider is **Supershuttle,** ☎ 415-558-8500 for transport to and from the airport.

- **Taxis** are also available at the airport. Budget about $30 for a downtown dropoff. Parking meters are strictly enforced and parking garages can run into the double digits for a few hours. Many hotels offer parking services but these may be pricey.

- **Amtrak** trains arrive in the Bay Area at the Jack London Square area of Oakland, where there is a handsome new Amtrak station. Call ☎ 800-872-7245 for details. Trains leave for Sacramento, the Sierra, and the Central Valley. In the Central Valley there is connecting bus service to Yosemite, one of the enjoyable ways to transport yourself to this distant treasure.

- The bus system known as **AC Transit,** ☎ 510-839-2882, transports people between San Francisco and the East Bay. AC Transit is the shortened name for Alameda-Contra Costa Transit, which refers to the two counties of the East Bay.

- **Golden Gate Transit**, ☎ 415-923-2000, offers bus and ferry service from The City to Marin and Sonoma Counties.

- Greyhound, the bus people, have a depot at 425 Mission Street in San Francisco. Call Greyhound at ☎ 800-231-2222.

- To get out on the Bay, a glorious experience, there are two services offering **excursion boats**. The Red & White Fleet, ☎ 800-229-2784, and Blue & Gold Fleet, ☎ 415-705-5444, send their boats out from three piers (41, 43, and 39). The two fleets offer competing Bay cruises and include land touring options via motorcoach to the wineries of Napa and to Muir Woods in Marin. Blue and Gold runs a ferry operation to Alcatraz and Angel Islands in the Bay as well as Tiburon and Sausalito in Marin County.

- **Ferries** link San Francisco to the North Bay and to Oakland. One goes from the Ferry Building, foot of Market Street, to Sausalito and Larkspur in Marin County. The ferry company is part of Golden Gate Transit. The Blue & Gold Fleet, mentioned above, operates daily commute service to Tiburon and Sausalito. Some specialized ferries can be an important part of your touring plan. For example, you can get a ferry out to Angel Island for a hike from Tiburon, ☎ 415-435-2131. There is ferry service to Oakland's Jack London Square (☎ 510-522-3300).

- South from San Francisco, the **Samtrans buses** cover San Mateo County (☎ 800-660-4287).

- The **CalTrain Peninsula Train Service** runs up and down the peninsula between San Francisco and San Jose. About 20,000 people use this commute rail each day. For a schedule, call ☎ 800-660-4287.

- **Rental cars** are available from all the major providers at the San Francisco Bay Area airports and in main cities. The critical skill needed by a motorist in San Francisco is remembering to curb the car sharply when parking on steep hills. For extensive exploring, a car is the most efficient means of transportation.

- Tours of San Francisco and the outlying regions, such as Muir Woods, are organized by Gray Line, 350 Eighth Street (☎ 800-826-0202).

Keep in mind one transportation strategy that may not immediately occur to you. **Oakland's International Airport** (☎ 510-577-4000), a few miles from downtown, is the easiest and most pleasant place in the Bay Area to fly into and out of. Ironically, it is the airport closest to San Francisco.

Also, know that there are a few critical stops to keep in mind when thinking of ground transportation. For BART, the excellent underground system between San Francisco and the East Bay, stations of most interest to travelers will be the Berkeley Station, Center Street and Shattuck Avenue, close to the University, and the 12th Street City Center Station in Oakland, in the heart of the downtown Oakland, or the Lake Merritt Station, near Oakland's Museum of California and Lake Merritt.

Bay Area Highways

As with most of America, the auto freeway is the main mode of transport in the Bay Area.

Highway 101 snakes up the San Francisco Peninsula, meanders across San Francisco, and heads north to the Redwood Country. Parts of this freeway in San Francisco were knocked down following the Loma Prieta Earthquake of 1989.

Freeway 80-880 stretches along the east side of the Bay, amounting to the main north-south artery. For the traveler, this is one of the routes north to the Wine Country.

From San Francisco an automobile traveler crosses to Oakland on the Oakland-Berkeley **Bay Bridge**, completed in 1936, the same year as the **Golden Gate**. The Bay Bridge is the workhorse of the two. Further south along the Bay, the San Mateo and Dumbarton bridges unite the East Bay with the Peninsula, as the land south of San Francisco is called.

Swinging around the south end of the Bay, Freeway 880 joins the East Bay to the San Francisco Peninsula. Major highways lead from Oakland east to Sacramento, the Gold Country, and the Sierra Nevada.

As in most of California travel, for better and for worse, the Silicon Valley has made the automobile the prime mode of transportation. It is difficult to see the sights in this region if you don't have your car or a rental vehicle.

The **San Jose International Airport,** ☎ 408-277-4759, at the south edge of San Francisco Bay, is a substantial airport, serviced by most of the major carriers and about an hour's drive from San Francisco.

Amtrak also has service to San Jose, a regular stop on its Coast Starlight run. A passenger train running from San Jose to San Francisco provides daily commuter service between the two towns. For schedules, call **CalTrain,** ☎ 800-660-4287.

San Jose's new light-rail train system now takes a visitor around the immediate downtown area. The train then runs out to the Santa Clara Convention Center and Paramount's Great America theme park.

For bus service, **Greyhound** (☎ 408-297-8890) connects San Jose with other cities in California. Within the Silicon Valley region, **Santa Clara County Transit** (☎ 408-287-4210) reaches the near and far corners, eventually.

Information Sources

For the most accurate weather predictions, contact the **National Weather Service.** They have a tape recording about Bay Area weather at ☎ 415-936-1212.

San Francisco

San Francisco Convention and Visitors Bureau, ☎ 415-391-2000; PO Box 429097, San Francisco, CA; 94142-9097; Web site: www.sfvisitor.org.

Marin County Area Immediately North of San Francisco

Marin County Convention & Visitors Bureau, ☎ 415-472-7470, Avenue of the Flags, San Rafael, CA 94903; Web site www.marin.org.

Point Reyes

Superintendent, Point Reyes National Seashore, ☎ 415-663-1092; Bear Valley Road, Point Reyes CA 94956.

San Francisco & the Bay Area

Marin Headlands Area

The Marin Headlands Visitor Center, ☎ 415-331-1540; Fort Barry Chapel in the Marin Headlands.

The popular close-in parks to visit on the way to Point Reyes are the redwoods at **Muir Woods National Monument**, ☎ 415-388-2595, and the grassy hillsides of **Mt. Tamalpais State Park**, ☎ 415-388-2070.

East Bay

The **Oakland Convention and Visitors Authority**, ☎ 800-262-5526; 550 10th Street, Suite 214, Oakland, CA 94607; Web site www.ocva.com.

The **Berkeley Convention & Visitors Bureau**; ☎ 800-847-4823; 2015 Center Street, 1st Floor, Berkeley, CA 94704.

The **East Bay Regional Parks District** provides information on the many distinguished parks in the hills east of Oakland-Berkeley, such as Tilden Park. Contact them at ☎ 510-635-0138.

South Bay

San Jose Convention & Visitors Bureau, ☎ 408-295-9600, 888-726-5673; 333 West San Carlos Street, Suite 1000, San Jose, CA 95110-2720; Web site www.san-jose.org.

San Jose

San Jose's 24-hour "For Your Information" **hotline** is ☎ 408-295-2265.

San Jose Visitor Information Center; ☎ 408-977-0900, San Jose McEnry Convention Center, Lower Level, 150 West San Carlos Street.

For more information about the surrounding area: **Santa Clara Convention & Visitor Bureau**, ☎ 408-244-9660; 1850 Warburton Avenue, Santa Clara, CA 95052; Web site www.santaclara.org.

San Mateo

San Mateo County Convention and Visitors Bureau, ☎ 650-348-7600; 111 Anza Boulevard, Burlingame, CA 94010; Web site www.sanmateocountycvb.com.

■ Touring the Bay Area

San Francisco

Even a selective touring list could not omit Golden Gate Park, Telegraph, Russian, and Nob hills; Chinatown, North Beach, Fisherman's Wharf, the Golden Gate National Recreation Area, and the scenic 49-Mile Drive (which takes you through all of the above).

Golden Gate Park

In 1887, Golden Gate Park comprised 730 acres of dunes and 270 acres of arable land dotted with oak trees. Today, the park encompasses lush meadows, lakes, dense stands of Australian eucalyptus, and more than 6,000 varieties of shrubs, flowers, and trees.

The park is both a cultural and recreational center of the city. Within its boundaries you can visit the **M. H. de Young Memorial Museum**, with its Rockefeller collection of American art, and the adjacent Asian Art Museum, with the unsurpassed Avery Brundage Collection of Asian art. (The de Young may move in the future.) Near the present de Young is the Japanese Tea Garden, the California Academy of Sciences, including the Steinhart Aquarium and the Morrison Planetarium, the 60-acre Strybing Arboretum, and the Conservatory of Flowers.

For recreation in Golden Gate Park you can rent horses, traditional skates and rollerblades, and bicycles, or put on your running shoes and join the multitude of joggers and walkers. Free guided walking tours of the park are provided by the **Friends of Recreation and Parks** organization, ☎ 415-263-0991.

San Francisco's Hills

Climb San Francisco's 43 hills and you will be rewarded with spectacular views of the city and surrounding bay. Atop Telegraph Hill sits **Coit Tower** (One Telegraph Hill Boulevard, ☎ 415-362-0808), the memorial built in 1934 to honor the city's volunteer firemen.

Russian Hill lies to the west. Here you'll find **Lombard Street**, the city's crookedest street with its notorious eight curves. The

San Francisco & the Bay Area

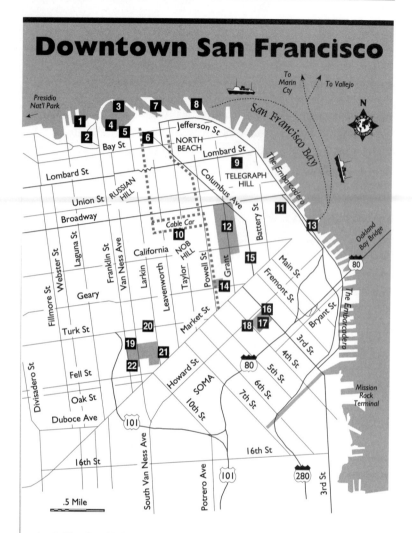

Downtown San Francisco

1. Golden Gate Nat'l Recreation Area
2. Ft. Mason Military Reserve
3. Hyde St. Pier, Balclutha
4. Aquatic Park, Nat'l Maritime Museum
5. Ghirardelli Square
6. The Cannery
7. Fisherman's Wharf
8. Piers 39 and 41
9. Coit Tower
10. Cable Car Barn Museum
11. Embarcadero Center
12. Chinatown
13. Golden Gate Ferry, World Trade Center Ferry Building
14. Union Square
15. Financial District
16. Museum of Modern Art
17. Moscone Convention Center, Yerba Buena Gardens
18. Hallidie Plaza & Visitors Info Center
19. War Memorial Auditorium
20. Civic Center
21. Library
22. Symphony Hall, Opera House

third famous hill is **Nob Hill**, once the site of mansions, today the home of famous hotels, including the **Mark Hopkins** and the **Fairmont**. Both offer panoramic views of the city from cocktail lounges on the top floor.

Chinatown/North Beach

San Francisco's **Chinatown** is the largest Chinese community outside the Orient. The community is best experienced on foot. Enter at the Dragon's Gate on Grant Street to browse through herb shops, temples, and fortune cookie factories. Grant Avenue is the main street to walk for general shopping. Stockton Street, between Washington and Broadway streets, is where you'll find the largest concentration of markets, exhibiting an amazing array of vegetables and meats, such as roasted ducks hanging in the windows. The Chinese New Year occurs in February, complete with a parade and firecrackers.

North Beach is the Italian district of the city, located between Chinatown and Fisherman's Wharf. Here you'll discover many Italian restaurants, bakeries, cafés, and Italian groceries, all within a few blocks of Washington Square, the heart of North Beach. The **North Beach Festival** in June is one of the oldest urban street festivals in the US. It celebrates the Beat heritage and Italian roots of the community with live poetry readings, as well as jazz and blues performances.

The birthplace of the Beat movement, North Beach is filled with bookstores, cafés, galleries, cabarets, and nightclubs. **City Lights Books** at 261 Columbus Street still thrives as a bookstore, publisher of local poets, and gathering place of writers.

Fisherman's Wharf/Golden Gate National Recreation Area

Once the center of the fishing and canning industry in the city, **Fisherman's Wharf** today attracts tourists with a wide variety of shops, galleries, and restaurants. Nearby Ghirardelli Square, first a woolen works, then a chocolate factory, was remodeled into a retail complex. **The Cannery**, originally a fruit and vegetable canning plant, houses restaurants, brew pubs, the **Museum of the City of San Francisco** and the **Redwood Empire Association**

San Francisco & the Bay Area

Visitor Information Center, which is well stocked with information for the nine-county area north of San Francisco.

Millions of visitors visit Pier 39, with its shops, resident sea lions, and new aquarium – which puts you in a transparent tunnel, with sharks and rays drifting overhead.

Attractions within the **Golden Gate National Recreation Area** (35,000 acres of land and water, ☎ 415-331-1540) include **Alcatraz**, **Aquatic Park**, and the **Golden Gate Promenade**. Guided tours of **Alcatraz Island**, a federal prison until 1963, leave from Pier 41. ☎ 415-705-5555 for reservations. The boat ride out to the "rock" offers a fine view of the city. Similarly, the large park island in the Bay, Angel Island, can be toured.

In the Fisherman's Wharf area, Aquatic Park includes the **National Maritime Museum**, with five historic vessels you can explore. The Golden Gate Promenade is a walk from the Marina to the Golden Gate Bridge. This three-mile path along the waterfront is a popular strolling and jogging area. The Golden Gate National Recreation Area is the umbrella organization that oversees all these resources.

The 49-Mile Drive

San Francisco is a city for walking, but for an overview of the major attractions, the scenic **49-Mile Drive** is recommended. The Visitor Information Center at Hallidie Plaza, Powell and Market streets, can assist you with a map. Allow half a day for the drive, which is well marked by blue and white seagull signs. The newest way to view the city skyline is from the **Embarcadero Center Skydeck** at One Embarcadero Center, ☎ 800-733-6318. For a few dollars you can survey the cityscape from 41 floors high.

Arts & Entertainment

In San Francisco the arts and entertainment life of the city is thickly textured. For one Saturday in July an "Only In San Francisco" event occurs. On that day comedians gather at the bandstand in Golden Gate Park, braving a bright sun that seldom penetrates their nightly comedy clubs. This free, all-day marathon of mirth, called the **Comedy Celebration Day**, is the performers' way of showing appreciation to their audiences. In some years, the superstar of American humorists, area resident Robin

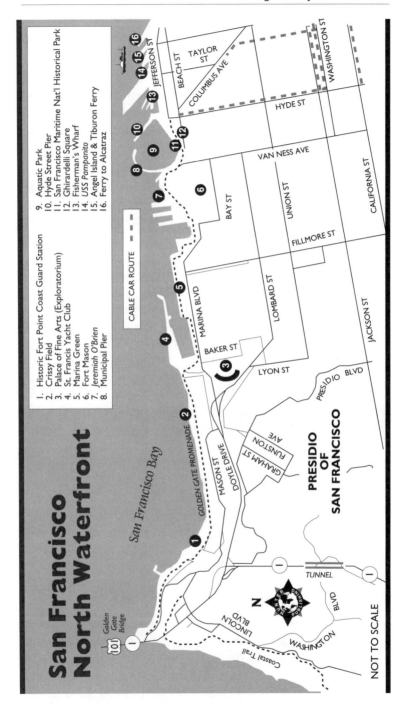

San Francisco North Waterfront

1. Historic Fort Point Coast Guard Station
2. Crissy Field
3. Palace of Fine Arts (Exploratorium)
4. St. Francis Yacht Club
5. Marina Green
6. Fort Mason
7. Jeremiah O'Brien
8. Municipal Pier
9. Aquatic Park
10. Hyde Street Pier
11. San Francisco Maritime Nat'l Historical Park
12. Ghirardelli Square
13. Fisherman's Wharf
14. USS Pampanito
15. Angel Island & Tiburon Ferry
16. Ferry to Alcatraz

CABLE CAR ROUTE

San Francisco Bay

Golden Gate Bridge

PRESIDIO OF SAN FRANCISCO

TUNNEL

Coastal Trail

LINCOLN BLVD

WASHINGTON

BLVD

NOT TO SCALE

GOLDEN GATE PROMENADE

MASON ST

DOYLE DRIVE

GRAHAM ST

FUNSTON AVE

PRESIDIO BLVD

LYON ST

BAKER ST

MARINA BLVD

LOMBARD ST

BAY ST

FILLMORE ST

UNION ST

VAN NESS AVE

HYDE ST

JEFFERSON ST

BEACH ST

TAYLOR ST

COLUMBUS AVE

WASHINGTON ST

JACKSON ST

CALIFORNIA ST

N

Williams, wraps up the evening as the twilight filters over San Francisco.

Comedy is but one thread of the arts and entertainment life of San Francisco. The degree of vitality in the local comedy club and comedy theater scene is special. Start a comedy evening at **Punch Line** (☎ 415-397-7573; 444 Battery Street) and perhaps move on to **Cobb's Comedy Club** (☎ 415-928-4320, The Cannery).

For full listings of comedy or other arts/entertainment possibilities during your visit, consult the Sunday *Datebook* section of the *San Francisco Chronicle-Examiner* or the daily *After Dark* section, or pick up a free copy of the *SF Weekly* or *Bay Guardian* newspapers.

Along with comedy, San Francisco is a good place to spend the evening enjoying music. You might want to ease into an evening of international jazz stars or Bay area talent in the **New Orleans Room** at the Fairmont Hotel (☎ 415-772-5259, 950 Mason Street). Jazz also flourishes at some of the better restaurants, such as the **Washington Square Bar & Grill** (☎ 415-982-8123, 1707 Powell Street) in North Beach. Salsa and other Latin rhythms are the fare at **Bahia** (☎ 415-861-4202, 1600 Market Street).

Topless in North Beach

To many past visitors, San Francisco meant topless. It was in North Beach, at the corner of Broadway and Columbus, that Carol Doda began a revered tradition. Doda descended from above on a white piano, her bare, silicon-injected figure displayed to titillate a generation of travelers. Similar clubs within view of the Columbus-Broadway intersection promise sexually oriented entertainment. There was a time when Doda needed a phalanx of lawyers to keep her out of jail, but the tastes of the 1990s have dealt an even crueler blow by declaring such acts passé – vice gone boring.

One refreshing North Beach entertainment is the music and comedy review called **Beach Blanket Babylon** at Club Fugazi, 678 Green Street, ☎ 415-421-4222. Year after year this musical theatre performance, originally created by the talented Steve Silver, plays to packed houses, partly because the material is constantly updated to parody the current political or sitcom scene.

Theater & Opera/Symphony

A spectrum of theater presents either a diverting or thoughtful evening depending on your tastes. The major company to watch for is the **American Conservatory Theater** (☎ 415-749-2228; 415 Geary Street) but there are also a dozen smaller and more experimental groups. Other theaters whose offerings you might check during your visit are the **Golden Gate Theatre** (☎ 415-551-2000; 1 Taylor Street), **Curran Theatre** (☎ 415-551-2000; 445 Geary Street) and the Tony Award-winning **Berkeley Repertory Theatre** (☎ 510-845-4700; 2025 Addison Street, Berkeley). Discount tickets to many theater, music, and dance events are available the day of the performance from **TIX Bay Area Booth** located on the Stockton Street side of Union Square (☎ 415-433-7827). TIX also sells full price, advance tickets.

Ever since 1848, when the first lucky prospectors brought their gold nuggets out of the Sierra foothills to San Francisco, certain elements of the population have generously supported the crowns of established culture, the opera and the symphony. In San Francisco, there is one element that defines the good life as an evening pubbing around the North Beach jazz joints referring to San Francisco with passionate familiarity as *Frisco*. But there is also another high-tone element given to black ties, furs, and limousines. These carriage-trade groupies tend to congregate at the **Opera House** (☎ 415-864-3330; Van Ness Avenue and Grove Street) for an evening with Marilyn Horne and other great divas. If you don't fancy taking in an opera, you might want to stop by **Max's Opera Café** (☎ 415-771-7300; 601 Van Ness Avenue) a classical music bar where the waiters and waitresses aspire to be opera singers and will regale you with arias. **The San Francisco Symphony** (☎ 415-864-6000) ranks among America's finest.

Only in San Francisco

What a visitor needs to comprehend, when thinking of the arts and entertainment world of San Francisco, is that there are many San Franciscos, and each is as authentic as the others. How would one classify such events as the annual **Bay to Breakers** run in May (about 100,000 participants each year, with many in costume or

San Francisco & the Bay Area

even clothing-free) or the annual **Gay Pride Celebration** in July (with attendance in the hundreds of thousands)? Not all the theater and performers in this city can be confined indoors.

The Great Museums

San Francisco enjoys its share of art museums, besides those in Golden Gate Park. South of Market Street on Third, the new **San Francisco Museum of Modern Art** (☎ 415-357-4000; 151 Third Street) has never been accused of lagging behind its audience. This museum also makes a special effort to show modern photography. The recently renovated **Palace of the Legion of Honor** (Lincoln Park, near 34th Avenue) hosts European and American shows. The **Ansel Adams Center** for **Photography** features changing exhibits as well as a permanent collection of works by Adams (☎ 415-495-7000; 250 4th Street). Many of the major modern art galleries in San Francisco are located downtown around Union Square. If you want to browse them, walk along Post and Sutter streets.

The City as Art Object

San Franciscans with a decided interest in art and entertainment also tend to argue passionately that the canvas of greatest interest here is the cityscape itself. The symphony with the most soothing sounds is the assembled foghorns, strategically placed around the bay, each with its own instrumentation. The laser light show that dazzles most in this urban disco is the sight of sunlight breaking through the fog bank. And the fitting center stage place for you, the traveler, to witness all this is an evening cruise out on the Bay, with the Red and White Fleet (☎ 800-229-2784; Pier 43) or the more posh Hornblower Yacht (Pier 33; ☎ 415-788-8866). The cruises amount to floating cocktail parties, some with a full dinner, music and dancing, plus a display of the most glorious work of US urban architecture – San Francisco, bathed in the setting sun, and framed with curls of fog.

Marin County

Immediately north of the Golden Gate, turn off the highway onto **Vista Point** to witness some unsurpassed views of San Francisco and the Bridge. The rambling Marin Headlands area can be hiked and enjoyed on the west side of the Bridge.

Back on Highway 101 and then west on Highway 1, pause first at **Muir Woods National Monument** (☎ 415-388-2595) to look at the redwoods. The drive is 15 miles, but allow plenty of time because the road twists and turns to Muir Woods and adjacent Mt. Tamalpais State Park. Muir Woods is clearly marked at the Panoramic Highway turnoff 2½ miles off Highway 1. Parking can be tight because of its popularity, so choose an off day if possible or prepare to walk a short distance to get to the entrance.

This impressive grove is named after John Muir, the patron saint of the environmental movement, who did so much around the turn of the century to popularize the cause of saving forests as national parklands. Muir Woods satisfies partly because it honors this great conservationist, who wrote eloquently about the California outdoors, helping to create the constituency needed to protect it. For the preservation of Muir Woods, we have Marin resident William Kent to thank. Theodore Roosevelt suggested at the 1908 dedication that the woods be named after this patron, but Kent declined and indicated that Muir's name would be a more appropriate title.

The redwood groves at Muir Woods have a hushed, sacral aura, with the choicest section appropriately called Cathedral Grove. The trees extend down a narrow valley with a stream, a typical redwood terrain with an undergrowth of sorrel and ferns. Deep within the grove the light diminishes and few other plants can compete. In late autumn you can see coho salmon and steelhead trout migrating up this stream, Redwood Creek. In summer the coastal fog drips off the redwood branches, providing a substantial amount of moisture.

After Muir Woods, drive further on Highway 1 to encounter Bolinas Lagoon, one of the richest estuaries along the coast, supporting an abundant fish and bird life. Stop at the **Audubon Canyon Ranch** (☎ 415-868-9244), three miles north of Stinson Beach, to see white egrets nesting in the tops of redwood trees. Trails at Audubon Ranch are an exciting introduction to nature in the area, especially if aided by naturalist literature from the excellent book shop.

San Francisco & the Bay Area

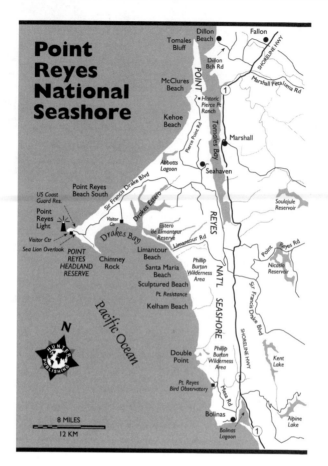

Point Reyes

The next stop, proceeding north, is the **Point Reyes National Seashore Visitor Center** (☎ 415-663-1092). If you have ever wondered what the April 17, 1906 Great Quake was like, the place to go is Point Reyes. Behind the large, modern barn-like structure that serves as Park Headquarters, you can take the **Earthquake Walk**. The spectacular display along this walk is an actual fence that split 16 feet apart as the earth's tectonic plates lurched past each other in the Great Quake. The walk circles for a mile through meadows and bay laurel trees along the San Andreas Fault, with markers alerting you to the Pacific and American plates grinding past each other at roughly two inches per year. Along the Earthquake Walk, you begin to imagine that Point

Reyes will be an island in time, destined to join the Aleutian chain off Alaska.

The Earthquake Walk is only the first of many discoveries at Point Reyes. Orient yourself at the displays in the headquarters building. Elaborate dioramas describe both natural history and the human story of Point Reyes, from the days of the Miwok Indians to the century of dairy ranching, which is still the main use of the Point Reyes land. Two million visitors a year make Point Reyes one of the most-used units in the National Park system. About 65,000 acres of Point Reyes is classified as wilderness.

Within the Point Reyes area, one of the more inviting and protected beaches has the beguiling name of **Heart's Desire**. Located in Tomales Bay State Park (☎ 415-669-1140), Heart's Desire is a safe and shallow beach whose waters, in protected Tomales Bay, become sufficiently warmed by late summer for pleasant swimming. The road to the beach curls down from the ridges, passing clusters of bay, madrone, and oak trees, to a protected cove, complete with a grassy area and picnic tables, an agreeable woodsy setting. The beach is ample, the ocean floor recedes gradually, rip tides and sleeper waves are unknown, and the water temperature becomes relatively comfortable. Heart's Desire is protected from wind. Moreover, the fog hangs up on the ridges. When the rest of the coast is foggy and windy, Heart's Desire will often be sunny.

Beyond Heart's Desire Beach, a **tule elk herd** can be seen if you drive further out Pierce Point Road. This big game species, so abundant in early California, survived a close brush with extinction and now climbs back to safe and stable numbers. Seeing the herds of antlered elk on the hillsides is an exciting wildlife spotting opportunity.

The East Bay

The short list of must-see things in the East Bay are as follows:

- Linger at the **Oakland Museum of California**, allowing enough time to see the separate floors devoted to California nature, history, and art.

- Visit **downtown Oakland**, including the Jack London waterfront complex, the vital **Chinatown** (better de-

San Francisco & the Bay Area

scribed as an Asia-town), the restored **Old Oakland** area around Ratto's restaurant and deli, and the art-deco **Paramount Theatre**.

■ Walk around the **University of California** campus, stopping in at the University Art Museum and the Lowie Museum. Then amble down Telegraph Avenue to survey the great **bookstores**, such as Cody's, and rub elbows with the **street artisans** and **crazies** for which Berkeley (aka Berserkely) is a code word.

■ Make a pilgrimage through the Berkeley **gourmet ghetto**, starting at Alice Waters' famous restaurant, **Chez Panisse**. Across the street is the noted cheese and bread co-op known as the **Cheese Board**. The **Fourth Street** area, near the Bay, is a newer trendy spot.

Jack London Square

The city of Oakland grew up along the waterfront, now **Jack London Square and Village**, a multi-block area of shops and restaurants struggling for identity, even as the author did. Jack London is the town's favorite son and the one luminary around whom you could build a themed waterfront area. Popular attractions here include shopping at places like Cost Plus, book browsing at Barnes & Noble, and dining at the good fish restaurant Scott's (☎ 510-444-3456). At the Square you can view Jack London's cabin, said to be his Yukon abode from the winter of 1897-98. Next to the cabin, quench your thirst at Heinold's First and Last Chance Saloon. Built in 1880, it is said that London acquired his self-made literary education at Heinold's. Inside you'll find Jack London photos and memorabilia. The bright night spot in the Jack London area is the jazz club known as **Yoshi's** (510 Embarcadero; ☎ 510-238-9200). Yoshi's also features Japanese dining, such as tempura or sushi dishes.

In recent years Jack London Square has shown new vitality. A **Sunday Farmer's Market** draws large crowds looking for everything from specialty apples to goat cheese. Franklin Roosevelt's Presidential Yacht, the *Potomac*, a National Historic Landmark, is now permanently berthed at Jack London Square. The public can sometimes tour the boat or participate in yacht excursions out on the bay. Call ☎ 510-839-8256 for reservations. A new Amtrak Train Station is the departure point for trips to Sacramento or Los Angeles. The Jack London Cinema features nine state-of-the-art theaters.

Downtown Oakland

From the Square, walk up Broadway into downtown Oakland. A civic group of volunteers sponsors free architectural walks around downtown Oakland. For reservations, ☎ 510-238-3234. At 9th Street between Washington and Broadway you'll see renovation and restoration in progress. This **Old Oakland** restoration consists of shops and restaurants, supplementing the excellent **Ratto's** deli and international grocery (821 Washington Street; ☎ 510-832-6503) a kind of culinary mirror of the city. Around Old Oakland are new office buildings that have changed the face of the downtown.

Much of the money coming in for the development is from Asia as well as from the public sector. Farther up Broadway, at 2025, is the **Paramount Theatre**, a lavishly gilded art deco movie palace of the 1930s. West toward the freeways is another dramatic Oakland development, Preservation Park, where 16 early Oakland Victorians have been restored. To complete the tour of Oakland, be sure to see the Oakland Museum and Lake Merritt.

The **Oakland Museum of California** (☎ 510-238-3401; 1000 Oak Street) was one of the first museums to present environments, such as the American kitchen in the 1940s, rather than static collections. Separate floors cover California art, California history, and nature in California. The museum architecture is noteworthy, with the building sunk into the ground and roof gardens atop each tiered floor. One of the popular annual shows is the mycological society's Fungus Fair, in November, which displays the season's offerings in wild mushrooms.

Lake Merritt Area

Lake Merritt, a 155-acre saltwater lake in the heart of Oakland, is a popular recreation area. On the north shore of the lake lies Lakeside Park and the country's oldest waterfowl refuge, founded in 1870. You can rent sailboats, rowboats, and canoes at the boat house on the west shore. Walking and jogging the 3½-mile shoreline around the lake is popular, as are the free summer band concerts. Youngsters enjoy the Children's Fairyland amusement park with its fantasy rides and puppet shows.

In June, 400 or so major artists, studio groups, and galleries open their spaces for two weekends of celebration and public interaction. The event, called Open Studios, is arranged by a spirited arts group called Pro Arts (☎ 510-763-4361; 461 Ninth Street).

Along the edge of Lake Merritt, at 666 Bellevue, you'll find one of the outstanding public gardens in California, the **Lakeside Park and Garden Center**, covering 122 acres that are intensely cultivated throughout the year. Permanent displays include a Japanese Garden, Herb and Fragrance Garden, Cactus and Succulent Garden, Polynesian Garden, and a tropical conservatory. The chrysanthemum displays each autumn are famous, but specialized appreciators might single out a preference for the bonsai show each autumn or the dahlia root sale each spring. Aside from this Lakeside Garden area, both Oakland and Berkeley boast impressive public rose gardens.

Another lakefront attraction is the **Camron-Stanford House** (☎ 510-836-1976; 1418 Lakeside Drive). This restored Italianate Victorian was built in 1876 and was owned by the brother of Leland Stanford, railroad tycoon and university founder. The other premier Victorian, in the Oakland Hills, is **Dunsmuir House** (☎ 510-615-5555; 2960 Peralta Oaks Court). Dunsmuir is a notable example of Victorian wealth and taste. Today it serves as a cultural, horticultural, and historical park open to the public.

Berkeley

Berkeley had its start as a modest land grant university town in the 19th century. A tour of the University is one of the major pleasures of Berkeley.

Beyond the crest of the hills there was little early development except for cattle ranching and some coal mining on the north slopes of Mt. Diablo. As during the time of the Miwok Native Americans, settlements tended to hug close to the shore of the opposite coast, or contra costa, as the Spanish called the area.

The visitor's focus in Berkeley tends to be the **University of California**, with its thousand-acre landscaped campus, a pleasant afternoon walk. For an impressive view of the East Bay, ride to the

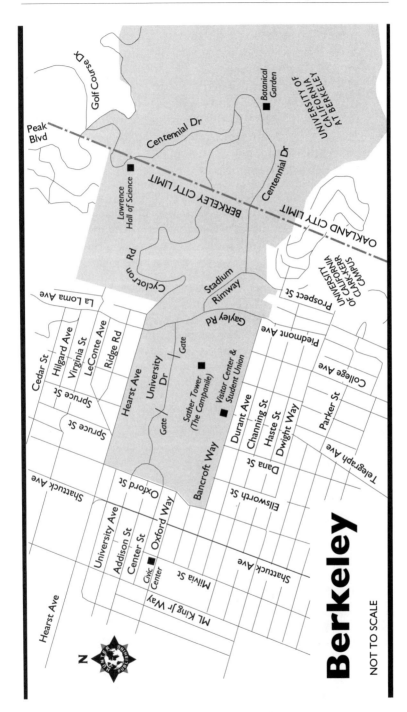

Berkeley

NOT TO SCALE

top of the campanile tower on campus. At the nearby **Visitor Center** (☎ 510-642-5215) in the main lobby of the Student Union you'll find maps of the campus. Be sure to see what's showing at the **UC Berkeley Art Museum** (☎ 510-642-0808; 2626 Bancroft Way) and the **Pacific Film Archives** (same building, ☎ 510-642-1412). The film library, the largest on the west coast, shows special interest and esoteric films daily. The **Robert Lowie Museum of Anthropology** on the campus often hosts impressive shows of archaeological finds.

Around the campus extend the vital streets, pulsating with craftspeople, dreamers, and gourmet groupies. **Telegraph Avenue**, which extends from Sather Gate, is the most active of these streets, populated by students, artisans, and the homeless. Several coffee shops offer places to sip a cappuccino and watch the parade.

Shattuck Avenue, between Cedar and Rose streets, puts you in the heart of trendy Berkeley, close to the latest in gourmet grocery stores and the landmark Alice Waters' **Chez Panisse** restaurant (☎ 510-548-5049; 1517 Shattuck Avenue).

College Avenue extends from the University all the way to Oakland's Broadway. For the walker, this is a pleasant stroll, with intermittent residential and shopping areas. The stores cluster around Ashby and from Alcatraz to Broadway, complete with several wine shops and specialty providers favored by carriage-trade gourmands. The Market Hall complex of restaurants and shops at the BART station on College Avenue is typical of the scene.

The University's **Lawrence Hall of Science** (☎ 510-642-5132) on Centennial Drive in the East Bay Hills, offers a quick immersion in the intricacies of science and technology. Built as a research facility for science education, the museum is filled with "hands on" displays and exhibits where you can test scientific principles and conduct experiments. An astonishing **Sunstone sculpture** in back of the Lawrence Hall will alert you to the time of day and your place in the universe, providing you ask for the brochure decoding the sculpture. If your wishes are less ambitious, simply gaze out at the elaborate view of the East Bay from this promontory. The view from the Lawrence Hall and all along the Grizzly Peak Boulevard is one of the better vistas in the East Bay, taking in both San Francisco and the Golden Gate Bridge.

As you drive up to the Lawrence Hall, you pass through Strawberry Canyon and the **University Botanical Garden** (☎ 510-642-3343) which has 8,000 specimens of arid vegetation from around the world. Picnic tables in this garden and in the California Redwood section across the road offer pleasant places to relax.

The South Bay

The region was first a rustic outpost, a Spanish mission and pueblo in the 18th century.

Today you can still visit the site of Mission Santa Clara de Asis, on the University of Santa Clara campus (☎ 408-554-4023; 500 El Camino Real). Based on the Franciscan padres' own measure of success, Santa Clara exceeded any other mission in California. That mark of success was the number of Indians who were baptized. A total of 8,536 went through the rites here.

San Jose was California's first official town. In November 1777 the order was given at the presidios, or forts, of Monterey and San Francisco for a march to San Jose. The stated purpose was the founding of a town. Sixty-six soldiers and their families formed the first community.

To glimpse their world, stop at the **Peralta Adobe**, 184 West St. John Street, in San Jose. When you enter the grounds, you'll see the adobe itself, whose empty interior can be viewed through barred windows. Other exhibits include a scale model of the original adobe complex and a detailed map of all early San Jose adobes.

Luis Maria Peralta and his wife, Maria Loreto Alviso, populated the countryside with 17 children, a not uncommon number for early California families. As a reward for military service, Peralta was given one of the largest and most valuable Spanish land grants, Rancho San Antonio, 44,000 acres. When he died in 1851, Peralta's net worth exceeded a million dollars.

Downtown San Jose

Two features of downtown San Jose are of special interest to the traveler.

The Romanesque-style post office building at 110 Market Street has become the **San Jose Museum of Art** (☎ 408-271-6840).

San Francisco & the Bay Area

Though much of earlier downtown San Jose has disappeared before the forces of modernization, this handsome old post office was saved. Constructed in 1892, this was the first federal building in San Jose. It served as a US Post Office from 1892 to 1923. Designed by Willoughby Edbrooke and constructed of locally quarried sandstone, this Romanesque style structure is the last of its kind on the West Coast.

If the building seems constructed of stone similar to that used for Stanford University's quadrangle buildings, your hunch is correct. The same quarry provided rock for both structures. The museum features changing shows in most of its galleries and rotating materials from its permanent collection in one upstairs gallery. A gift shop exhibits crafts and a judicious selection of books about the region.

As a counterpoint to the Romanesque post office/art museum, walk past a host of banks to 225 Almaden Boulevard, the corner of Almaden Boulevard and Park Avenue, to see the **San Jose Center for the Performing Arts**. In front you'll find a characteristic, granite Benny Bufano sculpture, called *California Bear*, reminiscent of his other sleek depictions of animals.

Performing arts are flourishing in San Jose even though the Symphony has its financial problems, as do symphonies everywhere, with the threat of a musician's strike on opening night a nightmare that became a reality during one season. However, the San Jose Symphony pulled through, without going bankrupt, something that could not be said for neighboring Oakland's symphony.

The San Jose Repertory Theater boasts sellout performance seasons. Civic Light Opera is also flourishing, with an incredible 25,000 season ticket sales.

High-Tech Encounters

One interesting high-tech tour of Silicon Valley is at the **NASA/Ames Research Center** in Mountain View (☎ 650-604-5000). On the tour of this 430-acre research facility you'll learn what NASA is now doing. You'll visit a wind tunnel where experimental aircraft are studied. Other stops on the tour include a centrifuge, a flight-simulation facility studying pilot error, and a hangar housing experimental aircraft.

The NASA facility is at Moffett Field, where you'll see immense hangars as long as football fields. These hangars were for dirigibles, those lighter-than-air craft that enjoyed brief popularity in the 1930s. The largest hangar was built in 1933 to house the *USS Macon*, fully 785 feet long. Five Sparrow Hawk fighter planes could be launched from the belly of the dirigible. Unfortunately, the *Macon* went down in a storm off the California coast near Big Sur. Its sister ship, on the east coast, suffered the same fate off New Jersey. These disasters closed the brief aviation chapter on dirigibles.

Another interesting perspective on the region can be gleaned with a stop at the **Intel Museum** (☎ 408-765-0503; 2200 Mission College Boulevard, in Santa Clara). The Intel Museum shows the technology development within the computer chip since the 1960s, portraying an only-yesterday wonder at the technologies that Intel has pioneered. Located in the ground floor of Intel's corporate headquarters, this small but very well designed museum manages to make the complex world of computer chips and Pentium processors fascinating and entertaining. There are hands-on exhibits and historical documents that trace the development of everything from the company's name to its breakthroughs in chip design and manufacturing.

The Silicon Valley's most complete celebration of technology is an entity known as **The Tech Museum of Innovation** (☎ 408-279-7150; 145 West San Carlos Street; Web site www.thetech.org). Since opening in 1990, the Tech Museum of Innovation has done an admirable job of capturing the creative spirit of Silicon Valley's entrepreneurs. Its modest home in downtown San Jose presents a fascinating array of displays that enable visitors to do everything from design a state-of-the-art bicycle to build a Web page. In the fall of 1998, the museum will move to a new $59 million, 112,000-square-foot facility that will both increase its exhibit space and add an Omnimax theater to its mix. Four galleries at The Tech focus on Silicon Valley innovations.

Santa Clara Wineries

Not all the passions of the Silicon Valley amount to discussions of RAM and ROM, however. Other debates center on the pleasures of Cabernet or Riesling. The more than 50 Santa Clara-based

San Francisco & the Bay Area

wineries with extensive plantings to the south in Monterey County include some of California's premier wine producers.

Within the San Jose area, one tasting-touring stop can be highly recommended. On the east side of the valley is the **Mirassou Vineyards** (☎ 408-274-4000; 3000 Aborn Road). The Mirassous go back five generations to the 1850s. They were pioneers in developing the grape fields in Monterey, to the south, but they kept their ancestral hearth and winery headquarters in San Jose. They run a hospitable tasting room and serve quality wines.

Three attractions are substantial parts of the South Bay tourism picture. They are Paramount's Great America amusement park, noted for its rides; the Rosicrucian Museum, legacy of a historical and spiritual cult; and the Winchester Mystery House, where the heir to the Winchester arms fortune created an endless, rambling Victorian.

Great America

When you look at a map, Great America, including the mammoth parking lot, occupies almost a town-sized area adjacent to Santa Clara. A hundred acres of family oriented entertainment cluster around the landmark carousel, Columbia, whose 103 prancing animals evoke a nostalgic, earlier America.

Constant performances by brass bands, stage musicals, an IMAX theater, trained dolphins, and an Americana theater group greet the visitor. Mascots of the entertainment complex include Hanna Barbera creatures, such as Yogi Bear, Huckleberry Hound, and Scooby Doo, plus the Smurfs and Fred Flintstone. There is a notable American effort at superlatives, with the Pictorium movie theater's screen billed as the world's largest. You can operate your own race car on the Barney Oldfield Speedway.

The most spectacular aspect of Great America (Highway 101 to Great America Parkway (☎ 408-988-1776) are its hair-raising rides. The new Drop Zone Stunt Tower plummets the rider from the world's tallest freefall ride.

Rosicrucian Museum

Of equal interest is a tour-de-force museum, a one-of-a-kind historical and spiritual experience known as the Rosicrucian Egyptian Museum, Park and Naglee avenues in San Jose, ☎ 408-287-9171.

Rosicrucians, known as "The Ancient, Mystical Order Rosae Crucis," operate here an Egyptian Museum, Planetarium, and Science Museum. The assembled ancient Near Eastern artifacts are stunning in their range.

This worldwide fraternal and educational order of men and women attempts to cultivate learning about man and nature that first flourished around 1400 BC. The organization encourages individuals to develop their own personal philosophies based on this knowledge and insights, which have ramifications in metaphysics, mysticism, philosophy, psychology, parapsychology, and science. Any pedagogic or propagandistic efforts at the museum are extremely low-key, almost as if the ancient artifacts should speak for themselves.

Winchester Mystery House

Also on the major curiosities list for the Silicon Valley is a phenomenon called The Winchester Mystery House (525 South Winchester Boulevard (☎ 408-247-2101).

Sarah Winchester's house is a tour de force, usually portrayed as a monument to her fears rather than to her eccentricity. The 160-room Victorian house, gardens, and historical museum of Winchester rifle paraphernalia include such oddities as stairs leading to dead ends and doors that open to solid walls.

For some 38 years between 1884 and 1922 Sarah Winchester employed a small army of workers, adding onto the eight-room farmhouse she purchased when she moved to San Jose. She devoted five million dollars to the project. As the heiress to the fortune made from the Winchester repeating rifle, the "gun that won the West," she had an income of about $1,000 per day and a fortune of around $20 million at her disposal. She died in 1922 at age 83.

Stanford University

Near the north end of Silicon Valley, at Palo Alto, stands a monument to another prominent Californian who shaped the future of the state – Leland Stanford. The monument is **Stanford University**, (☎ 650-723-2560) well worth a day of exploring. Stanford's motive for founding a university, in 1881, was to perpetuate the memory of the family's only child, Leland Jr., who had died of fever in Florence, Italy at the age of 16. As Stanford put it, "The children of California will be our children."

Little did Stanford, the railroad builder and Governor, dream that one day the technical departments in the University would nurture an entirely new industry. Graduates with names like Hewlett and Packard led these developments.

■ Adventures

On Wheels

Scenic Driving in San Francisco

 San Francisco is a city for walking, but for an overview of the major attractions, the scenic **49-Mile Drive** is recommended. Renting a car for a half-day will give you the mobility to make the drive, which skirts the perimeter of the city. The Visitors Bureau office at Hallidie Plaza, Powell and Market streets, can assist you with a map. The route is well marked by blue and white seagull signs.

One of the special scenic drives in San Francisco is a tour of the **Victorian architectural legacy**.

Touring the Victorians

Though 28,000 buildings were destroyed by the Earthquake and Fire of 1906, some 14,000 remained, mainly in the western half of the town, west of Van Ness Avenue.

Victorian Styles

There were basically three main Victorian design styles – Italianate, Queen Anne, and Stick, also known as Eastlake.

Italianate was in vogue from 1850-1875, and is characterized by bay windows whose side windows slant inward. Italianate design has pipe-stem columns flanking the front door and flat crowns over the doors and windows.

Queen Anne, patterned after a style popular in England in the 1860s, is marked by rounded corners, hooded domes, sinister-looking windows, and the use of shingles for siding material.

Stick, or Eastlake, is similar to Italianate, but from a later period, mainly the 1880s. Certain esoteric clues known to the architectural buff distinguish the style, mainly chamfered corners on pillars, incised decoration, and horseshoe arches.

From the Visitors Bureau office at Hallidie Plaza you can obtain a driving or walking tour map that will take you past the best of the Victorians.

Here are some directions that will seem obscure to read, but keep them in mind if driving. The streets suggested are precise because so many streets in the area are one-way. If you're walking, that's no problem, though the walk is long. If you're driving, the exact directions will be useful. Start at Franklin and California. From the right westbound lane on California turn right on Franklin, left on Pacific, left of Gough, right on Sacramento, right on Webster, left on Pacific, left on Scott, left on Clay, right on Steiner, right on Sacramento, left on Divisadero, left on Golden Gate, right on Scott skirting Alamo Square via Hayes and Steiner, left on McAllister, right on Divisadero, right on Bush, and left on Laguna to Union. With the map in hand, these turns will be obvious. Once you've planned the route, keep your eyes open to see all the structures.

The tour ends at Union Street, affectionately known as Cow Hollow because this was the city's first dairyland. Explore on foot the 1600 to 2200 blocks on Union Street, with its many intriguing alleyways and boutiques.

Inside a Victorian

You can tour one of the most striking and best preserved of these dwellings, the **Haas-Lilienthal House** (2007 Franklin Street; ☎ 415-441-3004) built in 1886. The classic Queen Anne building with its gables, bay windows, and turret tower, still houses much of the original decor, such as mahogany walls, marble hearths, and fine tapestries. Call ahead to see if you need a reservation.

For a leisurely look at the Victorians, also known as "Painted Ladies," there's a Victorian Home Walk given daily, year round (2226 15th Street; ☎ 415-252-9485).

Scenic Driving in Marin County

The entire Highway 1 through Marin County is the area's prime scenic drive and has been described under *Touring*. Here we'll focus on a close-in scenic drive around the **Marin Headlands** and the adjacent small towns of Sausalito and Tiburon.

The Marin Headlands

Take the Alexander Avenue exit just north of the Golden Gate Bridge and proceed to Bunker Road. The road passes through the Barry-Baker Tunnel to Rodeo Valley. The different entities within the area that you can see are the Headlands, the Tennessee Valley, the Forts (Baker, Barry, and Cronkite) and Rodeo Beach.

The Marin Headlands, north of Golden Gate Bridge.

The Marin Headlands is studded with gun emplacements from the era when a vision of Japanese storming east from Hawaii to make a surprise strike at San Francisco fanned the local passions. Much of the Marin Headlands can now be hiked, offering pleasing views, with over 100 miles of trails. The land is managed by a federal park agency known as the Golden Gate National Recreation Area (☎ 415-331-1540) which supplies trail maps.

The Visitor Center at Fort Barry Chapel will inform you about the area and how to enjoy it. There's plenty of parking at Rodeo Beach for a beach walk. Hikers enjoy the Miwok, Coast, and Tennessee Valley trails.

Other interesting places to stop here are the **Marine Mammal Center** (☎ 415-289-7325) which specializes in animal recovery after disasters, and the **Golden Gate Energy Center** (Building 1055, Fort Cronkite) which shows alternative energy devices, especially wind electric generators so feasible in this area. The Point Bonita Lighthouse, guiding ships in through the Golden Gate, provides splendid views of the Golden Gate Bridge.

Sausalito/Tiburon

Alexander Avenue also drops east down the hill to Sausalito and Tiburon. Make this the second aspect of your scenic drive. Both towns are good shopping, dining, and gallery-browsing places, with trendy small spots on the waterfront, sister cities to the likes of Carmel and Mendocino. A ferry can also take you here from Pier 41 in San Francisco if you don't want to drive. In Sausalito, which means "little willow," walk the main street, Bridgeway, and note the restaurants, shops, and galleries. The Village Fair houses some 30 shops on four stories. Among galleries, for example, photographer Mark Reuben (12 Princess Street) provides lovely views of the most obvious San Francisco-region scenes at moderate prices.

Two special Sausalito attractions are a long walk or a short drive from the downtown. The first is an immense two-acre model of the San Francisco Bay and the Delta, complete with a hydraulic system with which to run tests on tidal surge and freshwater flows. Be sure to see this curiosity, which helps explain the complex water dynamics of the region. Stop in at the **Bay Model Visitor Center** (☎ 415-332-3870; 2100 Bridgeway, foot of Spring Street; open Tuesday-Saturday). The handsome Visitor Center, a successful public relations gesture by the Army Corps of Engineers, includes picnic tables at the waterfront, where you can gaze at restorations-in-progress as work proceeds on the historic ship *Wapama*, which will eventually return to its family of historic ships at the Hyde Street Pier in San Francisco.

The second attraction is an armada of hundreds of live-in **houseboats** at Waldo Point, 3030 Bridgeway. You can walk out on the elaborate piers that serve as sidewalks to this on-the-water neigh-

San Francisco & the Bay Area

borhood. This fleet of houseboats shows a notable absence of conformity to any pre-conceived idea about what the proper shape, size, or appearance of a dwelling on the water should be. The houseboats represent, depending on the perception of the observer, either a fresh breath of affordable housing or a ragtag lapse of zoning enforcement.

Scenic Driving the East Bay

Scenic drives in the East Bay would include excursions to explore the East Bay Regional Parks, the wine world of Livermore, the peak known as Mt. Diablo, and the home of the great conservationist, John Muir.

Justly celebrated as one of the special suburban park systems in the country, the **East Bay Regional Parks** (☎ 510-562-7275) boast 53,000 acres of land with excellent trails for the walker.

Tilden Park in the Berkeley hills is representative of these pleasures. Inspiration Point amounts to one of the lovelier walks. The Environmental Education Center is excellent for nature interpretation. The Botanic Garden, also known as the California Native Plant Garden, recreates the biotic regions of California, alpine to seashore, with representative plants from each. This garden is a wonderful spot for a picnic and a superb introduction to the diverse landscapes of the Golden State.

The **Livermore Valley**, east of Oakland along Highway 580, is the home of a small but honorable wine region. Wente and Concannon are the wineries to visit. German and Irish ancestors in these families began making wine here in the 1880s. Try a Wente Riesling or a Concannon Petite Sirah. Wente is the more visible of the two, at 5565 Telsa Road (☎ 510-456-2300) with tastings and winery tours daily.

Mt. Diablo looms over the increasingly urbanized corridor of rolling hillsides, dotted with oak trees. For a panorama of the area, drive to the top of 20,000-acre Mt. Diablo State Park (☎ 510-837-2525). The view from the summit offers a regional perspective, allowing you to see in all directions. On a clear day you can see the Sierra to the east, the web of channels in the Sacramento Delta, and the coast mountain ranges to the west, all the while charting the flow of the Sacramento River through the Bay. Walk the chaparral trails, especially in the months of February-April, to see lovely displays of spring wildflowers.

John Muir's house (☎ 510-228-8860; 4202 Alhambra Avenue, Martinez) is now a National Historic Landmark. The house recalls the era when Muir managed a fruit ranch into which the impoverished wanderer married. Muir was a successful businessman, but he regarded work as only a necessary provider of sustenance to support his trips to Yosemite and other wilderness areas, about which he wrote so eloquently. At this shrine to the founder of the environmental movement, you can see a movie on Muir's life and work.

Scenic Driving the South Bay

One enjoyable scenic outing in the area south of San Francisco would be a look at the great institution of learning, **Stanford University** (☎ 650-723-2560).

In 1881, after the tragic death from typhoid fever of their 16-year-old son in Florence, Italy, Leland Stanford and his wife turned their 8,200-acre stock farm in Palo Alto into the Leland Stanford Jr. University so that "the children of California may be our children."

Today this cerebral farm, home for 14,000 students and an establishment of medical and technical professionals, is well worth a visit.

Drive south from San Francisco along Highway 101 and turn onto University Avenue, which takes you through the heart of Palo Alto, once known as Professorville. University Avenue becomes Palm Drive after you cross the El Camino Real. As you proceed up Palm Drive, stop at the University Museum of Art. The Museum shows memorabilia of Stanford and describes how he rose from a Sacramento hardware man to become the railroad builder and governor. One of the appealing California Indian exhibits is a Yurok canoe carved from a single redwood log.

The Stanford Campus

Continue on Palm Drive to the oval parking area. Immediately in front of you is the most historic part of the University, the Main Quadrangle, a sandstone-enclosed courtyard in the Romanesque style, with archways and thick walls. Red tile roofs inadvertently echo the missions. Memorial Church, dedicated in 1903, was Mrs. Stanford's memorial to her husband.

Walk east from the main quadrangle to the Hoover Tower, the 285-foot landmark. You can take an elevator to the top daily from 10 am to 4:30 pm. The tower houses the Hoover Institution on War, Revolution, and Peace, which has substantial collections of papers and books related to world conflicts. At the base of the tower you'll find a museum room honoring Herbert Hoover, the Stanford graduate and engineer whose enduring legacy was not his presidential years, but his earlier feat, as Secretary of the Interior, when he negotiated successfully among the Southwestern states the agreement to construct the Hoover Dam. Without the dam's Colorado River water, hydro-electrical power, and flood control, life in California and the West would be substantially different today.

To get a feel for campus life, walk from the Hoover Tower to Tresidder Union and stop for a cup of coffee. You'll pass such landmarks as the Main Library, Encina Hall, and the Campus Bookstore. If you haven't visited Stanford in recent years, the addition of outdoor sculptures has changed the physical look of the campus.

Bicycling San Francisco

One of the great San Francisco bike rides is out over the **Golden Gate Bridge**. Start at the Marina Green, where you can park your car if you are carrying a bike. If you want to rent a bike or more powerful two-wheeled vehicles, one provider in the Marina area is **American Bicycle, Scooter & Motorcycle Rentals** (☎ 415-931-0234; 2715 Hyde Street). **Bay Bicycle Tours**, located on the first level of the Cannery (☎ 415-923-6434; 2801 Leavenworth Street) also rents bikes and coordinates tours to Sausalito.

Bicycling the Golden Gate

This bike trip winds west from the Marina Green parallel to the bridge along the Golden Gate Promenade path. At the bridge, you cross to the Marin County side. You can then either return on the same route or make a circular trip by going into Sausalito and catching a ferry back to the Ferry Building.

Bicycling along the San Francisco Waterfront.

The main subject to consider during this magnificent ride is the Golden Gate Bridge.

The Golden Gate is one of America's best-loved landmarks. Whether seen from the south and north end visitor viewpoints or from special vantage points, such as the deck of an excursion boat, the Golden Gate Bridge is a pleasing sight. From a bike you get a special close-up feel for the bridge and can cover the distance in little time.

The gracefulness of its suspension construction, the bridge's proportion alongside the green hills of Marin County to the north, and the orange-vermilion color of the bridge against the blue sky and sea add to the effect. The shiplane below the Golden Gate has become its own bridge to the Orient, adding to the mystique of the site.

Building the bridge required both political vision and technical imagination. A San Francisco character of the 1860s, named Emperor Norton, is credited with the first public proposals for a bridge. In the 1870s railroad magnate Charles Crocker presented plans for a bridge. However, the task was enormous and public interest dwindled until 1916, when newspaperman James Wilkins launched an editorial campaign favoring a bridge. The idea appealed to North Bay residents who were transporting their cars across on time-consuming ferries. Spanning the Golden Gate, however, seemed more like a dream than a possibility. In 1917, San Francisco's chief engineer, M. M. O'Shaughnessy, enlisted the aid of a Chicago engineer, **Joseph B. Strauss**, to design and build the bridge.

Strauss followed the project attentively for the next two decades. A distinguished bridge builder, Strauss engineered over 400 bridges from Leningrad to New Jersey in his lifetime. A statue at the south end of the bridge acknowledges his role as *The Man Who Built The Bridge*.

The political hurdles required to build the bridge were considerable. In 1930 voters in the six counties making up the Bridge District approved issuing the bonds to finance it. This act required some vision as the nation waded through the Depression. In January 1933 Strauss broke ground for construction of the towers. Admirably, the bridge was built on time and under its $35 million budget, with the last bridge bond paid off in 1971. Today's toll goes entirely towards maintaining the bridge, including its never-ending schedule of painting.

The first technical challenge in the 1930s construction involved the 4,200-foot length of the span, which many said could not be bridged successfully. Strauss weighed plans for a suspension bridge, which risked being too flimsy, and a cantilever bridge, which might be too heavy for the site. His original plans called for a design incorporating both ideas. From an aesthetic point of view, his later decision to focus just on the suspension approach proved far superior. At that time, a suspension bridge of this length had not yet been built.

The location of the bridge, bearing the full brunt of the ocean elements, exaccrbated potential problems of design. Winds of 20-60 miles per hour are commonplace. A broadside wind at 100 miles per hour produces a midspan sway of 21 feet, which had to be allowed for. Heat and cold cause expansion and contraction of the bridge, which creates a movement of 10 feet up and 10 feet down. The depth of the water underneath the bridge and the speed of the current are major technical challenges. Pacific tidal pressures are enormous in the narrow outlet, especially when the 7½ knot tidal outrush combines with the swift-flowing waters of the Sacramento and San Joaquin Rivers emptying through this gap into the ocean. Strauss decided to anchor one of the 65-story towers right in the waterway, 1,215 feet from shore.

Bicycling Golden Gate Park

Another good bicycle outing in San Francisco would be a tour through Golden Gate Park. Rentals are possible from **Golden Gate Park Skate and Bike** (☎ 415-668-1117; 3038 Fulton Street and Sixth Avenue). The best plan is simply to meander through the park from the Haight Ashbury entrance out to the ocean. With any local city map, such as one procured from the Hallidie Plaza Visitor Center at Powell and Market streets or the Beach Chalet building at 1000 Great Highway, you can find the paths in the park and enjoy this huge urban amenity.

Bicycling Marin County

Marin County is an excellent mountain biking area. For example, there are more than 35 miles of trails open to cycling at Point Reyes National Seashore and another 10 miles in the adjacent Golden Gate National Recreation Area. The Marin Headlands, Muir Woods, and Mt. Tamalpais all are great biking areas.

Two contrasting rides that we've enjoyed in Muir Woods and Point Reyes epitomize the biking experience available in Marin County. In **Muir Woods**, you can get information and a good map at the Visitor Center and then begin a bike trip nearby up the **Dipsea Trail**. This trail is fairly steep, so the ride will be definitely aerobic, but the terrain eventually levels off. You pass through ridgeline meadows, redwood forests, and oak/bay tree forests. The ride can go on into Mt. Tamalpais State Park or over to the ocean at Stinson Beach.

By contrast, the **Coast Trail** in **Point Reyes**, starting from the Youth Hostel, offers a gentle and level ride of 5.6 miles round-trip. You will want to take this ride slowly to enjoy the deer, the families of quail chicks, and finally the expansive views of the shoreline and cliffs. On the day of our ride a redtail hawk flew past us with a snake in its claws. The area is recovering from wildfires of October 1995. Get information on the ride and a map from the Visitor Center at Point Reyes. This is a superb hike, also, if you don't want to bike. You can bike in Point Reyes in all the developed areas with roads, colored tan on Point Reyes maps, but not in the wilderness trail areas, indicated in green.

Bikes can be rented in the Point Reyes area at **Trailhead Rentals** (88 Bear Valley Road, Olema; ☎ 415-663-1958). Another bike rental supplier, in Point Reyes Station, is the **Building Supply Center** (☎ 415-663-1737).

Bicycling the East Bay

The East Bay Parks system amounts to a magnificent resource for various outdoor adventures, including bicycling. One of the best bike trips is on the ridge path from **Inspiration Point** in **Tilden Regional Park**, along Wildcat Canyon Road in the Berkeley hills. The paved path proceeding out from Inspiration Point offers some of the loveliest panoramic vistas in the Bay Area, presenting a swath of greenery from the Golden Gate Bridge to the North Bay waters approaching the Delta. Mount Diablo looms on the horizon and San Pablo Reservoir pops up in the foreground. On a clear day the distances visible are striking. If you're looking for a sunny biking ridge with a fairly level paved path and ample picnic places, this is hard to beat. There are plenty of dirt paths off the paved path for the bicycle explorer, and the end of the paved path transforms into an extended dirt path with some steep grades. Detailed maps can be obtained from the East Bay Regional Parks (☎ 510-635-0138). Bikers share the paved path for four miles with inline skaters, who find this one of the most satisfying places for their sport. Also on the path are hikers, couples pushing baby strollers,

Bicycling from Inspiration Point at Tilden Park in the Berkeley Hills.

and dog-walkers. It can be busy, but people on the path are courteous and camaraderie is strong, especially since the path is a full two lanes wide. While close in to the urban area, the vistas remind a biker of just how many square miles of green open space have been set aside as public land in the East Bay. This is not a wilderness, however, but rather a grazed cow pasture terrain, something of a disappointment. You may need to park some distance from the trailhead on weekend days, when the small parking lot at Inspiration Point fills up fast. There is no fee for using the trail.

Bicycling the South Bay

Five special parks in the South Bay area offer excellent biking, as well as hiking, backpacking, and camping.

Three of the parks are clustered on the mid-peninsula on the sea-facing slopes of the mountains in San Mateo County. The first is **Memorial County Park** (☎ 650-879-0212; 9500 Pescadero Road, 5½ miles southwest from La Honda). Adjacent is **Sam McDonald County Park** (☎ 650-879-0238; 13435 Pescadero Road, near La Honda). From Sam McDonald you can access **Pescadero Creek County Park**, which is largely undeveloped.

The other two parks are south of San Jose in rustic and remote terrain. **Mt. Madonna County Park** (☎ 408-842-2341; Hecker Pass Road, Highway 152) has substantial redwood forests in its 3,093 acres. **Henry Coe State Park** (☎ 408-779-2728; East Dunne Avenue from Morgan Hill) is a vast grasslands park covering 80,000 acres.

As the sport of mountain biking has advanced, each of these parks has opened its roads to the biker. The three San Mateo County Parks have miles of old logging roads now open to the bicyclist, meandering through the redwood and Douglas fir forests. Henry Coe State Park, a cattle ranch in the earlier days, has over 100 miles of back-country roads through its grassland domain. Call each of these parks to get details on the biking pleasures.

To rent bikes in the region and get support, contact the Stanford Campus Bike Shop, ☎ 650-325-2945; 551 Salvatierra, Stanford.

San Francisco & the Bay Area

Railroading

Fans of the early-day horse-and-train transportation will enjoy a visit to **Ardenwood Historic Farm** (☎ 510-796-0663; Patterson House, 34600 Ardenwood Boulevard) in the East Bay community of Fremont. Ardenwood has an historic, single-car, horse-drawn train, one of the last of its kind. Belgian draft horses pull the car along a half-mile branch of the Southern Pacific Railway.

For contemporary railroading, of course, the **Amtrak** trains depart from the new station at Jack London Square in Oakland to various touristic points in California. With Amtrak you could ride out to the Central Valley and catch a bus up to Yosemite. You could also ride east through the Sierra and contemplate the momentous task of building the transcontinental railroad. You could take a day trip from the Bay Area on Amtrak up to Sacramento and immerse yourself in the great Railroad Museum at Old Sacramento, which portrays the sociological story of the railroad and shows the rolling stock that made it possible. All these details can be arranged by calling Amtrak at ☎ 800-872-7245.

Three of the best railroad experiences in Northern California are beyond the Bay Area and are discussed in their sections of the book. Besides the **California State Railroad Museum** (☎ 916-445-7387; Second and I streets) in Old Sacramento, there are two nostalgia train trips not to miss. See the Sierra and Gold Country chapter for Old Sacramento. The nostalgic trains are the **Skunk Train** (☎ 800-777-5865) from Fort Bragg to Willits, discussed in the North Coast chapter, and the **Roaring Camp Railroad** (☎ 408-335-4484) described in the Monterey-Santa Cruz chapter.

On Foot

Hiking & Backpacking in San Francisco

Some of the best hikes in San Francisco are urban walks along the Golden Gate Promenade, in Golden Gate Park, at Fisherman's Wharf, through Chinatown/North Beach, and around Angel Island, the most rustic of these options. It is also possible for a backpacker to stay overnight on Angel Island, a special treat.

Hiking the Golden Gate Promenade

The Golden Gate Promenade is a glorious hike or bike path extending from the Marina Green to the Golden Gate Bridge. This is a bracing walk, filling the lungs with sea air, and presenting the superb landscape of the bridge and Marin County headlands. Walk onto the Golden Gate Bridge from the south side. Pause to salute the statue of the Man who Built the Bridge, Joseph Strauss. Gaze at the structure from the gardens on the south side, then amble out on the Bridge to see the San Francisco skyline and the many small sailboats scudding along below.

Hiking Golden Gate Park

To hike Golden Gate Park, sit down with a map and plot a course. Maps are available at the Hallidie Plaza visitor center. You could begin at the Japanese Tea Garden, especially if you are here in the spring when the cherry blossoms are out. Then allow time for a walk through the Park.

In 1887 Golden Gate Park comprised 730 acres of dunes and 270 acres of arable land scattered with oak trees. Today the park is a landscape of lush meadows, lakes, dense stands of Australian eucalyptus, and thousands of different shrubs, flowers, and trees. This popular park is both a cultural and recreational center. When you look at Golden Gate Park today, it is difficult to imagine how in the 19th century much of the western half of San Francisco was a shifting sand dune. Expert landscapers, such as Frederick Law Olmstead, despaired of ever taming the dunes. Yet the city fathers, showing much foresight, set aside $800,000 for the purchase and development of the acres that would be known as Golden Gate Park. Like the great hotels and the Opera House, the Park was both a gesture and a legacy to the future, an index of the confidence that San Franciscans had in the city's growth and destiny, a sense that the city would later need the civilizing and recreational opportunities afforded by a major park.

There are perennial walking appeals here, such as an outing amidst the tranquil garden settings at the 75-acre **Strybing Arboretum** (☎ 415-661-1316). The Arboretum is an encyclopedia of world plants, especially of trees. Because of its mild climate, San Francisco can grow an unusually large spectrum of plants.

San Francisco & the Bay Area

Walking Fisherman's Wharf

Walk Fisherman's Wharf to see the crab sellers, the many shops, and the seafood restaurants. The historic ships at the Hyde Street Pier are adjacent to Fisherman's Wharf and are worth an hour of exploring. They include the last of the Bay hay scows, the *Alma*, and a classic example of the small schooners that brought lumber to San Francisco from ports on the North Coast, the *C. A. Thayer*.

Walking Chinatown

Explore North Beach/Chinatown with a hike the length of Grant Avenue through Chinatown and Upper Grant, starting at Bush and walking until the street ends, north of Columbus. With a walk you'll get a feel for the Chinese and Italian districts and the pleasure of listening to different dialects.

San Francisco's Chinatown is a 16-block community best experienced on foot. The **Chinese Cultural Center** (☎ 415-986-1822) offers walking tours of the area Saturday afternoons.

Grant Avenue is the main street for a general overview, starting at Bush. Stockton between Washington and Broadway is where you'll find the largest concentration of markets, exhibiting an amazing array of vegetables and meats. The food markets stock vegetables such as Chinese bok choy, and live birds, including pigeons. Numerous fat ducks hanging raw or cooked and paper-thin dried fish are two unusual sights. On Stockton you may even see a butcher carve up a turtle.

A temple on Waverly is open to visitors and instructs on the spirituality of the Chinese. Visit the **Tin How Temple** (125 Waverly) to see the offerings of oranges, rice, and tea to ancestors and to the gods. Incense burns constantly in this restful and meditative setting of carved Buddhas and red lanterns. The building housing the temple exhibits a colorful facade, as do the other temples, such as the Norras Temple, on this quiet street running parallel to Grant.

Jade and ivory carving can be seen at many shops, such as **Jade Empire** (832 Grant). The oldest grocery here is **Mow Lee** (774 Commercial) dating from 1856.

Hiking Angel Island

The most rustic walk available close to San Francisco is an outing to Angel Island State Park (☎ 415-435-1915), a large island inhabited by deer and packed with picnic sites, 12 miles of hiking trails, 10 miles of biking trails, and recreational facilities for volleyball, fishing, and camping. The island is littered with gun emplacements that, fortunately, were not needed in the 1940s. Two electric-powered trams circle the eight-mile perimeter of the island daily from May-October. Ferries to Angel Island leave from Pier 39-41 and from Tiburon (☎ 415-435-2131). The Alameda/Oakland Ferry (☎ 510-522-3300) offers service. Call ahead for schedules and information.

Backpack campers on Angel Island in San Francisco Bay.

Hiking & Backpacking in Marin County

The choicest hike in Marin, arguably, would be a trek through **Muir Woods National Monument** and beyond to the Pan Toll Ranger station in Mt. Tamalpais State Park. Muir Woods charges only $2 for admission, something of note when it now costs $20 to drive your car into Yosemite. Parking at Muir Woods can take some time, but there is ample parking down the road toward Highway 1. Allow sufficient time for the walk back to the monument and the start of your hike. Muir Woods has a splendid grove of old growth redwoods. You would have to drive hours north to Humboldt State Park or south to Big Basin State Park to equal the experience.

As you walk into the redwood area of Muir Woods, there is a cathedral hush to the cool, moist environment, which is also exceptionally clean, giving you an impression that people can actually be trained to manage their gum wrappers and film boxes if given enough coaching. The ancient redwoods tower above you. A stream passes through Muir Woods. Sword fern and oxalis cover the forest floor. Near the entrance there is an easy paved path if you want just a short walk among these towering giants. However, if you want a substantial hike, there are plenty of options.

Muir Woods Trails

Get a map of the Monument and adjacent Mt. Tamalpais State Park, but be aware that the maps passed out are not terribly accurate, and double check your directions with the ranger if you want an all-day outing. One option would be to go up the **Bootjack Trail** to the Pan Toll Ranger Station, which takes you on a steady climb through a redwood, Douglas fir, and oak forest terrain, much of it a wilderness area. This is a cool, shaded, dark environment, as is true of all redwood habitats, since the towering trees darken the ground and even cool it by condensing water on their leaves, dripping several inches of moisture in the course of a year.

At the Pan Toll Ranger Station check with the rangers and get the best maps available, then set off on the **Dipsea Trail**, taking a sunny, exposed ridges as you make your way back toward the Muir Woods entrance. The sunny Dipsea Trail contrasts with the shady Bootjack Trail. The Dipsea Trail is both a hiking path and a separate fire-road used by bikers, separating these sometimes competing interests. Muir Woods and Mt. Tamalpais form a contiguous area, so where they begin and end is almost invisible. The terrain has a pleasing variety, including some steep stretches that will delight a hiker who wants a mini-mountain climbing experience. The area is also an entirely wild environment, which contrasts with the grazed world of the East Bay Parks, which are pleasant open spaces but have the man-made stamp of a cow pasture on them.

If you'd like a guided walk in Muir Woods, one provider is **Tom's Scenic Walking Tours** (☎ 510-845-0856). The tours depart daily from San Francisco and take in the scenic trails of Marin. Tom Martel, a former Sierra Club guide, leads the walks through Muir Woods or other choice Marin County areas.

Point Reyes Trails

At Point Reyes walking and hiking are major activities. The **Bear Valley Trail** is a 4.4-mile walk from park headquarters to the sea. This is a pleasant half-day walk with time for a picnic at the coastside. The slope of the wide trail is gentle and the terrain varies from oak forest to streambank.

One of our favorite hikes in all of Northern California is a spring wildflower walk in April or May at **Chimney Rock** in Point Reyes. This large bluff area, rich with vegetation and scenic views, shows such a profusion and variety of wildflowers that you will be dazzled. California poppies are numerous, as are deep blue and purple Douglas iris. Lupines and yellow mustard, wild radish and various yellow composites are among the treats here. More of a stroll than a rigorous hike, the trip is perfect for someone who wants to meditate on the combined beauty of the wildflowers, the sea, and the bluffs of Point Reyes. To reach Chimney Rock, stop at the Point Reyes Visitor Center and obtain a good Point Reyes map. Chimney Rock is at the farthest point on the peninsula, near the Lighthouse. Chimney Rock is also a good birding habitat and a promontory for whale watching.

Backpacking is also excellent at Point Reyes. Be sure to call ahead (☎ 415-663-8054) to make a reservation. You can walk or bike in to the Glen, Wildcat, Sky, or Coast camps, where you'll find water and pit toilets. Point Reyes offers miles of back-country wilderness to the backpacker.

Hiking & Backpacking the East Bay

The East Bay presents some of the Bay Area's finest and most accessible hiking. **Briones Park** in the East Bay Regional Parks system offers one of the more satisfying hiking situations. The park occupies a huge chunk of the map of the East Bay. It is located on the Bear Creek Road turnoff from San Pablo Dam Road. Visitors arriving from Highway 24 take the Orinda exit. Briones is an ex-urban immersion, almost a wilderness feel of total isolation. The area is grazed, but it is often possible at Briones to imagine yourself in a Bay Area with no people. The terrain is also varied, which will please a hiker who enjoys some up and down hill trekking. The plant communities are also complex, from open grasslands to oak woodlands. From some of the higher hills, you get clear views of San Francisco Bay. Any of the hillsides could serve as a picnic site. This is more of a hiker-friendly than a biker-easy park. Bikers tend to park here and enjoy riding the San Pablo Dam Road, where they can open up, rather than strike out on the heavily rutted paths of the park. There is a modest entrance fee to the park.

Briones is but one element of the many parks in the East Bay Regional Park system. For a packet of maps and brochures on all these parks, send a $5 check to East Bay Regional Parks, 2950 Peralta Oaks Court, Box 5381, Oakland, CA 94605-0381; ☎ 510-562-7275. After looking through the packet of maps and park brochures, you might be inspired to hike a section of the Skyline National Recreation Trail that runs along 31 miles of the crest of the East Bay Hills. At many elevated positions on this trail you get stunning, panoramic views of the Bay Area.

Tilden Park in the Berkeley Hills is further representative of these fine hiking parks. The Botanic Garden (☎ 510-841-8732), also known as the California Native Plant Garden, is a quiet place for a stroll. The garden recreates the biotic regions of California, alpine to seashore, with representative plants from each. If you have time for only one short hike, walk through this superb introduction to the diverse landscapes of the Golden State.

Hiking & Backpacking the South Bay

Leave the valley floor and climb into the foothills for an earthquake hike at **Los Trancos Park**. This lovely walk amidst rolling grasslands and oak trees acquaints you with the infamous San Andreas Fault, which rumbles occasionally underneath. A self-guided tour pamphlet describes in detail the geology of the fault. Ominous warnings, however, are little heeded by valley residents, as they raise a glass of Chardonnay to a high-tech future. For info on Los Trancos call the Mid-Peninsula Open Space District (☎ 650-691-1200) that manages substantial public lands here. Call them to receive a packet on all the lands they manage. Los Trancos Park is off Page Mill Road, seven miles west of Highway 280.

The Baylands

Another enjoyable South Bay hike takes you out along the Bay in Palo Alto to see the remarkable natural environment and bird life of the Bay. This park is simply called the Baylands (☎ 650-329-2506). At Embarcadero Road you turn towards the Bay and park at the end of the road. The diverse flora and fauna of this shallow, open bay has all the appeal of a California redwood forest for an informed observer. Moreover, the absence of man-made structures on the Bay adds an important spatial dimension to human feeling in the region, especially for the seeker of solitude.

At Palo Alto Baylands, you can make the acquaintance of salt marsh flora and birds. A trail system of boardwalks and levees allows the special experience of walking in the marsh, even during high tide. The main boardwalk leads out from the interpretive center to an observation deck near the water's edge. Connecting boardwalks installed originally for maintaining utility towers add to the potential walking territory.

At the **Lucy Evans Baylands Nature Interpretive Center**, on the fringe of the salt marsh, there is a lecture room, a library, exhibits, and an observation deck. The mounted birds, from a great blue heron to sandpipers, are a few examples of the many species found here. Trained naturalists manage the operation. Guided bird and plant walks, slide shows, movies, and ecology workshops are some of the activities here. Programs emphasize seasonal migration patterns and the interdependence of plants and animals.

Birds are a special treat here. The 1,500 total acres of preserve along a 2½-mile frontage allow for a sufficiently large habitat to maintain a range of species. Marsh hawks, black-shouldered kites, canvasback ducks, goldeneye ducks, and burrowing owls are just some of the winged residents. Migrating, overwintering, and permanent-resident birds can be seen. For birdwatchers, this is an excellent place to see secretive California clapper rails at high tide. About half of the 200 species of birds common to the region can be seen in the shallow waters and marshes of the bay.

South Bay Parks

Five special parks in the South Bay area offer excellent hiking/backpacking, as well as biking and camping.

Three of the parks are clustered on the mid-peninsula on the sea-facing slopes of the mountains in San Mateo County. The first is **Memorial County Park** (☎ 650-879-0212; 9500 Pescadero Road, 5½ miles southwest from La Honda). Adjacent is **Sam McDonald County Park** (☎ 650-879-0238; 13435 Pescadero Road, near La Honda). From Sam McDonald you can get access to **Pescadero Creek County Park**, which is largely undeveloped.

The other two parks are south of San Jose in rustic and remote terrain. **Mt. Madonna County Park** (☎ 408-842-2341; Hecker Pass

San Francisco & the Bay Area

Road, Highway 152) has substantial redwood forests in its 3,093 acres. **Henry W. Coe State Park** (☎ 408-779-2728; East Dunne Avenue from Morgan Hill) is a vast grasslands park covering 80,000 acres.

Hikers/backpackers can envision the three San Mateo County parks as one unit because they have interconnected trails, over 50 miles of paths and old logging roads. The four-mile Ridge Trail in Sam McDonald offers good views of the Pacific. Sam McDonald also has a hiker's hut, which can be reserved, reducing the need for backpacking equipment. Pescadero Creek has several backpacking sites, such as Shaw Flat and Tarwater Flat. Memorial Park's Mt. Ellen Nature Trail and Tanoak Nature Trail offer a good introduction to the regional flora.

Mt. Madonna Park's Giant Twins trail takes you past two large redwood trees that escaped the loggers' saws. The Merry-Go-Round trails skirts the entire perimeter of the park, showing the madrone and tan oak forests as well as redwood forests for which Mt. Madonna is noted.

Henry W. Coe Park has over 22,000 acres of wilderness ready for the hiker. The spring wildflowers on these grassy slopes are a special treat. Thirty-one backpack camping sites have been designated in remote areas.

On Horseback

Horseback riding occurs in San Francisco in Golden Gate Park and along Ocean Beach. **Golden Gate Park Stables**, John F. Kennedy Drive and 36th Avenue, is San Francisco's equestrian facility (☎ 415-668-7360). A 1½-hour ride takes you through the park and then out onto the magnificent beaches along the west side of the City.

In Marin County one of the main horseback riding opportunities is at **Five Brooks Ranch** in Point Reyes National Seashore. They offer guided rides of one, two, and 3½ hours, plus all-day rides. The trails traverse Point Reyes National Seashore. Be sure to make reservations (☎ 415-663-1570) and check with them the day before if weather conditions are bad. Rides can be canceled if trails become impassable. Five Brooks Ranch is located near Olema at the Five Brooks Trailhead entrance to Point Reyes National Seashore, 3½ miles south of the Highway 1/Sir Francis Drake Boulevard junction.

In the East Bay you can ride through the regional parks with horses from the **Chabot Riding Stables**. They rent horses for guided rides through Chabot Regional Park, year round, weather permitting. Chabot Riding Stables is at 14600 Skyline Boulevard, Oakland, ☎ 510-638-0610.

On Water

Excursion Boats on the Bay

Take an excursion boat ride on San Francisco Bay to view the cityscape and enjoy the open expanse of the bay.

One of the most pleasurable ways to see the sights is aboard the 103-foot-long **Hawaiian Chieftain** (☎ 415-331-3214) that sails from Sausalito and offers sunset cruises, Sunday brunch trips, and adventure sailings when the full sail power of this sleek ship is engaged. This 1790s-style tall ship carries its passengers in style as it glides underneath the Golden Gate Bridge.

Other providers are the **Blue & Gold Boat Fleet** (Pier 39; ☎ 415-705-5444 for departure times and information) and the **Red & White Fleet** (Pier 43; ☎ 415-546-2628 for recorded schedule information). Besides a classic tour outing on the Bay, these fleets offer various other options, such as a ride over to Tiburon and back or round-trip rides to Angel Island.

The extensive **ferry system** on the Bay can also combine sightseeing with transportation. For example, you could take the ferry from San Francisco to Larkspur and back. For details, call the ferries at Golden Gate Transit (☎ 415-923-2000).

Hornblower offers posh trips out of San Francisco and Oakland on its upscale yachts, providing great views, good food, and live entertainment. Hornblower's programs include dinner dances and champagne Sunday brunches. Call ☎ 415-788-8866 for details.

San Francisco & the Bay Area

Kayaking Tomales Bay in Marin County.

Kayaking/Canoeing

Tomales Bay in the Point Reyes area offers a special kayak experience. You kayak out from Inverness along the forested Tomales Bay shoreline and enjoy the forests that stretch down to the water. Small and secluded beaches are good for a swim break in summer. Extraordinary bird life can be observed during the migration periods. On Tomales Bay it's often best to head northwest into the prevailing wind and then sail back to your starting point. Tomales Bay is fairly protected and calm if you stay close to the Point Reyes shoreline. You might see some special sights, such as rays eating mussels amidst the rocks near shore. The yellow chalk cliffs and heavy vegetation of forest are a pleasing contrast with many other kayaking situations, where the terrain is relatively flat. The provider of kayaks here is **Blue Waters Kayaking Tours and Rentals**, ☎ 415-669-2600; 12938 Sir Francis Drake Boulevard, Inverness.

On San Francisco Bay, **Sea Trek Ocean Kayaking Center**, in Sausalito, is a leading kayak provider (☎ 415-488-1000).

In Oakland the kayak/canoe enthusiast will find an elaborate provider in the Jack London Square shop known as **California Canoe and Kayak** (☎ 510-893-7833; 409 Water Street). They sell kayaks and offer classes in kayaking skills. From their Oakland base, they rent kayaks and do tours of the nearby Oakland estuary. Their other tours take in the San Francisco waterfront, Angel Island, and various areas along the California coast. They also do kayaking river trips in the Sierra and to the north on the Klamath River.

Sailboats/Powerboats/Windsurfing

For sailboat charters, with or without a skipper, the **Modern Sailing Academy** in Sausalito rents to non-members who pass an on-the-water checkout (☎ 415-331-8250).

At Stinson Beach, contact **Off the Beach Boats** (☎ 415-868-9445) for boat rentals.

Windsurfers congregate at Point San Quentin, near the Larkspur Ferry Terminal on East Sir Frances Drake Boulevard. There is usually a mobile windsurf-rental truck there if you want to try a board. Chances are you will also want to rent a wetsuit because the waters are chilly.

At the Berkeley Marina there are also active sailing and windsurfing providers. Contact the **Cal Sailing Club** (☎ 510-287-5905), which is open to the public. They rent an extensive range of boats and offer lessons.

In the East Bay one relaxing lake sailing opportunity is at Oakland's **Lake Merritt Boating Center** (☎ 510-444-3807; 568 Bellevue Avenue). They rent El Toro, Sunfish, Capri, and Hobie Cat sailboats as well as canoes for excursions around this unusual saltwater lake in the middle of Oakland.

Fishing

Fishing in the Bay Area tends to concentrate on charter boat activities in search of salmon and halibut. Beyond the Bay Area, in the more inland region, the quarry changes to bass in the reservoirs and trout in the streams.

At all the major ports in the Bay Area charter boats go out for salmon (March-September), halibut (June-September), and rock or ling cod (all year). The fishing boats may become whale watching boats in winter and early spring.

There are many charter boat fishing operations at Fisherman's Wharf in San Francisco. **Miss Farallones Sport Fishing**, based at Space 6 along the Wharf, offers daily departures, weather permitting, on a 50-foot charter boat. Everything you need is provided, including licenses, rods and tackle. Reservations are required and may be made by calling ☎ 415-346-2399.

Caruso's Café (☎ 415-332-1015) at the Sausalito Yacht Harbor has been offering sport fishing trips and selling fishing supplies since 1957. This cozy place does a good mealtime business of fresh fish and crab sandwiches.

One exception to the dearth of freshwater lake fishing in the Bay Area is at **San Pablo Dam Reservoir** (☎ 510-223-1661) in the East Bay at 7301 San Pablo Dam Road. This extensive reservoir has good trout, crappie, bass, and sunfish fishing. The concessionaire at the reservoir sells all the necessary gear and fishing licenses. Over 5,000 anglers caught their limits of trout last year at San Pablo Dam Reservoir.

There is more trout fishing for those who seek it out. The Mt. Tamalpais watershed encompasses five lakes in its 20,000 acres. The state Department of Fish and Game (☎ 415-459-0888) keeps the lakes stocked with trout.

Whale Watching

Whale watching is a major pleasure along the Northern California coast. The whales in question are the Pacific gray whales, which proceed on one of the longest migrations of any mammal. The whales swim 6,000 miles from their Arctic feeding grounds to the protected lagoons of Baja California to give birth and mate. This southward trek occurs December-February. From March-May they are making the northward trip back to the summer feeding grounds off Alaska. The migration takes them six to eight weeks each way, traveling alone or in groups up to 12. During the southward migration they may swim for 20 hours per day, covering 100 miles. Brought to the edge of extinction, the Pacific gray whale population now hovers comfortably at about 30,000 individuals.

One of the foremost sponsors of whale watch boats led by expert naturalists is **Oceanic Society Expeditions**, which maintains an office in the Fort Mason Center in San Francisco. Call their whale watch phone (☎ 415-474-3385) to make reservations for their charter boats leaving from San Francisco or from Half Moon Bay on frequent sailings from late December to early April. The chartered boat *New Superfish* carries 49 passengers from San Francisco. The *Salty Lady* carries 48 on trips out of Pillar Point Yacht Harbor in Half Moon Bay.

Many other fishing boats, from Monterey to Crescent City, lead whale watching expeditions. A knowledgeable naturalist on board is helpful to understand the whale migration.

You can also see whales from the shore all along the coast. One of the choicest sighting places is Point Reyes at the Lighthouse, especially in January. Bring your binoculars during any excursion along this coast. The Lighthouse can also be visited, but there is a 312-step walk down and back to negotiate.

In the Air

Scenic Flying

 The nostalgia buff, yearning for a scenic aerial perspective of the Bay Area, will enjoy a DC-3 flight. A company called **Otis Spunkmeyer Air** (☎ 800-938-1900) operates the vintage DC-3 from the North Field at the Oakland Airport.

San Francisco Seaplane Tours (☎ 415-332-4843) with departures from Pier 39 and Sausalito, offers conventional sightseeing flights as well as sunset champagne sweeps of the Bay.

For a different experience, climb aboard a jet helicopter available through **San Francisco Helicopter Tours and Charter**. Flights are from the San Francisco International Airport. Call ☎ 800-400-2404 for reservations.

Hang Gliding

Bird's eye views of the San Francisco area are available at Fort Funston on the western shores of San Francisco. A lively hang gliding community congregates at this park. With proper instruction, tandem rides are sometimes possible. One provider for the sport is the **San Francisco Hang Gliding Center** (☎ 510-528-2300; 977 Regal Road, Berkeley).

■ Where to Stay & Eat

Accommodations in San Francisco

 San Francisco has always been able to serve up satisfying experiences in its lodgings. There are grand hotels, major chains, boutique small hotels, B&Bs, and economy lodgings. Weekend rates can sometimes be a fraction of weekday charges in the hotels that host many business travelers.

A visitor is advised to call ahead to the **Visitor Bureau** (☎ 415-391-2000) to receive a copy of the *Lodging Guide*, which has a thorough listing of hotels, including many budget options.

Grand Hotels

Among the grand hotels, the establishment with the most favored location is the **Westin St. Francis** (☎ 415-397-7000 or 800-228-3000) on Union Square, complete with its own cable car stop. "Meet me at the St. Francis" has been the slogan for generations of celebrities and the well-to-do, referring to a rendezvous at the Compass Rose Room off the lobby. The Compass Rose is famous for the way the hours of the day proceed from tea at 4 pm to champagne at 5 pm and 10-oz. martinis at any time. The Westin St. Francis is at 335 Powell Street, San Francisco, CA 94102. $$$

For the traveler who wants the finest, another good choice is **The Clift Hotel** (☎ 415-775-4700 or 800-652-5438; 495 Geary Street, San Francisco, CA 94102. $$$). The Redwood Room at the Clift, with its wood decor and piano music, is one of the elegant bars and dining rooms of the city.

The **Renaissance Stanford Court Hotel** (☎ 415-989-3500; 905 California Street, San Francisco, CA 94108. $$$) parallels the Clift in the higher echelon of hotels for service, rooms, and overall quality, including its distinguished restaurant, **Fournou's Ovens** (☎ 415-989-1910).

Also in this league is the **Ritz Carlton** (☎ 415-296-7465 or 800-241-3333; 600 Stockton Street, San Francisco, CA 94108. $$$).

The outdoor patio at the Ritz Carlton is noted for its Sunday brunches.

Two grand hotels reflect the ethnic flair of the city in a highly stylized manner.

Hotel Nikko (☎ 415-394-1111 or 800-645-5687; 222 Mason Street, San Francisco, CA 94102. $$$) is an example of contemporary Japanese-style influencing the hotel world. The Nikko also has a health club and a heated indoor pool.

The **Mandarin Oriental** (☎ 415-885-0999; 222 Sansome Street, San Francisco, CA 94104. $$$) offers an elegant Financial District location with view restaurant on top. The Mandarin Oriental is known for the impeccable service one might expect to find in Hong Kong or Singapore.

Another premier example of a luxury hotel is the nostalgic **Huntington Hotel** on Nob Hill. The Huntington (☎ 415-474-5400; 1075 California Street, San Francisco, CA 94108. $$$) was constructed as a posh residence hotel in the 1920s. The property was converted to a hotel in the 1940s, but the lavish apartment rooms remained intact. Individually decorated rooms, comfortably formal public rooms, and attentive service are hallmarks of the Huntington. Students of California history will recognize that the name refers to Colis P. Huntington, one of the movers and shakers in the railroad-building days of 19th-century California.

The **Fairmont Hotel and Tower** (950 Mason Street, San Francisco, CA 94108; ☎ 415-772-5000 or 800-527-4727. $$$) offers quality from atop Nob Hill. Complete with health club and view restaurants, the Fairmont is a venerable San Francisco institution.

The **Mark Hopkins Inter-Continental** (1 Nob Hill, San Francisco, CA 94108; ☎ 415-392-3434 or 800-327-0200. $$$) honors a California founding father, appropriate in its Nob Hill location. The Mark Hopkins presents a genteel atmosphere with panoramic views.

The **Pan Pacific Hotel** (500 Post Street, San Francisco, CA 94102; ☎ 415-771-8600 or 800-533-6465. $$$) is an airy edifice, built around a massive atrium, architecturally distinctive. The spacious rooms are known for their marbled amenities.

San Francisco & the Bay Area

Chain Hotels

Most of the major chain hotels are represented in San Francisco. They can often be good values on the weekend, when business travelers have deserted them and rates fall dramatically.

For example, the well-located **Grand Hyatt San Francisco** on Union Square (☎ 415-398-1234 or 800-233-1234; 345 Stockton Street, San Francisco, CA 94108. $$$) has romantic getaways, golf and shopping packages as well as a rooftop jazz club.

The **Hyatt Regency** is famous for its lobby (5 Embarcadero Center, San Francisco, CA 94111; ☎ 415-788-1234 or 800-233-1234. $$$) whose 17-story atrium, complete with hanging plants and exotic birds, has become a friendly gathering place in the city. The Hyatt anchors the Bay end of Market Street, San Francisco's parade street and main thoroughfare.

The **San Francisco Hilton** near Union Square (333 O'Farrell Street, San Francisco, CA 94102; ☎ 415-771-1400 or 800-445-8667. $$$) is a mammoth hotel, almost a city in itself, with 1,914 rooms. The lobby is an international crossroads buzzing with the sound of languages from far-off places.

Holiday Inn Union Square (480 Sutter Street, San Francisco, CA 94108; ☎ 415-398-8900 or 800-243-1135. $$$) has a choice downtown location, close to Union Square. Some rooms are studios, offering good mid-price value in the downtown area.

The **San Francisco Marriott** (55 Fourth Street, San Francisco, CA 94013; ☎ 415-896-1600 or 800-228-9290. $$$) is a tall, south-of-Market hotel known as the "Jukebox" because of its stylized art deco architecture.

Boutique and B&B Hotels

San Francisco has many options in this category.

In the moderate to upscale price range, one cluster of stylish boutique hotels are those developed by the Kimco Group, which has almost 2,000 restored hotel rooms in recycled buildings usually adjacent to a fine restaurant.

One Kimco choice would be the **Galleria Park Hotel** (191 Sutter Street, San Francisco, CA 94104; ☎ 415-781-3060 or 800-792-9639. $$$) next to the Galleria and only two blocks from Union

Square. **Perry's**, the adjacent restaurant, is a favorite watering hole.

Another popular, newer Kimco property is the **Hotel Monaco** (501 Geary Street, San Francisco, CA 94102; ☎ 415-292-0100 or 800-214-4220. $$$) and its adjoining Grand Café.

Often the desire of the traveler is for a central location, dependable hotel amenities, but still a feeling of B&B intimacy, complete with breakfast. One such effort to meet this need in San Francisco is the **White Swan Inn** (845 Bush Street, San Francisco, CA 94108; ☎ 415-775-1755 or 800-999-9570. $$$).

The traveler looking for a Victorian feel in an upscale lodging in San Francisco could be directed to the **Archbishop's Mansion** (1000 Fulton Street, San Francisco, CA 94117; ☎ 415-563-7872 or 800-543-5820. $$$) where each room creates an atmosphere reminiscent of a 19th-century opera. The property is a handsome Victorian in the Alamo Square area, surrounded by other notable survivors of the 1906 quake.

Budget to Moderate Hotels

There are a surprising number of budget to moderate hotels, many of which are listed in the *Lodging Guide*.

The **Atherton Hotel** (685 Ellis Street, San Francisco, CA 94109; ☎ 415-474-5720 or 800-474-5720. $$) is a restored small hotel with reasonable rates, near the Civic Center and the Performing Arts Center. With its cozy lobby and Abbey Room bar, the Atherton also has its Atherton Grill restaurant serving American food.

The **Hotel Richelieu** (1050 Van Ness Avenue, San Francisco, CA 94109; ☎ 415-673-4711 or 800-295-7424. $$) is located near the Opera House and Civic Center. The Richelieu has the charm of an old San Francisco hotel, a resurrected minor Grande Dame, in a central location at a reasonable price.

 Lest the budget traveler despair, know that illusion and reality are not always the same in hotel rates. The $$$ published rack rate we quote is often not the actual rate paid. Almost every hotel has some kind of discount or deal, bringing that to $$ or even $. Few commodities are more perishable than an

San Francisco & the Bay Area

unsold hotel room, so don't be afraid to bargain, which can be done politely, with the solicitation, "Do you have any room tonight you could offer me at xx dollars?" You may find the answer surprisingly positive.

The *Lodging Guide* lists a number of hotels and reservations services with published rates of $60 and under.

At $55 per night, consider **The Amsterdam** (749 Taylor Street, San Francisco, CA 94108; ☎ 415-673-3277 or 800-637-3444. $). Recently renovated, The Amsterdam provides a continental breakfast.

At $49, the **Grant Plaza Hotel** (465 Grant Avenue, San Francisco, CA 94108; ☎ 415-434-3883 or 800-472-6899. $) places you near the entrance to Chinatown.

If you have been happy with a budget chain hotel, expect that it will have a San Francisco location. For example, the **Econolodge** (825 Polk Street, San Francisco, CA 94109; ☎ 415-673-0411. $) has a published rate of $45 and children stay free.

Hostels

Travelers comfortable with the hostel travel style of shared rooms, bathrooms, and chores can find good options in San Francisco.

Hostelling International San Francisco-Fort Mason (Building 240, Fort Mason, San Francisco, CA 94123; ☎ 415-771-7277. $) enjoys a choice location, includes laundry facilities, and charges $15 per night.

When considering adventure travel lodgings in Northern California, the hostels are an economical alternative. Hostellers provide their own food and bed linen, usually a sleeping bag, though linen can sometimes be rented. Everyone participates in some morning cleanup chores before going out for day adventures. The cost per night is typically $10-$20. The central hostel information source is **San Francisco Travel Center**, 308 Mason Street, San Francisco, CA 94102; ☎ 415-788-2525. They have complete information on membership in this organization. The San Francisco Travel Center can acquaint you with many other hostels scattered over Northern California, often in terrific locations, ranging from the middle of Point Reyes to the Pigeon Point Lighthouse on the San Mateo Coast. Adjacent to their office is **Hostel at Union Square** (312 Mason Street, San Francisco, CA 94102; ☎ 415-788-5604. $) with lodging for $16 per night.

Green Tortoise Hostel & Guesthouse (494 Broadway, San Francisco, CA 94133; ☎ 415-834-1000. $) includes breakfast and sauna in its $20 fee.

Accommodations in Marin County

 Marin County is especially noted for its B&Bs in the Point Reyes/Inverness area and its view lodgings in Sausalito.

B&Bs

Sandy Cove Inn, in Inverness, epitomizes the Point Reyes area B&Bs. Quiet and peaceful, the inn has modern country-decor rooms that are self-contained, with everything from robes to a walking stick for hiking. Natural blond wood, tiles, Southwest designs in the sofa cushions, and fresh flowers are examples of the detail. Breakfast is served in your room, so this is a good B&B for people who want to be by themselves, enjoying a glass of wine on their own deck. The red iron stove for warmth, the tranquil set of tapes and CDs for easy listening, and direct access from the inn to nearby Tomales Bay beaches and hikes, are a delight. The proprietors are knowledgeable about the area and can guide you to all activities. Sandy Cove Inn is at 12990 Sir Francis Drake Boulevard, Inverness, CA 94937; ☎ 415-669-2683. $$$.

Each B&B has its own style, which is part of the fun of B&B travel. For example, **Holly Tree Inn & Cottages** consists of rooms in a large house, each with private bath, where part of the ceremony is the communal, gourmet morning breakfast. Holly Tree also has several special cottages. One cottage, Sea Star, is on a pier over the water. At Sea Star Cottage you even have your own hot tub and telescope for spotting birds at dawn. As you reside there, at the end of a 75-foot dock, the tide goes in and out underneath you. Sea Star has a full kitchen and its own breakfast room, with the breakfast discretely packaged and delivered to you the afternoon before so as not to disturb the tranquility of the morning. Holly Tree Inn & Cottages is at 3 Silverhills Road, Point Reyes Station, CA 94956; ☎ 415-663-1554. $$-$$$.

Bear Valley Inn (88 Bear Valley Road, Olema, CA 94950; ☎ 415-663-1777. $$) is an 1899 Victorian Ranch House, close to the Point Reyes Visitor Center. The inn has three decorated guest rooms, full breakfast, a large parlor with a fireplace, and nearby bike or horse rental.

Ten Inverness Way Bed & Breakfast Inn (10 Inverness Way, Inverness, CA 94937; ☎ 415-669-1648. $$-$$$) is a restored 1904 house, surrounded by English gardens. There are five rooms and stone fireplaces.

Roundstone Farm (9940 Sir Francis Drake Boulevard, Olema, CA 94950; ☎ 415-663-1020. $$-$$$) is on a 10-acre horse ranch and offers views of the surrounding Olema Valley. Five cozy bedrooms have been built in this ranch-style setting.

Blackthorne Inn (266 Vallejo Avenue, Inverness, CA 94937; ☎ 415-663-8621. $$-$$$) is a carpenter's fantasy - a giant treehouse, complete with a fireman's pole, spiral staircase, and hot tub. The inn has five rooms and serves a buffet breakfast.

The B&Bs, restaurants, and other travel service providers of West Marin have joined together in a **West Marin Visitor Bureau**, PO Box 869, Inverness, CA 94957. They can send you a brochure.

Information and referral services include **The Inns of Point Reyes** (PO Box 145, Inverness 94937; ☎ 415-663-1420) representing seven inns, and **Point Reyes Lodging** (PO Box 878, Point Reyes Station, CA 94956; ☎ 800-539-1872) representing about two dozen properties.

An economical alternative to lodging in Marin would be a stay at the **Point Reyes Hostel**, located in the middle of the Point Reyes wilderness. The hostel is a handsome house, adjacent to the Coast Trail, from which you can walk or bike to some of the loveliest Point Reyes beaches. There are accommodations for 44, including a family room. The hostel has hot showers, a country kitchen, a dining room, and rates under $20/night. Contact Point Reyes Hostel, PO Box 247, Point Reyes Station, CA 94956; ☎ 415-663-8811. $. Note that there is also a **Marin Headlands**

Hostel, Bldg. 941, Fort Barry, Sausalito, CA 94965; ☎ 415-331-2777. $.

In Sausalito

Aside from Point Reyes area B&Bs, the other special lodgings in Marin County are the hotels in Sausalito with a view of the Bay, San Francisco, and the Golden Gate Bridge.

Within Sausalito, the **Hotel Sausalito** (16 El Portal, Sausalito, CA 94965; ☎ 415-332-4155. $$-$$$) has a convenient downtown location. A convivial staff and comfortable antique-filled surroundings make this a distinctive, yet reasonably priced lodging. The Sausalito Hotel puts you in the heart of downtown, but a level above the street.

The **Alta Mira Hotel** (125 Bulkley Avenue, Sausalito, CA 94966; ☎ 415-332-1350. $$-$$$) lodges you above the bustle of the city in rooms that provide a spectacular view of San Francisco, Angel Island, and the Bay. Whether or not you stay at Alta Mira, squeeze in time for a drink or meal at its terrace restaurant.

Upscale travelers to Sausalito will enjoy the **Casa Madrona Hotel** (801 Bridgeway, Sausalito, CA 94965; ☎ 415-332-0502 or 800-567-9524, $$$) which begins at Bridgeway and sprawls over a hillside in a mock-Victorian cluster of houses, cottages, and aeries.

In Larkspur

In the urban eastern area of Marin, if you take the ferry from San Francisco to Larkspur, one convenient lodging near the landing is the **Larkspur Courtyard Marriott** (2500 Larkspur Landing Circle, Larkspur, CA 94939; ☎ 415-925-1800, $$).

Accommodations in the East Bay

One of the grand places to lodge in the East Bay is the **Claremont Resort & Spa** (41 Tunnel Road, Berkeley, CA 94705; ☎ 510-843-3000 or 800-551-7266. $$$). This white *fin-de-siècle* palace of gentility has been renovated and repositioned by its owners as an *urban resort*, complete with a spa.

Another dependable lodging is the **Berkeley Marina Marriott** (200 Marina Boulevard, Berkeley, CA 94710; ☎ 510-548-7920. $$-$$$) at the foot of University Avenue in the Berkeley Marina. This lodging, surrounded by sailboats and water, is a reassuring spot for the visitor who has been overly panhandled by crazies on Telegraph Avenue or trended to death by California cuisine at Chez Panisse. There's plenty of open space, two indoor pools, rooms with views and patios, the presence of sailboats, and an on-site restaurant/bar, The Bay Grille, where you can sit around the fireplace and watch the sailing life.

Gramma's Rose Garden Inn (2740 Telegraph Avenue, Berkeley, CA 94705; ☎ 510-549-2145. $$-$$$) is a large B&B inn in a converted 1905 Tudor-style house with a folksy atmosphere, located a few blocks from the University. This establishment is indeed like grandma's. Think floral patterns on overstuffed sofas. Homelike without being precious, this B&B's rooms look like places you might relax and sleep in rather than an antique store where you could accidentally break something.

The **French Hotel** (1538 Shattuck Avenue, Berkeley, CA 94709; ☎ 510-548-9930, $$) offers a personable, small-scale, modern environment in the culinary mecca, opposite Chez Panisse. The café on the ground floor is a neighborhood favorite, serving espresso, fresh orange juice, and croissants.

Hotel Durant (2600 Durant Avenue, Berkeley, CA 94704; ☎ 510-845-8981. $$) offers dependable, modern hotel rooms close to the University. This recently restored structure includes a lively bar and restaurant, **Henry's**.

The premier downtown Oakland lodging is the handsome **Oakland Marriott City Center** (1001 Broadway, Oakland, CA 94607; ☎ 510-451-4000. $$) close to Old Oakland, Chinatown, and the Oakland Museum.

The choice Jack London Square lodging is **The Waterfront Plaza Hotel** (Ten Washington Street, Jack London Square, Oakland, CA 93607; ☎ 510-836-3800 or 800-729-3638. $$$). Their rooms overlook the water and put you within easy walking distance of the Square's attractions. **Jack's Bistro** offers fine dining.

Another dependable Jack London Square lodging offering good value is the **Best Western Inn at the Square** (233 Broadway, Oakland, CA 94607; ☎ 510-452-4565 or 800-633-5973. $$) which has a pleasant enclosed courtyard with pool.

An unusual option is **Dockside Boat & Bed** at Jack London Square and Pier 39 in San Francisco. They provide private yachts, from 34-68 feet, for overnight stays with breakfast. For details, ☎ 510-444-5858 in Oakland; ☎ 415-392-5526 or 800-436-2574 in San Francisco. $$$.

For an intimate and exotic spot, the **East Brother Light Station**, on East Brother Island, offers four rooms with views and the nightly serenade of foghorns (no extra charge). Guests are welcome Thursday through Sunday nights (117 Park Place, Point Richmond, CA 94801; ☎ 510-233-2385. $$$).

Accommodations in the South Bay

The luxurious **Fairmont Hotel** (170 South Market Street, San Jose, CA 95113; ☎ 408-998-1900 or 800-527-4727. $$-$$$) is a gracious 541-room structure that anchored the restoration of modern San Jose. In few cities could it be said that a hotel recreated the area downtown, but San Jose and the Fairmont are an exception. The pink-granite hotel, which opened in October 1987, commands the most prominent location in the city, downtown on the historic city plaza park. The massive set-back design of the hotel, topped by triangular motifs echoing other structures in the downtown area, creates a distinguished architectural signature for San Jose. This $150 million five-star facility, an investment of the Swig family, brought a major after-hours vitality to the urban center. The **Lobby Lounge Bar** of the Fairmont has become the fashionable and cheerful meeting place of the city, with piano music drifting through the expanse. Four restaurants leading off the lobby have transformed the gastronomic scene here. The **Pagoda Restaurant** (☎ 408-998-3937) is classy Chinese. The choice rooms at the Fairmont are the fourth floor lanai suites, complete with their own patios fronting a large outdoor pool, flanked by palm trees.

San Francisco & the Bay Area

Sculptor Benny Bufano's California Bear at the entrance to the Performing Arts Center in San Jose.

Another beautifully restored gem in San Jose is the **Hotel De Anza**, dating back to 1931. The De Anza delights its guests with an Art Deco design and lots of special touches. Conveniently located in downtown San Jose, it is within walking distance of the museums, historic sites, cultural venues and a growing number of restaurants and nightspots. Since undergoing a multi-million dollar refurbishing a few years ago, the hotel has a contemporary look that is mixed with nostalgic touches like the handheld shower head in the spacious bathrooms. Guests with late-night appetite attacks can take advantage of the hotel's "Raid Our Pantry" resource that is open from 10 pm to 5 am. Make a sandwich or enjoy fresh fruit, but be sure to save room for the appetizing breakfast buffet served in the hotel's dining room. The Hotel De Anza is at 233 W. Santa Clara Street, San Jose, CA 95113; ☎ 408-886-1000 or 800-843-3700. $$$.

If lodging in the **Palo Alto** area, it is possible to stay at B&Bs created in early Victorians. Try the **Cowper Inn** (705 Cowper Street, Palo Alto, CA 94301; ☎ 650-327-4475. $$) or the **Victorian on Lytton** (555 Lytton, Palo Alto, CA 94301; ☎ 650-322-8555. $$$).

Restaurants in San Francisco

Fisherman's Wharf

The renaissance of food at Fisherman's Wharf is one of the pleasant culinary stories of San Francisco in the late

1990s. Candid observers will concede that Fisherman's Wharf did go into decline, with over-priced fast food the norm for awhile. But the place has made a turnaround. In part, competition from the rest of the city forced this. Additonally, it simply took some time as Fisherman's Wharf went through a franchise phase until the movers and shakers concluded that they had to go back to their roots, with the Italian families offering a high quality product and asking a fair price.

Two leaders in the restaurant rebirth are Alioto's and A. Sabella's. **Alioto's** gets the nod as the romantic, fine-dining choice on the Wharf. Smooth career waiters bring out a platter of the various fresh fish available for the day. At sunset the light plays on the fishing boats immediately beyond the dining room. The house wine is a winery-bottled vintage designated as the Alioto recommendation. A family of 42 Aliotos – yes, that's 42 – works at the restaurant, with patriarch Joe Alioto guiding the performance. Alioto's is at 8 Fisherman's Wharf and reservations are recommended. ☎ 415-673-0183. $$-$$$.

Across the street, the Sabella family has created a parallel upgrade of Fisherman's Wharf cuisine. Mike Sabella is in the kitchen managing some of his specialties, such as swordfish or abalone. They have a huge tank in which abalone and crab are kept fresh. **A. Sabella's** (3766 Taylor Street; ☎ 415-771-6775. $$-$$$) sits in an elevated position with a view of the bustle of the wharf and of the Bay. Live music plays nightly, and the bar has a cozy fireplace.

Another player in the culinary renaissance on the Wharf is the **Franciscan** (☎ 415-362-7733. $$-$$$) which gives a diner the pleasure of a panoramic view of San Francisco Bay, the bridges, and the sailboat action on the water. The Franciscan is a light and airy place, with large glass windows and a yellow-pastel color scheme. There's not a bad seat in the house because the dining levels are tiered back. The Franciscan has a modern and urban feel to it, with a wavy decor on its ceiling, posts, and carpets, following a recent renovation. Try the roast snapper or blackened shrimp.

Green's is a tour de force in the vegetarian culinary world, raising vegetarian cooking to an art form. Supplied by its own gardens at the Green Gulch Farms in Marin County, Green's concentrates

San Francisco & the Bay Area

on creating a few distinguished dishes each evening. Such delicacies as baby golden beets and beet greens are to be expected here, but would rarely make their way into a mainstream restaurant. Aside from the food, Green's has a lovely view of the adjoining yacht harbor. The restaurant is bright, with huge windows, and a cavernous open space, legacy of the military architecture of Fort Mason. Try the goat cheese tart. The lunch menu emphasizes sandwiches and salads. Green's also operates a lively takeout business (Fort Mason Building A; ☎ 415-771-7955. $$).

Ethnic

San Francisco also offers many ethnic restaurants. For a spicy Chinese meal, try the **Hunan Restaurant** (924 Sansome Street; ☎ 415-956-7727. $$). Try the Henry's Special (chicken, shrimp, and scallops) named for chef-founder Henry Chung. Another style of Chinese food is the dim sum lunch, featuring bite-size delicacies. One good choice for this would be the **Hang Ah Tea Room** (1 Hang Ah Street; ☎ 415-982-5686. $$). For the most elegant Chinese, try **Tommy Toy's** (655 Montgomery; ☎ 415-397-4888. $$$).

Chinese is, of course, only one of the spectrum of ethnic groups here. Thai would be another. **Racha** (771 Ellis Street; ☎ 415-885-0725. $-$$) is an excellent example of unpretentious ethnic restaurants in San Francisco. This Thai establishment serves imaginative food at moderate prices. Thais themselves give it hearty patronage. Try the fried noodles with dried shrimp, hot spices, and bean sprouts or a pork, shrimp, and mushroom concoction served on a bed of rice in a clay pot, called kow opp mor din.

Neighborhood Dining

Another approach to San Francisco restaurants is to make a choice of a place in a favored neighborhood you plan to visit, such as North Beach. If just browsing around, try an excellent bakery here with two North Beach locations, **Cuneo**, at 1501 Grant Street and 523 Green Street, $$. For a cappuccino or glass of wine, stop in at **Mario's**, on the corner of Columbus Avenue and Union Street, $$. Two North Beach institutions recommended for dinner are **Little Joe's** (523 Broadway; ☎ 415-433-4343. $$), with its open kitchen, and **Caffe Sport** (574 Green Street; ☎ 415-981-

1251. $$), which requires reservations. The food and atmosphere of both restaurants are the essence of North Beach. Little Joe's motto is, "Rain or shine, there's always a line." Watch the master chefs prepare food at the open kitchen. Try the pastas, such as gamberoni Napoli, prawns and vegetables in pasta, or the carbonara a la Franco, mushrooms and pasta.

Some North Beach places offer exceptional value for price. An example is **Des Alpes** (732 Broadway; ☎ 415-391-4249. $-$$) where a multi-course French dinner is served family-style. **North Beach Pizza** (1499 Grant Street; ☎ 415-433-2444. $-$$) has pizza, pasta, and veal in a convivial setting.

One distinct neighborhood to explore would be the Mission, where the Mission Dolores church is the oldest building in San Francisco. The Mission has many inexpensive Mexican and other Latin restaurants. **La Taqueria** (2889 Mission Street; ☎ 415-285-7117. $) offers a casual, authentic culinary encounter in the Latino Mission area, where you watch the experts prepare your food, perhaps a shredded chicken burrito with dollops of guacamole and spicy tomato sauce. The house specialties include refreshing fruit drinks.

If looking for a restaurant to hang out and converse in, one choice would be the **Cadillac Bar and Grille** (Howard between 4th & 5th streets; ☎ 415-543-8226, $$). Another, near Fisherman's Wharf, is the **Buena Vista** (2765 Hyde Street; ☎ 415-474-5044. $$) where, the proprietors claim, Irish Coffee was invented. This is a fitting drink for San Francisco, a city of brisk weather.

Classic Dining

One of the distinguished and dependable old-line restaurants is **Tadich's Grill** (240 California Street; ☎ 415-391-2373. $$). Tadich's is known for its grilled seafood and career waiters. Some of the diners will tell you how their grandfathers once ate here. Tadich's has been serving food since 1849 and claims to be one of the first 100 businesses in California. The endless wood counters and booths on one side offer no irrelevant frills, no cute gimmicks, just expertly grilled sole, petrale, and sea bass. Each day a new menu is printed, so don't hesitate to take a menu as a souvenir. If you've ever wondered what it takes to run a San Francisco restaurant, take a look at Tadich's daily shopping list: 200 pounds each of rex sole, petrale, and sand dabs; 40 pounds each of shrimp and abalone; 50 pounds flounder; 100 pounds crab meat; 25 pounds each of sea bass and halibut; and 80 pounds salmon. They accompany this cornucopia of seafood with 250 half-pound loaves of the sourdough bread so highly prized in San Francisco.

A restaurant steeped in literary history is **John's Grill** (63 Ellis Street; ☎ 415-986-3274. $$). This landmark eatery was part of the setting for Dashiell Hammett's famous novel, *The Maltese Falcon*. Try the fresh seafood and shellfish, such as the *fruits de mer* pasta or the prawns and scallops en brochette.

The restaurants in the great hotels, discussed under Accommodations, include some exquisite San Francisco eating spots. These include the **Redwood Room** at the Clift, **Fournou's Oven** at the Stanford Court, the Sunday brunch on **The Terrace** at the Ritz Carlton, and **The Big Four** at the Huntington.

Another one-of-a-kind restaurant, offering arguably the best aerial view in San Francisco, is the **Carnelian Room** on the 52nd floor of the Bank of America. Open at dinner time for drinks or a meal, the Carnelian Room has the steaks, seafood, and wine list that would warm a banker's heart. The daily pageant of fog creeping over the city is presented at no charge. The Carnelian Room is at 555 California Street, ☎ 415-433-7500. $$-$$$.

Innovative Fine Dining

But it is the evolving fine dining scene in San Francisco at independent restaurants that is the glory of the city. This is the new California cuisine, created by chefs who are artists and who sometimes become celebrities.

An example is Jeremiah Tower's **Stars** (555 Golden Gate Avenue; ☎ 415-861-7827. $$$). There are not many awards left for Jeremiah Tower to win. Try the grilled Chilean swordfish or the oven-roasted breast of capon.

Wolfgang Puck's **Postrio** (545 Post Street; ☎ 415-776-7825. $$$) combines California cuisine with Asian and Mediterranean accents. Chinese duck and roasted lamb are the patrons' favorites.

Washington Square Bar & Grill (1707 Powell Street; ☎ 415-982-8123. $$-$$$) is a favorite power lunch site for the political and literary heavyweights. This established North Beach eatery features modern Italian cuisine and offers piano-jazz and late night dining.

Moose's (1652 Stockton Street; ☎ 415-989-7800. $$-$$$) is a North Beach establishment with an ideal vantage point on Washington Square, offering exemplary service and a menu that ranges from pastas to lamb, inventive salads to grilled salmon.

Restaurant Lulu, (816 Folsom Street; ☎ 415-495-5775. $$-$$$) lures patrons to its country-style Southern French/Northern Italian ambiance, where the rosemary rotisserie chicken is a favorite.

Zuni Café (1658 Market Street; ☎ 415-552-2522. $$-$$$) is a contemporary restaurant with artful appetizers, specialty entrées, and a wine-by-the-glass bar. Zuni is Southwest by name, but a California original by cuisine.

The Grand Café (501 Geary Street; ☎ 415-292-0101. $$-$$$) flourishes in a grand and elegant room where the artful decor matches the creativity of the menu. Consider starting with the puff pastry mushrooms, then proceed to the rack of lamb.

Restaurants in Marin County

 The special restaurants of Marin County tend to be either in West Marin in Point Reyes, where they are close to the B&Bs and the fresh oysters, or back in Sausalito, where they offer good food and a view of San Francisco Bay and The City.

Point Reyes

Oyster lovers at Point Reyes can go directly to the source. The Lighthouse Road at Point Reyes includes a turnoff to Drake's Bay and the enterprise known as **Charlie Johnson's** oyster farm (☎ 415-669-1149. $-$$) the most substantial aquaculture effort in the area. It is not possible to tour the actual oyster beds, but they are nearby. Charlie Johnson pioneered the hanging culture method of oyster production, growing 140 oysters on a string in the open water, as opposed to the mud bottom of the bay. The Drakes Bay waters are exceptional for their purity. Oysters grow to full size in about 18 months. At Charlie Johnson's you can purchase jars of freshly shucked oysters, perfect for picnics. Our favorite beach at Point Reyes, perfect for a picnic with a jar of oysters and a bottle of chilled Chardonnay, is **Limantour**. Access to the beach is easy from your car.

The **Station House Café** (Main Street, Point Reyes Station; ☎ 415-663-1515. $$) is a good example of an old-line local-favorite restaurant where West Marin residents gather in unpretentious surroundings to enjoy fresh oysters and fish. Try chef Dennis Bold's many skilled ways of presenting the fresh oysters from Charlie Johnson's and the Hog Farm's oyster beds in Drake's Bay. Besides oysters on the half shell, Bold offers oysters barbecued in butter, garlic, and parsley. The fettucini with local mussels or a simple platter of local clams are superb. The trout salad is a favorite salad selection.

Olema Farm House is another cozy and friendly restaurant favored by the locals. If oysters continue to be the theme of choice, you could try their oyster stew or oysters Waldo, named after a local customer who enjoyed his oysters sautéed in a mix of herbs and garlic. Olema Farm House is at 10005 State Highway 1 in Olema; ☎ 415-663-1264. $$.

Two Czech restaurants at the small town of Inverness in Point Reyes are well known. At **Manka's** (☎ 415-669-1034. $$-$$$) try the roast duckling with caraway seeds or the chicken paprikash. Located in a brown-shingled structure set amidst oak trees on a ridge in the woods, above the water and away from traffic, the restaurant also includes a small inn for the traveler who wants dining and lodging together.

The owner of **Vladimir's** (☎ 415-669-1021. $$-$$$) is a former Czech Olympic equestrian champ, as the photo decor of the restaurant testifies. He now turns his attention to loin of pork in a rosemary sauce. Tasty chocolate cake topped with raspberries is a favorite dessert.

If you want to dine on the way to Point Reyes, or even choose some sophisticated take-out food for your trip, make a stop at **Insalata's** in San Anselmo. At this Mediterranean and Middle Eastern flavor restaurant, start with the Mediterranean platter, a tapestry of intriguing tastes, such as hummus, carrots with cumin, and spiced eggplant. The grilled lamb or prawns with pasta are tasty dinner entrées. Barbecued ribs are a takeout item especially good for a picnic on the beach. Insalata's is at 120 Sir

Francis Drake Boulevard in San Anselmo; ☎ 415-457-7700. $$-$$$.

Sausalito & Tiburon

When looking for views in Sausalito, try **The Spinnaker** (100 Spinnaker Drive; ☎ 415-332-1500. $$) which offers stunning water-level perspectives of San Francisco. From the long menu, which includes many selections each from fish, shellfish, meat, and poultry, try the fresh fish of the day.

Alta Mira Hotel's restaurant (125 Bulkley Avenue; ☎ 415-332-1350. $$) offers the premier bird's-eye view of San Francisco, Angel Island, and the Bay. This unsurpassed panorama can be enjoyed on an outdoor terrace or at an indoor bar-restaurant. The Alta Mira emphasizes celebrating its location with menu selections such as fresh Pacific Salmon Delice, which is salmon poached with fresh lime and dill.

The Caprice (2000 Paradise Drive, Tiburon; ☎ 415-435-3400. $$-$$$) is another choice water-level restaurant, this time in Tiburon. Caprice is a romantic getaway, with candlelight, linen tablecloths, and the twinkling lights of San Francisco as a distant backdrop. Try the lamb curry. From the restaurant you get a view of Angel Island, the Golden Gate Bridge, and the San Francisco skyline.

One of the good bargain eateries and warm-weather outdoor dining spots in Sausalito is unpretentious **Caruso's Café** (foot of Harbor Drive; ☎ 415-332-1015. $). They sell fresh fish and a nice assortment of soups, salads, sandwiches, and grilled fish. Either take out or settle in at their outdoor deck and dream of joining the houseboat dwellers docked nearby.

If you want to grab a bite in casual surroundings in Sausalito, get a shrimp fajita at **Margaritaville** (1200 Bridgeway; ☎ 415-331-3226. $$). The parallel eatery would be **Sam's** (27 Main Street; ☎ 415-435-4527. $$) in Tiburon, where the drink of choice is a gin fizz.

San Francisco & the Bay Area

Restaurants in the East Bay

Alice Waters' innovative restaurant, **Chez Panisse** (1517 Shattuck Avenue; ☎ 510-548-5525. $$$) has put Berkeley on the world culinary map. Equipped with imagination and fresh ingredients, the restaurant has developed into a place of pilgrimage, partly for readers who have enjoyed the various Chez Panisse cookbooks. The restaurant is surprisingly small and compact, divided into a downstairs serving fixed-price, single-choice dinners and a more casual upstairs café. The dinners are five-course, leisurely affairs and the offerings change daily. A typical menu would be: fennel and boletus mushrooms vinaigrette, soup of crab and leeks, stuffed Krout Farm pheasant breast with sweet potatoes, garden salad, and tarte tatin with muscat raisins. If the downstairs restaurant is a bit much, consider lunch or dinner at the more casual upstairs Chez Panisse Café, where inventive offerings are moderately priced. The grilled swordfish Moroccan-style, with sweet potatoes and peppers, and the calzone, consisting of goat and mozzarella cheese with herbs, would be good choices.

A walk in the Chez Panisse environs on Shattuck Avenue provides a tantalizing immersion in the so-called gourmet ghetto of Berkeley. Along Shattuck Avenue you pass the superb Thai restaurant **Cha-am** (1543 Shattuck; ☎ 510-848-9664. $$) and the cheese and bread shop **The Cheeseboard** (1504 Shattuck; ☎ 510-549-3183). **Andronico's** supermarket (1550 Shattuck) has a take-out operation that would dwarf most delis. **Virginia Bakery** (1690 Shattuck) is the premier croissant-birthing place. A fitting destination for this gustatory journey is **Triple Rock Brewery** (1920 Shattuck; ☎ 510-843-2739. $$) which epitomizes a widespread 1990s trend in California culinary travel – the brew pub. They make their own porters and ales on the premises.

If you explore Telegraph Avenue and long for a quiet counterpoint, here are two options. **The Musical Offering** is a classical music CD shop with wine and appetizing salads (2430 Bancroft Way; ☎ 510-849-0211. $-$$). **Jupiter Jam** presents jazz music and a large selection of beers on tap in a quiet courtyard (2181 Shattuck Avenue; ☎ 510-843-8277. $-$$).

Other East Bay restaurants augment the Berkeley-Oakland dining scene:

Juan's Place (941 Carleton Street at Ninth Street; ☎ 510-845-6904. $-$$) is a festive and popular Mexican restaurant, where the shrimp or crab enchiladas would be a good choice. Juan's consistently wins awards as Best Mexican Restaurant in various local publications.

Ratto's (821 Washington Street; ☎ 510-832-6503. $$) in downtown Oakland, is an excellent international-food deli, serving a tasty sit-down lunch. The Friday night pasta dinner comes complete with opera arias as entertainment.

Scott's (2 Broadway, ☎ 510-444-3456, $$) is the quality seafood restaurant in the Jack London Square area. Try the fresh grilled fish of the day.

Nan Yang (6048 College Avenue, Oakland; ☎ 510-655-3298, $$) is a distinctive Burmese restaurant guided by the culinary artistry of Philip Chu. Try the ginger salad, curry prawns, and garlic noodles.

The **Gingerbread House** (741 Fifth Street, Oakland; ☎ 510-444-7373. $$) specializes in jambalaya, gumbo, red beans, and rice in a cozy candlelight setting.

Restaurants in the South Bay

 Downtown San Jose is filled with gleaming modern buildings that are testaments to the cutting edge endeavors of this Silicon Valley business district, but what about restaurants? A fitting contrast to the steel and glass structures is the French restaurant, **Rue de Paris**. The intimate interior and linen-covered tables make the atmosphere more hushed than rushed. The wine list is notable for depth and decent prices. For a special treat, top the meal off with one of the more than 100 varieties of vintage port that the restaurant stocks. Some dishes to try at this classical French cuisine restaurant include duck pâté with cognac, salad of spinach leaves, smoked salmon and goat cheese, Grand Marnier soufflé for two or the chocolate almond torte. Since opening in 1983, Rue de Paris has flourished as neighboring eating establishments have struggled and sometimes failed. Rue de Paris is at 19 North Market Street; ☎ 408-298-0704. $$-$$$.

In San Jose, try **Scott's Seafood Grill & Bar** (185 Park Avenue; ☎ 408-971-1700. $$) the main fish and shellfish restaurant of the city.

For California cuisine, try Steve Borkenhagen's **Eulipia Restaurant** (374 S. First Street; ☎ 408-280-6161. $$). The grilled trout is a specialty.

The landmark Italian restaurant is still **Original Joe's** (corner of First and San Carlos streets; ☎ 408-292-7030. $$). There are 156 items on the menu to paralyze a tentative chooser.

A diner longing for breaded veal and red cabbage should select the premier German restaurant, **Hochburg von Germania** (261 North Second Street; ☎ 408-295-4484. $$).

Downtown Palo Alto comes alive at lunchtime with an outpouring of people. One eatery to try is the **Good Earth** (185 University Avenue; ☎ 650-321-9449. $$). Good Earth caught the cresting wave of demand for natural, wholesome, yet attractive food, and rode that surge to a chain with national ambitions. Try their garden patch salad, which has nine seasonal vegetables.

Liddicoat's (340 University Avenue, Palo Alto. $-$$.) was formerly a select grocery store, but now houses a dozen specialized fast-food booths, from Japanese fish tempura to Filipino sweet and sour pork. There are plenty of chairs and tables upstairs for seating.

Cenzo's (233 University Avenue, Palo Alto; ☎ 650-322-1846. $$) is a lively Italian trattoria.

The most historic restaurant is delightful **McArthur Park** (27 University Avenue, Palo Alto; ☎ 650-321-9990. $$). You can miss the restaurant entirely because of its secretive location. Continue on University Avenue from Palo Alto toward Stanford University and turn right after you pass under the railroad trestle. The restaurant is located next to the train station. The ample, white-painted structure was a World War I hostess house, designed by Julia Morgan in 1918 for Camp Fremont, in Menlo Park. The structure was later moved to its site in Palo Alto, where it served community recreational needs. A bronze marker in the front tells the story, adding that this is the only building remaining from that World War I camp. Try the smoked babyback ribs or the mesquite-charcoal swordfish.

Another cluster of interesting restaurants can be found near the San Francisco airport or in the city of San Mateo.

Empress Court (433 Airport Boulevard; ☎ 650-348-1122. $$-$$$) is an elegant Chinese penthouse restaurant featuring foods from four provinces of China.

Less formal and right on the water is **Kinkaid's** (60 Bayview Place; ☎ 650-342-9844. $$) where the oyster bar and sashimi are favorites.

Slightly farther north, good choices for the moderate expense traveler would be **El Torito** for Mexican food (1590 Old Bayshore Highway; ☎ 650-692-3113. $-$$) or **Benihana** for Japanese (1496 Old Bayshore Highway; ☎ 650-342-5202. $$).

Two locations in San Mateo and Burlingame rank high on the local gastronome's short list. The French restaurant **231 Ellsworth** (between Second and Third streets, San Mateo; ☎ 650-347-7231. $$$) has ever-changing fish, pasta, and salad specialties. **Isobune** (1451 Burlingame Avenue; ☎ 650-344-8433. $$) serves sushi from an endless sushi boat parade.

Camping & RV

 Keep in mind, throughout Northern California, that camping reservations for state parks can be made on a reservation system (☎ 800-444-7275).

If you want to camp near San Francisco, **Samuel P. Taylor State Park** (☎ 415-488-9897) would be one option. The park, 15 miles west of San Rafael on Sir Francis Drake Boulevard, has 2,700 acres of wooded countryside in the steep hills of Marin County.

Angel Island State Park has nine special hike-in backpack campsites accessible after you ferry out to the island. The view from Angel Island (☎ 415-435-1915) surpasses any view a commercial hotel could offer of the Golden Gate Bridge and the San Francisco Skyline. The easiest ferry access is from Tiburon (☎ 415-435-2131).

When thinking of camping in Marin County, here are some options:

Point Reyes National Seashore has backpack campgrounds only, and reservations are required. Call the Bear Valley Visitor Center at ☎ 415-663-1092.

Marin Park (2140 Redwood Highway, Greenbrae; ☎ 415-461-519) offers RV travelers in Marin full hook-ups, heated pool, laundry, restrooms and showers. The park is within walking distance of the Larkspur Ferry and Golden Gate Transit buses to San Francisco.

Near Point Reyes at Olema, the **Olema Ranch Campground,** (10155 Highway 1; ☎ 415-663-8001) has full RV and camping resources with showers and laundry facilities on the premises.

There is a **KOA** in Petaluma at Stony Point and Rainsville Road (☎ 707-763-1492) offering all the full-hookup resources expected of this national chain of campgrounds.

Mt. Tamalpais State Park has walk-in camping sites but no car camping. ☎ 415-388-2070.

Tomales Bay State Park (☎ 415-669-1140) has hike-in or bike-in campsites, first-come, first-served, but no car camping.

Camping is available in the East Bay at **Chabot Park** (Oakland Hills; ☎ 510-676-0192) and at **Mount Diablo State Park** atop Mt. Diablo (five miles east of Highway 680 at Danville, on Diablo Road; ☎ 510-837-2525). Both operate on a first-come, first-served basis. Chabot Park has access to a pleasant lake. Mt. Diablo has an extraordinary 360° view from its summit, allowing you to see from San Francisco Bay to the Sierra.

Five special parks in the South Bay area offer excellent camping, as well as hiking/backpacking, and biking.

Three of the parks are clustered in the mid-peninsula on the sea-facing slopes of the mountains in San Mateo County. The first is **Memorial County Park** (☎ 650-879-0212, 9500 Pescadero Road, 5½ miles southwest from La Honda). Adjacent is **Sam McDonald County Park** (☎ 650-879-0238, 13435 Pescadero Road, near La Honda). From Sam McDonald you can get access to **Pescadero Creek County Park**, which is largely undeveloped. Memorial has 140 drive-in camping sites available on a first-come, no-reservation basis. Using Memorial as a camping base, you can explore these three contiguous parks.

The other two parks are south of San Jose in rustic and remote terrain. **Mt. Madonna County Park** (Hecker Pass Road, Highway 152; ☎ 408-842-2341) has substantial redwood forests in its 3,093 acres. **Henry W. Coe State Park** (East Dunne Avenue, 14 miles east of Morgan Hill; ☎ 408-779-2728) is a vast grasslands park covering 80,000 acres. Henry Coe has 20 shaded car-camping sites near its park headquarters from which you can explore the back country.

Information Sources

Bureau of Land Management, 2800 Cottage Way, Sacramento, CA 95825; ☎ 916/979-2800.

For California fishing licenses and regulations:

California Department of Fish and Game, **License and Revenue Branch**, 3211 S Street, Sacramento, CA 95816; ☎ 916-653-7664; Web site www.dfg.ca.gov.

It is possible to purchase a one-year fishing license over the phone, using your charge card.

Ski enthusiasts should contact the major ski sites noted in the Sierra and Shasta Cascade chapters. There is also an umbrella group for the ski providers:

California Ski Industry Association, 74 New Montgomery Street, Suite 750, San Francisco, CA 94105; ☎ 415-543-7036

📖 When looking at wildlife around Northern California, one helpful resource is the *California Wildlife Viewing Guide*, available at bookstores or from Falcon Press, ☎ 800-582-2665.

San Francisco & the Bay Area

Chapter 3

North Coast & Redwood Country

The region north of San Francisco has two special attractions for travelers – a glorious coast extending from Bodega Bay to Mendocino and an inland Highway 101 route that features stately redwoods from southern Humboldt County all the way to the Oregon border.

North of Point Reyes, enjoy pristine views of the Sonoma-Mendocino Coast. The coast meanders from Bodega Head, an appealing promontory, past Fort Ross, the major historical entity, to the artsy community of Mendocino.

Russians were the dominant people here from 1812-1841. Stop at Fort Ross to see the well-developed fur-gathering outpost they established on this coast. With the help of skillful Aleut Indians in small kayaks, the Russians harvested the sea otters almost to the point of extinction. Today, Fort Ross has been rebuilt to resemble its appearance during the Russian era.

Lumbering has been the steadiest income provider along the northern stretches of this coast since 1850. In Fort Bragg, stop in at the **Guest House Museum**, 343 North Main Street, to become acquainted with the lumbering story.

The other prominent industry has been **fishing**. Bodega Bay is a major center for commercial fishing, an occupation that OSHA ranks as one of the most dangerous in the country.

The pleasures of the coast compete with the attractions of the inland route, especially the redwoods. Though the California imagination can sometimes suffer from inflation, certain facts of nature here are indisputable. The redwood trees, *Sequoia sempervirens*, north of San Francisco, are magnificent and are the world's tallest trees. Similarly, the most massive living thing on earth is the inland relative of the coastal redwood, the giant sequoia. The best example of the *Sequoia gigantea*, the General

Sherman Tree, can be seen at **Sequoia National Park**. If superlative trees stir your sense of adventure, California offers yet another wonder of nature – the oldest living thing on earth. This distinction goes to the **bristlecone pines**, which can be seen high in the **White Mountains**, south and east of Yosemite.

The park service visitor center in **Redwood National Park**, at Orick, can provide you with a better understanding of the special environment of the redwoods. UNESCO deemed Redwood National Park a World Heritage Site in 1982, recognizing that redwoods are a phenomenon of worldwide interest. These monarchs of the mist have been flourishing for around 20 million years in a long, thin band along the coast, from southwest Curry County in Oregon to south Monterey County, about 10 miles north of Hearst castle.

■ The Coastal Route: Highway I

The Russian colonial incursion into California occurred at what is now called **Fort Ross State Historic Park** (☎ 707-847-3286) on Highway 1, 11 miles north of Jenner. Be sure to allow time to see the restored Russian fort, a gem of historic reconstruction and interpretation. Guide yourself through the displays with narrated interpretation at 10 stations on the grounds.

Below the fort is **Fort Ross Cove**, the original sandy beach where the fur-gathering Russians landed and constructed ships. Lumber traders later in the 19th century loaded their boats here with redwood for the San Francisco market, using long chutes. This beach, complete with a meandering stream, is a seldom-appreciated aspect of the impressive Fort Ross restoration. As you explore this historic spot, it's intriguing to think of the Russians bringing their supplies ashore, or the nimble Aleut Indians in the Russians' employ casting off in small kayaks in search of sea otters.

The Russians actually built four ships on this sandy beach between 1816-1824, using redwood and Douglas fir from the forests in the hills. The Russians' failure at growing a surplus of wheat and vegetables here, plus the decline in the otter population, caused them to pull back and return to Sitka, Alaska, in 1841. Eventually, the Russians retreated to their homeland.

Coastal Highway 1 has something for every taste and for many adventure travel passions. The lighthouse buff will want to stop at the magnificent 115-foot tall structure at **Point Arena**. The botanist with an interest in California plants, especially the azaleas and rhododendrons of the redwood forests, will want to stop at the **Kruse Rhododendron State Reserve** or the **Mendocino Coast Botanical Gardens**. Lovers of contemporary art and fine woodworking will want to browse the shops at Mendocino.

More energetic pursuits might mean a hike to the **Pygmy Forest**, a canoe ride up **Big River** near Mendocino, or a bike trip into **Russian Gulch State Park** to a discreet waterfall at the end of the trail. The **Skunk Train** ride from Fort Bragg to Willits is one of the classic California rail adventures. Many places along this coast have multiple adventure travel aspects. For example, **MacKerricher State Park**, extending eight miles along a sandy coastline north of Fort Bragg, is excellent for camping, fishing, scuba diving, biking, hiking, jogging, and horseback riding.

■ The Redwood Route: Highway 101

The inland route, like the coastal ride, focuses on one long road – Highway 101. Along this route, be sure to savor the following experiences:

- First, linger a half-day along the **Avenue of the Giants**, looking at the impressive groves of trees, the tallest towering as high as a 36-story skyscraper.

- Second, tour the **Pacific Lumber Company** mill at Scotia, an example of a company lumber town. Take the self-guided tour to comprehend the process of turning trees into lumber.

- Third, enjoy the Victorian and urban pleasures of **Eureka, Ferndale, and Arcata**, with their shops, art studios, restaurants, and historic structures.

North Coast & Redwood Country

- And, finally, after visiting the **Redwood National Park Interpretive Center** at Orick, allow a day of outings to see trees at the **Lady Bird Johnson Grove**, elk at **Prairie Creek Park**, and beaches within the park or at Trinidad Head.

Redwoods flourish both south and north from San Francisco, but the northern forests are most worthy of the name, **Redwood Country**, which refers generically to the more than 400 miles between San Francisco and the Oregon coast. Actually, only about 3-5% of the primeval redwood forest remains today. About half of that resource is on protected public lands. Disposition of the old grove redwoods now in private hands is one of the major political controversies in the region.

The first reports of European contact with redwoods were from south of San Francisco when a priest-botanist in the expedition of Portola noted them in his diary of 1769. The tree was unknown to Europeans. The first American to observe redwoods was the intrepid explorer, Jedediah Smith, who saw the trees in 1822. He is now honored in Redwood Country with a river and a state redwood park named after him.

The native Californians were well aware of the redwoods and the redwood environment, but they did not consider the groves a hospitable habitat. Because the trees cast such shade, forage foods did not flourish beneath them as abundantly as in meadow or oak woodland terrain. The bark did not burn well and the trunks of the trees were too massive for the Native Americans to cut for firewood. However, Yuroks of the north coast split redwood planks for their shelters. They also hollowed canoes out of redwood logs.

The Lumber Era

Lumbering has been the main historical story associated with redwood country. The tree's wood is soft and easy to saw. Though not as strong as Douglas fir, it has an attractive red color that can be stabilized to remain red or will weather naturally to a pleasing gray. It is widely used in house siding, decks, and garden lumber. The biggest virtue of redwood is its ability to withstand weathering and termites rather than deteriorating. Prolonged moisture will cause most woods to rot, but redwood will endure. Redwood is one of the most weather-resistant woods found in North America, competing with the cypress of the South.

When thinking of the lumber baron era, the place to stop and gaze at is the **William Carson Mansion** in Eureka. This lavish gingerbread Victorian, the finest 19th-century architectural legacy along the north coast, was built in 1884 at the corner of Second and M streets. Today it is a private club but remains an elegant testament to the fortunes made from the giant trees.

The Resilient Lighthouse

The **Battery Point Lighthouse** in Crescent City, built in 1856, serves as a repository for local history, especially regarding the fate of wayward ships whose captains were inattentive to the treacherous shorelines. The sturdiness of this lighthouse, perched on a rock, sometimes cut off from land during high tide, became apparent in 1964. On Good Friday of that year, an earthquake in Alaska created a 20-foot-high tsunami that washed over the lighthouse, but failed to dislodge the structure, despite devastating the buildings in Crescent City.

■ Getting to the North Coast & Redwood Country

A private car is the most practical method of travel along the coast, allowing flexibility of planning. A scheduled van, operated by the **Mendocino Transit Authority** (☎ 800-696-4682) provides service between Mendocino, Fort Bragg, and Santa Rosa, where it is possible to catch a Santa Rosa Airporter (☎ 707-545-8015 or 800-228-8015) for transport to the San Francisco and Oakland airports.

Similarly, you need a car to see the redwoods on the inland route. The famous redwoods are not difficult to locate. Simply head north from San Francisco along Freeway 101. Within an hour and a half you reach the first awesome forests, which stretch from Garberville to the Oregon state line.

North Coast & Redwood Country

The initial redwoods you'll encounter are at the 1,500-acre **Richardson Grove State Park** (☎ 707-247-3318). Like so many public parks in this region, it has multiple uses for camping, swimming, fishing, hiking, and biking. The first substantial groves are at **Humboldt Redwoods State Park** (☎ 707-946-2409).

Information Sources

Mendocino

Fort Bragg-Mendocino Coast Chamber of Commerce, 322 N. Main Street Fort Bragg, CA 95437; ☎ 707-961-6300 or 800-726-2780.

Sonoma

The **Sonoma County Convention and Visitors Bureau**, 5000 Roberts Lake Road, Suite A, Rohnert Park, CA 94928; ☎ 707-586-8100; Web site www.visit-sonoma.com.

Within the county, contact the **Russian River Region Visitors Bureau** at 14034 Armstrong Woods, Guerneville, CA 95446; ☎ 707-869-9212 or 800-253-8800; Web site www.rrrvb.com.

Coastal State Parks

Department of Parks and Recreation, Mendocino Area State Parks, PO Box 440, Mendocino, CA 95460; ☎ 707-937-5804.

Nine state parks in the area have camping, with **Manchester Beach** one of the choice places.

The Mendocino National Forest has hiking resources and eight campgrounds to offer. Contact the **Mendocino National Forest Headquarters**, 420 E. Laurel Street, Willows, CA 95988; ☎ 916-934-3316.

The Redwood Country

This territory, both coastal and inland, falls under the purview of the Redwood Empire Association, an organization of attractions and service providers in the redwood region, stretching from San Francisco through the Wine Country and north. For more travel information on Redwood Country, write the **Redwood Empire Association**, 2801 Leavenworth, Second Floor, San Francisco, CA

94133-1117; ☎ 888-678-8502; Web site www.red-woodempire.com. Send for their excellent *Redwood Empire Adventures Travel Guide* (cost for shipping and handling is $3 in the US and $5 internationally).

The most active tourism information source in the northern Redwood Country is the **Eureka/Humboldt County Convention & Visitors Bureau**, 1034 Second Street, Eureka, CA 95501; ☎ 707-443-5097; Web site www.northcoast.com/~redwoods.

■ Touring the North Coast

Coastal Route Highway I

Proceeding south to north along the coast, you may want to:

- See the crashing surf at the Bodega or Mendocino headlands, two of the rugged coastal promontories.

- Enjoy the fresh fish catch at one of the coastal restaurants, such as **The Tides Wharf Restaurant & Bar** (☎ 707-875-3652) in Bodega Bay or **Café Beaujolais** (☎ 707-937-5614) in Mendocino.

- Visit the historic Russian Fort at **Fort Ross** (☎ 707-847-3286) along the Sonoma Coast and learn about the Russian sea otter hunting era 1812-1841.

- Visit the artsy coastal town of **Mendocino**, a popular stop for its art galleries, restaurants, and B&Bs.

- Linger over some of the **Mendocino coast state parks** (☎ 707-937-5804), which have particularly lovely beach wildflower showings in spring and summer. Consider Manchester Beach, south of Mendocino, and Russian Gulch, north of Mendocino.

- Explore the working coastal town of **Fort Bragg**, home of lumber and fishing operations. Visit its Noyo Harbor to see the fishing boats and fish restaurants. Take a day trip on the **Skunk Train** (☎ 707-964-6371 or 800-777-5865) from Fort Bragg to Willits and back.

North Coast & Redwood Country

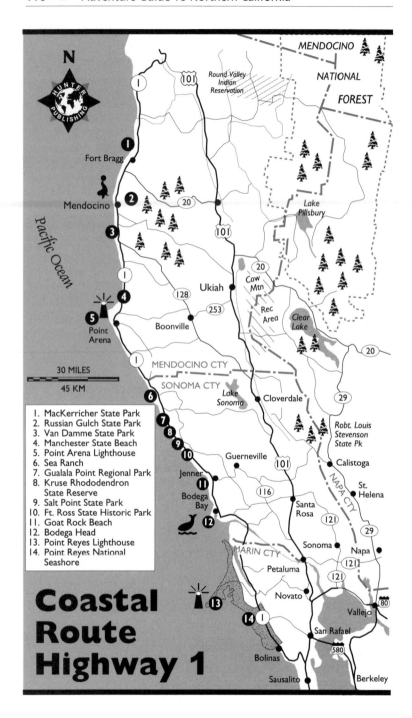

N

Coastal Route Highway 1

MENDOCINO

NATIONAL

FOREST

Round Valley
Indian
Reservation

Fort Bragg

Mendocino

Pacific Ocean

Point
Arena

30 MILES

45 KM

1. MacKerricher State Park
2. Russian Gulch State Park
3. Van Damme State Park
4. Manchester State Beach
5. Point Arena Lighthouse
6. Sea Ranch
7. Gualala Point Regional Park
8. Kruse Rhododendron
   State Reserve
9. Salt Point State Park
10. Ft. Ross State Historic Park
11. Goat Rock Beach
12. Bodega Head
13. Point Reyes Lighthouse
14. Point Reyes National
    Seashore

Lake
Pillsbury

Ukiah

Cow
Mtn

Rec
Area

Clear
Lake

Boonville

MENDOCINO CTY

SONOMA CTY

Lake
Sonoma

Cloverdale

Robt. Louis
Stevenson
State Pk

Guerneville

Calistoga

Jenner

St.
Helena

Bodega
Bay

Santa
Rosa

NAPA CTY

Sonoma

Napa

MARIN CTY

Petaluma

Novato

Vallejo

San Rafael

Bolinas

Sausalito

Berkeley

Sonoma Coast

The Sonoma Coast is an extension of the coastal wonders in Marin County at Point Reyes.

Sonoma and Mendocino present a more remote and rugged appearance than the cattle-grazing pastures of Marin.

The Sonoma Coast begins just south of **Bodega**, a 19th-century town that once boasted seven sawmills, but which now relies on fishing and tourism. Bodega Bay presents a fairly protected harbor for fishing boats. This is a dangerous business, however, and the celebrative Fisherman's Festival each April honors fishermen lost at sea, tragedies which persist. Bodega boasts the largest fishing fleet between San Francisco and Eureka.

West of the town, drive out to **Bodega Head** for one of the most magnificent coastal views in California. This is a fine whale-watching promontory in January, when the whales swim south, and again in March, when the California gray whales proceed north. Bodega Head is also a site at which to admire crashing surf on a sunny summer day.

Bodega Head starts some 10 miles of coastline that comprises **Sonoma Coast State Beach** (☎ 707-875-3483). Fishing, picnicking, and walking are favorite activities all along this kelp-strewn strand. At low tide, observe the exposed tidepool life, but don't disturb it. Swimming is not advised along any of these beaches because of treacherous surf.

Goat Rock Beach

The Russian River empties into the ocean midway up the Sonoma Coast at a beach called Goat Rock, one of the more appealing beaches of the region because of its diversity. Goat Rock Beaches, at the mouth of the Russian River, extend out on a peninsula between the river and the ocean. Here you can watch waves crashing against the rock pedestals, called seastacks, slowly eroding the softer rock perimeters. Picnicking on grassy slopes and sunset viewing are superb from this west-facing beach. Driftwood collecting at the mouth of the Russian River also draws travelers here. (Park officials encourage driftwood collecting because the wood debris becomes a potential fire hazard. Inveterate beachcombers and firewood gatherers scrounge the area. Periodic burning by the parks staff reduces the uncollected volume.)

To get to Goat Rock Beaches, which are not visible from the road, watch for the clearly marked sign and take State Park Road off Highway 1,near Jenner. You'll find a string of parking lots with access to the beach. The northern edge puts you closest to the mouth of the Russian River. The most southerly parking lot locates you near the most protected beaches. However, these beaches are too dangerous for swimming, due to sleeper waves and rip tides.

About 300 resident harbor seals rest at the mouth of the Russian River in the spring and give birth to their young. Fishing for salmon and steelhead in winter is popular near the mouth of the river. Rockfish are plentiful in the surf in summer. Smelt netters are also successful here.

North From Jenner

Back along the coast, north of Jenner, the next major stop is **Fort Ross State Historic Park** (☎ 707-847-3286). As mentioned, the Russians occupied Fort Ross from 1812 to 1841 as a sea otter hunting outpost. Today the restored stockade, houses, barracks, storehouses, and Russian Orthodox chapel present an accurate picture of Russian life in early California. Fortunately, Fort Ross had sufficient artifacts and adequate state funding to become a first-rate historical interpretive center.

Pushing onward, several attractive parks occupy chunks of the Sonoma County coast.

Stillwater Cove Regional Park has a redwood trail to the beach.

The **Kruse Rhododendron Reserve** (☎ 707-865-2391) 10 miles north of Fort Ross, consists of 317 acres of wild rhododendrons. These tall shrubs bloom with pink flowers from April to June. Call ahead to check the blooming time.

Gualala (pronounced wa-la-la) **Point Regional Park** (☎ 707-527-2041 or 707-785-2377) at the mouth of the Gualala River, is another good place for hiking and nature study, with camping by the ocean.

Mendocino Coast

Between Salt Point and Gualala, you pass the elaborate **Sea Ranch** coastal home development. The beauty of the coast is such that any use of it for up-scale and exclusive homes now requires substantial political clout. Sea Ranch, one of the last of the major coastal home developments, won awards for its skill at blending in with the environment. Private road designations in the developed area tend to exclude travelers, but the California Coastal Commission forced Sea Ranch to allow several beach access routes through the property. Some of the Sea Ranch homes can be rented. Call **Ocean View Properties and Rentals** at ☎ 707-884-3538 or **Ram's Head Realty** at ☎ 800-785-3455.

The Mendocino Coast.

Point Arena Lighthouse (☎ 707-882-2777) immediately south of Manchester Beach, is worth a tour. Point Arena ranks as one of the more photogenic of the lighthouses along the California coast. Climb the 146 steps to the top and see the Fresnel lens that focused a small kerosene flame – visible from up to 20 miles at sea. On weekends the spirited citizens of the region act as docents at this lighthouse-museum.

Traveling north, **Manchester State Beach** (☎ 707-937-5804) has miles of sand, huge sand dunes topped with European beach grass, a stream cutting through the dunes to the water, and plenty of driftwood. The size (650 acres) of Manchester Beach permits seclusion. Wildflowers abound here, especially Douglas iris.

All along the hillsides of this coast, such as the steep hills above Jenner, there are many wildflowers in spring, especially a small yellow flower called goldfields (*Baeria chrysostoma*). This flower appears to thrive in spite of sheep grazing.

North Coast & Redwood Country

Artsy Mendocino

Next stop is the town of Mendocino, one of the more picturesque places in California. Because many travelers favor it as a destination, an active artists' colony has emerged, catering to the travelers. This is also quintessential bed-and-breakfast territory, where you stay in a quaint Victorian house in an individually decorated room and hobnob with the owner-proprietor.

Among places to explore in Mendocino are, the **Mendocino Art Center** (45200 Little Lake Street; ☎ 707-937-5818) and the **Artists Co-op of Mendocino** (45270 Main Street; ☎ 707-937-4307) which features local artists' portrayals of the region.

Travelers to Mendocino should anticipate fog in summer and may confront many rainy days in winter, but the afternoons of summer and the crisp winter days after the storms have cleared make the trip exceptional.

Two Coastal Parks

The entire Mendocino coast, from Point Arena to Rockport, is a joy to drive. Two special state parks, flanking the town of Mendocino, are **Van Damme** and **Russian Gulch** (☎ 707-937-5804 for both). Van Damme's main feature is its lush Fern Canyon, where an extraordinary variety of ferns grow. The beach at Van Damme attracts divers searching for abalone and rockfish. Van Damme also offers good camping and a bike trail. Russian Gulch boasts a hospitable sunning and swimming beach, though the water is chilly. The promontory on the north side of Russian Gulch provides one of the most pleasing coastal views, looking south toward the Mendocino headlands. Russian Gulch's moist, elevated headlands support lavish displays of coastal wildflowers, including seaside daisy, Indian paintbrush, and pink mallow varieties.

Fort Bragg

North from Mendocino is Fort Bragg, a logging and fishing town. Fort Bragg was once a military outpost, but gradually became a lumbering site. Over the Labor Day weekend, a series of events known as Paul Bunyan Days includes contests involving many lumberjack skills. Fort Bragg's Noyo Harbor celebrates what is billed as the world's largest salmon barbecue each July 4. Celebrants receive a full plate of salmon, plus plenty of down-home corn, beans, and salad. Also in the area, the **Mendocino Coast**

Botanical Gardens (☎ 707-964-4352) feature a spectrum of native plants.

North of Fort Bragg, after Rockport, the coast highway turns inland to Highway 101 and the Redwood Country.

Redwood Route 101

Southern 101: Santa Rosa to Eureka

Redwood Country's main trees begin along Highway 101 north of Leggett at the Richardson Grove, as mentioned.

A few miles further north, you enter a 31-mile stretch appropriately called **The Avenue of the Giants**. This extended landscape consists of over 100 memorial and picnic groves, all part of the 51,222-acre Humboldt Redwoods State Park. Follow the side road at Phillipsville along Highway 101 to several turnoff areas that invite you to pause and walk through the groves. Be sure to see all the groves on both sides of Highway 101 from Phillipsville to Redcrest. **Founder's Grove** is one of the better stops, with trees about 2,500 years old. The Founder's Tree is 346.1 feet high and was once thought to be the highest.

The drive along the 10,000-acre **Rockefeller Forest** on Bull Creek Flats Road is a poignant example of the need to protect whole watersheds to save prize redwoods. Clear-cut slopes upstream from the prize Rockefeller trees exposed ground that washed into the creek in 1955 and 1964, subsequently undermining some of the giant trees. Silting of streams has also damaged the salmon-spawning habitat. Albee Camp, located in an abandoned apple orchard near the Rockefeller Grove, is a lovely camping and picnic site.

The **Humboldt Redwoods Visitor Center** (☎ 707-946-2263) at the Burlington Campground is open May-October to dispense park information, maps, and books.

Driving north, both the towns of **Ferndale** and **Eureka** are worth exploring for their Victorians, shops, inns, bed-and-breakfast, and logging-era mementos. At Eureka, stop to visit **Fort Humboldt**, an 1850s military outpost with many exhibits about the lumber harvesting craft. One amazing tool of the trade was a huge winch, called a slackliner, used to bring large logs down steep

North Coast & Redwood Country

slopes. An excursion boat called the *Madaket* (☎ 707-445-1910) gets you out on the water in a 1910 ferry boat for a view of Humboldt Bay.

Eureka

Eureka's **Clarke Museum** (240 E. Street; ☎ 707-443-1947) showcases Indian artifacts, especially basketry and dance regalia of the Hoopa, Karook, and Yurok tribes. The museum, housed in the white-marbled, columned former Bank of Eureka, contains a model of the steamers that plied these waters in the latter half of the 19th century, connecting San Francisco to this isolated outpost. A traveler interested in Indian culture can drive the backcountry road through the Hoopa Reservation northeast of town and stop at the **Hoopa Tribal Museum** (☎ 916-625-4110) 11 miles north of Willow Creek on Highway 96 in the Hoopa Shopping Center.

Eureka's **Old Town** boasts intriguing shops, such as **Angelus Clockwork Music** (420 Second Street), a store devoted to antique music scores and music-making machines. The city nurtures an arts and crafts tradition, especially in its Old Town area, the place where traffic from travelers creates a market. At the **Humboldt Cultural Center** (422 First Street) you can see pottery, paintings, sculpting, and crafts. **The Indian Art & Gift Shop** (241 F Street) deals exclusively in authentic creations from the Indians of the Northwest. The gallery has been established by the Northern California Indian Development Council. **Old Town Art Guild** (233 F Street) is a co-op venture with changing one-person shows. **Blue Ox Mill Works** (foot of X Street; ☎ 707-444-3437, 800-248-4259) deals in the wood trimmings used to restore Victorians in the historical district. For a rest stop while exploring, try a cappuccino and dessert at **Ramone's Bakery** (209 F Street) or a huge scoop of ice cream at **Bon Boniere** (215 F Street). Finally, the city boasts a folk-art tour de force comparable to Simon Rodia's Watts Towers in Los Angeles. This Eureka entity is **Romano Gabriel's Sculpture Garden** (317 2nd Street), a collection of wooden folk art created by the local sculptor from 1940-1970. The garden makes a visual commentary on social issues, politics, and religion.

Eureka can be enjoyed via a driving tour that takes in 125 structures from the Victorian era. An excellent example, as mentioned earlier, is the **Carson Mansion** at Second and M streets. A good walking-tour brochure, readily available from the Convention and Visitors Bureau, outlines all the noted Victorians and assists in explaining the nuances of styles described as Queen Anne, Eastlake, Stick, New England, Carpenter Gothic, and even Islamic.

Two opportunities to become familiar with the maritime traditions, early shipbuilding legacy, and ocean environment at Eureka should also be mentioned. **The Humboldt Bay Maritime Museum** (1410 2nd Street, 707-444-9440) describes the picturesque bay's history in photos and artifacts. The **Humboldt State University Marine Lab & Aquarium** (Edwards and Ewing streets, Trinidad; ☎ 707-826-3671) presents some of the ongoing research in coastal waters off Northern California. A touch-and-feel tank at the Marine Lab displays some of the denizens of the sea.

Ferndale

Ferndale, south from Eureka, specializes in Carpenter-Gothic Victorians, such as the **Shaw House** at 703 Main Street; ☎ 707-786-9958. A handy foldout map, called *The Victorian Village of Ferndale Visitors' Guide and Walking Tour*, can be your companion for a stroll down the four blocks of Main Street from Ocean to Shaw streets. With the map you can distinguish the Eastlake-style **Ferndale Meat Co.** (376 Main Street), now a deli, from the Roman Ferndale Bank (394 Main Street). Several Victorians, as you might suspect, have been turned into B&B's, such as the **Gingerbread Mansion Inn** (400 Berding Street), **Ferndale Inn** (619 Main Street) and the **Shaw House Inn** (703 Main Street). For an historic overview, stop in at the **Ferndale Museum** (3rd and Shaw streets; ☎ 707-786-4466).

The **Eel River Delta** around Ferndale can provide some interesting back country drives. Pause at the small town of Loleta to see its famous **Loleta Cheese Factory**, where they transform some of the area's abundant milk production into flavored cheeses, such as jalapeño Monterey jack or smoked salmon cheddar. The Loleta Cheese Factory is at 252 Loleta Drive; ☎ 707-733-5470 or 800-995-0453. Drive on to **Table Bluff County Park,** where you can watch the crashing surf from above and venture down to the driftwood-rich beach.

North Coast & Redwood Country

The futures of both logging and fishing, the economic mainstays of the region, are uncertain. Depletion of the old-growth supply, rather than a slowing demand, is a restricting factor in lumbering. However, redwood is the fastest-growing softwood species suitable for this climate. Young forests are more productive than old forests, from a board-per-foot yield point of view. Fishing for salmon has been banned in the waters off parts of this coast for some years because the annual run of salmon in the Klamath River was perilously low. If you happen to pass the south of the Klamath River when the salmon are spawning, you'll find a small army of RVs with salmon fishermen lined up reel-to-reel along the bank. Upstream, in the Hoopa Native American Reservation, the residents are allowed to net the fish. The politics of salmon fishing and logging are equally intense.

Scotia

The best way to get a feel for the lumber era today is to drive to the small town of Scotia, 27 miles south from Eureka on Highway 101, and take a tour of the **Pacific Lumber Company** (125 Main Street; ☎ 707-764-4200). At Scotia you get a perspective on how people and trees relate in the region. The town has the largest redwood lumbermill in existence, which you can tour self-guided on weekdays. The tour puts you directly in the midst of the operation. Powerful waterjets first strip the bark from the trees. Then huge saws cut the logs into board thickness. Finally, the boards are carefully graded for sale. Few industrial tours in these litigious times put you so close to the dramatic working machinery of a major enterprise. At a park in the center of Scotia you can see a cross-section of a redwood tree 1,285 years old. The tree yielded 69,000 board feet of lumber. Children can scramble over an old logging railroad on display at the park. Scotia is a classic company town, with the lumber company controlling all aspects of life. Be sure to see the Company Museum, full of photos of the Scotia Baseball Team of 1923 or of the ox-drawn logging trains of the 19th century. Within town the company also maintains a salmon and steelhead rearing pond. The **Scotia Inn** offers a hospitable and rustic lodging and dining opportunity. South of town, the company demonstration forest at the Jordan Creek exit shows re-forestation practices.

Redwoods have a capacity to inspire wonder because of their height, beauty, and age. Even a 1,285-year-old tree may in fact be eons older. Most redwoods sprout clonally from the roots of their parent tree rather than from seeds. This same tree may have perpetuated itself in this fashion for thousands of years.

At shops throughout Redwood Country you can often see **burls** for sale. Burls are masses of tree tissue that form around a bud. They are attractive ornamentally and, if put in water, will sprout as a miniature tree. The shoots will grow for years, living off the nourishment stored in the burl.

One element of grand natural beauty in the region is the rhododendron bloom in the forest. Eureka hosts a **Rhododendron Festival** in April at the height of the blooming time, complete with a parade.

Most of the festivals in Redwood Country are folksy small-town affairs, such as the **Trinidad Fish and Art Festival** in June or the **Fortuna Country Music Showdown** in July.

The Kinetic Sculpture Race

This festival is in a class by itself. The zany race is run over the Memorial Day Weekend across land, water, and marsh from Arcata to Ferndale. The event captures the levity of the region. For further information, contact the **Ferndale Chamber of Commerce** (PO Box 325, Ferndale, CA 95536; ☎ 707-786-4477). Past vehicles from the race can be seen in a museum and art gallery at 580 Main Street in Ferndale.

The race has become a cult tourism attraction. For three days, contestants scramble over a 36-mile course in contraptions of their own design. The race was begun in 1969 by Hobart Brown, an artist who arrived in Ferndale in 1965 as the first resident artist. Brown bought his gallery and living space in downtown Ferndale, then a rundown place, and proceeded with his metal-welding sculpture. Today there are about 100 artists among the 1,700 residents of Ferndale.

When Brown announced the first race, he was surprised to find that seven entrants and 10,000 spectators showed up. The vehicles contrived for the race must be human-

> powered and must be all-terrain contraptions. The race now attracts over 50 entrants per year, including contestants from Tokyo and Canada. The race is a kind of performance art, a concourse rather than a marathon.
>
> "We race for glory alone," says Hobart Brown. "The prize money for winning one year was a check for $6.75."

Northern 101: Eureka to Oregon

North of Eureka is **Arcata**, which hosts the major seat of learning in the region, Humboldt State University, founded in 1913. The university has grown to some 7,500 students enrolled in 43 different degree programs. With that many students, and the requisite university employees as potential consumers, the current explosion in micro-breweries around California has found a local expression. Sample the goods at the **Humboldt Brewery** (856 Tenth Street; ☎ 707-822-2739). Like Eureka and Ferndale, Arcata boasts a number of Victorian structures of note, such as **927 J Street**, where a young writer named Bret Harte resided during the 1880s. As editor of a local paper, *The Northern Californian*, he was known for writing scathing editorials deploring a white massacre of innocent Indians. Local tempers ran high and Harte shipped out, at age 24, to San Francisco and subsequent literary fame. The waterfront area of Arcata is home of the **Arcata Marsh & Wildlife Sanctuary** (600 G Street; ☎ 707-826-2359) a restored estuarine habitat with rich fish, bird, and plant life. Vistas and views of Arcata are possible from this walking and jogging trail.

Redwood National Park

Beyond Arcata, the road swings close to the coast and passes through major state redwood parks, such as Prairie Creek, Del Norte, and Jedediah Smith, located in the foggy and rainy environment so conducive to optimal redwood growth. These parks were combined in 1968 to create Redwood National Park. Prairie Creek Park is noted for its Fern Canyon and herds of Roosevelt elk. Del Norte Park contains attractive showings of rhododendrons and azaleas. Jedediah Smith Park, with its wild Smith River, is appreciated for its trout, salmon, and steelhead fishing.

The **Redwood Visitor Information Center** is worth a stop on Highway 101, just west of Orick. The center is perched right on

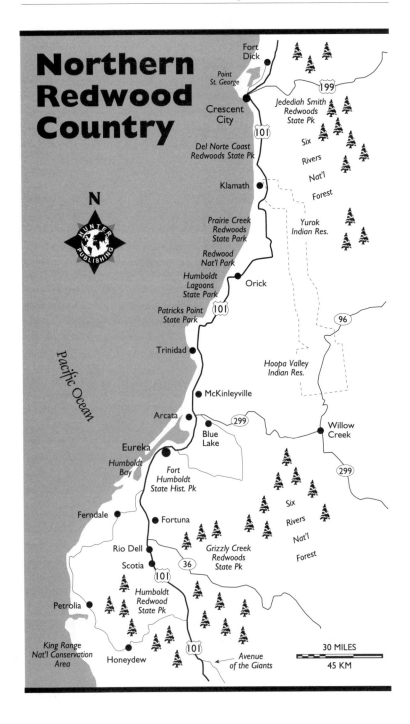

Northern Redwood Country

Fort Dick

Point St. George

Crescent City

199

Jedediah Smith Redwoods State Pk

Del Norte Coast Redwoods State Pk

101

Six

Rivers

Nat'l

Forest

Klamath

N

Prairie Creek Redwoods State Park

Yurok Indian Res.

Redwood Nat'l Park

Humboldt Lagoons State Park

Orick

Patricks Point State Park

101

96

Trinidad

Hoopa Valley Indian Res.

Pacific Ocean

McKinleyville

Arcata

299

Willow Creek

Eureka

Blue Lake

Humboldt Bay

Fort Humboldt State Hist. Pk

299

Ferndale

Fortuna

Six

Rivers

Nat'l

Rio Dell

Grizzly Creek Redwoods State Pk

Forest

Scotia

36

101

Humboldt Redwood State Pk

Petrolia

King Range Nat'l Conservation Area

Honeydew

101

Avenue of the Giants

30 MILES

45 KM

The Carson Mansion in Eureka is the Victorian architectural masterpiece of the Northern Redwood Country.

the coast. Headquarters for Redwood National and State Parks is 1111 Second Street, Crescent City, CA 95531; ☎ 707-464-6101.

One of the most enjoyable walks in Redwood National Park is a loop in the **Lady Bird Johnson Grove**, which shows the range of vegetation, such as the 12 kinds of ferns that grow in this environment.

Wander through the string of units that form the park to make your own private discoveries, such as the Roosevelt elk, mentioned earlier, at Prairie Creek. You may see as many as 30 wild elk at Prairie Creek, part of the 200-strong herd in the region.

There are two ways to get close to the tallest trees, which are in **Tall Trees Grove**. You can take a park service bus from the **Redwood Information Center** (☎ 707-488-3461) to within 1.3 miles of the grove and hike down (and back up) to see the trees. Alternatively, you can make a 15-mile and relatively level hike up and back Redwood Creek for the same view.

Redwood Country Exploring

Redwood Country is itself so spread out along Highway 101 that concentrating on the parks alone would make for an interesting trip. Side trips can be made on the scenic roads that parallel the main route, such as the Old Coastal Highway near the mouth of the Klamath River. The red elderberry, red alder, and scenic views of the ocean at marked turnouts make this a particularly choice back road. The side road, hugging the coast north and south of Trinidad, offers exhilarating vistas, such as Houda Point.

At present, the Redwood National Park covers 106,000 acres, of which about 70% is federal land; the remainder is state-owned park land. The National Park boasts important estuarine and beach environments as well as the hushed grandeur of the red-woods. In the watery beach habitats, some 300 species of migrating birds rest each autumn on their southward migration. Whale watching, January-March, is popular at the **Crescent Beach Overlook**, following the progress southward of the Pacific gray whales as they move from chilly Arctic waters to the warmth of Baja, Mexico lagoons. Roosevelt elk are often seen at Gold Bluffs Beach and Boyes Prairie. Guided tidepool walks with rangers are possible at Endert Beach.

Nature lovers consider the **Trinidad Head Trail** one of the spectacular vista walks along the North Coast. Park at the beach area below Trinidad Head and walk up the marked trail, a sacred area to the family of Tsurai Indians who once flourished here. Few locations in California display the grandeur of the coast more fully.

Throughout Redwood Country there are roadside attractions that curious youngsters in the back of the car will never let you get past, such as the **Tour Thru Tree** at Highway 169, Klamath Glen Exit. Another attraction, **Trees of Mystery** (☎ 707-482-2251, 800-638-3389) at first appears to be largely a tourist memento store, but be sure to see their **End of the Trail Indian Museum**, with its elaborate Native American basketry and costume collection. Besides the Native American artifacts, such as a Crow elk-tooth-adorned dress, you'll see a distinguished collection of Edward Curtis photos.

■ Adventures

On Wheels

Scenic Driving

The coast Highway 1 and the inland Highway 101 through the redwoods are such scenic routes in themselves that they capture all your attention at first. But the connecting roads between the two routes make interesting side trips.

A drive up the **Russian River Road**, Highway 116, takes you through several small resort communities. One of those towns, **Guerneville**, boasts a major redwood park, **Austin Creek State Recreation Area**, two miles to its north.

Just south of Mendocino, consider a drive on **Highway 128** between Cloverdale and the coast, passing the town of Boonville. Highway 128 is a twisty road as it leaves Highway 101 at Cloverdale, but it eventually becomes less curvy. You pass grasslands and oak forests, then orchard country, before finally driving through a long redwood state park along the Navarro River. The Navarro is a favorite winter steelhead fishing stream. One pleasant picnic stop here is the **Hendy Woods State Park** (☎ 707-937-5804). Canoeing/kayaking fans rate the stretch of Navarro River from Hendy Park to Dimmick as one of the lovelier streams in California.

Boonville is a proud little town with its own colloquial language. It is also a festive site with an art show in March, wildflower celebration in April, Buck-a-roo rodeo in June, and sheep raiser's barbecue in July.

Highway 20 is another through-the-forest drive between the coast and the inland area. Joining Fort Bragg to Willits, Highway 20 is a twisty road with numerous logging trucks. The road from Fort Bragg keeps you fairly immersed in the forest until the vistas open up a few miles west of Willits.

In the northern Redwood Country, Highway 101 is the main scenic drive from Willits north. Be sure to linger along the Avenue of the Giants roadway paralleling the main road to see examples of the giant redwoods, especially the Founder's Tree at Founder's Grove.

The bucolic dairying region south of Eureka along the **Eel River Delta** can be pleasant to explore by car. Turn off at Ferndale and then drive north and west on the small roads to Loleta. From Loleta you can drive on to **Table Bluff County Park**, which offers crashing surf and a five-mile stretch of beaches.

North of Eureka, the **Trinity Scenic Byway** is an engaging scenic drive on Highway 299 east. This designated Scenic Byway in the Bureau of Land Management system twists through logging country with steep mountains and many vistas. The route follows the Trinity River and heads farther east to Weaverville, once a major gold mining area.

A circular loop trip on the small roads north from Willow Creek can take you through the wilds of the **Trinity Alps**, a mountain range as stark and steep as the Sierra. Consult a detailed local map and follow the circular route from Willow Creek to Weitchpec, Somes Bar, Etna, Weaverville, and back to Willow Creek.

Bicycling

The Coast Highway 1 is a vigorous ride, from Bodega north to Mendocino, but the traffic can be challenging, especially with the wide logging trucks. Locating yourself at a B&B or campsite in the region as a bicycling base would be one strategy. The **Stanford Inn by the Sea**, in Mendocino, rents bikes and has a full-service bike mechanic available in their **Catch a Canoe & Bicycles, Too!** on-site program (☎ 800-320-2453). Managed by Jiro Tulley, this rental, information, and bike repair source is complete. Tulley can advise you on a ride into Russian Gulch State Park, with a final hike to one of the region's loveliest waterfalls. **Van Damme State Park** also has a good bike trail. Tulley is developing maps of bike trails in the **Jackson State Forest**, which presents much good back-country riding if you have adequate information on where to ride.

Backroads (801 Cedar Street, Berkeley, CA 94710-1800; ☎ 510-527-1555 or 800-462-2848) are the experts on a fully organized bicycling or bicycling/hiking trip in this region. Contact them if you want everything provided, from bikes and helmets to comrades, support vehicle, lodging, and dining.

Mendocino Mountain Bike Tours (10450 Nichols Lane; ☎ 707-937-3069). They offer custom, guided tours, ranging from an hour to a full day.

Adventure Rents (behind the Gualala Hotel; ☎ 888-881-4386) rent bikes, canoes and kayaks.

Ocean Trail Bikes & Rental in Fort Bragg (1260 N. Main; ☎ 707-964-1260). After you rent your bike, you can access an extensive paved bike path near the store. This path runs along the ocean and includes a stretch through **MacKerricher State Park**.

North Coast & Redwood Country

Northern Redwood Country

South of Eureka, the small towns of the **Eel River Delta** can be explored, possibly while staying at the Southport Landing B&B. The Southport area, Humboldt Bay Wildlife Refuge, Table Bluff Park, Loleta, and Ferndale are places to visit on your bike outing along peaceful, back country roads.

Bike rentals are possible at **Hum-Boats** near Old Town Eureka, where you can also rent kayaks and sailboats. Hum-Boats, run by Jay Dottle, is at the foot of F Street in Eureka; ☎ 707-444-3048.

The city of Arcata has a 600-acre **Community Forest** with 9.85 miles of roads and trails, seven miles of which can be used by mountain bikes. A map can be obtained from City of Arcata Environmental Services (☎ 707-822-8184).

Redwood National Park (☎ 707-464-6101) has a 22-mile bike loop through a redwood forest to the coast and back. Begin at the Ossagon Trailhead off Newton B. Drury Parkway, using the national park brochure as your map.

Railroading

Fort Bragg, the blue collar balance to Mendocino's artsiness, is known for its **California Western Railroad** (the *Skunk Train*, named for the smell of its diesel smoke that is now a mere memory) and the museum of the lumber industry in the **Guest House**,

Riding the Skunk Train from Fort Bragg to Northspur.

adjacent to the train depot. This steam train makes a daily narrated run inland along the Noyo River to Northspur and beyond to Willits. You can rest in enclosed cars if you wish, or stand in open-air viewing cars allowing for an intimate look at the redwoods, the streams, and occasional wildlife. Call ☎ 707-964-6371 for the train schedule or write ahead to California Western Railroad, PO Box 907, Fort Bragg, CA 95437. The 40-mile round-trip to Willits takes 7½ hours and passes extensive redwood and Douglas fir forests, crisscrossing the Noyo River. The half-day trip out to Northspur and back covers the western part of the scenic terrain with a shorter time commitment.

On Foot

Hiking & Backpacking

 The parks in the region offer outstanding hiking and backpacking opportunities. Here are a few of our favorites:

At **Bodega Head**, a trailhead sign alerts you to a three-mile hiking trail linking Bodega Head with the miles of shifting sand dunes. Walk north on this loose-sand trail for as long as you wish, allowing time for the walk back. The trail passes a University of California Biological Research Station, but the tidepool and population studies are not open for public scrutiny.

For a direct route to the dunes, after you've viewed the splendid rocky promontory at Bodega Head, return to Highway 1, drive north a half-mile, and turn west into the **Bodega Dunes Campground**. Besides camping, a day-use area locates you right in the dunes. A boardwalk allows you to cross the dunes to the glorious, expansive beach. Eight miles of crisscrossing trails in the sand dunes behind the beach afford plenty of hiking opportunities.

Another fine hiking park along the coast is **Manchester Beach State Park** (☎ 707-937-5804), accessible by three roads north of Point Arena. Alder Creek, Kinney, and Stoneboro roads lead to parking lots behind the dunes. The beach stretches the full five miles from Alder Creek to just north of Point Arena. Hiking trails crisscross the area. Fishing is popular for snapper and sea trout. The Alder Creek entrance at the north end crosses a San Andreas

Hiking the Jughandle Reserve along the Mendocino Coast.

fault line that jumped 16 feet in 1906. After passing a marsh with abundant bird life, you reach the beach. Kinney Road leads you through sand dunes to the state parks campground and the beach. Stoneboro Road leads to the major bird habitat at Hunter's Lagoon.

In the Mendocino region the **Jughandle State Reserve** (☎ 707-937-5804) is an enjoyable five-mile roundtrip hike. Five wave-cut terraces intersected by Jughandle Creek expose 500,000 years of beach history. You can climb from sea level to a Pygmy Forest, where plant growth has been stunted because of the meager nutrients in the rain-washed sandy soil. Offshore, the underwater park is used by scuba divers.

Hikes Near Eureka

In the northern Redwood Country, hiking around the **Humboldt Bay Wildlife Refuge** is a delight in winter when the major migrations of ducks and geese fill the bay. The **Hookton Slough Trail** locates you close to the birds and harbor seals. Any time of the year you are likely to see plovers, night herons, egrets, and resident Canadian geese, but the abundance of migrating birdlife makes the refuge enticing in winter. This is also a good kayaking and biking area. Nearby, the **Table Bluff County Park** has five miles of driftwood-strewn beach and plenty of crashing surf, if you want an ocean beach walk.

Nature lovers will enjoy the **Trinidad Head Trail**, one of the compelling vista walks along the north coast above Eureka. Park at the beach area below Trinidad Head and walk up the marked trail, a sacred area to the family of Tsurai Indians who once flourished here. Few locations in California display the grandeur of the coast more fully.

The most spectacular walk in the redwood region is the stroll to glimpse the tallest tree in the world, at Redwood National Park. There are two ways to get a glimpse of the tallest trees, which are in **Tall Trees Grove**, as mentioned also under Touring. You can take a park service bus from the Redwood Information Center (☎ 707-464-6101) at Orick to within 1.3 miles of the grove and hike in the final steep stretch. This is the way most people do it. Alternatively, you can make a 15-mile round-trip hike to see the trees by walking up the relatively level Redwood Creek.

The state parks and the national park that form the north coast redwoods parks complex have many miles of hiking trails. **Prairie Creek State Park** alone has 75 miles of trails.

Within the city of Arcata the **Arcata Marsh & Wildlife Sanctuary** (☎ 707-826-2359) is intriguing to explore for its trails, its shorebirds, and the revolutionary transformation of this wastewater management area into a wildlife habitat.

On Horseback

Chanslor Riding Stables (2660 Coast Highway 1, Bodega Bay; ☎ 707-875-2721) offers a horseback riding experience on Sonoma area beaches. The trail winds through the dunes until you reach the ocean, at which point you can gallop along adjacent to the waves. The horses at Chanslor are more spirited than the somnolent beasts one usually finds at horse-riding operations.

In the Mendocino area, the dependable horseback riding provider is **Ricochet Ridge** (24201 North Highway One, Fort Bragg; ☎ 707-964-7669). Their lively horses can be

Horseback riding in the old growth forests of Redwood National Park.

North Coast & Redwood Country

taken on escorted rides that include cantering along the beach. Ricochet is a large operation, with about 35 horses, offering everything from 1½ hour beginner rides to a week's immersion in horse riding, which includes trips into the adjacent mountains. Ricochet Ridge Ranch lies adjacent to MacKerricher Beach State Park, one of the choice horseback riding areas along this coast.

In the northern Redwood Country an outstanding horseback ride is offered by **Tall Trees Outfitters**, run by Nancy Fiddler. Fiddler guides you on trails ascending through the red alders, then the second-growth redwoods, and finally into the old-growth redwoods of Redwood National Park, all the while illuminating you on the environmental and political nuances of the region. Riding a horse in the fog amidst the thousand-year-old trees is an experience you will long remember. Tall Trees Outfitters also conducts overnight and multi-day trips. On an overnight trip you see the tallest trees in the world, the redwoods carefully measured along Redwood Creek. Tall Trees Outfitters operates only in summer, Memorial Day to Labor Day, because rain on the trails in the other months makes the riding too dangerous.

On Water

Rafting/Kayaking/Canoeing

Canoeing is popular along the Russian River in spring and early summer. The main provider is **Trowbridge Canoe Trips** (Healdsburg; ☎ 707-433-7247). You canoe a section of the Russian River above Healdsburg and then put out near the Trowbridge facility in town.

The **Catch a Canoe & Bicycles, Too!** program (☎ 800-320-2453) in Mendocino at the Stanford Inn offers an unusual canoe experience. You launch the canoe in Big River as the tide goes upstream. Riding the tide, you can travel several miles inland, turning around to catch the flow of the tide going out. Catch a Canoe has kayaks, canoes, and special handmade outrigger canoes designed to resemble redwood from the region. On a paddle upriver we saw a doe and fawns, osprey hunting for fish, a merganser duck with over a dozen chicks, and numerous herons feeding in the shallows.

The **Albion River** is another engaging small river to canoe on the Mendocino Coast. You can rent a canoe from **The Boathouse Rents** (☎ 707-937-5153) at Schooners Landing. They rent canoes, kayaks, paddle boats, and camping gear. The Boathouse Rents also conducts tours with an historical or birdwatching interest.

If you want to do **sea kayaking** along this coast, Catch a Canoe can provide the vessels and information on where to go. Kayaking is especially popular at Van Damme State Park.

Lost Coast Adventures (☎ 800-961-1143) offers Mendocino sea-cave kayak tours at Van Damme State Park.

Canoes and kayaks can be rented in Gualala from **Adventure Rents** (behind the Gualala Hotel; ☎ 888-881-4386). They also rent bikes.

WHITEWATER CLASSIFICATION CHART		
CLASS	SKILL LEVEL	WATER CONDITION
I	Easy	Calm, moving water with occasional riffles.
II	Intermediate	Little bursts of bouncing rapids in clear, wide channels between long stretches of calm.
III	Difficult	Irregular waves through narrower channels where maneuvering around rocks is required.
IV	Very Difficult	Rapids are intense, loud, and long, with complex, rocky obstacles in the way.

Watersports Near Eureka

In the northern Redwood Country the main rivers to raft or kayak are the **Trinity** and the **Klamath**. A stretch of the Trinity known as the Pigeon Point Run offers good Class III rapids in the warm summer time, when most people like to raft. On a typical trip you will see turtles, merganser ducks, osprey, and deer. The steep hillsides and sculpted rock patterns along the river make Trinity rafting memorable. Many other rivers and creeks in the region offer rafting or kayaking in winter, when rains swell the streams. One dependable and experienced outfitter is **Bigfoot Rafting Company** (19 Willow Way, Willow Creek; ☎ 916-629-2263 or 800-722-2233). Another is **Aurora River Adventures** (Willow Creek; ☎ 916-629-3843, 800-562-8475).

North Coast & Redwood Country

Kayaking is popular in Humboldt and Arcata bays. **Southport Landing B&B** has its own kayaks for guests to explore the quiet environs of the Humboldt Bay Wildlife Refuge. A central rental place in Eureka is **Hum-Boats**. You can rent kayaks or canoes and paddle immediately across the bay to Indian Island, where there are dozens of white egrets nesting in the trees. Jay Dottle, owner of Hum-Boats, also leads moonlight kayaking excursions and other celebrations of the watery resources of the bay. Hum-Boats is at the foot of F Street in Eureka; ☎ 707-444-3048.

Some **surfing** on the ocean side and windsurfing on the protected eastern side of the breakwater occurs at Humboldt Bay. The local organizer is **Pro Sport Center**, 508 Myrtle, Eureka; ☎ 707-443-6328. A limited amount of diving occurs for abalone, but this activity is more popular along the Mendocino Coast, where the water is clearer.

Boating

The protected Humboldt Bay provides some sailing and boating opportunities, though sailing on the ocean requires advanced skills.

Hum-Boats in Eureka can rent sailboats, powerboats, and even drive you around in their water taxi, a lovingly restored wooden craft from 1938, made of redwood. Hum-Boats is at the foot of F Street, ☎ 707-444-3048.

Naturalist Bruce Slocum (☎ 707-786-4187) provides a competent natural history boat excursion on the Eel River. You meet Slocum at Fernbridge on the Eel River, near the Ferndale turnoff. He then motors you in an open boat through the Eel River Delta, stopping to show you the harbor seals and the ospreys. Slocum, an expert on the flora and fauna of the river channels and salt marshes, calls his outfit the **Camp Weott Guide Service**.

Fishing/Whale Watching

All the coastal towns have charter fishing boats that welcome anglers hoping to catch salmon, halibut, and rock cod. At Bodega Bay, one provider is **New Sea Angler** (☎ 707-875-3495). Many of the fishing boats of the region become whale watching boats in the winter season. New Sea Angler is an example.

Whales can also be watched from shore promontories, such as **Bodega Head** or the **Mendocino Headlands**.

Mendocino and Fort Bragg hold **Whale Festivals** in March, with activities ranging from a marine art exhibit to a Whale Run.

Anchor Charter Boats (☎ 707-964-4550) in Fort Bragg offers salmon fishing, deep sea bottom fishing, and open ocean tuna excursions. In winter, they become a whale watching charter.

Shore fishing for rockfish is good all along the coast, but especially in the Mendocino-Rockport area. Abalone diving, prying the abalone off rocks during free dives (no tanks) is a special form of fishing here.

The runs of steelhead, an ocean going trout, enter streams such as the Garcia, Eel, and Gualala rivers in winter and are sought by fly fishermen.

The main fishing gear store supporting the sport in the Mendocino coast region is **North Coast Angler** (1260 North Main Street, Fort Bragg; ☎ 707-964-8931).

The *Noyo Belle* (☎ 707-964-3104) out of Fort Bragg specializes in scenic cruises and whale watching.

In the northern Redwood Country a similar pattern of fishing and whale watching persists. Fishing is good in the northern rivers, such as the Trinity or the Eel, for salmon and steelhead trout during the runs. Charter boats leave Eureka and Trinidad for sport fishing catches of salmon and halibut. Whale watching is popular in winter from the charter boats or from the cliff locations, such as Patrick's Point or Table Bluff.

Fishing paraphernalia and local expertise is available from **Eureka Fly Shop**, 505 H Street; ☎ 707-444-2000. **Trinidad Bay Charters** (☎ 707-839-4743) handles both deep-sea fishing and whale watching, depending on the season.

Scuba Diving/Snorkeling

Though the waters are not always clear and are extremely cold, requiring a wet suit, much scuba and snorkel occurs on the north coast, especially at **Van Damme State Park** near Mendocino. Van Damme is the single best scuba/snorkel site because an offshore reef breaks up the waves, presenting fairly calm waters for the

North Coast & Redwood Country

diver/snorkeler. Divers can also camp at Van Damme, offering ready access to the water.

For diving equipment and information, contact **North Coast Divers**, ☎ 800-961-1143.

Some scuba divers go to enjoy the sea life, even though the waters can be murky. Snorkelers dive for abalone, which can be pried off the rocks if they have reached a certain size. Abalone can only be taken by snorkelers doing *free dives*, meaning diving without tanks.

Salt Point State Park has an underwater reserve for divers who want to explore the coastal flora and fauna. Call ☎ 707-847-3221 for complete information, ☎ 707-847-3222 for surf and tide questions. Salt Point is a large holding, 5,970 acres, with miles of wave-sculpted shoreline and rich intertidal life. Salt Point's underwater area is called the Gerstle Cove Underwater Reserve.

The **Point Arena Lighthouse** (☎ 707-882-2777) has an offshore underwater preserve where scuba divers view the marine flora and fauna as well as the remains of a sunken freighter. The offshore entity is known as the **Arena Rock Underwater Preserve** and is used also for surfing, kayaking, and rowing.

The waters at Van Damme (☎ 707-937-5804) are clearer and more inviting than the diving opportunities off the other coastal parks north of Eureka.

In the northern Redwood Country the sources for diving instruction and equipment are **Big Blue Dive** (☎ 707-725-1318) and **Pro Sport Center** (☎ 707-443-6328).

■ Where to Stay & Eat

Accommodations on Coast Highway I

 The opportunity to serve travelers has been a major impetus for the restoration of historic buildings as lodgings and restaurants along this coast.

Here are some representative lodgings, both old and new:

The Bodega Bay Lodge (103 Coast Highway 1, Bodega Bay, CA 94923; ☎ 707-875-3525 or 800-368-2468. $$$) is a deluxe coastal lodge with fireplaces, heated pool, and spa.

The Inn at the Tides (800 Coast Highway 1, Bodega Bay, CA 94923; ☎ 707-875-2751. $$-$$$) boasts 86 units in a clustered village atmosphere on a hillside overlooking Bodega Bay.

Vacation Rentals US, (☎ 800-548-7631. $$-$$$) offers beach-front homes in the Bodega Bay region for rent. The homes may have anywhere from one to five bedrooms. For families or family reunion celebrations, this can be an excellent option.

Fort Ross Lodge (20705 Coast Highway 1, Jenner, CA 95450; ☎ 707-847-3333. $$-$$$) emphasizes a coastal environment with panoramic ocean views. The units include fireplaces and hot tubs.

River's End Resort (11048 Coast Highway 1, Jenner, CA 95450; ☎ 707-865-2484. $$-$$$) is a comfortable eight-unit facility on cliffs overlooking the Russian River. The resort features private decks, ocean views, and its own restaurant.

Some of the **Sea Ranch** development homes can be rented. Call **Ocean View Properties and Rentals** (☎ 707-884-3538, $$-$$$) or **Ram's Head Realty** (☎ 800-785-3455. $$-$$$).

One of the more romantic of the upscale lodgings in the region is **The Whale Watch Inn** (five miles north of Gualala at 35100 Highway 1, Gualala, CA 95445; ☎ 800-942-5342. $$$) located strategically on bluffs overlooking tidepools and a rocky coast. Mesmerized by the crashing surf, the silence, the dance of light in the fireplace, the in-room jacuzzis, and the creative breakfasts, couples discover and re-discover each other here. Each room has a little book where guests have been leaving their memoirs and pledges of love to each other since 1985. The contents of these books would make a romance novelist blush and require that a cynic recant any notion that true love does not exist.

Old Milano Hotel (38300 South Highway One, Gualala, CA 95445; ☎ 707-884-3256, $$-$$$) boasts a view of the coast over-looking Castle Rock. This superbly sited bed and breakfast allows

North Coast & Redwood Country

you to soak in the hot tub with a view of the ocean. At their restaurant, try the grilled lamb or braised prawns.

Stanford Inn By the Sea, one of the stately lodgings along the coast (Coast Highway One and Comptche-Ukiah Road, PO Box 487, Mendocino, CA 95460; ☎ 707-937-5615 or 800-331-8884. $$$) offers a pleasing view of the rugged Mendocino coast and proximity to the picturesque town of Mendocino. Several of the buildings are newly constructed units emphasizing pine wood and decks with sea views. Stanford has a solarium-enclosed pool and hot tub, plus a separate exercise room. In addition to lodging, the inn runs a substantial organic farm. Hors d'oeuvres at wine time are made of vegetables collected from the garden. The breakfast is hearty, made to order. Llamas on the property are family pets. Of considerable interest to adventure travelers is their Catch a Canoe outfitter that provides all you need to paddle kayaks and canoes as far as eight miles up Big River, timing the trip with the tidal surge. Paddlers see wildlife and experience tranquillity in this wooded habitat. The same business also rents bicycles.

In Mendocino, **MacCallum House** (45020 Albion Street, Mendocino, CA 95460; ☎ 707-937-0289. $$-$$$) is one of the prominent Victorian lodgings, typical of the artsy B&Bs along this coast. A driftwood whale sculpture adorns the front yard. MacCallum House has lodgings in the main house, outlying cottages, and a barn. It is also noted for its elegant, fine-dining restaurant.

One of the most charming seaside destinations of all is **Heritage House Country Inn** at Little River. This large property has luxury rooms and some separate houses, plus an outstanding dining room with a view. Guests can walk the bluffs along the coast and enjoy a glass of wine with sunset. Lodging includes an exquisite dinner and full breakfast. Heritage House is at 5200 North Highway One, Little River, CA 95456; ☎ 707-937-5885 or ☎ 800-235-5885. $$-$$$.

Joshua Grindle Inn (44800 Little Lake Road, Mendocino, CA 95460; ☎ 707-937-4143. $$-$$$) is a typical Mendocino inn. They have 10 rooms in the 1879 structure. Country Victorian with a New England coastal feel describes the setting.

Another nearby B&B with deep roots in history is the **Little River Inn**, just south of Mendocino. This home was built by lumber baron Silas Coombs, who arrived here in 1853. Little River Inn (7751 N. Highway One, Drawer B, Little River, CA 95456; ☎ 707-937-5942, $$-$$$) also has one of the premier dining facilities in the region. The inn is immediately south of Van Damme Park, which has a fine fern canyon walk.

The Inn at Schoolhouse Creek (7051 N. Highway One, Little River, CA 95456; ☎ 707-937-5525. $$-$$$) offers a cluster of comfortable, separate cottages, most with full living room, kitchen, and bedrooms. Some cottages have decks and ocean views. Besides the cottages, there is a small motel. The proprietors can send you on a peaceful hike to the creek in the redwoods at the back of the property. They can also point out the walk-in access across the road and a few steps south to a hidden cove, Buckhorn Cove, where the tidepools are engaging at low tide.

The Mendocino Hotel and Garden Suites (45080 Main Street, Mendocino, CA 95460; ☎ 707-937-0511. $$-$$$) now an inviting garden bar and restaurant, typifies another aspect of the recycling pattern converting early structures to tourist use.

About 60 ocean-view vacation homes in the Mendocino area can be rented through **Mendocino Coast Reservations** (☎ 707-937-5003 or 800-262-7801).

Farther north at Westport there is a lodging with roots deep in the ranching culture of the region. The gardens, the family ranch atmosphere, the wildlife, the rural charm, and the sumptuous ranch breakfast are all attractions at **Howard Creek Ranch Inn** (40501 North Highway 1, Westport, CA 95488; ☎ 707-964-6725. $-$$$). You know you are in a remote area when the evening talk turns to the mountain lions in the nearby hills.

For budget accommodations in Fort Bragg, try the **Tradewinds Lodge** (400 South Main Street, Fort Bragg, CA 95437; ☎ 707-964-4761 or 800-524-2244. $-$$). They sometimes offer packages that combine lodging, breakfast, dinner, and admissions to various area attractions.

North Coast & Redwood Country

The Gingerbread Mansion Inn, a B&B in the Victorian village of Ferndale.

Accommodations on Highway 101

 Lodging options on Highway 101 range from the stately Benbow and Eureka inns, near the south and north end of the highway, to the picturesque Gingerbread Mansion Inn, a quintessential Victorian in Ferndale. Many styles of B&B can be found here.

On the way up to Redwood Country, as you pass through the Sonoma Wine Country, a comfortable lodging would be the **Vintner's Inn** (4350 Barnes Road, Santa Rosa, CA 95403; ☎ 800-421-2584. $$$).

At the south edge of Redwood Country, the dependable choice lodging is the Tudor-style **Benbow Inn** (445 Lake Benbow Drive, Garberville, CA 95542; ☎ 800-355-3301. $$-$$$), which emphasizes outdoor activities at its lake and is noted for its cuisine.

As you drive toward Eureka, the historic company lumber town of Scotia offers 12 lodging rooms at its rustic and economical **Scotia Inn** (100 Main Street, Scotia, CA 95565; ☎ 707-764-5683. $$), a historic redwood building with both casual dining and fine dining restaurants.

South of Eureka is Judy and Dana Henderson's **Southport Landing B&B** (444 Phelan Road, Loleta, CA 95551; ☎ 707-733-5915. $$-$$$). This bed and breakfast is especially focused on adventure travel. It is an early shipping family's house set in relative isolation on the south side of Humboldt Bay. In the 1890s, the area was a busy shipping point for potatoes, salmon, and lumber from the Eel River Delta. From the house you can kayak, hike around the wildlife refuge on the bay, and bike out to the ocean or to the nearby town of Loleta. Kayaks and bikes are available at the house. The Hendersons delight in sharing their interest in the natural history of the region. Winter is the busy birding season because of the major migrations.

Eureka boasts some cozy lodgings, especially the Eureka Inn and the Hotel Carter.

The **Eureka Inn** (518 7th Street, Eureka, CA 95501; ☎ 707-442-6441 or 800-862-4906. $$-$$$) is an elegant and historic English Tudor structure from 1922 that welcomes children. Now on the National Register, the building includes a plushly furnished lobby, a fine restaurant known as the Rib Room, a lively Rathskeller Bar, and comfortable accommodations. The lobby is a venue where the region celebrates Christmas in a public way. From late November through New Year's Eve, the lobby hosts many singing groups and entertainers.

The **Hotel Carter** (301 L Street, Eureka, CA 95501; ☎ 707-445-1390. $$$) and across-the-street **Carter House** are run by folksy entrepreneur Mark Carter and his wife Christi. The Carters built the Carter House structure in the 1980s, based on a floor plan and design from the 1880s. Those plans were drawn by the same architect who guided construction of the classic Carson Mansion, within easy view a block away. When the Inn overflowed, Carter proceeded to acquire his Hotel. Their restaurant, known as Restaurant 301, is arguably the most elegant in Redwood Country.

The **Eagle House Victorian Inn** (139 2nd Street, Eureka, CA 95501; ☎ 707-444-3344. $-$$$) is a downtown Eureka establishment with rooms, a comedy club, and a relaxed ambiance. Lodging here puts you close to old Town.

The **Doubletree** (1929 4th Street, Eureka, CA 95501; ☎ 707-445-0844 or 800-547-8010. $$-$$$) is the largest property in

North Coast & Redwood Country

town, offering good-quality motel-type rooms and an elaborate Sunday brunch.

The Victorian Village of Ferndale has seen several of its historic structures transformed into B&Bs.

The **Gingerbread Mansion Inn** (400 Berding Street, Ferndale, CA 95536; ☎ 707-786-4000 or 800-952-4136. $$$), a block off Main Street, is a restored Victorian filled with antiques by a couple who were smitten by the structure and idea of relocating here in the early 1980s. Another prominent B&B is the **Shaw House** (703 Main Street, Ferndale, CA 95536; ☎ 707-786-9958. $$-$$$), the oldest structure in the city, dating from 1854.

Restaurants on Coast Highway I

 In Bodega, the restaurants that put you close to the fishing fleet and the bustle of the harbor are **The Tides** (☎ 707-875-2777. $$) and **Lucas Wharf** (☎ 707-875-3522. $$). You can see the boats unload their catches right in front of the restaurants.

At the mouth of the Russian River, the restaurant of choice is **River's End** (☎ 707-865-2484. $$), where Chef Wolfgang Gramatzki offers German-continental cuisine and Sonoma area wines. This is a choice location for watching the sunset and admiring the coast, along with its resident wildlife in season.

For a meal or bed and breakfast in Jenner, try **Murphy's Jenner-By-The-Sea** (☎ 707-865-2377. $$), a turn-of-the-century inn. Seafood is the dinner specialty, washed down with an ample selection of North Coast wines. The Sunday champagne brunch draws a crowd.

When price is no object and fine dining is sought, the choice candidate along this coast is **St. Orres** (☎ 707-884-3335. $$$) just north of Gualala. Housed in a distinctive wooden building with a dome that seems to echo the Russian church at Fort Ross, St. Orres pleases the palate with boar and deer, as well as salmon and halibut. The appetizer might be warm goat cheese in pastry or mixed organic greens with the house raspberry dressing.

The **Sign of the Whale** restaurant (☎ 707-882-2259, $$) in Point Arena features prime rib and seafood.

Three Mendocino-area restaurants are in the upper strata of fine California cuisine.

Café Beaujolais (961 Ukiah Street; ☎ 707-937-5614. $$-$$$) enjoys a solid reputation for its French-California style. Try the fresh coho salmon.

The intimate **Little River Inn Restaurant** (Little River; ☎ 707-937-5942. $$-$$$) is located in one of the most historic buildings in the region. Try the Mendocino mussels, followed by either the margarita swordfish or the fresh lamb.

MacCallum House Restaurant (45020 Albion Street; ☎ 707-937-5763. $$-$$$) in Mendocino emphasizes chef/owner Alan Kantor's seasonal menu. Starters include grilled quail or field greens. The grilled portabello mushroom or duck breast in tangerine sauce are tasty entrées.

For picnic fixings in Mendocino, stop at **Good Taste** (☎ 707-937-0104), which makes its own jellies and pickles as well as the usual deli salads. They offer a selection of cheeses, meats, pâtés, bread, and wine that could inspire a picnic on the Mendocino Headlands.

For breakfast in Mendocino, you might try an omelet at the **Bay View Café** (☎ 707-937-4197. $-$$) where you have a view of the grassy headlands. Hawks can be seen swooping over the area in search of their breakfasts. For a soup-and-sandwich lunch, try **Cultured Affair** (☎ 707-937-1430. $-$$).

For breakfast or lunch in Fort Bragg, drop in at the **Egghead Restaurant** (326 North Main Street; ☎ 707-964-5005.$-$$). Omelets and crepes are the specialty.

Farther north, one of the rural restaurants with strong ties to the farming and ranching heritage of the area is **DeHaven Valley Farm Inn** (39247 North Highway One, Westport, CA 95488; ☎ 707-961-1660. $$-$$$), north of Westport. They have a fixed menu dinner for guests of the inn, but welcome additional diners on a space-available basis. Call at least a day before to enjoy their home cooking, such as red bean soup, salad greens, poached salmon, and inventive custard desserts.

North Coast & Redwood Country

Restaurants on Highway 101

 A Eureka restaurant that takes you back to the lumber-jack days is the **Samoa Cookhouse** (on Samoa Boulevard in Samoa; ☎ 707-442-1659. $-$$). Generous-sized portions are served family-style on long tables with red-checkered oil-cloth table covers. Look for a whole pie to be set before you. No one has ever left the economical and fixed-price Samoa Cook-house still hungry. The adjacent museum has examples of the cooking apparatus that kept the loggers fueled.

The dining room at the **Benbow Inn** (445 Lake Benbow Drive, Garberville 95542; ☎ 707-923-2124 or 800-355-3301. $$-$$$), at the south end of Redwood Country, has a solid reputation.

The Scotia Inn's **Redwood Dining Room** (100 Main Street, Scotia; ☎ 707-764-5683. $$) has both a regular menu and a monthly ethnic one, which may be Southwestern or Greek. Try the flaming goat cheese appetizer. Salmon or filet are specialties on the regular menu. Owner John Schleef offers his knowledge of wines along with his decent wine list. In the basement, at the more casual restaurant, the **Steak and Potato Pub**, try one of the seven different types of steaks. For the no-red-meat partisans there is salmon or chicken.

Curley's Grill (460 Main Street, Ferndale; ☎ 707-786-9696. $$) presents culinary magic in a friendly and unpretentious setting, where you can order a full dinner or just linger over wine and an appetizer. Owner Curley Tait guides the operation. Try the grilled tortilla and onion cake appetizer, perhaps followed by a Caesar salad or the roast pork loin in beer. Consider a local Humboldt wine such as a merlot from Oliviera.

The **Eel River Brewing Company** (1777 Alamar Way, Fortuna; ☎ 707-725-2739, $-$$) exemplifies the proliferating brew pub scene, with brewmaster Dave Hiett's award-winning ales and porters, plus pub fare, such as Cajun shrimp or baked snapper, served either indoors or on the patio built on the site of a former lumber mill. The decor of the restaurant includes historic photos of the devastating 1964 flood, when the Eel River set records for destruction. Flooding is so prominent in the minds of people who live in the Eel River Delta that many of the houses near the river are built on elevated foundations.

Within Eureka, another brew pub to consider is the **Lost Coast Brewery** (617 4th Street; ☎ 707-445-4480. $-$$) known for its Downtown Brown light brown ale, presented with distinctive modern graphics when bottled. Try the Asian sesame chicken salad or vegetarian chile. On weekend evenings, Lost Coast Brewery becomes the happening place in Eureka with a live band.

Eureka Inn's Rib Room (7th and F streets; ☎ 707-442-6441 or 800-862-4906. $$-$$$) is a stately place for a leisurely dinner. Try the crab cioppino, in season, followed by the elaborate dessert tray.

Hotel Carter's Restaurant 301 (301 L Street, ☎ 707-444-8062. $$$) gets the nod as the fine-dining standard for the region. Chef Rodger Babel creates a *garden-to-kitchen* style from his extensive herb garden, a block from the restaurant, that can be toured. Aside from the regular menu, Chef Babel's Discovery Menu offers a fixed-price evening of several courses showing considerable culinary artistry.

"We aim at clean and straightforward taste," says Chef Babel. "We let the ingredients show their own taste rather than manipulate the taste."

The small towns in the region present some good local restaurants, such as Trinidad's **The Eatery** (☎ 707-677-3777. $-$$), where a crab sandwich amounts to a tasty lunch.

In Redwood National Park, though you are out in the woods, there is gourmet dining at Rolf Rheinschmidt's place, known as **Rolf's Park Café** (☎ 707-488-3841. $$). You will find it at the Fern Canyon exit off Highway 101. Try the smoked salmon or the restaurant specialty, a combo plate of buffalo, elk, and boar. The complex includes a motel.

Inland, at Willow Creek, the paraphernalia-strewn **Cinnabar Sam's** restaurant is the place to stop after rafting or a scenic drive. Try the chicken fajitas. Cinnabar Sam's is at 19 Willow Way in Willow Creek; ☎ 916-629-3437. $-$$.

North Coast & Redwood Country

Camping & RV on Coast Highway I

 Numerous state parks along the coast offer excellent camping opportunities. Commercial operations, such as KOAs, cater to the RV traveler who needs electricity and hookups.

Write the **Department of Parks and Recreation**, Mendocino Area State Parks, PO Box 440, Mendocino, CA 95460, ☎ 707-937-5804 to learn more about nine state parks in the area that have camping. Manchester Beach, Van Damme, Russian Gulch, and MacKerricher are all good choices. Some state park camps can be reserved (☎ 800-444-7275).

The **Mendocino National Forest** has eight campgrounds to offer. Contact the Mendocino National Forest Headquarters, 420 E. Laurel Street, Willows, CA 95988; ☎ 916-934-3316.

Along the Sonoma coast, good camping is possible at **The Bodega Dunes Campground** (☎ 707-875-3483), which puts you in a coastal sand dune environment. The entrance is a mile north of Bodega along Highway 1. Besides camping, a day-use area locates you right in the dunes. A boardwalk allows you to cross the dunes to the glorious, expansive beach. Eight miles of crisscrossing trails in the sand dunes behind the beach afford plenty of hiking opportunities.

Another good beach camping site, moving north along the Sonoma Coast, is at **Wright's Beach** (☎ 707-875-3483) south of Goat Rock Beaches. If this is too chilly or windy, try the **Casini Ranch Family Campground** (☎ 800-451-8400) a few miles inland, at Duncans Mill, along the Russian River road.

For travelers wanting full RV hookups and hot showers, Manchester Beach has a **KOA** with all desired facilities and is located in a pine forest. The contact is Manchester Beach KOA, Highway 1 at Manchester State Beach; ☎ 707-882-2375.

Casper Beach RV Campground in Mendocino is open all year and is right on the beach. It is good for abalone diving, fishing, surfing, and scuba direct from your campsite. The contact is Caspar Beach RV Campground, 14441 Point Cabrillo Drive, Mendocino, 95460; ☎ 707-964-3306.

One unusual camping opportunity along the coast is called **Adventure in Camping**. They will set up for you at MacKerricher Beach State Park or other park sites a fully self-contained travel trailer. You arrive with your food and bedding material and focus your energy on camping activities. They have various model trailers that sleep from three to six people. They offer a similar service at Lake Tahoe or Mammoth Lakes. Call ☎ 619-648-7509 or 800-417-7771 for details.

Camping & RV on Highway 101

 Along the inland redwood route, Highway 101, one good camping choice would be at the Rockefeller Forest on Bull Creek Flats Road. The Rockefeller Forest is a magnificent grove and a poignant example of the need to protect whole watersheds to save prize redwoods. The choice camp here is **Albee Camp** (☎ 707-946-2409) in an abandoned apple orchard near the Rockefeller Forest. Besides camping, you could stop here for a picnic.

Along the coast, north of Eureka, consider **Patrick's Point State Park** (☎ 707-677-3570) for camping. It's a quiet place, a little-known state park with a re-created Yurok village. The campsites are lovely and there are trails down to fine beaches. It is also a relatively allergen-free environment. Patrick's Point boasts handsome stands of spruce and hemlock, plus some 350 varieties of mushrooms.

Remember that some state park camps can be reserved (☎ 800-444-7275). Similarly, there is a national parks camp reservation number (☎ 800-365-2267).

Redwood National Park has excellent campgrounds. The contact is ☎ 707-464-6101.

Along scenic Highway 299 traveling east from the coast there are many forest service campgrounds, some with hosts, managed by the **Six Rivers National Forest** (☎ 707-442-1721).

Self-contained RVs park at Orick in large numbers on the beach immediately south of the Visitor Center for Redwoods National Park.

A new **KOA** at Fortuna (1660 Kenmar Road, Fortuna, CA 95540; ☎ 707-725-3359) has all the facilities expected of this national RV chain. Additional KOAs are located in Eureka and Crescent City.

At the south end of Redwood Country, the **Benbow Valley RV Resort & Golf Course** (7000 Benbow Drive, Garberville, CA 95542; ☎ 707-923-2777) is a full-service RV establishment in a country club atmosphere.

■ Coniferous California

By Lee Foster

Though the California imagination sometimes suffers from inflation, certain facts of nature here stand out as indisputable. In California you can meet the tallest, the most massive, and the oldest living things on earth.

The tallest life forms on earth are the redwoods (*Sequoia sempervirens*) along the coast north from San Francisco. Three tallest specimens, measuring 367 feet high, flourish in Redwood National Park, near Orick, in the northwestern corner of the state.

Most massive of living things are the coast redwoods' inland cousin (*Sequoiadendron gigantea*), found in pockets along the western foothills of the Sierra at midstate. The giant is the General Sherman Tree in Sequoia National Park, east of Fresno.

Oldest living creatures on this planet are the bristlecone pines (*Pinus longaeva*) that survive in the White Mountains, a range east of Bishop. Bristlecone Pines exist in other mountain settings in the Southwest, but the California trees rank as the oldest, around 4,500 years, based on core samples that can be ring dated.

The Tallest

A quest to see the tallest of the tall trees will take you to Redwood National Park in the far northwest corner of the state.

Seeing the *Sequoia sempervirens* is easy because the trees are distributed in a cool, moist band along 400 miles of the California coast from Big Sur north to beyond the Oregon border. Some favorite viewing sites are near San Francisco at Muir Woods or at

Big Basin State Park. On the road north of San Francisco impressive groves can be enjoyed at the Avenue of the Giants, along Highway 101, on the route to Redwood National Park.

Unlike the other two special trees, you can see the coast redwoods in many locations, if seeing the type of tree, as opposed to the prime specimen, satisfies your passions. But, for me, only the tallest tree itself would do, so I drove the five-six hours north from San Francisco to Redwood National Park.

The drive gave me time to meditate over the marvel of the coast redwood. Though huge, these trees flourish in a fairly narrow environmental niche. They grow naturally only within 30 miles of the coast and at elevations below 3,000 feet, requiring a substantial amount of moisture from rain and fog.

Fortunately, some of the most valuable examples of coast redwoods are now protected in parks. Only 5% of the primeval forest of these trees escaped the loggers' saws. Redwood lumber is one of the most durable wood building materials available, resistant to rot and insect damage, though not as strong as Douglas fir.

You are close to the final destination when you reach the Redwood Information Center (☎ 707-488-3461) the handsome interpretive center at Orick.

There are two ways to get a glimpse of the tallest trees, which are, appropriately, in Tall Trees Grove. You can take a Park Service bus from the Redwood Information Center to within 1.3 miles of the grove and hike the final stretch.

Either way, you will be amply rewarded. The redwood forest exhibits a cathedral hush. So dense and dimly lit is this reverential area, so moist and cool and strewn with oxalis flowers, so calm and eternal in aura as compared with the frenetic and ephemeral acts of daily human life, that you may find tears coming to your eyes and experience a certain relaxing release as you commune with the arboreal giants all around you.

The Most Massive

Out of deference to Civil War generals, who appeared at the time as the most substantial figures around, the giant inland sequoias are known as the General Sherman Tree, General Grant Tree, and other "general" trees.

North Coast & Redwood Country

You can see these marvelous and massive objects in Sequoia and Kings Canyon National Parks, twin parks comprising 1,300 square miles in the Sierra foothills, at mid-state, east of Fresno.

Unlike the tallest of the coast redwood trees, which require a hike in, the inland sequoias are drive-in wonders. The largest tree, **General Sherman**, stands only a short walk from your car. Standing before the General Sherman tree is akin to swimming next to a dozen blue whales in the ocean. Many of the inland sequoia trees are fully 30 feet in diameter and rise over 200 feet high.

As you proceed through the parks, it is possible to prepare yourself for the climactic encounter with General Sherman. First, pay your respects, in Kings Canyon National Park, to the third largest, the **General Grant Tree** (267 feet high, 107.6 feet circumference). General Grant gets the nod from many observers as the most classic illustration of this tree species because it stands alone in magnificent grandeur, beautifully proportioned. Then proceed to the second most massive tree, the **General Lee**. Finally, in an area of Sequoia National Park called the Giant Forest, you meet 2,500-year-old General Sherman (275 feet high, 103 feet in circumference, and 36½ feet maximum diameter). The volume of its trunk is estimated to be 52,500 cubic feet. In 1890 this tree wonderland was set aside as a National Park for future generations to enjoy.

The propensity to turn those cubic feet into board feet of salable lumber proved to be an understandable, if shortsighted, temptation of lumber interests. At the Grant Grove Visitor Center you can learn how close these priceless natural gems came to feeding a pedestrian lumber mill before the creation of the park. In fact, a 300-foot Sequoia was cut so that a cross-section could be taken to Philadelphia for the national Centennial in 1876. Most observers at the Centennial dismissed the purported cross-section of a tree as a California hoax, a tall tree tale. Trees just didn't grow this large. It is comforting to know that the remaining giant sequoia trees will now survive for at least as long as there are people to appreciate them.

To get the full benefit of the trees, scenic terrain, and many potential hikes, spend a day wandering the "Generals" Highway, entering on 180 from Fresno, snaking through the park, then turning down 198 to Visalia. Your vistas will include the sharp-toothed granite peaks of the Sierra, especially the view from Moro Rock. For a good hike, try the two-mile Congress Trail in the General Sherman locale.

The Oldest

Not until 1957 was the startling discovery made that trees 4,000 years old, trees even older than the sequoias, existed in the White Mountains of eastern California.

The surprising discovery was that some gnarled bristlecone pines ring dated to that early period. Moreover, a 9,000-year chronology of weather patterns could be established by matching the ring dates of living trees, dead trees, and downed wood.

Some bristlecones living today were already ancient when Socrates posed his penetrating questions in early Greece. The tenacious bristlecones silently maintained their vigil, living in the inhospitable conditions of the White Mountains, where moisture is minimal and is locked up for long periods as snow, where wind constantly prunes adventuresome branches, and where alkaline soils present as spare a nutrient base as plant life can survive on. The longevity of the twisted, ravaged bristlecones seems to stand as a metaphor of adaptation to adversity.

Communing with the bristlecones makes the passing fashions, the everyone-is-famous-for-15-minutes philosophy, the capsulized soundbite mentality of our time, seem fleeting indeed.

A ranger on duty at Schulman Grove can acquaint you with two self-guided trails, the Discovery Trail and the Methuselah Trail. Take the mile-long Discovery Trail, which has plenty of photogenic trees and the Pine Alpha, the first tree that Dr. Edmund Schulman determined was over 4,000 years old. The Methuselah Trail is longer, taking several hours, and is recommended only for the extremely fit who can hike some distance in the rarefied air.

The Bristlecone Forest is a special 28,000-acre preserve within Inyo National Forest. Transport yourself to the aerie from your support base along Highway 395 at Bishop or Big Pine, the convenient places for lodging and dining. Consider the outing to the bristlecones as an assault on a peak, for you will rise to almost 10,000 feet, so make sure your car is in good condition and pace yourself, taking only very short walks. You would need to accli-

North Coast & Redwood Country

mate yourself for a day or more before hiking here strenuously. Fill the tank with gasoline at Bishop, take plenty of protective clothes, and carry a gallon of water per person in your vehicle.

From Big Pine make the 23-mile drive to the bristlecones by starting east on Highway 168, also known as Westguard Pass Road. After two miles, stay left at the junction with Eureka Valley. Eleven miles later, a sign will direct you to the bristlecones. You pass through a forest of pinon pine and Utah juniper until you reach the nearly pure forest of bristlecones, starting at 9,500 feet. Within the Bristlecone Pine Forest, visit the Schulman Grove, at the south edge. Another grove, the Patriarch Grove, lies at the north end, but the drive in to this moonscape environment takes over an hour on a dirt road.

California is a special place, subject often to public scrutiny and speculation in the national press. Whatever the veracity of reports on the lifestyle of the natives, the state can boast of this arboreal natural wonder. Even the most dispassionate scientific observers support the notion that California offers you the tallest, most massive, and oldest living things on this planet.

Information Sources

Tallest Living Thing

Superintendent, Redwood National Park
1111 2nd Street, Crescent City, CA 95531
☎ 707-464-6101

Most Massive Living Thing

**Superintendent, Sequoia and
Kings Canyon National Parks**
Ash Mountain, Three Rivers, CA 93271
☎ 209-565-3456

Oldest Living Thing

White Mountain Visitor Center
798 Main Street, Bishop, CA 93514
☎ 619-873-4207

Write ahead for brochures.

Chapter 4

The Napa-Sonoma Wine Country

The Napa and Sonoma wine regions are among the more romantic getaways in Northern California. Noted for their wines and history, both areas have also developed lodgings and restaurants that make them inviting destinations. Both regions are north of San Francisco and are distinct from one another. Napa dominates as *The Wine Country*, which causes Sonoma to wince. However, Sonoma benefits from this close association more than do places such as Santa Clara or Monterey. Much to the envy of other wine-producing areas in California, the Napa-Sonoma region, especially Napa, retains its position in the imagination of wine travelers as California's premier wine area.

The **Napa-Sonoma** area acquired the reputation because it was so important in the era when Americans re-discovered wine, circa 1950-1970. The compact 35-mile stretch of Napa vineyards from Carneros to Mt. St. Helena also possesses extraordinary natural beauty as a well-proportioned valley between the Mayacamas and Howell Mountains. Today, the more than 250 Napa wineries and 145 Sonoma wineries welcome visitors and continue to produce much of California's outstanding wine. Moreover, the wineries themselves are often handsome architectural statements.

■ Napa

Of the many grapes grown on the 24,000 acres planted in the Napa Valley, several stand prominently above the crowd. They are Cabernet, Merlot, and Zinfandel among the reds, and Chardonnay, Sauvignon Blanc, and Riesling among the whites. Napa is the premier region in California for Cabernet, partly because of the dependable sun and moderate warmth, which is somewhat similar to the maritime Bordeaux region. Chardonnay also does very well here. Similarly, Amador County is a good place for Zinfandel and Monterey County for Riesling.

California Wine Varietals

Cabernet produces a more consistent wine in Napa than in its native Bordeaux because the vintners of Napa (and California generally) manage the vines more actively. In Bordeaux, if there is drought, the vineyard manager can do nothing more than genuflect before the forces of nature and the legal restrictions of the 1855 law that prevents irrigation. In Napa, drought prompts the vineyard manager to turn on the sprinklers. Frost is another threat to vines in Bordeaux, but not in Napa, where overhead sprinklers eliminate the frost problem. The long, dry summers of the Napa Valley are ideal for grape development in Cabernet and other varietals. Only the occasional unseasonal rain, especially as the harvest time nears in late August and in September, causes concern for the vineyard manager. In Napa, Cabernet is made into either a big wine or a more accessible wine, soon drinkable, depending on the marketing goal and aesthetic position of the winemaker. All the wineries of the Napa region benefit from technological changes in vineyard management and wine production, advanced at the California agricultural colleges, with the University of California at Davis the leader in matters oenological.

Chardonnay, the premier white wine from Napa, tends to produce a fruitier wine than the typical Chardonnay of Burgundy. The low yield of Chardonnay grapes and the high demand for white wines, an international trend, make Chardonnay as expensive as Cabernet in Napa.

Zinfandel or **Merlot** among the reds and **Sauvignon Blanc** or **Riesling** among the whites are the second grapes of Napa. One experiment in winemaking has been *White* Zinfandel, created by removing the skins from the juice quickly after pressing. Red wines get their color from the pigment in the grape skins when the skins are left with the juice. White wines remain white because the juice is drawn off the skins immediately after the press. A dozen other grapes have lesser roles in Napa, such as Pinot Noir.

The ritual of wine tasting in the Napa Valley begins when you drive to the winery and enter the tasting room. You may be invited to taste directly or you may be escorted for a tour of the wine-making operation first. The tour, typically, is a one-hour event that explains the entire wine-making process, from fermentation through aging. A tour is highly recommended for the first-time visitor. If you have gone to Napa before, you will probably wish to bypass the tour entirely or take no more than one tour per day. Visiting hours at Napa wineries are generally 10 am-4:30 pm, seven days a week, and some of the tastings are free, part of the winery's public relations effort. At the tasting room you can also purchase the company's wines, but often at a price similar to the liquor store price. The wineries can usually arrange shipment to your home.

The best way to experience the Napa Valley is to drive up the valley, touring and tasting at wineries. Our favorite time here is an autumn weekend in October when the vines have turned flaming red, the harvest is in frenetic process, and there is a nip of autumn chill in the air. However, this is also a busy time, and you will get more personal attention at other times of the year. Part of the pleasure of the Napa Valley is its pleasing proportion, its manageable size, and its human scale, when compared with the vastness of other areas of California.

■ Sonoma

If there is one preeminent theme in Sonoma County, it is food, in all its aspects. Sonoma County ranks as one of the primary gourmet and culinary travel destinations in California. The completeness of a food encounter is what makes Sonoma special. Here, an environmentalist and ex-vegetable gardener can see organic gardening in mainstream competition with traditional farming. The oenophile can find as many award-winning wineries to visit here as in Napa, though Napa is still "The Wine Country" because of its geographic integrity. Sonoma County's 145 wineries have 19,000 acres in red varietals and 16,000 acres in white varietals. Local restaurants serve Sonoma wine in special blue-stemmed glasses as a way of fostering local pride. A baby boomer can pile the kids in the Volvo and tour the Farm Trails. The nature lover can catch the spring flowering of the Gravenstein apples. A political activist can observe here working models of small-scale, producer-owned food-raising enterprises competing effectively. The gourmand who wants shiitake mushrooms, the finest oysters, goat cheese, and every conceivable type of eggplant can find it here. Sonoma has the soils, microclimates, and proximity to appreciative Bay Area markets to make it a food capital. The area might be seen as the kitchen garden for San Francisco's celebrity chefs, though Sonoma has its own fine restaurants. You can grow almost everything here, as horticultural whiz Luther Burbank proved decades ago.

■ Getting Here

The Napa Valley is an hour by car from San Francisco or the East Bay. There are two routes up. From San Francisco, drive north on Highway 101 and turn east onto Highway 37, then 121-12, connecting with Highway 29 in the Napa Valley. From the East Bay, the Oakland-Berkeley region, drive north on Interstate 80, then west at Vallejo, until you reach Highway 29. Once in the Napa Valley, you will need a car to drive around to the various wineries and to explore the small towns.

Sonoma is an easy hour's drive from San Francisco north along Highway 101, east on Highway 37, and north on Highway 121. For exploring, you'll need a car.

Information Sources

Napa Valley Conference & Visitors Bureau
1310 Napa Town Center, Napa, CA 94559
☎ 707-226-7459
Web site www.napanet.net

Napa Chamber of Commerce
1900 Jefferson St. , Napa, CA 94558
☎ 707-226-7455

Calistoga Chamber of Commerce
1458 Lincoln Avenue, Calistoga, CA 94515
☎ 707-942-6333
Web site www.napanet.net

For the Sonoma County Farm Trails map
and area information:

Sonoma County Convention and Visitors Bureau
5000 Roberts Lake Road, Suite A, Rohnert Park, CA
94928
☎ 707-586-8100
Web site www.visitsonoma.com

Sonoma Valley Visitors Bureau
453 First Street East, Sonoma, CA 95476
☎ 707-996-1090
Web site www.sonomavalley.com

The wineries of Sonoma have joined together as:

Sonoma County Wineries Association
5000 Roberts Lake Road, Rohnert Park, CA 94928
☎ 707-586-3795
Web site www.sonomawine.com

■ Touring

Napa

Wine is the single dominant subject here today, but that has not always been so. Stop at the **Bale Grist Mill** in Bothe-Napa State Park to learn about the early wheat and corn heyday of the valley. This grist mill ground wheat to feed hungry goldminers after the 1848 discovery of gold. In 1848 flour sold for 1½ cents a pound. By 1850, flour had risen to $1.50/pound as hundreds of thousands of miners descended on California. Wheat was the first major crop in the Napa Valley. The wheat boom lasted until 1869 when the transcontinental railroad pushed across the Sierra, allowing the trains to bring back the superior hard winter red wheat of the Great Plains. The hard winter wheat had a higher gluten content that produced a lighter bread, which put California wheat growers out of business overnight.

However, the wine story also started early. Gustave Niebaum, a Finnish sea captain, traveled inland to build the **Inglenook Winery** in the 1880s. The German Beringer Brothers and Charles Krug were other planters in the 1860s and '70s. Some vines had been planted at the most northerly California mission, in

Napa & Sonoma Wineries

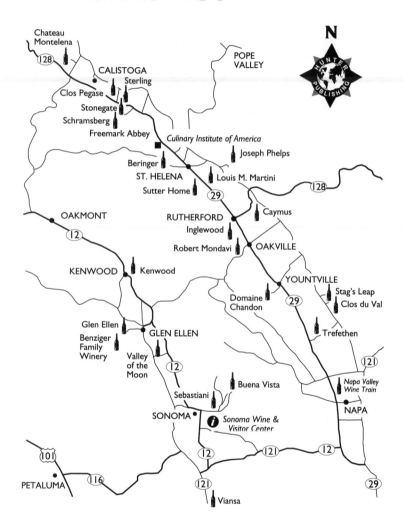

NOT TO SCALE

Sonoma, but they were not grapes of the vinifera class associated with modern gustatory pleasures. It is instructive to read a small book by **Frona Waite**, written in the 1870s, describing California wine production. Already then, wine was a big business here.

One of the charming early observers was **Robert Louis Stevenson**, who stayed here 1880-1881, and whose memorabilia are gathered in a small museum in St. Helena. The **Silverado Museum** (1490 Library Lane, St. Helena; ☎ 707-963-3757) is well worth a stop. Stevenson wrote a bucolic little volume called *The Silverado Squatters* that described his stay here, including his visit to the **Schramsberg Winery**, an early maker of champagne. You can still visit Schramsberg today (Calistoga; ☎ 707-942-4558). Stevenson tasted about 15 champagnes with the proprietor of Schramsberg. Seven miles northeast of Calistoga along Highway 29 there is a lovely undeveloped park, named after Stevenson, near the summit of Mt. St. Helena. Here, in a rude cabin, Stevenson regained his health, celebrated his marriage, and launched himself on his literary career. You can hike up to his cabin site.

Ravages of Prohibition

Prohibition dealt a severe blow to the Napa valley. As single-crop farmers, the growers felt the harshness of The Great Experiment to its fullest impact. Even after this 1919-1933 aberration passed into history, the vineyards suffered a generation of neglect. Winemakers were not seen then as artists, but as gangsters. The vines planted were rough grapes like Carignane, tough enough to ship on boxcars to families who were allowed to make their 50 gallons per year of household wine during Prohibition. Ambitious young men in wine families went on to other pursuits. Fortunately, all this has changed, but only since the 1960s.

Wine Touring Strategies

Your challenge, when traveling through Napa Wine Country, is which of the valley's many wineries to visit. Usually it is prudent to visit about three wineries in a day's outing. For a good map, pick up the free *Wine Country Review*, available everywhere in the valley.

One plan for visiting Napa Valley wineries would be to choose four or five well-known names with strong tours, tastings, and attractive architecture. Domaine Chandon, Mondavi, Beringer, Sterling, and Clos Pegase, in that order, are ones we highly recommend.

- **Domaine Chandon** (☎ 707-944-2280) in Yountville offers its sparkling wines for a nominal charge in an outdoor café, with or without a tour. They also maintain an excellent restaurant with dishes such as salmon with Champagne cream sauce and candied ginger. Chandon is a French-owned enterprise, founded in 1973. Out of deference to the Gallic Champagne region, their sparkling wine will always be called just sparkling wine.

- **Robert Mondavi** (☎ 707-259-9463), in Oakville, sprawls over a Cliff May mission-style building, offers instructive tours, and entertains on some Sunday afternoons with music concerts. The Mondavis have been a crucial name in the resurgence of the Napa Valley, both because of their quality Cabernets and because of their energy in promoting the valley. Try the Mondavi Cabernets and Zinfandels. The most recent Mondavi venture is a joint Cabernet with the French Rothchild label, called Opus One, located across the road and south. At Opus One you can taste a few ounces of wine, but at a fairly hefty price.

- The tour at **Beringer** (☎ 707-963-7115), on the north edge of St. Helena, takes you through their palatial Rhine House, from 1876, emphasizing the historical wine story as you visit elaborate caves cut in limestone hills and used to store and cool wine. Try their Riesling.

- **Sterling** (☎ 707-942-3344), south of Calistoga, charges a nominal fee. You ride up in a gondola to witness the modern high-tech operation on a self-guided tour. This Greek Mediterranean-style winery was deliberately laid out with the traveler in mind. From Sterling you also enjoy sweeping views of the valley. Try their Merlot, a red that is as important as Cabernet at some Bordeaux wineries. Some of the most famous Bordeaux wineries, such as Petrus, use Merlot exclusively in their wine, while others use Cabernet predominantly, with some measure of Merlot.

■ **Clos Pegase** (☎ 707-942-4981) is a tour-de-force at 1060 Dunaweal Lane, south of Calistoga. Built as a showcase for both fine art and fine wine, Clos Pegase has the capital to do everything right. Stroll the grounds to enjoy the modern sculptures. Then sample in the tasting room their superb Merlot and Cabernet. If you have time, take their tour, which shows caves sunk deep into the hillside to keep the wines cool.

Two other major wineries should also be mentioned.

■ Stop to see the **Niebaum/Coppola Winery**, in Rutherford, ☎ 707-963-9099. Niebaum/Coppola is one of the most historic and charming properties in the valley. It is also an illustration of how celebrities like Francis Ford Coppola, co-owner of the winery, and other entertainment people have bought into the wine country. Try their Cabernet.

■ The former Christian Brothers Greystone Winery, along the highway at St. Helena, is now the **Culinary Institute of America**, ☎ 707-967-2303. This massive stone warehouse was one of the largest stone buildings in the world when constructed in the 19th century. It now houses a restaurant and a cooking paraphernalia store.

Touring the Smaller Wineries

As an alternative strategy, visit three smaller producers. They provide a more intimate tasting experience and may appeal more to the experienced wine drinker. They sometimes offer a tour only if you call ahead to make arrangements. Some good winery choices would be **Heitz Cellars** (☎ 707-963-3542), **Joseph Phelps** (☎ 707-963-2745), **Grgich Hills** (☎ 707-963-2784), and **Stag's Leap** (☎ 707-944-2020).

Since your main task on a Napa Valley wine tour will be choosing where to go, here are more wineries that we would recommend for possible touring and tasting. All are open for tasting, but call ahead if you also want a tour:

- **Chateau Montelena**, Calistoga, ☎ 707-942-5105.
- **Cuvaison**, Calistoga, ☎ 707-942-6266.
- **Freemark Abbey**, St. Helena, ☎ 707-963-9694.
- **Louis Martini**, St. Helena, ☎ 707-963-2736.
- **Rutherford Hill**, Rutherford, ☎ 707-963-7194.
- **Villa Mt. Eden**, St. Helena, ☎ 707-963-9100.
- **Whitehall Lane**, St. Helena, ☎ 707-963-9454.

Autumn is the classic time of year to visit the Napa region, both to enjoy the vine leaf color and to witness the harvest in progress. However, other seasons are also rewarding here. In winter the winemaker or winery owner will more likely be present in the tasting room or otherwise accessible if a special appointment is made. In spring the budding out of the vines and the light green color of new leaves is engaging. Spring is a favorite bicycling time in the Napa region, with bicycle rentals easily available. Summer is a popular touring time because of vacation periods, with Napa often one element of the California vacation pattern. The warm sun is then swelling the developing grapes, creating the sugars that yeasts will transform into alcohol.

Other Than Wine

Spas and mudbaths are a further attraction of the Calistoga area. The mud baths and mineral baths, such as **Dr. Wilkinson's** (1507 Lincoln Avenue; ☎ 707-942-4102) are heavily patronized. Dr. Wilkinson has been in the business of mineral and mud baths for over 50 years. **EuroSpa** offers an alternative to the mud baths and hot mineral pools. Treatments here range from facials and massages to stimulating scrubs and soothing wraps. With only six treatment rooms, there's never a crowd and the backyard pool that overlooks a vineyard is the perfect place for a post-spa picnic or nap. Packages include overnight stays, treatments, breakfast and a dinner voucher. Or simply enjoy the treatments at EuroSpa (1202 Pine Street; ☎ 707-942-6829).

Each spa has its own style. **Calistoga Spa Hot Springs** (1006 Washington Street; ☎ 707-942-6269) is quite modern.

Indian Springs Spa & Resort (1712 Lincoln Avenue; ☎ 707-942-4913) is a big, old-fashioned place with a large outdoor pool.

Mount View Spa (1457 Lincoln Avenue; ☎ 707-942-5789) offers many esoteric treatments.

Roman Spa Hot Springs Resort (1300 Washington Street; ☎ 707-942-4441) has cozy landscaped grounds.

North of Calistoga is **Old Faithful Geyser** (1299 Tubbs Road; ☎ 707-942-6463), said to be one of three geysers in the world that erupts on a regular timetable. The Tubbs Road geyser spews forth every 17 to 40 minutes, but on a predictable timetable. The entire region has much geothermal activity, with electricity production taking place farther north at a Pacific Gas and Electric installation called The Geysers, which is the world's largest geothermal electrical production site.

Five miles west of Calistoga on Petrified Forest Road is the **Petrified Forest** (☎ 707-942-6667), a remarkable sight. The huge redwoods that lie solemnly pointing away from Mt. St. Helena remind the viewer that violent volcanic eruption, from Lassen in northern California to St. Helens in Washington, is always a possibility in this chain of fire mountains. Though vulcanism is the basis for the area's geology, don't allow the names to confuse you. Helena, the ancient erupter, is in California, while Helens, the 1980 pyrotechnic displayer, is in Washington state.

Each of the small towns in the area has some features other than wine to mention.

Napa boasts an attractive collection of Victorian architecture. Get a brochure when there or write ahead for one to Napa City Hall, Second and School streets, Napa CA 94558; ☎ 707-226-7455.

Yountville was the former home of valley-founder George Yount. The park in Yountville is a pleasant place to relax, picnic, or let kids loose at the playground. **Vintage 1870** is an elaborate shopping and dining complex adjacent to Yountville Park.

Calistoga, besides the mud baths and spas already mentioned, is a busy soaring port. **Rides** can be arranged by calling **Calistoga Gliders** at ☎ 707-942-5000. Located at 1546 Lincoln Avenue in Calistoga, the operation has gliders that can be booked for rides ranging from 20-30 minutes. The gliders hold a pilot and one passenger. Tours proceed over the vineyards in the center of the Napa Valley, across a rugged and arid land formation called the Palisades on the east side of the Napa Valley, and atop a more water-rich forest of pines on the west side of the valley.

Sam Brannan's Legacy

In Calistoga there is also a small museum, called the **Sharpsteen Museum** (☎ 707-942-5911), recalling the contributions of Sam Brannan, a Mormon, who envisioned a resort here as early as 1859. Brannan pushed through a rail spur to the area. Perhaps appropriately, Brannan is said to have raised a glass of the local liquid sunshine to his vision and pronounced that this would be *the Saratoga of California*, thinking of the great spas in upper New York State. However, the glass may not have been his first glass of liquid sunshine that day because the words came out as *the Calistoga of Sarafornia*. The name Calistoga stuck. Calistoga has some of the most enjoyable street life of the wine country as visitors stroll up and down Lincoln Way. The main street is off the highway and the community has a small-town friendliness, with food and wine sophistication.

St. Helena, aside from its mentioned Stevenson Museum, also has an interesting beeswax candleworks, the **Hurd Candle Factory**, 2½ miles north at the Freemark Abbey Winery.

Sonoma

The village square in Sonoma is steeped in some of the most attractive historical traditions of California. Overseeing the setting is the figure of General Mariano Vallejo, the Spanish-Mexican lord of the area before the American period. Vallejo set a pattern of generous hospitality and openness to the foreigner that has become a hallmark of the California character. He was also astute enough to finesse his way through the political changes following the Gold Rush. Around the square in Sonoma be sure to visit the Spanish Mission, the Bear Flag rebellion statue and Vallejo's house.

Contemporary Sonoma County's diversity has much to offer the explorer. As mentioned, be sure to get a copy of the *Sonoma Farm Trails Map* and spend a day driving through the back country, vis-

Napa-Sonoma Touring

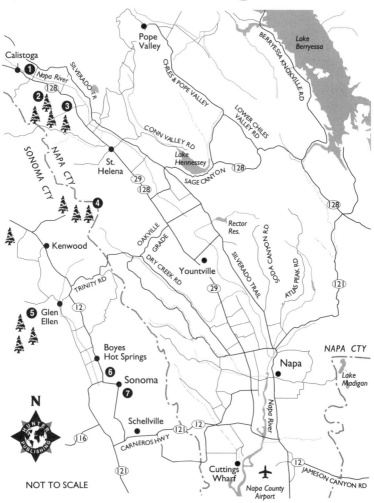

1. Calistoga Airport Soaring Center
2. Bothe-Napa State Park
3. Bale Grist Mill
4. Sugarloaf Ridge State Park
5. Jack London State Historic Park/ Jack London Village
6. Sonoma Mission
7. Gen. Vallejo Home

iting the farmer-direct operations that will sell you everything from apple juice to olallieberries. The map is fairly ingenious in its layout, dividing the county into areas, so you can see which producers are on your itinerary. Another part of the map is organized by producers, so you can determine just where to go for edible flowers or emu meat. A handy calendar on the map alerts you to the appropriate months for various specialty products.

Around the village square in Sonoma you can immerse yourself in this most northerly reach of Spanish influence in California.

The **Sonoma Mission** (☎ 707-938-1519) was founded in 1823 by impatient, ambitious Father Jose Altimira, but was doomed because of the impending collapse of the entire mission system a decade later. Today the mission is part of a state historic park, whose museum gathers many interesting early artifacts.

On the square itself you'll see a heroic bronze statue to the **Bear Flag patriots**. The Bear Flaggers were a group of hotheads who expressed the uncertainty of the political twilight in the Mexican period. In 1846 a faction wanted California declared independent as the California Republic, and they hoisted the Bear Flag.

A mile or so from the Plaza is the home of **General Mariano Vallejo**. This Gothic-Revival New England-style house from the latter part of his life is an interesting museum (☎ 707- 938-1519). Near the house there are tables where you can enjoy a picnic lunch.

Sonoma Wine

Appreciators of California wine should also taste wine at the **Buena Vista Winery** (☎ 707-938-1266) on 18000 Old Winery Road near the square. This winery was the original domain of one Colonel Agoston Haraszthy. More than any other individual, Haraszthy pioneered bringing European grape cuttings to California. He founded the winery here in 1857. The European cuttings of noble vinifera species far surpassed the wines made from the so-called Mission grape, which may have satisfied sacramental purposes, but was of little interest to the secular drinker with purely gustatory intentions. The other major winery to visit in Sonoma is **Sebastiani**, on Fourth Street East. One branch of the Sebastiani family, Sam and Vicki Sebastiani, now operate a complete food and wine sampling spot along the highway south of

Sonoma, called **Viansa**, a good one-stop immersion in the wine and food scene of the region. The rationale is to see wine in the context of food and conviviality. Viansa (☎ 707-935-4700) is located on a hill overlooking the Sonoma marshlands. Viansa, a wonderfully euphonious word, lest you strain your Latin or Spanish vocabulary resources, means Vicki and Sam.

Two wineries north of Sonoma worth exploring are Kunde and Benziger.

- **Kunde** (10155 Sonoma Highway, Kenwood; ☎ 707-833-5501) epitomizes the new wineries. Kunde boasts a lovely tasting room set against their impressive 2,000 acres of hill vineyards, mainly planted in Chardonnay. There is a picnic area outside the tasting room. Tours are available on weekends.

- **Benziger** (1883 London Ranch Road, Glen Ellen; ☎ 707-935-4046) rests high in the hills at Glen Ellen. This winery offers an exceptionally informative tour of the vineyards, showing innovative organic gardening techniques. The tasting room pours a spectrum of quality wines, including their Imagery series, which is their tastiest production. The latest Benziger expansion is into beer-making on a large scale. The brewery and hops-growing trellises can be seen on Highway 12 north of Sonoma.

Sonoma has many small producers, such as Cale, Kaz, Arrowood, and Ravenswood. There are 36 wineries with a total of 13,000 acres in the Sonoma Valley. Nine of the small producers, which are also family wineries, have banded together to create a common tasting room along Highway 12, called the **Family Wineries Tasting Room**.

For picnic fixings while exploring in the town of Sonoma, be sure to stop at the **Sonoma Cheese Factory** on the square, where you can watch jack cheese being made and stock up at what may be the most complete deli in the west. Sonoma Cheese Factory is at 2 Spain Street; ☎ 800-535-2855.

Beyond the charming town of Sonoma, here are more of our favorite pleasures in the region.

Jack London & Luther Burbank

Jack London, the noted fiction writer, built his home in the Valley of the Moon north of Sonoma. It is now an 800-acre state historic park. London's celebrated Wolf House, which sadly went up in flames after he built it, remains a ruin. Another house on the property, called the House of Happy Walls, now serves as a museum for London memorabilia, especially artifacts from his Alaska and South Seas adventures. You'll see editions of his works, mementos from his travels, some of the 600 rejection slips he got before he became famous, and a 1916 newsreel taken a few days before he died. London, who was famous for his urban novels, such as *Martin Eden*, as well as his man-against-the-elements tales, such as *Call of the Wild*, was a gifted and paradoxical man, an entrepreneur and a socialist. He died young, of kidney failure, at this property, fulfilling his wish that, "I would rather be a superb meteor, every atom of me in magnificent glow, than a sleepy and permanent planet." This bucolic shrine to the writer, in Glen Ellen, is officially known as the **Jack London State Historic Park** (☎ 707-938-5216). Call ahead to see if London impersonator Mike Wilson will be giving one of his Jack London shows during your visit.

Down the road from the park is the extraordinary **Jack London Bookstore** (☎ 707-996-2888), run by Winnie Kingman. She and her late husband, Russ Kingman, developed this labor-of-love store honoring London. The Kingmans published an appreciative book, *A Pictoral Life of Jack London*, and spent much time examining original editions and generally keeping the flame burning for fans of London, who arrive in droves. As you drive into the state park, you pass Glen Ellen Winery, makers of an affordable, yet delicious Chardonnay, as well as the Benziger Winery, which has an excellent tour.

The road into Jack London Park passes **Jack London Village**, a shopping, art, and dining complex at 14301 Arnold Drive in Glen Ellen. The Glen Ellen Winery maintains a tasting room here. Of special interest here is the **Olive Press** (☎ 707-939-8900), an establishment that makes and sells a range of specialty olive oils. Here you can do an olive oil comparative tasting, as one might taste wines, and see olives being pressed.

In Santa Rosa, the **Luther Burbank Gardens** commemorate the innovative work of this horticulturalist, who symbolized the skill with which California agriculturalists have developed fruit, nut, and flower varieties that thrive here, producing a third of the nation's food. Anyone with a delight in growing things will enjoy the Luther Burbank Home and Gardens, Santa Rosa and Sonoma avenues, ☎ 707-524-5445.

The Long Shadow of Napa

As with the Napa Valley, Sonoma is a notable wine region, as the locals will emphasize. Sonoma does not always enjoy living in the long shadow of Napa. Similarly, it galls the winemakers of Monterey or Santa Clara, for example, to have Napa and Sonoma referred to as The Wine Country. California wine is now so diverse and there are so many new producers, hundreds making excellent wine, that a journalist could spend a lifetime following this one subject. What it comes down to is the individual wine producer. This is not a battle of regions, but of individual wine-making artists. As an example of one of the progressive wineries, consider Hank and Katie Wetzel's **Alexander Valley Vineyards** in Alexander Valley. Call ahead to be sure they are open for tasting and bottle sales (☎ 707-433-7209). They make an excellent Cabernet and Chardonnay. It is a sign of the maturity of California wine that the company concentrates on a few select grape varietals rather than a large spectrum of production.

■ Adventures

On Wheels

Scenic Driving

In Napa, be sure to drive the road along the east side of the valley, **The Silverado Trail**, at some point in your outing. This elevated road from Calistoga to Napa City shows the beauty of the area to best advantage, minus the traffic of Highway 29. Consider driving up the Napa Valley's main artery, Highway

Vineyards with mustard in the spring along the Russian River Road in Sonoma County.

29, to Calistoga and then back along the Silverado Trail, which is especially lovely in October as the vine leaves turn yellow and red.

An enjoyable drive north and east of Napa, passing oak-woodland hillsides, takes you to **Lake County**, noted for its large lake, Clear Lake, and the rustic feel of its walnut and pear agriculture. The major resort here is Konockti Harbor. Bass fishermen rank Clear Lake among the best in the west. Geologists are also fascinated by Clear Lake, the largest natural lake entirely in California, because of evidence that it is one of the oldest lakes in the world. The best introduction to the natural history of the area is at the Visitor Center for Clear Lake State Park. The area also nurtures some good wineries, such as Kendall-Jackson. South of the lake lies the largest gold mine in California, run by Homestake Mining. This high-tech operation can extract one ounce of gold from seven tons of crushed rock. For the itinerant traveler, Lake County has the undeveloped feel that perhaps Napa/Sonoma had some 50 years ago.

The roads between Napa and Sonoma make engaging country scenic drives. From Calistoga you could take **Petrified Forest Road** and then **Calistoga Road** over to Highway 12 in Sonoma. Slightly farther south the Oakville Grade becomes Dry Creek Road and then Trinity Road, another winding passage across the mountains, a pleasure if you are not pressed for time.

In western Sonoma County, drive the **Russian River Road** from Highway 101 to the ocean, passing the many resorts of the region. Lodging and dining in Guerneville puts you in the center of activities here. The Russian River is a favorite canoeing stream in the spring, with commercial operators providing the boats and the shuttles. The drive is also particularly lovely in the spring, when yellow mustard balances the green of the new leaf. Wolfgang Gramatski runs a gourmet restaurant, **River's End** (☎ 707-865-2484. $$) in Jenner, overlooking the mouth of the Russian River. Try his tomato basil soup, salmon in filo dough with crushed hazelnuts and spinach, salads of exotic greens, and other subtle culinary wizardry.

Another town worth exploring in the area is **Healdsburg**, notable for its appealing square and shops. The town square is a classic of 19th-century city architecture, where greenery and trees in the center created a public space for all. Around the square are boutique shops, such as Wildrose Gifts, Spoke Folk Cyclery, and Impressions Gallery.

If you would rather be driven than drive, fresh-air jeep tours of the backroads, byways, and vineyards of either Napa or Sonoma can be arranged through **Wine Country Jeep Tour**, ☎ 707-584-9120 or 800-539-5337. They offer customized tours emphasizing anything from parks to wineries.

Bicycling

In the Napa Valley, the town of St. Helena would be a good central base to start from. From the town you can bicycle east to the Silverado Trail and then north or south to see vineyards. Traffic on the Silverado Trail is light, compared to Highway 29, which is a killer. North from St. Helena along the Silverado Trail you can bike to Calistoga. If you want a bicycle shop for support, one knowledgeable local source is **St. Helena Cyclery**, 1156 Main Street; ☎ 707-963-7736. The ambitious bicyclist could make a 33-mile loop over little-used roads east of St. Helena by bicycling out Howell Mountain Road, then south on Pope Valley Road, and west again on Sage Canyon Road. If you want some remote country terrain on good roads, this is a congenial trip.

For bike rentals or a fully organized bicycle tour, another provider is **Getaway Adventures & Bike Shop** (1117 Lincoln Avenue, in Calistoga; ☎ 707-942-0332). Their day bicycle trips range from wine tastings and a gourmet lunch, to "extreme dirt" mountain biking adventures. They also offer other adventure trips, such as canoeing the Russian River. Owners Randy and Tina Johnson

Bicyclists leaving Clos Pegase Winery in the Napa Wine Country.

specialize in small groups and individual attention, whether it's for a day of biking back roads to various wineries and enjoying a gourmet lunch on some scenic picnic grounds or driving clients to the top of Mount St. Helena for great views and a 12-mile bicycle ride – or bike-coast – back to Calistoga.

Another provider in Calistoga is **Palisades Mountain Sport** (1330-B Gerrard Street; ☎ 707-942-9687).

Two dependable bike rental and riding information sources in the Sonoma area are **Goodtime Bicycle Company** (18503 Sonoma Highway, Sonoma; ☎ 707-938-0453) and **Sonoma Valley Cyclery** (20093 Broadway, Sonoma; ☎ 707-935-3377). Farther north in Sonoma is **Spoke Folk Cyclery** (249 Center Street, Healdsburg; ☎ 707-433-7171).

Railroading

A wine train through the Napa Valley, offering both a view of the wine country and fine dining, presents a genial way to see the area. Contact the **Napa Valley Wine Train** (1275 McKinstry Street, Napa; ☎ 707-253-2111). You drink wine and eat fine food while riding up the Valley. You may get off at some locations, such as Grgich Winery, for a tour and tasting.

Train motifs are an interesting part of the Napa and Sonoma area. Rail buffs delight in the **Sonoma Traintown Railroad**, which has plenty of vintage cars. Traintown is in Sonoma on Broadway, a mile south of the town plaza. ☎ 707-938-3912.

On Foot

Hiking

The state parks offer some of the best hikes in the region.

Bothe-Napa State Park (☎ 707-942-4575) has trails in the oak and pine forests at the north end of the Napa Valley. The park is three miles south of Calistoga on Highway 29.

Robert Louis Stevenson State Park (☎ 707-942-4575) has a trail that proceeds up the mountain to the cabin where the author stayed during his 19th-century visit. Only the foundations of the cabin remain today. The view from the top of Mount St. Helena is one of the more striking perspectives of the Napa Valley. The park is eight miles north of Calistoga on Highway 29 en route to Clear Lake.

Jack London State Historic Park (☎ 707-938-5216) in Sonoma has good hiking trails on its 800 acres, plus plenty of Jack London mementos in the Visitor Center. A trail takes hikers past the remains of London's Wolf House, which burned shortly after it was built. Jack London State Park is at 2400 London Ranch Road in Glen Ellen.

Sugarloaf Ridge State Park (☎ 707-833-5712) is another favorite hiking place in Sonoma. The park is northeast of Kenwood in the Mayacamas Mountains, between the Sonoma and Napa valleys. Elevations in this 2,700-acre holding range from 600 feet at the entrance to 2,729 feet at the top of Bald Mountain. In spring there is a 25-foot waterfall and plenty of wildflowers. The park is at 2605 Adobe Canyon Road.

Also in the Sonoma Valley, **Annadel State Park** (☎ 707-539-3911) has pleasing hiking trails. The park is at 6201 Channel Drive in Santa Rosa.

On Horseback

The **Sonoma Cattle Company & Napa Valley Trail Rides** (PO Box 877, Glen Ellen, CA 95442; ☎ 707-996-8566) organizes rides in the Sonoma region in both Jack London State Park and Sugarloaf State Park. Riders travel through carpets of wildflowers in spring. Some rides are barbecue or picnic outings, while on others you'll watch magnificent sunsets. All rides are guided.

On Water

Canoeing

The main water experience in the region is canoeing down the Russian River, which is organized by **Bob Trowbridge Canoe Trips** (20 Healdsburg Avenue, Healdsburg; ☎ 800-640-1386). You put in at the Alexander Valley Campground above Healdsburg and take out in Healdsburg at Memorial Beach, near the Trowbridge shop. This stretch of river is scenic and remote. Resort operators below Healdsburg on the river sometimes have individual canoes for rent so you can float a stretch of the river.

Boating

Boating is popular on the two large lakes, **Clear Lake** and **Lake Berryessa**. Boat rentals, fishing, water skiing, and jet skiing can all be arranged. For Clear Lake, contact the **Lake County Visitor Information Center** (875 Lakeport Boulevard, Lakeport, CA 95453; ☎ 800-525-3743). For Lake Berryessa, contact **Lake Berryessa Marine Resort** (5800 Knoxville Road; ☎ 707 966-2365).

Fishing

The large lakes of the region, such as Clear Lake and Lake Beryessa, are noted for their largemouth bass catches as well as crappies and sunfish. For fishing supplies and guides at Clear Lake, contact **Konocti Harbor Marina**; ☎ 707-279-4281. For the same at Lake Berryessa, contact **Lake Berryessa Marine Resort**, 5800 Knoxville Road; ☎ 707-966-2365.

The **Russian River** has seasonal runs of coho salmon and steel-head. The steelhead are becoming endangered, but fishing was still legal as of 1997. The river also has some warm water species, such as black bass and blue gills. The bass are biting May to mid-October. With the first rains of October, the river swells and the steelhead runs begin.

Along the coast, sport fishing boats leave from Bodega Bay in search of Salmon, Pacific snapper, and rock cod, depending on weather and season. For charter boat parties, contact **New Sea Angler** (☎ 707-875-3495).

In the Air

Ballooning

Ballooning is popular in both Napa and Sonoma as a way to savor the landscape. Typically, your flight will begin shortly before dawn so as to take advantage of the relatively windless conditions. The balloon floats aloft, carried up by the heat of its propane burners, which swell the envelope of the balloon with hot air. From then on you are in the hands of the pilot, who knows that winds move in different directions at varying altitudes. The FAA-certified balloon pilot will guide the craft for an hour or so of 10 mph flying. At the end of the flight the pilot will seek out a hospitable landing site and communicate the position to the chase vehicle, which will meet you on the ground. Once secure on terra firma, chances are you will sip some champagne and receive a certificate commemorating your

Balloon prepares for ascent in the Napa Wine Country.

adventure. Some balloon companies also include breakfast.

Providers include **Adventures Aloft** (☎ 707-944-4408); **Balloon Aviation** (☎ 707-944-4400); **Napa Valley Balloons** (☎ 800-253-2224); **Aerostat Adventures** (☎ 707-579-0183); **Air Flambuoyant** (☎ 800-456-4711); and **Bonaventura Balloon Company** (☎ 800-359-6272).

Scenic Flying

If you've ever had an urge to indulge in the nostalgia of a bygone era and fly in an historic open cockpit biplane, that dream can be realized in Sonoma at the **Aero Schellville** bi-plane and glider facility. The flights leave from the Schellville Airport, 23982 Arnold Drive, Sonoma; ☎ 707-938-2444.

Soaring

Soaring rides can be arranged in Calistoga by calling the **Soaring Center** at the Calistoga Airport (☎ 707-942-5592). Soarers catch the thermals rising along the flanks of Mt. St. Helena. Calistoga is one of the busier soaring places in northern California.

■ Where to Stay & Eat

Accommodations in Napa

For lodging, the Napa Valley has an ample number of full-service hotels and bed and breakfast inns.

Napa boasts the first resort in California, **White Sulphur Springs**, opened in 1852. When Buzz and Betty Foote accidentally stumbled upon this historic retreat, nestled in a quiet corner of the Napa Valley in the 1980s, they were lost. Mesmerized by the place and given a good purchasing deal by the owner, a guru who had sent his spiritual flock to Australia, they moved in. They have spent years trying to reverse decades of neglect to make it into the popular getaway it once was. The Footes have managed to maintain a rustic feel to the cabins, but have been savvy enough to add new facilities such as a swimming pool, sulphur hot springs soaking pool, and amenities like outdoor massages. Since its humble beginnings, White Sulphur Springs has gone through a

Opposite: *Vineyard along Russian River.*

Above: *Cross-country skiing in the Yosemite High Country.*
Opposite: *Biking at Mt. Shasta Ski Park in summer.*
Below: *Lassen Peak and Manzanita Lake.*

number of transformations; it went from a ritzy resort that enticed Hollywood stars to a church camp for youngsters. Today it functions as a retreat for corporate groups, a serene escape for stressed-out souls, and a hiking and biking haven for outdoor enthusiasts. White Sulphur Springs is at 3100 White Sulphur Springs Road, St. Helena, CA 94574; ☎ 707-963-8588. $$.

Chateau Hotel (4195 Solano Avenue, Napa, CA 94558; ☎ 707-253-9300. $$) provides complimentary evening wine tastings from 5-7 pm. Your host will assist you in choosing a restaurant from the hotel's collection of menus. In the heat of summer, the Chateau Hotel pool is a welcome amenity. In the chill of winter, their hot tub allures.

Meadowood is a luxury resort on the east side of the Silverado Road north of Rutherford. This is a full-facility resort with a restaurant, pool, tennis courts, and a golf course. In CA, call ☎ 800-458-8080; outside CA call ☎ 707-963-3646. Their address is 900 Meadowood Lane, St. Helena, CA 94574. $$$.

An intimate luxury lodging is **Rancho Caymus Inn** (1140 Rutherford Road, Rutherford, CA 94573; ☎ 707-963-1777. $$$). Artist and owner Mary Tilden has supervised the coordinated decor of the establishment.

Unsurpassed for its view, luxury lodging, creative restaurant, and price is **Auberge du Soleil** (180 Rutherford Hill Road, Rutherford, CA 94573; ☎ 707-963-1211. $$$). When you're ready for the best, try chef Andy Sutton's orchestrations in the kitchen. The lodgings and restaurant are an excellent site for watching the sun set over the valley.

Typical of the quaint bed and breakfast inns is the four-room **Ambrose Bierce House** (1515 Main Street, St. Helena, CA 94574; ☎ 707-963-3003. $$-$$$). The structure, formerly the home of the curmudgeonly philosopher and author of *The Devil's Dictionary*, has been decorated to recall his work and friends, such as Lillie Coit, who built Coit Tower in San Francisco.

The **Vintage Inn** (6541 Washington Street, Yountville, CA 94599; ☎ 707-944-1112. $$$) presents an accessible location near the south end of the Valley. Strategically located, the Vintage Inn offers one-stop lodging, putting you adjacent to a large swimming pool, within walking distance of eight restaurants, and close

Opposite: *Big Sur at Rocky Creek Bridge.*

to tennis courts or bike rentals. The Vintage Inn is also a short walk from a shopping complex called Vintage 1870, where you can see a light and sound show about the area, titled *Napa Valley Experience.*

The **Wine Country Inn** (1152 Lodi Lane, St. Helena 94574; ☎ 707-963-7077. $$-$$$) is at the other end of the spectrum. This small, rustic country inn, with views over the hills and vineyards, exists as "an inn for lovers," says the proprietor. It was built by the Smith family; their grandmother stitched quilts for the brass beds. The lobby is filled with the aroma of nut breads baking for tomorrow's breakfasts. Wine Country Inn has no TV, no phone in the rooms, no briefcases strewn about, and no gift shops with T-shirts, but entices with romantically decorated rooms and a spa-swimming pool, plus the peace and quiet of a location off the highway.

Art deco enthusiasts will want to stay and dine at the **Mount View Hotel** (1457 Lincoln Avenue, Calistoga, CA 94515; ☎ 707-942-6877. $$-$$$). Innovative chef Jan Birnbaum is considered one of the top chefs in the Golden State.

The grand old-line resort is the **Silverado Country Club** (1600 Atlas Peak Road, Napa 94558; ☎ 707-257-0200. $$-$$$). This fully contained resort community offers condo-like lodgings fronting a championship golf course.

For a French touch, try **Maison Fleurie** (6529 Yount Street, Yountville, CA 94599; ☎ 707-944-2056 or 800-788-0369. $$-$$$). This hundred-year-old brick farmhouse, decorated in the French tradition, has 13 rooms and a pool. Bicycles are available for a two-wheel tour of the nearby wine country.

The **Calistoga Country Lodge** has a homespun charm that carries through right down to the anatomically correct black and white cow-motif chairs located at its entrance. Along with six rooms, four with private baths, there is a pool looking out on the Mayacamas Mountains and a large, comfortable common area filled with Navajo rugs, eclectic antiques, games, books, music and an inviting fireplace. Innkeeper Rae Ellen Fields offers guests a glass of wine in the evenings and a spread of baked goods, fresh fruit, and cereal in the mornings. Calistoga Country Lodge is at 2883 Foothill Blvd., Calistoga, CA 94515; ☎ 707-942-5555, $$.

For clean, comfortable rooms with shared baths that are a great value ($), check out the **Calistoga Inn** at 1250 Lincoln Avenue, Calistoga, CA 94515. Rates for the 18-room inn, which has been welcoming guests for more than 90 years, include breakfast.

Accommodations in Sonoma

 Among the more than 50 small B&Bs in the Sonoma Valley, the **Gaige House Inn** shows how each inn reflects its owners. It is a contemporary antidote to those who have seen one too many stuffed bears or rubber ducks at other bed and breakfast establishments. Its light colors and sleek modern furniture gives it an open, airy feel that makes a pleasing minimalist statement. Owners Ken Burnet and Greg Nemrow take pride in the place, greeting callers inquiring about the inn, sharing insights into their favorite area restaurants and wineries, and even serving a hearty breakfast to guests who are seated at tables covered with linen cloths and adorned with fresh-cut flowers. Flower and herb gardens enhance the setting as well as the open deck that overlooks the backyard swimming pool. On Saturday evenings, a local wine expert hosts a private sampling for guests. Flashlights are thoughtfully provided for anyone who wishes to walk to one of the fine dining establishments located nearby in this small community. The Gaige House Inn is at 13540 Arnold Drive, Glen Ellen, CA 95442; ☎ 800-935-0237. $$-$$$.

The **Sonoma Mission Inn and Spa** (18140 Highway 12, Sonoma, CA 95476; ☎ 800-862-4945. $$-$$$) has 170 rooms and is the biggest establishment in the Sonoma area. Built around an elaborate hot springs and spa, it offers a spectrum of treatments and pampering, plus fine dining.

The **Sonoma Valley Inn** (550 2nd Street West, Sonoma, CA 95476; ☎ 800-334-5784. $$-$$$) is a dependable Best Western a block from the town plaza in Sonoma. The courtyard rooms have fireplaces and private balconies.

El Dorado Hotel (1st Street West, Sonoma, CA 95476; ☎ 800-289-3031, $$-$$$) is on the plaza in Sonoma and has 26 rooms, with complimentary wine on arrival, a heated pool, and a continental breakfast.

Restaurants in Napa

A fitting expression of the Napa Valley dining style can be seen at the **All Seasons Café** in Calistoga. Laid-back Calistoga does not take its food lightly. Guests may ride up to the front door and lean over their bikes to look at a menu or even stroll in from a neighboring spa still wearing a bathrobe. All Seasons owner Gayle Keller knows that it takes something special to pull people inside. She and her husband have created that magic at their restaurant and the **Hydro Bar and Grill** located just across the street. Both places present sophisticated food and wine, yet also emphasize relaxation. Menus change with the seasons to provide timely tastes of locally produced favorites such as grilled rabbit with a mustard glaze, herbed goat cheese, and spring garlic with wild mushrooms. From the café-smoked salmon and homemade pumpernickel bread to the outstanding and affordable list of wines by the glass or the 20 microbrews on tap at Hydro Bar and Grill, either establishment is sure to please and keep choosy Calistoga residents and visitors alike coming back. All Seasons has a café-on-the-corner casualness, but aspires to world-class food. The style has a certain bistro earthiness, but with ambition. Wines from the wine shop are only $7.50 above retail in the restaurant or a penny a milliliter. All Seasons Café & Wine Shop are at 1400 Lincoln Avenue in Calistoga; ☎ 707-942-9111. $$-$$$.

All Seasons is just one of many good places to dine here. Your lodging proprietor can alert you to the ever-changing restaurant scene in the valley, as well as to special wine tastings, hot air ballooning, and the mud baths at Calistoga.

For a restaurant reflecting the exuberance of the valley, try **Mustard's Grill** (north of Yountville on Highway 29; ☎ 707-944-2424. $$) where the dining is casual, the prices reasonable, and the style is mesquite-grilled fish or ribs, plus house vegetable specialties.

For a quieter restaurant, try **Hoppers** (6518 Washington Street, Yountville; ☎ 707-944-1500. $$) which emphasizes its mesquite grill rotisserie. Start with the Caribbean country ribs or prawns with fresh mozzarella. Salads include mixed Napa greens or Caesar. Entrees from the rotisserie are chicken, pork loin, and rack of lamb.

The Napa Valley invites picnicking with wine and deli purchases. The **Oakville Grocery** (☎ 707-944-8802), along Highway 29 in Oakville, stocks a complete assortment of picnic fare. Many wineries have picnic facilities (Joseph Phelps, Chateau Montelena, and Rutherford Hill are examples). The area parks are also favorite picnic destinations (George Yount Park in Yountville, Crane Park in St. Helena, and Bothe-Napa State Park north of St. Helena). Another good picnic supply source is the **Napa Valley Olive Oil Co.**, 835 Charter Oak Avenue, St. Helena; ☎ 707-963-4173.

One of the inviting coffeehouses in the Napa area is the **Napa Valley Coffee Roasting Company** (1400 Oak Avenue, St. Helena; ☎ 707-963-4491). The indoor-outdoor ambiance of the establishment meets the need for your latte, soft classic music, fresh baked goods, and a free book exchange for used paperbacks.

Café Sarafornia (1413 Lincoln Avenue in Calistoga; ☎ 707-942-0555. $-$$) in Calistoga typifies the special, small restaurants that are one-of-a-kind in the up-country towns of the Napa Valley. Located on Calistoga's walkable street, with indoor seating that opens to the sun, this café serves delicious sandwiches, such as curried chicken on sourdough.

The historic Mount View Hotel in Calistoga houses the **Catahoula Restaurant & Saloon**, a place as appealing to the eye as it is to the palate. Executive Chef/Owner Jan Birnbaum has hit culinary heights in New York, Denver and San Francisco during his career, but relies on his Cajun roots for inspiring dishes at his latest venture. Bienville cakes with poached oysters and cascabel aioli, a rich tasting appetizer that includes wild mushrooms, scallions, and bacon, may be the perfect start to any meal. For a light entrée, try the grilled quail with cumin pinto bean brandade and corn maque choux. That should leave room for the very decadent espresso crème brulée. Catahoula (named after the official dog of Louisiana) is located at 1457 Lincoln Avenue; ☎ 707-942-2275. $$$.

For casual dining, especially if the weather is nice enough to sit outdoors, the **Calistoga Inn Restaurant & Brewery** excels at barbecue and homemade brews from the award-winning Napa Valley Brewing Company. Lighter fare includes a spinach Waldorf salad that features honey-roasted walnuts and dried cranberries. Several fresh fish dishes change with the season. The Calistoga

Inn Restaurant is at 1250 Lincoln Avenue; ☎ 707-942-4101, $-$$.

Restaurants in Sonoma

An example of the quality dining establishments in Sonoma is the **Glen Ellen Inn** (13670 Arnold Drive, Glen Ellen; ☎ 707-996-6409. $$-$$$), which has added a few more tables, created a wine bar for waiting customers, and enlarged the closet-sized kitchen area. One thing that does not need to change is its food. Every dish is a visual delight and every taste lingers long after the plate has been cleared away. Christian and Karen Bertrand are a charming young couple who have managed to spark a special magic that translates into such dishes as the fire and ice salad, lamb ravioli with sweet and spicy mustard mint sauce, and prawn croquettes in a light lemon herb sauce, topped with a spicy chipotle sauce. Anyone who enjoys a little zing in their meal will delight at the number of offerings flavored with wasabi or jalapeño peppers. The dishes can be extra spicy if requested, but don't let even these favorite flavors overpower the mix of ingredients that make the difference between a good dinner and a truly memorable meal.

Chefs Karen and Christian Bertrand of the Glen Ellen Inn.

Babette's (464 1st Street East; ☎ 707-939-8921. $$-$$$), located in an alley off the square in Sonoma, serves a five-course meal with wine.

Della Santina's (133 East Napa Street; ☎ 707-935-0576. $$) is an Italian eatery just off the square in Sonoma, known for its tortellini.

Café Citti, 9049 Sonoma Highway; ☎ 707-833-2690. $$) is a family owned place in Kenwood, known for its pastas and chicken.

In Santa Rosa, try **John Ash & Company** (4330 Barnes Road, Santa Rosa; ☎ 707-527-7687. $$-$$$), a nationally lauded eatery in a 45-acre vineyard, with wine country regional cuisine under the artistry of chef John Ash.

Camping & RV

 Bothe-Napa Valley State Park is a favorite camping place in the Napa Valley. The park is three miles south of Calistoga along Highway 19. Call ☎ 707-942-4575 for details; 800-444-7275 for reservations.

Sugarloaf Ridge State Park (2605 Adobe Canyon Road; ☎ 707-833-5712) is a popular camping place in the Sonoma area.

The **Petaluma KOA**, (20 Rainsville Road, Petaluma; ☎ 800-992-2267) has full camping and RV facilities, including a pool and spa.

■ The Wine Country Renewing Itself

By Lee Foster

The adventure traveler in Napa-Sonoma will want to pause for an adventure in taste. The Napa-Sonoma wine country of California continually renews its taste component, just as a vine goes through an annual cycle of renewal.

I've watched this process of renewal in the California wine country since the 1960s. From the traveler's perspective, the wine country of the late 1990s is better than ever. While some areas of the world are declining in terms of the quality of the travel experience, the wine country of California offers an ever more enhancing travel adventure, especially when one thinks of food and wine. Sometimes the reasons for the wine country's success are subtle.

For example, consider food. The wine country has always been on the cutting edge of California cuisine, especially in the small towns, such as Calistoga and St. Helena. One reason for this is that the small towns have fought the entry of chain restaurants. No Taco Bells here. Consequently, even modest lunch places, such as Café Sarafornia in Calistoga, strive to create inventive sandwiches.

Moving to higher levels of culinary ambition, such as at All Seasons Café in Calistoga, chef John Coss aims at world-class cuisine with grilled duck breast in black currant sauce or grilled rabbit with wild mushrooms, both exquisitely presented. And down the street, at chef Jan Birnbaum's Catahoula Restaurant in The Mount View Hotel, absolute food magic is at work. Birnbaum is recognized, even by the other chefs, as one of the major food creators in contemporary California.

One aspect of the current renewal is that the number of boutique suppliers of fresh ingredients to these restaurants increases every year, with goat cheese or specialized salad greens now commonplace. And there is no timidity on the part of many young people who want to enter the food business.

Typical of young people with dreams of culinary artistry are Christian and Karen Bertrand, owners of the Glen Ellen Inn, a restaurant in the Sonoma Valley. Working in the tiniest kitchen I have ever seen, they create dazzling food artifacts that dance in your mouth. On a recent visit there I savored their creations. The dinner started with their fire and ice salad, which blended a jalapeño chutney with small chunks of apple, not a small taste risk. Every dish they served had the same level of well-executed novelty, from the lamb ravioli to the seared ahi tuna. Ingredients, preparation, and presentation were all part of the performance.

Of course, Napa and Sonoma have always had restaurants, but in the earlier times of renewal, the 1960s and 1970s, the chef was not seen in such an elevated and celebrity position as today. The maître d' might have set the tone of the restaurant more than the chef. The chef was important, but was still a functionary. Now, the chef is seen as an artist, as is the winemaker. But the entire scene is not getting too precious. In fact, it is quite egalitarian, partly because there are always fresh, new people interested in stepping in, putting their names on the restaurants, in the same manner that many small wineries arose in the 1970s and 1980s.

This spirit of renewal in the Napa-Sonoma wine country also shows itself in other aspects of life, such as wine and lodging.

The good news for consumers is that California wine continues to move to higher levels of quality. This is inevitable, given the current scene. Increasing numbers of young enology graduates from the University of California at Davis and other schools move into stronger positions in the wineries. Technological advances, such as disease-free grape root stock and more adept grafting of buds, cloning the tastiest varietals to the root stock, insure that vines planted today will yield the most luscious grapes tomorrow. Moreover, the competition is fierce. Only quality will sell.

Fortunately, for those of us who love wine, the price of Napa-Sonoma valley wines has not increased much in recent years. That's partly because the neo-temperance movement in the US today has taken out a portion of the potential wine drinkers. Moderation is also on the rise. Hence, supply and demand remain relatively stable, despite a population increase.

The spirit of renewal in wine production is a very personal story and can best be told with two examples that I recently enjoyed in the Sonoma Valley.

The first was a visit to the Kunde Winery near Glen Ellen. Kunde is a respected name in California wine, but you may not know it. In fact, one of the special pleasures of visiting the wine country is that there are many small producers whose best bottles never leave the valley. I will not tease you with an extensive list of names. There are a total of over 650 commercial wineries now in California, so the opportunities for a spectrum of taste styles is extraordinary. And Kunde is a good example.

The Kunde family has been growing grapes since 1904. They have amassed a sizable holding, about 2,000 acres. Later came the urge to bottle under their own label and build a handsome tasting room in their vineyards. All this came about by the early 1990s. The setting is dramatic, with steep hills of vineyards extending in back of the tasting room. I enjoyed their Chardonnay, Sauvignon Blanc, and Cabernet at a recent tasting. Kunde is one more family with wine dreams that are being fulfilled as the Napa-Sonoma region continues to renew itself.

I also witnessed recently a second aspect of wine-production renewal at the Benziger Winery in Glen Ellen. Though I have taken a number of winery tours in my day, I have never enjoyed a tour as much as I did at Benziger. The tour takes place on a tram that trundles its way around the picturesque, hill-country vineyards. What is fascinating is that you learn on the tour how the Benzigers represent a radically new approach to grape growing. The Benzigers have taken organic farming and sustainable agriculture beyond the boutique phase to an industrial level in their agricultural operations.

A nitrogen-fixing vetch plant grown between the vine rows puts enough nitrogen back into the soil to eliminate the need for nitrogen fertilizer. An "insectary" of host plants creates enough predator insects to keep down the damaging bugs, such as leaf eaters, eliminating the need for pesticides. Anyone with concerns about the long-term survivability of the soil, the local fauna, and the human consumer of wine can't help but be cheered to see what the Benzigers are doing. It takes knowledge and progressive thinking, key aspects of renewal, to make these changes come about. Just as soon as the bottom line of the Benzigers shows favorably the effect of these changes, the bandwagon will follow. And the Benzigers are not merely virtuous. They also make terrific wine, especially their Imagery series, sometimes with specialized grape varietals, such as Cabernet Franc.

Part of the joy of making wine in the late 1990s is a happy convergence of the art of winemaking and the advances in agricultural technology. Matters haven't always been so rosy or optimistic. The earlier times of renewal that I have witnessed in the Napa-Sonoma region and other California wine areas have been more somber. I remember, back in the late 1960s, talking with some of the young wine leaders, such as Michael Mondavi of Napa and Dan Mirassou of the Mirassou family in Santa Clara. Both these young men were proud of the leadership roles their families were playing in California wine. But they were far from exuberant. They had seen their fathers struggle through the post-Prohibition era. They had watched their comrades go into other businesses because winemaking was seen as low-class. A generation of talented wine technicians was lost. The winemaker was seen as something less than an artist. In fact, the winemaker was just emerging from the taint of association with the criminal class, which extended far beyond the Prohibition era. The activity of the winemaker was under the control of the Bureau of Alcohol, Tobacco, and Firearms, and the presence of the authority was apparent. Today that same bureau manages the wine industry, but the issues are less concerned with gangsters and more with such nuances as labeling to indicate the presence of sulfites in wine.

Both Michael Mondavi and Dan Mirassou were leading their family efforts to re-create a wine consumer who enjoyed wine. It was an uphill struggle, but by the late 1960s they were succeeding, and many people came to enjoy wine in the 1970s and 1980s, as we all know. Wines from California in those decades became technically sound wines, which still can't be said of many French wines. In the 1980s the quality of varietal wine taste in California became the chief story. With the current period of renewal, refining the last nuance of taste is the quest. I remember fondly on my most recent visit to Napa savoring a particular Petite Sirah, a Guenoc North Coast 1994, and thinking to myself – have I ever tasted a spicier, more delicious Petite Sirah?

The current phase of renewal in the California wine country means more delicious cuisine and tastier wines. Only a curmudgeon could pass this way and quarrel with the assertion that life is good.

Chapter 5

Shasta Cascade Region

The multiple adventure travel pleasures of **Lassen Volcanic National Park** and the placid 30,000-acre surface of **Shasta Lake**, the premier houseboating lake in the west, are major aspects of travel to the Shasta Cascade region.

Ironically, the tranquility of the park and the lake belie their tumultuous histories. One was shaped by the explosive forces of nature and the other by man's restless need to control water supplies. Both are part of the Cascade chain of fire mountains stretching down the West Coast.

The eruption of northern California's Lassen Peak on May 30, 1914 far exceeded the 1980 eruption of Mt. St. Helens in Washington. On that remarkable Memorial Day, the "extinct" plug volcano spewed the first of 150 spectacular eruptions. The greatest show of all occurred on May 19, 1915, when a river of lava poured a thousand feet down the mountain and created a mud flow a quarter-mile wide and 18 miles long. Three days later, a dramatic upheaval, called the Great Hot Blast, shot debris five miles into the air and felled pine trees like bowling pins around the base of the mountain. Some two inches of ash fell on towns as far away as Reno, Nevada. To some people, it appeared that the day of judgment had arrived. The Loomis Museum near the park's northwest entrance houses a dramatic display of historic photos of the catastrophhe.

Vulcanism means more than brimstone and devastation at Lassen. All life in Lassen, whether a struggling whitebark pine, a scurrying ground squirrel, or an interloper such as man, exists precariously, at the pleasure of the more powerful underlying geologic forces.

Lassen today shows how succession in nature covers the scars of volcanic activity. The high meadows, trout streams, exceptional

The Shasta Cascade Region

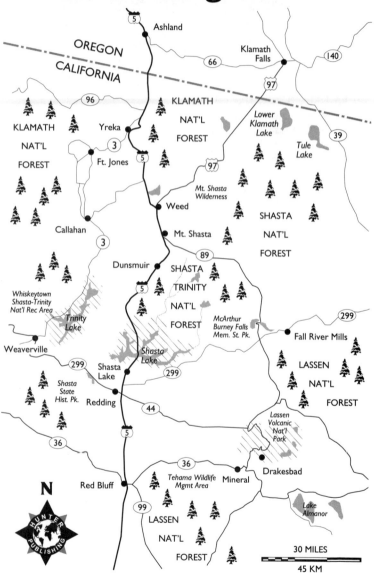

stands of pine and fir trees, and 150 miles of hiking trails draw visitors to Lassen in summer. In winter, cross-country skiing is popular.

The building of **Shasta Dam** (1938-1945) as part of the Central Valley Project has been the defining economic event in the area during this century, setting up the region's agricultural and recreational roles. Three major state rivers – the Pit, McCloud and the Sacramento – were corralled to form California's largest man-made reservoir. Free tours of the dam's interior are a fascinating experience. The spillway of the dam is three times higher than Niagara Falls. For information, contact the visitor center at 16349 Shasta Dam Boulevard, Shasta Lake; ☎ 916-275-4463, for details and tour times.

■ Diversity of the Region

Though Lassen is a special treat, the entire Shasta Cascade region is rich in history and immense natural resources. The historic story begins with the various **Native American** groups, the Wintu, Yana, Chomawi, and Atsugewi tribes. In the 1820s, mountain men like Jedediah Smith and Peter Skene Ogden led fur trappers into the region. In 1844, Pierson B. Reading obtained the northernmost Mexican land grant in the region and in 1848 he discovered gold along Clear Creek, setting off a gold rush that lasted through the 1850s in the town of Shasta, west of Redding. Copper mining and logging boomed later.

Museums

Several small museums tell the historic story. All are listed in a brochure available from the Redding Convention & Visitors Bureau. Some are in remote areas and are special discoveries.

For example, the **Fort Jones Museum** (11913 Main Street, Fort Jones; ☎ 916-468-5125) houses an elaborate Native American collection of basketry, ceremonial rocks, mortars and pestles.

The **Weaverville Joss House State Historic Park** (Highway 299 in Weaverville; ☎ 916-623-5284) recalls that there were 2,500 Chinese seeking gold along the Trinity River in 1852. The Joss House was their site of Taoist worship.

The **Kelly/Griggs House Museum** (311 Washington Street, Red Bluff; ☎ 916-527-1129) is a Victorian showplace built in the 1880s by sheepman Sidney Allen Griggs.

The **William B. Ide Adobe State Historic Park** (21659 Adobe Road, Red Bluff; ☎ 916-529-8599) interprets the pioneer and later Victorian era in this region, with rangers in period costumes. Ide was the first and only president of the California Republic, an 1846 anomaly that occurred when spirited rabble-rousers in Sonoma briefly envisioned California as an independent nation.

■ Getting Here

The Shasta Cascade region is five hours by car north from San Francisco along Interstate 5.

Lassen Volcanic National Park is a farther drive east. From Red Bluff, turn east on Highway 36, then north through the park on Highway 89. From Redding take Highway 44 east to Lassen.

The nearest fly-in point for commercial commuter aircraft is Redding. United Airlines flies in from San Francisco and Horizon arrives from Portland. The Medford, Oregon and Sacramento airports have better commercial jet access, but are 2½ hours away. Car rentals from the major suppliers are available at all these airports.

The main reservoir, Shasta, is on Interstate 5. The other major reservoirs, Trinity and Whiskeytown, lie west of Interstate 5 from Redding on Highway 299.

Information Sources

Redding Convention & Visitors Bureau
777 Auditorium Drive, Redding, CA 9600
☎ 916-225-4100 or 800-874-7562.

Shasta Cascade

Shasta Cascade Wonderland Association
14250 Holiday Road, Redding, CA 96003
☎ 800-474-2782
Web site www.shastacascade.org

The organization also has an office in the new California Welcome Center at the Deschutes Exit along Interstate 5.

Lassen

Superintendent, Lassen Volcanic National Park
PO Box 100, Mineral, CA 96063-0100
☎ 916-595-4444

When in the area, stop for interpretive information at park headquarters near the southwest entrance, outside the park, at Mineral. There is also a ranger-staffed interpretive center at the northwest entrance to the park near Manzanita Lake. This facility, known as the **Loomis Museum**, has nature literature, photos of the explosion of Lassen 1914-1917, and a video on volcanic realities. Lassen is a seasonal park accessed by roads that may be covered by snow for much of the year. The park is generally open from Memorial Day to mid-October, but be sure to call to verify dates; excessive snowpack in some years keeps the park closed until July 1.

Request a price list of the literature they have available. Send for publications in advance to enhance your trip. Our favorite small books on the region, all available from the Superintendent, are *Road Guide to Lassen National Park*; *Birds of Lassen*;, *Trees and Shrubs of Lassen*; *Geology of Lassen*; *Indians of Lassen*; and *Lassen Trails*.

Forests

The local **Forest Service Shasta Information Office** (☎ 916-275-1589) offers tips about many adventure travel resources within its jurisdiction, especially hiking, camping, backpacking, and fishing. The main forests are the **Shasta-Trinity National Forest** (☎ 916-246-5222), the **Klamath National Forest** (☎ 916-842-6131), and the **Lassen National Forest** (☎ 916-257-2151).

Road Conditions

These can be tricky on the high passes in winter, especially during snowstorms. For road conditions in the region, ☎ 800-427-7623.

Shasta-Cascade Region

■ Touring

The Highway 5 Corridor

When driving through this vast region, one longs to grasp it in miniature. The central focal point tends to be the city of Redding. One helpful new interpretive and educational effort is the **Turtle Bay Park and Museum** (800 Auditorium Drive in Redding; ☎ 916-243-8850 or 800-887-8532), which uses wise resource management along the 375-mile Sacramento River as its theme. The facility is designed to explore the region's special environment and history. Interactive exhibits on water, wildlife, forestry, and history will acquaint visitors with the region and challenge the viewer to participate in sustainable stewardship of the resources. The positive and negative tradeoffs involved in development, such as the building of Shasta Dam, are the subject. A children's interactive center known as the **Paul Bunyan Forest Camp** opened in 1997 and serves as an introduction to the logging industry of the region. There are replicas of logging equipment as well as a logging train with a Shay engine. As the $35 million park and museum complex at Turtle Bay develops, it will be the major visitor orientation center for the region. An artistic glass bridge will cross the Sacramento River, joining Turtle Bay with the **Redding Arboretum By The River**. While walking the wild shoreline of the Sacramento River (only 4% of the river still boasts such an undisturbed, forested shoreline) visitors will be able to see salmon spawning.

Events

The main annual events in the region are on the I-5 corridor. Redding celebrates with its **Cool April Nights** fest in April. Red Bluff sponsors a major **rodeo** in April. The main musical event in the region is the **Shasta Jazz Festival** each September in Redding.

Waterfalls

A major theme of the Shasta Cascade area is its waterfalls. The most impressive of these is the fall located in **McArthur-Burney Falls State Park**. These 129-foot falls are best viewed and photographed in early morning when the light hits the cascading water.

Get there by driving east from I-5 on Highway 299 to the intersection of Highway 89. Drive north on 89 and follow the signs to the falls. The Redding Convention & Visitors Bureau has a brochure on McArthur-Burney and seven additional falls that you could visit in a falls circuit. The brochure even indicates the best time to photograph each of the falls. Some of the falls require a hike, such as **Mill Creek Falls**, a 700-foot drop in Lassen Volcanic National Park accessible via a 4.6-mile round-trip hike.

Shasta Lake

Be on the lookout on I-5 for the choice scenic view points. One is a lookout above Shasta Dam. From this point you can see the Three Shastas – Shasta Lake, Shasta Dam, and Mt. Shasta. Shasta Dam is the highest and second largest concrete structure in the United States. Construction began in the 1940s, resulting in impounded and dependable water for California agriculture and 370 miles of recreational shoreline behind the dam. The lake has numerous forest service campgrounds, houseboat resorts, and facilities for launching your canoe or boat. To reach this choice vista point, take Interstate 5 north from Redding approximately 12 miles and

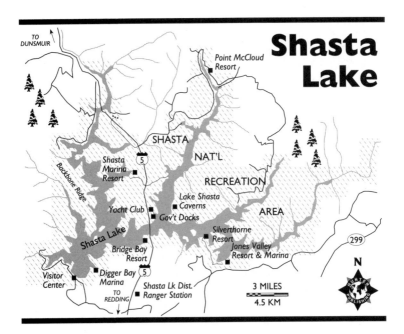

turn off at the Shasta Dam Boulevard exit, watching for the lookout sign.

Dunsmuir

Redding is the main travel stop on this route, but each minor town also vies for your attention. If you make one more choice for a stop, consider Dunsmuir at the foot of Mt. Shasta. Dunsmuir has appealing small lakes nearby, including such strangely named spots as Picayune Lake. There are lots of small lodgings and restaurants in this brick-storefront town, which flourished as a tourism focal point in the earlier railroad era. Like all the small towns, Dunsmuir begs you to stop. For further information, contact the Dunsmuir Chamber of Commerce & Visitor's Center, PO Box 17, Dunsmuir, CA 96025; ☎ 916-235-2177 or 800-386-7684.

Wild Rice

One of the interesting agricultural crops in the region is wild rice, which grows in the water-rich flatlands. East of Shasta Lake, the Fall River Valley produces about 25% of the world's wild rice. You can tour a wild rice processing facility, the Fall River Wild Rice facility (Osprey Drive, Fall River Mills; ☎ 916-336-5222) and learn how the rice is roasted and prepared for packaging. Wild rice is an aquatic grain that formerly grew wild in Minnesota, Canada, and a few other North American locations. Now California is the leading producer of this nutty, flavored treat, which grows best in acidic soils with plenty of water and a clay base. The tour includes a tasting of wild rice in some gourmet food, such as asparagus soup, and plenty of tips on how to cook it yourself. The harvest is mid-July to mid-October. Call ahead to be assured of a tour time.

The Shasta-Whiskeytown Area

Shasta State Historic Park

West of Redding, the Shasta State Historic Park offers an intriguing look into a northern expression of the Gold Rush. Most of the Gold Rush activity occurred east of Sacramento in the Sierra foothills, but there were bursts of frantic activity in other areas, including west of Redding and near Jacksonville, Oregon, across the state border. Shasta State Historic Park is a short, three-mile drive west of Redding on Highway 299. You see a row of old red brick buildings, what remains of the thriving town of Shasta, "Queen City" of the northern mines in the 1850s. There is a fine **museum** (☎ 916-243-8194) in the old Courthouse with a strong California art collection. The Kitsch General Store has been restored to its original condition. The town of Weaverville, further west, has a restored Joss House, mentioned earlier, recalling the Chinese contributions to the gold mining effort.

Whiskeytown Lake

Whiskeytown Lake, eight miles west of Redding on Highway 299, is one of the three major reservoirs that are part of the Whiskeytown-Shasta-Trinity National Recreation Area. Whiskeytown Lake offers sandy beaches, marinas, camping, and numerous hiking trails. The scenery in the area, the interplay of water and forest in an alpine setting, is a constant delight.

Lassen Volcanic National Park

The main historic drama at Lassen is geologic. Massive eruptions a few centuries ago created a pile of debris called Chaos Jumbles. At the northeast corner of the park lies a textbook-perfect cinder cone formed from 19th-century volcanic sputtering. The park was originally purchased because of this cinder cone, an excellent geologic specimen. Taxpayers received a bonus with their investment when everyone learned, much to their surprise, that the volcano was active.

The Atsugewi Indians followed the deer herds back into Lassen each spring and ate venison, trout, salmon, acorns, seeds, and lily bulbs that they foraged.

A branch of the **Nobles Emigrant Trail** that brought early settlers to California passes through Lassen Park. Rangers at the park recreate the early wagon-train scene.

Our main suggestions for an approach to Lassen are as follows:

- Drive the **Loop Road** through the park.
- Walk into the **Bumpass Hell** cauldron area.
- Hike to the top of **Lassen Peak** if you are reasonably fit and able to handle high altitudes.

Shasta-Cascade Region

- Drive to the northeast corner of the park to see the **cinder cone**.

- Drive around the edge of the park to the southeast entrance and visit **Drakesbad**, the historic lodging.

Lassen is both a driving and a hiking park. The Loop Drive presents spectacular promontory views, including a fairly close position near Lassen Peak. Be sure to purchase the *Road Guide* booklet at the entrance headquarters for orientation. Most people enter the park at its southwest corner from Red Bluff, proceed to the center, and exit through the northwest corner.

Other access points by car require rather circuitous drives around the park. A northeast entrance leads to the cinder cone. A southeast entrance leads into Drakesbad, a rustic old lodge.

For information on the park and its camping prospects, write the **Superintendent, Lassen Volcanic National Park**, PO Box 100, Mineral, CA 96063-0150; ☎ 916-595-4444.

All the entrances lead to attractive campgrounds and picnic spots, with centrally located Summit Lake Camp a favorite. From Summit it is possible to make day hikes to various perimeters of the park. Lassen is a park of manageable size, one of its attractions. You get the feeling in a week that you truly know the park. **Juniper Lake** at the southeast corner of the park is another lovely, isolated place to visit.

 When hiking in Lassen Park, especially when making the climb to the peak, take it easy. You are already at about 8,000 feet and may be climbing another 2,000 feet. The air is thin. Hikers unaccustomed to these altitudes commonly push too hard.

The park's 150 miles of trail include a 17-mile section of the Pacific Crest Trail.

Lassen Peak

The central physical experience of the park is Lassen Peak, with its aura similar to Mt. Rainier for a Seattleite, or Mt. Fuji for a Japanese. There is always another view with a different light to meditate over. Make a climb to the top to peer into the crater. From wherever you are in the park, Lassen Peak is clearly visible. The park visitor can collect memorable views of Lassen Peak from different locations, sometimes mirrored in the high lakes, and at different times of the day or year.

Bumpass Hell

Stop at Marker 17 along the Loop Road and make the 1.3-mile walk along relatively level ground to Bumpass Hell, a cauldron of boiling mudpots, sulfurous fumaroles, and junior-size volcanoes – the whole possible range of hissing hydrothermal experiences. Those not wishing to purchase a guidebook can bring their dog-eared copies of Dante's *Inferno* as an introduction.

An Undeveloping Park

The current management policy reflects a change of thinking in the National Park system. Lassen is an undeveloping park. The former lodgings in the park have gradually been phased out, partly to protect people from possible eruptions and partly because the park managers have determined that lodging is not a proper activity within this wilderness park. Also, fish are no longer stocked in the lakes of Lassen, so the only fish caught are the resident trout that persist.

Animal and plant life in this wilderness setting are abundant and varied. Blacktail deer can be observed everywhere. John Muir called the hemlock trees on the south slopes of Lassen the finest stands of that species he had seen anywhere. Golden mantled ground squirrels scurry about. Western tanager birds dart among the trees. Mountain fritillary butterflies flit among the red columbine wildflowers. The lifecycle of all living things here must accommodate the 20-foot snowpack that locks up the park from October through April.

Lassen is a quiet place of nature whose main festive moment is the first show of wildflowers in June after the chilling winter snows have melted. Lassen is a summer-use park with a June-September season.

■ Adventures

On Wheels

Scenic Driving

 Even Interstate 5 is an especially scenic drive along here because of the presence of Mt. Shasta and the forests and lakes. From Sacramento north there is the pageant of California agriculture, from tomatoes to alfalfa. Once you arrive in the Shasta Cascade area and turn off the main road, the side trips present you unexpectedly with views of the dominant mountain, Shasta.

The drive through Lassen Park is a major scenic treat. The most usual route is to turn east on Highway 36 at Red Bluff, enter the park through its southwest corner, drive through the park, and return on Highway 44 to Redding.

Many side trips in the area are delights. Consider a loop drive that can be made from Yreka on **Highway 3** through Fort Jones and Etna, then down to Weaverville and east to Redding on Highway 299. This drive takes you through ranching country, past large reservoirs and rivers with good trout fishing, and close to such pine-filled wilder-nesses as the Marble Moun-tains. The region is small-town California at its best, full of discoveries, such

Mt. Lassen, as seen from Manzanita Lake.

as the historic gold mining dredges on the Trinity River or the barbed-wire collection at the Scott Museum in Trinity Center.

Another satisfying drive could take you east from Mt. Shasta City on Highway 89 to McArthur-Burney Falls State Park, with a side trip to see the wild rice production around Fall River Mills. Then proceed west on Highway 299 past Burney and back to Redding.

Bicycling

The **Sacramento River Trail** in Redding is an eight-mile stretch of paved biking and walking paths along the river. The generous 12-foot width of the trail makes it a pleasant riverside experience. Access the trail from Riverside Drive off Market Street. A bro-chure on the trail is available from the Redding Convention and Visitors Bureau.

Like the major ski venues around Tahoe, the Mt. Shasta Ski Park re-invents itself in summer for the biker and hiker, offering chair-lift rides to the top to view the scenery before making the swift 1½-mile ride down the mountain on your bike. For information, contact **Mt. Shasta Ski Park**, 104 Siskiyou Avenue, Mt. Shasta,

Shasta-Cascade Region

CA 96067; ☎ 916-926-8600. The Ski Park rents bikes and arranges tour rides from the park to Dunsmuir. From the bike rental site it is also possible to make a multi-day, 35-mile bike trip around Mt. Shasta, camping along the way.

For bicycle support in Redding, contact **Bikes Etc.**, 2400 Athens Avenue, ☎ 916-244-1954.

Another interesting bicycle trip would start at the new California Welcome Center at the Deschutes Exit. Stop for information on how to make the ride from here to the **Coleman National Fish Hatchery** (☎ 916-365-8622) where there is also a picnic area. The hatchery was founded in 1942 to mitigate the loss of the chinook salmon's natural spawning grounds. Four runs of salmon can be seen spawning as the year progresses. Call for more details on the ride.

The **Shasta Cascade Wonderland Association** has produced a free guide covering 40 of the best bike trails in the region. Call ahead (☎ 800-474-2782) for a free copy as you plan your trip.

Railroading

The **Blue Goose Excursion Train** out of Yreka offers one of the most stunning scenic train trips in Northern California, largely because white-domed, 14,162-foot Mt. Shasta looms in the background. The Blue Goose recaptures the sights and sounds of a working steam locomotive on the historic short-line Yreka Western Railroad for the three-hour excursion. An heirloom 1915 Baldwin Steam Locomotive pulls the train through the Shasta Valley. You see sawmills and wood-processing plants in operation, as well as Mt. Shasta. This is cattle ranching country, with a stop at the historic cattle town of Montague. The venue is about 35 miles north of Mt. Shasta on Interstate 5. Take the Central Yreka/Miner Street exit to locate the depot, which is adjacent to the freeway on the east side. Contact **Yreka Western Railroad**, Yreka; ☎ 916-842-4146 or 800-973-5277. The train operates Wednesdays through Sundays, mid-June to early September, and continues weekends only through October.

A nostalgic dinner train ride is available on the **Shasta Sunset Dinner Train** out of McCloud. On some days the train also makes lunch and excursion rides. Check by phone for precise details. The train travels over tracks of the McCloud Railway Company, which built the line originally for logging in Siskiyou County. Today, the restored 1920s passenger cars offer a posh dining and scenic viewing opportunity on evening runs, June through September. Call ☎ 800-733-2141 for details. The clickety clack of rails begins at McCloud, east on Highway 89 from Interstate 5, for a 40-mile, three-hour journey. The scenic opportunity includes views of Mt. Shasta, Castle Crags, and the Trinity Alps.

Rail buffs may want to lodge in vintage cabooses at **Railroad Park Resort** (100 Railroad Park Road, Dunsmuir, CA 96025; ☎ 916-235-4440 or 800-974-7245). The cabooses have been modernized and outfitted as lodging rooms. There is even a restaurant in two former rail dining cars. For an immersion in rail Americana, this has few equals.

On Foot

Hiking & Backpacking

Lassen Volcanic National Park, discussed in detail earlier, offers 150 miles of excellent hiking and backpacking opportunities. The hike to the summit of Lassen Peak can be made in a 4½-hour round-trip. For more information on hiking Lassen, ☎ 916-595-4444.

Castle Crags State Park, 35 miles north of Redding along Interstate 5, offers backcountry hiking trails up its soaring spires, where views of Mt. Shasta are one of the rewards. Castle Crags has backpack and car camping sites as well as swimming and fishing in the Sacramento River. Contact Castle Crags at ☎ 916-235-2684.

Near the city of Redding, walking trails have been developed along the Sacramento River. The scenery of the river on the eight-mile **Sacramento River Trail** is rustic. Also in Redding, the **Arboretum By The River**, now part of the Turtle Bay complex, has a 2.2-mile trail with labeled flora. Brochures describing the flora and attractions of both Redding trails are available from the Redding Convention and Visitors Bureau.

Whiskeytown Lake has many pleasing trails around its perimeter. Detailed maps are available at the visitor center on the turnoff

Hiking at Bumpass Hell thermal area in Lassen Volcanic National Park.

to Whiskeytown, where Kennedy Memorial Drive meets Highway 299. Because this lake is never drained down, as is Shasta Lake, the aesthetics of hiking around its perimeter, with the pine trees extending to the water, is superior.

McArthur-Burney Falls State Park (☎ 916-335-2777) boasts an attractive nature trail skirting the falls. This one-mile walk has signs interpreting the flora in the geological context.

One of the engaging local guide services specializing in hikes and all other outdoor activities is **Jack Trout's Scenic & Nature Tours** (PO Box 94, Mt. Shasta, CA 96067; ☎ 916-926-4540). They lead hiking tours to the area's waterfalls, take you on a trek along the Pacific Crest Trail, assist with photo expeditions, or show you the remote high lakes in this alpine wilderness.

Spelunking

Arguably, the most interesting caving experience in Northern California is a visit to **Lake Shasta Caverns**, 15 miles north of Redding on Interstate 5. The limestone magnificence of these caves has been little altered by man, except for the addition of a walkway and indirect lighting in the caves. The marbled appearance of the stalactites and stalagmites in large, open rooms thrills visitors. Slowly flowing deposits frozen into miniature waterfalls, white limestone rivers, and crystal-studded crevices add to the allure. The caverns are open year round with guided tours. To get there, take Interstate 5 north from Redding the 15 miles to the O'Brien/Shasta Cavern exit. The tour operators (☎ 916-238-2341 or 800-795-2283) ferry you across the McCloud arm of Shasta Lake to reach the caverns.

Another intriguing cave experience is possible at **Subway Caves**, a series of tubes or tunnels formed when molten lava on the surface cooled and hardened while the molten lava underneath continued to flow. The caves are safe and can be explored by all ages, but bring a jacket to ward off the chill and a flashlight to find your way. There is no charge for the self-guided tour at Subway Caves, just off Highway 44-89, about 15 miles northeast of Manzanita Lake.

Mountain Climbing

The two mountains to climb are Lassen and Shasta.

Lassen Peak, at 10,457 feet, can be climbed with relative ease in a 4½-hour round-trip effort from the trailhead in the park. The climb is a manageable 2,000 feet on a good trail and is routinely done by people in good physical condition.

The ascent of 14,162-foot **Mt. Shasta** is more complicated and should be undertaken only with an expert guide. One provider is Michael Zanger, **Shasta Mountain Guides**, 1938 Hill Road, Mt. Shasta, CA 96067; ☎ 916-926-3117. Another is Leif Voeltz of **Fifth Season**, 300 North Mt. Shasta Boulevard, Mt. Shasta, CA 96067; ☎ 916-926-3606. June is considered the safest month for a Shasta climb. Climbing Mt. Shasta is a 12-mile round-trip from the 7,300-foot level to the summit. The climb is strenuous and requires planning, proper equipment, good weather, and superb physical conditioning.

On Horseback

 One unusual horseback experience is at the **Wild Horse Sanctuary**, founded by Jim and Dianne Clap. They initially rescued 80 wild horses from BLM (Bureau of Land Management) destruction in 1987 and set up a foundation for the first wild horse refuge. The non-profit foundation dedicates itself to preserving America's wild horses. Today you can go on two- and three-day pack trips in the Mt. Lassen foothills to track and photograph some of the 300 wild horses. The rugged habitat is shared with black bear, bobcat, mountain lion, wild turkey, and deer, plus over 150 species of songbirds. Overnights are spent in frontier-style sleeping cabins. Hearty meals are cooked over a woodburning stove. The night sky, dotted with stars, is illuminated further with sparks from the campfire. Wild horses in the sanctuary are a sample of the wild horses found throughout the west on remote lands, especially in Nevada and Utah, where wild horses still roam. For details, contact the Wild Horse Sanctuary, PO Box 30, Shingleton, CA 96088; ☎ 916-474-5770. Shingleton is east of Red Bluff off Interstate 5. Proceed on Highway 36 to Lassen Volcanic National Park. At Dale's Corner, turn left to Manton, then left to Shingleton. Confirm all details by phone before proceeding.

In Lassen Volcanic National Park horseback riding is a favorite activity at **Drakesbad Guest Ranch** (Warner Valley Road, Chester, CA 96020; ☎ 916-529-1512).

The **Trinity Alps Resort** (1750 Trinity Alps Road, Trinity Center, CA 96091; ☎ 916-286-2205) at Trinity Lake features rustic cabins and horseback riding in its scenic, alpine location.

Spanish Springs is a dude ranch with horse riding in Lassen County. This working cattle ranch provides an adventure for the whole family, including riding, swimming, and fishing. Cabins, a full service restaurant, and cattle drives are some of the attractions. Contact Spanish Springs Ranch, PO Box 70, Ravendale, CA 96123; ☎ 916-234-2050 or 800-272-8282.

On Water

Scenic Boat Trips

Osprey Excursions (8587 Future Drive, Redding, CA 96001; ☎ 800-294-3683) offers guided excursions in a six-person jet boat on your choice of waterways, either the Sacramento River or one of the reservoirs. The tour concentrates on sightseeing, scenery viewing, nature and wildlife photography, or fishing, as you wish.

Rafting & Kayaking

Rafts can be rented in Redding for a pleasant 12-mile float trip on the Sacramento River. The providers include the raft, paddles, life jackets, a map of the river, and shuttle pickup at the other end to bring you back to Redding. The service is offered by **Park Marina**

Raft Rentals (2515 Park Marina Drive, Redding; ☎ 916-246-8388). Many rafters float down to the Amigos Mexican restaurant (☎ 916-365-6142) in Anderson for lunch or dinner.

Rafting also occurs on the Trinity and Klamath rivers with the **Turtle River Rafting Company**, PO Box 313, Mt. Shasta, CA 96067; ☎ 916-938-1056 or 800-726-3223.

Cutting Edge Adventures leads rafting trips on the Salmon, Scott, Klamath, and Upper Sacramento rivers. They also do kayaking schools, which start you with skill-building on placid Lake Siskiyou. After you learn the "Eskimo roll," enabling you to recover from an overturned kayak, they'll lead you down the rivers. Contact Cutting Edge Adventures, PO Box 1334, Mt. Shasta, CA 96067; ☎ 916-926-4647 or 800-594-8435.

Houseboating the Shasta-Trinity Reservoirs

Houseboating is a major part of tourism in the Shasta region, which calls itself the Houseboating Capital of the West. Only the scale of houseboating on the Colorado River comes close to the number of boats and the miles of shoreline to roam on Shasta and Trinity lakes.

The modern houseboat is a wonder to behold, fully equipped with shower, bathroom, refrigerator, freezer, microwave, VCR, and even a trash compactor. All you bring is your food and drink, bedding, and sports gear, such as fishing rod to capture the trout, bass, and catfish that flourish in the reservoirs. As a platform for relaxation and a viewpoint for savoring sunrises and sunsets in the isolation of some remote wilderness location, a houseboat is hard to beat. Houseboats are usually rented for a week, but operators will rent for shorter periods if they have boats available.

The operators of houseboats on Shasta Lake, the largest man-made reservoir in California, with 370 miles of serpentine shoreline, have banded together and will send you a brochure with all the major suppliers. Study it to find the type of boat and services appropriate for your group. Lodging, camping, and services are included in the brochure, besides house boating. All together, there are 10 providers of houseboating with about 350 boats for rent. Write the **Redding Convention and Visitors Bureau** for the bro-

Houseboating on Shasta Lake.

chure (777 Auditorium Drive, Redding, CA 96003; ☎ 916-225-4100 or 800-874-7562), or contact the **Shasta Lake Business Owner's Association**, PO Box 709, Lakehead, CA 96051.

Shasta Houseboating

One substantial provider is **Bridge Bay Resort** (10300 Bridge Bay Road, Redding CA 96003; ☎ 916-275-3021 or 800-752-9669). This is a complete resort with houseboating, powerboats, on-shore lodging, dining, and fishing support. Bridge Bay is 15 minutes from Redding, off Interstate 5.

Another supplier is **Antlers Resort & Marina** (PO Box 140, Lakehead, CA 96051; ☎ 916-238-2553 or 800-238-3924). Antlers is also a multi-facility property, with houseboats, powerboats, cabins, plus RV and tent camping on property. There is a primitive forest service campground nearby.

The complete source for watersport toys on Shasta Lake is appropriately named **The Toy Box**. It's at the Holiday Harbor Resort, Shasta Caverns Road, O'Brien, CA 96070; ☎ 916-238-2383 or 800-776-2628. The Toy Box motto is, "If it floats, we rent it." They provide ski boats, skis, jetskis, and canoes, as well as party barges and houseboats. They also run the only parasail operation on the lake in case you want to be taken aloft.

The only drawback to the houseboating pleasure on Shasta Lake is that the water in the lake gets drawn down for agricultural purposes as the summer progresses. This drop in lake level creates an ever greater ringed effect around the shore, which detracts from the aesthetic appeal of the lake. Recreational providers on the lake find themselves at odds with the agricultural interests that would like to buy Shasta water.

Powerboating & Sailing

The three major reservoirs have ample launch sites for the traveler with access to a powerboat or sailboat. There are also power and sailboat rentals at many marinas on Shasta Lake. See the houseboating section to learn of the suppliers.

Lake Britton at McArthur-Burney Falls State Park (☎ 916-335-2777) is a special, smaller boating lake. Not only is the peaceful setting appealing, with its pine-filled vistas, but there is also a sandy swimming beach. A lakeside concession rents motorboats, canoes and pedal boats for fishing or cruising along the waters from June-September. The lake is a short walk away from the campground, one of the loveliest in the region.

Fishing

In the large reservoirs there is good fishing for trout, bass, and catfish. The rivers and small streams of the area are excellent for trout.

Some streams, such as **lower Hat Creek** east of Burney, are particularly well known for trout fly fishing. Other favorite fly fishing locations include the McCloud River below Lake McCloud and Fall River near the town of Fall River Mills.

The **Fly Shop** in Redding (4140 Churn Creek Road; ☎ 916-222-3555) is an example of the dedicated fishing store with just the right trout gear and knowledge of local waters. They also control four lodging situations on good fishing streams and organize drift fishing trips on the Sacramento River.

A source on Shasta Lake with knowledgeable advice and appropriate tackle is **Bridge Bay Resort**, 10300 Bridge Bay Road, Redding, CA 96003; ☎ 916-275-3021 or 800-752-9669.

Some lodgings focus primarily on fishing. **Lava Creek Lodge** (Glenburn Star Route, Fall River Mills, CA 96028; ☎ 916-336-6288) is a full service lodge with wide lawns, a lake, and food service, catering to fishermen, hunters, and nature viewers. Lava Creek can arrange guides to help you fish or point you in the direction of nature trips, perhaps an outing northward to Tule Lake to see migrating waterfowl such as snow geese from December to February.

Clearwater House (PO Box 90, Cassel, CA 96016; ☎ 916-335-5500) is a B&B with many specialized packages for fly fishing, including trips for women and children. This fly fisher's haven is on the banks of legendary Hat Creek. The inn offers full meal packages, instruction, and guide.

The Sacramento River has seasonal runs of steelhead, an ocean-going trout, and salmon, as well as year-round trout, striped bass, and catfish fishing. In August 1997 the steelhead runs from the Russian River south along the California coast were declared threatened, so check with Fish and Game authorities to determine if steelhead fishing remains legal on the Sacramento River in future years.

Hundreds of small lakes in the northern area are good for brown and rainbow trout. Frenchman, Davis, and Bucks lakes are some of the possibilities.

There are many guide services for fishermen in the area. **Jack Trout Fly Fishing & Guide Service** (☎ 916-926-4540) specializes in guided fishing on the Upper Sacramento and McCloud rivers.

Scuba Diving in Whiskeytown Lake

The clarity of Whiskeytown Lake has led to scuba activity in the Shasta Cascade. The main local organizer of the sport is the **Camps Diving Adventure Center**, 3048 South Market Street, Redding; ☎ 916-241-4530.

On Snow

The Shasta-Lassen Snow Playground

Downhill Skiing

Though the vertical drop (1,380 feet) does not compare with the skiing around Lake Tahoe, the **Mt. Shasta Ski Park** offers the special experience of skiing this major volcanic mountain. The park has three triple chairs. Lift lines will never be long because this ski area is too far to drive for the maddening crowds from San Francisco. The drive is longer (five hours) from the Bay Area than the comparable drive to Tahoe, though the flat Interstate 5 road is easier.

About 25% of the terrain at Mt. Shasta Ski Park is advanced, 55% intermediate, and 20% beginner. The ski park has night skiing and snow-making capacity. Rentals and lesson packages are available both for skiing and snowboarding. Lift tickets are somewhat less than at Lake Tahoe. For information on Mt. Shasta skiing, contact Mt. Shasta Ski Park, 104 Siskiyou Avenue, Mt. Shasta, CA 96067; ☎ 916-926-8600. At the base of the lift there is also a Climbing Tower for those who want to engage in the sport of climbing on an artificial rock surface.

Ascending the outdoor climbing wall at Mt. Shasta Ski Park in summer.

Cross-Country Skiing

Cross-country skiing takes place at **Lassen Volcanic National Park** (☎ 916-595-4444) and at the **Mt. Shasta Ski Park**, which has a separate nordic center with 25 miles of groomed trails. The cross-country skier at Mt. Shasta will feel a reverence for the massive white mountain, sacred to the Modocs and other tribes who lived here. Most of Lassen is closed in winter, making its roads excellent cross-country trails. Cross-country skiing takes place at the northwest entrance to the park in the vicinity of Manzanita Lake. The roads are not groomed trails, but the many skiers create a track. At Lassen there are also ranger-led hikes on showshoes.

Dogsledding

Dogsledding is a special adventure here when the weather conditions permit. Gliding over the snow, pulled by a trained team of huskies or Alaskan malamutes, you feel the special bond that exists between man and dog in the harsh winter environment. **Dogsled Express** (PO Box 15, Etna, CA 96027; ☎ 916-467-5627) is ready to take you around Mt. Shasta, the Trinity Alps, or the Marble Mountains. They can limit the outing to a short track ride or stretch it to the ultimate with a high-altitude back country camping trip in winter, with you handling your own dog team. They pack a freight sled to provide the comforts possible in winter camping.

In the Air

Ballooning Mt. Shasta

Land and water adventures are more abundant in this area than air sports, but the **Mt. Shasta Balloon Company** (PO Box 216, Yreka, CA 96097; ☎ 916-841-1011 or 800-841-1011) of Siskiyou County offers year-round opportunities for hot air balloon rides over this sparsely populated area.

■ Where to Stay & Eat

Accommodations

One of the comfortable lodgings in the region is the **Best Western Hilltop Inn** (2300 Hilltop Drive, Redding, CA 96002, 916/221-6100. $$). Their C.R. Gibbs Alehouse & Restaurant has the region's best salad bar, plus good fish or meat entrées.

Another suitable site is the **Doubletree Hotel** (1830 Hilltop Drive, Redding, CA 96002; ☎ 916-221-8700. $$).

Either property would make a good base of operations for day trips in the region or to Lassen Volcanic National Park.

At Lassen Park, the distinguished lodging is **Drakesbad Guest Ranch** (Warner Valley Road, Chester, CA 96020; ☎ 916-529-9820. $$), an interesting old-line lodge, but accessible only from the remote southeast corner of the park and open only for the summer. Drakesbad requires advance reservations, as much as a year ahead.

Near the northwest entrance to Lassen an engaging B&B with a stunning view, swimming pool, woodsy setting, hot tub, and flower gardens is **Weston House** (PO Box 276, Shingletown, CA 96088; ☎ 916-474-3738. $$-$$$). Proprietor Angela Weston manages Weston House, one of the more tranquil scenic settings in the region.

One quaint, historic lodging at the foot of Mt. Shasta is the **McCloud Bed & Breakfast Hotel** (408 Main Street, McCloud, CA 96057; ☎ 800-964-2823. $$). With 14 guest rooms and four suites, this National Historic Register property also offers good value and a sense of humor. There's a 20% discount for anyone arriving in a pre-WW II car.

If lodging in pure Americana is your taste, then try the **Railroad Park Resort** (100 Railroad Park Road, Dunsmuir, CA 96015; ☎ 916-235-4440. $$) in Dunsmuir. You sleep in an authentic caboose. This vintage-rail-car lodging has other amenities, from a cocktail lounge to laundry services, but what is special is the caboose lodging, even if somewhat modernized for comfort. Two former dining cars create a restaurant on the premises. The setting, at the base of the magnificent spires of Castle Crags, is appealing.

The **Mt. Shasta Resort** (1000 Siskiyou Lake Boulevard, Mt. Shasta, CA 96067; ☎ 916-926-3030. $$) has modern one- or two-bedroom chalets located in a woodsy setting, plus an 18-hole golf course and fine dining with a view of Mt. Shasta.

For lodging near skiing, consider the **Strawberry Valley Inn** (1142 South Mt. Shasta Boulevard, Mt. Shasta, CA 96067; ☎ 916-926-2052. $-$$). The rate includes breakfast and complimentary beverage in the evening.

Another unusual area lodging is the **Brigadoon Castle Bed & Breakfast** (PO Box 324, Igo, CA 96047; ☎ 916-396-2785 or 888-343-2836. $$$).

Built by an eccentric doctor as his private home, this composite Elizabethan castle, created tastefully from his recollections of many European castles, later came into the hands of ex-banker Geri MacCallum. Ms. MacCallum's dream was to turn the house into a small B&B. Today the stately castle has four guest rooms and one outlying cottage. Hot tub, gardens, and hikes along a creekbed are among the amenities on the 86-acre property, which is 20 minutes from Redding on narrow, winding back-country roads. Be sure to call ahead to get careful directions to the property.

Shasta-Cascade Region

Restaurants

 In Redding, try **C. R. Gibbs** at the Best Western, 2300 Hilltop Drive; ☎ 916-221-2335. $$). Their signature dish is a bowl of boiled shrimp, which is offered to every diner. C. R. Gibbs has a sumptuous salad bar and tasty entrées, from calamari to New York steaks.

For a good Mexican restaurant in Redding, consider **Pio Loco's** (1135 Pine Street; ☎ 916-246-2111. $-$$). Start with a margarita and perhaps proceed to the crab enchiladas or chicken fajita salad.

If you want a hearty breakfast in Dunsmuir, stop by the **Old Rostel Pub and Café** (5743 Sacramento Avenue; ☎ 916-235-2028. $-$$). Owners Tim and Joan Elam will serve up their smoked trout omelet or Rostel *mess*, which consists of a medley of vegetables with cheese. The Elams have dreams of making Dunsmuir the focus of tourism that it formerly was in the railroad heyday. Until the 1960s and the advent of air travel, there were sometimes 20 trains a day stopping at Dunsmuir on the coastal route between San Francisco and Portland/Seattle.

Food is available in Lassen Park at the **Chalet Café**, near the southwest entrance (☎ 916-595-3376. $-$$). The Chalet offers sandwiches, salads, and a pleasant setting on its open deck.

To dine with a stunning view of Mt. Shasta in the background, choose the contemporary setting of the **Mt. Shasta Resort** (1000 Siskiyou Lake Boulevard, Mt. Shasta; ☎ 916-926-3030, $$). Try the Greek/spinach salad or the rack of lamb.

Camping & RV

 Lassen Volcanic National Park has seven campgrounds with guided nature walks and campfire programs in the summer months. The park is closed during winter, except for cross-country skiing from the Manzanita Lake entrance. Get to Lassen by taking Highway 44 east from Redding or Highway 36 east from Red Bluff. For camp reservations, contact ☎ 916-595-4444 or 800-280-2267.

The two state parks mentioned for hiking (**Castle Crags**) and waterfall watching (**McArthur-Burney Falls**) are good camping options. Both can be reserved at ☎ 800-444-7275).

Castle Crags, 35 miles north of Redding on Interstate 5, has 64 campsites with tables, stoves, and storage lockers. Hot showers here are welcomed by campers. Some of the sites are large enough for motorhomes.

McArthur-Burney Falls State Park, with 118 campsites, is a particularly good off-season camping site. Though most campers arrive in summer, McArthur-Burney is delightful in the lush new vegetation period of May and again in September and October, when the leaves of the black oak and white oak trees provide fall color. Miraculously, the 129-foot falls, with their million gallons per day flow, did not become a power plant. The setting is a delight, though Theodore Roosevelt may have spoken too freely when he called McArthur-Burney Falls the eighth wonder of the world.

There is a **KOA** in Redding at 280 Boulder Drive; ☎ 916-246-0101. Though located in the city, the setting is rustic and has all the features expected of this chain.

Other dependable RV facilities in the area with full hookups include the **Sacramento River RV Park** (8900 Riverland Drive; ☎ 916-365-6402) on the Sacramento River south of Redding. The **Rancheria RV Park** (☎ 800-346-3430) is on a trout-stocked lake near the town of Hat Creek. **Antlers RV Park & Campground** (☎ 800-642-6849) has RV sites and tent camping adjacent to Shasta Lake.

■ Coyotes at Midnight

Backpacking the California Wilderness

By Lee Foster

Shortly after midnight the wilderness callers began their song. I was startled awake by a long, plaintive "Aroooohhh" on the slope above our backpack camp. Before the wail had ceased, another caller on a neighboring ridge answered. Soon a half-dozen singers at distant points were calling to each other. For 15 minutes the serenade continued. The entertainers, of course, were coyotes.

For this I had come to the wilderness. In the previous two days I had put one foot patiently in front of the other, climbing through California's wilderness, to this wooded shoulder at 8,500 feet, about a thousand feet below Mokelumne Peak. I had entered the wilderness at the Silver Lake Trailhead near Bear Valley Reservoir, on Highway 88 east of Jackson, with a party of six other enthusiasts. I had made similar trips farther north, in the Shasta Cascade, especially into the Marble Mountain Wilderness.

Even without the coyotes, I had already been amply rewarded that night. The stars were bright and clear enough to shock a citified sensibility whose stargazing is usually obscured by urban lights. It was easy to imagine how shepherds and other night vigilants could weave legends about these light points in the sky.

Besides the coyotes and stars, the wildflowers alone were worth this wilderness trip, especially those growing on the bare slope below the rock talus of Mokelumne Peak. Clusters of Indian paintbrush, bush lupine, and tiny gilia carpeted the slope. Deep in the forest the red wildflower called snow plant, actually a mushroom-like saprophyte, brought color to the duff below pine trees. In the moist meadows the corn lily, blue larkspur, and red columbine proliferated.

The botanical richness of Tanglefoot Canyon in the Mokelumne Wilderness is a major treat. In moist Tanglefoot Canyon the bracken fern attain six-foot heights and in neighboring Cole Creek the aspens grow to six-foot diameters. As we gradually climbed the flanks of Mokelumne Peak, our party took much pleasure in keying out the trees, watching as the ponderosa pine gave way to jeffrey pine, the white fir were succeeded by red fir, and the lodgepole pines yielded to silver pines. Stately red fir and mountain hemlock regally dominated the higher slopes. Finally, on the most exposed and windswept locations, struggling dwarfed whitebark pines clung tenaciously to the rocky soil. Though a massive fir tree standing straight up is impressive, equally poignant is a dead fir tree on the ground, disintegrating slowly, with the help of fungi and termites re-forming the organic soil.

This wilderness enticed me with views of the mountains in their granite splendor. The Sierra and the Shasta Cascade have numerous parallel views. From the top of Mokelumne Peak I looked north to the Desolation Wilderness and Pyramid Peak near Lake

Tahoe, east to the Carson Range in Nevada, south to the High Country of Yosemite, and west to the Mokelumne Gorge, which happens to be the watershed where dams impound the daily drinking water of my East Bay community. When I made the trip, in July, there were scattered snow patches in the mountains. It is easy to imagine how *snowy mountains*, or Sierra Nevada, struck the Franciscan Padre Font as an appropriate name when he looked east from the Central Valley in April 1772. The brief summer growing period here offers only 40-70 frost-free days, so the fecund plant growth is a frenetic race to perpetuate the species between the times of heavy winter snowpacks. In the Mokelumne Wilderness, which lies roughly east of the Golden Gate, the snowpack is heavier than at any other section of the Sierra, due to the climate pattern. Consequently, glaciers during the ice age reached their maximums here, fully 80 by 40 miles at one time.

Everywhere the glacier-scraped granite face of the Sierra was apparent. Sheer granite, and a summer climate with minimal rain are the two most distinguishing characteristics of the Sierra, compared to other mountain ranges. At night, the granite of the Sierras, washed in moonlight, presents an alluring aura that contrasts sharply with the majestic look of the mountains in strong sunlight.

Wilderness backpacking affected me deeply because for four days I saw no people other than our party. We were not misanthropes or even weary of civilized life, as John Muir was when he called on wilderness to help him throw off "the galling harness of civilization." No, the wilderness was simply an alternative view, a surprising, satisfying solitude. Such landscapes still exist in California, despite more than 31 million inhabitants, where you can walk four days in an inviting botanical garden and find images only of nature. The Mokelumne Wilderness happens to be one of the less visited wildernesses of California. At the top of Mokelumne Peak there is a small brown notebook where climbers record their thoughts. Though the first entries were from 1977, the notebook was not yet filled. Apparently, macho backpackers bypass the 9,000-foot Mokelumne Wilderness in their rush to stand in line at the higher-elevation trailheads.

I came to the wilderness also to see how self-reliant I could be, how well I could survive in a simplified existence with all my life-support systems on my back. With what self-confidence would I emerge? Two backpackers in our group (my son, Bart, and another adult, Larry Lamoreux) were expert, and I benefited from their skills. At the higher altitudes they found two water sources that we had not counted on. Rich with water, we could be luxurious in our consumption. We found our way during two days of bushwhacking in trailless areas along Cole Creek, navigating around giant boulders and through buckbrush tangles, stopping occasionally to watch the wild trout disport themselves while searching for caddis fly larvae and other foods. When the heat oppressed us, we too swam in the clear mountain pools. After four days on the trail, our party emerged from the wilderness with no incident more serious than a couple of small blisters. However, the severity of this wilderness was such that an inept, reckless, or unlucky hiker could die in a day in the hot sun without water. If you broke a leg in the wilderness, jumping from boulder-to-boulder with a 40-pound pack, only a helicopter could get you out.

The wilderness has many pleasures, and I wish they were more than vicariously available to all. Enter the Sierra or Shasta Cascade wildernesses only if you are in good shape, able to carry yourself and a backpack over distances at high altitude. Gear up adequately with attention to detail. Seek out an experienced fellow backpacker as your initiator in this drama rather than go it alone. And then listen shortly after midnight for the serenade of the coyotes high on the slopes.

Chapter 6

The Sierra & Gold Country

Lake Tahoe & Yosemite

The mountains and foothills of eastern California present some of the great adventure playgrounds of the state, starting with the alpine jewel of a lake, **Tahoe**, and continuing on to the distinguished national park, **Yosemite**. On the eastern slopes of the mountains, the **Mammoth** area presents many delights, from the natural phenomena at Mono Lake to the horseriding behind Mammoth Mountain. As you drive to the mountains, you pass the foothills, the **Gold Country**, where the momentous discovery of precious metal was made 150 years ago.

■ Lake Tahoe

Mark Twain, who was not given to easy superlatives, felt that an exception was appropriate when speaking of **Lake Tahoe**. He called the lake "the fairest picture the whole earth affords."

Twain, who had a remarkable ability to turn a phrase, went on about Tahoe, noting, "The water is clearer than the air, and the air is the air that angels breathe."

Clarity (97% pure), deep bluish color, elevation (at 6,229 feet), a mountainous and wooded setting in the Sierra Nevada, and size (22 miles long and 8-12 miles wide) combine to make Lake Tahoe one of the most attractive freshwater lakes in North America. The extraordinary blue color occurs because of the lake's remarkable depth, as much as 1,645 feet, with about 1,000 feet as the average. This third deepest lake in North America could cover a flat area equal to the size of California with 14 inches of water.

The Sierra & Gold Country

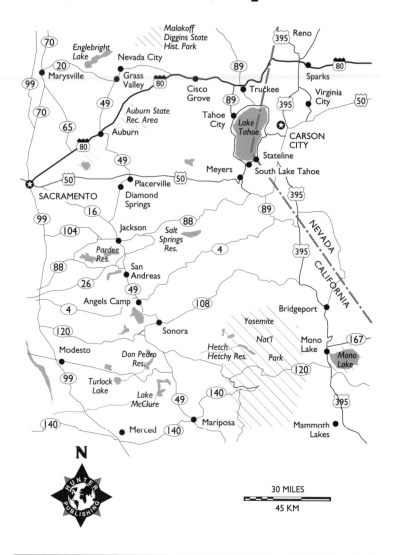

N

30 MILES

45 KM

When **John Fremont** became one of the first white men to see the lake, in 1844, the area was sparsely populated by Washoe Indians. It is thought that Tahoe comes from a Washoe Indian word meaning "water in a high place" or "lake in the sky." The lake is indeed in the sky, easily the largest alpine lake in North America.

Appreciated in the summer for its hiking opportunities and natural beauty and in winter for its ski areas, the Tahoe basin has its year-round enthusiasts. If you visit in spring or autumn, you'll find that the crowds have thinned.

The political struggle to achieve sensible, but restrained development of the Tahoe area is an ongoing challenge. Ruining the natural beauty, over-drawing the available fresh water supply, and polluting the water are major concerns. The political decisions must be agreed upon by the two states, six counties, and perhaps 20 agencies with various authorities. A third of the lake lies in Nevada, with the rest in California. The lake nestles between the main north-south Sierra Nevada and an eastern offshoot, the Carson Range.

■ Yosemite

"As I looked, a peculiar sensation seemed to fill my whole being," wrote the militiaman. "And I found my eyes in tears with emotion."

Such were the sentiments of the first white man to see **Yosemite**, a mountain retreat of awesome beauty in east central California. The year was 1851. Our observer was not a poet, but a rough militiaman, and the simple eloquence of his recorded thoughts testifies to the universal experience of Yosemite. So many travelers feel the same when first encountering Yosemite Valley, an eight-mile funnel with a flat base and 3,000-foot granite walls. There's a subdued grandeur about the place, a sense of nature's cathedral, even a spare and enobling aura.

Today there are many ways to experience the best of Yosemite. You can circle the valley in the park service tram, walk the easy trails leading out of the valley, rent a bicycle to explore the valley floor, join a guided horseback ride, hike the high country in summer, cross-country and alpine ski in winter, take classes with the

Yosemite Mountaineering School, rock climb the granite faces (with an experienced guide) and attend ranger walks or talks.

Yosemite Valley, which 90% of the visitors never leave, is only a miniscule part of Yosemite National Park. The valley is seven of the total 1,169 square miles of the park. Make an effort to get out of the valley to Wawona to see the big trees, the sequoias, or to the high country to see Tuolumne Meadows. There are 196 miles of primary roads and about 800 miles of trail to entice you beyond Yosemite Valley.

Yosemite sustained $178 million in damages during the severe floods of January 1997 that closed the park for two months. The park opened to a new era of substantially higher user fees, with the charge set at $20 per car per day.

■ Mammoth Lakes

Partisans of California's Mammoth Lakes region in the eastern Sierra can argue persuasively that it competes for the honor of the most diverse outdoor summer region of the Golden State.

The scenery is stunning, starting with the basalt columns at **Devils Postpile National Monument**. A traveler arrives right in the mountains, with no foothills as a prelude, and with many small alpine lakes as a setting.

The natural history of the region intrigues, especially at **Mono Lake**, immediately north of Mammoth Lakes. Remnants of volcanoes and earthquakes, tufa formations, and an abundant food supply for birds make Mono Lake special.

Day hikes or ambitious backpacking can easily take a visitor into the wilderness, such as the **John Muir Wilderness**, perhaps on the John Muir or Pacific Crest trails. In few places will a traveler find so many accessible trails.

Elaborate horsepacking outfits can remove the huff and puff from traversing this granite terrain, ranging from 4,000 to more than 12,000 feet high. A full-day pack trip, for example, takes you six miles to **Duck Lake**, revealing a back-country wilderness that only a hiker in superb condition could experience.

Mountain bikers delight in the more than 300 miles of cycling routes partly because of the numerous bikable roads, and partly because the great winter mountain, **Mammoth**, so noted for its ski runs, becomes a mountain biking park in summer. You take the gondola to the top and then bike down the switchbacks, through the trees, to the bottom.

Fishermen get the style of trout fishing they desire. Some seek out the trophy trout in **Crowley Lake**. Others fish for the numerous planted "catchables" in the cluster of **Mammoth Lakes**. Purists angle with barbless hooks in world-class catch-and-release **Hot Creek**.

A traveler will find the requisite tourism infrastructure in this modern little mountain town of 4,500 people. Abundant mid-range condos, such as Snowcreek, serve the needs of the family traveler and can be arranged through central reservation services. Local restaurateurs offer ethnic dishes and everything from family style to elegant dining.

All considered, Mammoth has appeals that equal its famous competitors, Yosemite and Lake Tahoe. Both those regions are better known than Mammoth, partly because they are more accessible. Already popular as a winter ski destination, Mammoth now attracts an increasing share of summer visitors. Summer travelers tend to echo the comments of the transplants in the local population who explain, "I came for the winter, but stayed for the summer." Mammoth is a six-hour drive from San Francisco or from Los Angeles.

Mammoth Lakes is one of those special California places that confirms how satisfying the Golden State can be for travelers. Unlike Yosemite and Lake Tahoe, with their focused identities, conjuring up immediate images of El Capitan or the blue lake, Mammoth Lakes offers a more diffused range of impressions. This may be a marketing problem, but it can be a plus. Today's travelers are hard to define. They may demand scenery, natural history, hiking, biking, horsepacking, fishing, all in a single destination. Mammoth responds effectively to these demands.

The Sierra/Gold Country

■ Gold Country & Sacramento

The monumental discovery of gold in California in 1848 provoked one of the most frenzied voluntary migrations in human history. California's Gold Rush Country marks its 150th birthday in 1998.

This anniversary is an opportune time to retrace the routes to riches chased by the hundreds of thousands who came to California. A statewide celebration offers visitors special events, exhibits, and activities now through the year 2,000 to commemorate the Sesquicentennial of the Gold Rush.

What would be a fitting approach to exploring the Gold Country during this time of celebration? Consider a visit to the four major historic parks that dramatically recall the Gold Rush experience.

The **Marshall Gold Discovery Site** in Coloma is where the shiny nuggets were first found. **Columbia State Historic Park** recreates the brief, democratic period when the common man, if lucky, could get rich by panning for nuggets in chilly mountain streams. The **Empire Mine State Historic Park** is a memorial to the later period in gold extraction, when highly capitalized companies mined the quartz rock deep underground in search of veins of gold. The fourth park, **Malakoff Diggins**, is a tragic testament to how man can, and will, destroy the environment in the name of greed.

The Gold Country, a three-hour drive east from San Francisco, still conjures up the excitement that James Marshall felt when he first noticed gold nuggets at a sawmill he was building on the banks of the American River in 1848. You can trace the path that miners from the eastern US and from around the world took along Highway 49 as they searched for instant wealth.

Gold Rush Country functions as a massive outdoor living museum, 300 miles long and about 20 miles wide if you begin at Mariposa in the south and drive north beyond Sierraville.

Today you can bathe in the nostalgic memories of the wild mining era while gazing at the many preserved buildings from the Gold Rush. You can lodge in old Gold Rush era hotels and Victorian houses, now B&Bs. You can visit the intriguing museums, poke about the small towns, and, if you are ambitious, even pan for flakes of your own.

■ Getting Here

Lake Tahoe

Lake Tahoe lies between the two main routes that emigrants took to California. Today these routes are Interstate 80 and Highway 50. Sacramento is the Central Valley metropolis from which both highways reach into the mountains. Lake Tahoe is four hours (200 miles) from San Francisco, allowing for the mountain climb and depending on weather conditions.

Commuter planes fly directly into **South Lake Tahoe Airport**. A dozen major carriers fly into **Reno-Cannon Airport**, located east of the lake. **Greyhound** buses can take you to Truckee on the north side of the lake. **Amtrak** (☎ 800-872-7245) can carry you from San Francisco to Truckee on the north side of the lake.

The major resorts of the region offer shuttle services between pickup points and area lodgings. The 45-minute drive from Reno to the South Shore can be made via local shuttles.

One low-cost public transportation option is the **Lake Lapper** (☎ 916-542-5900) which circles the lake. For $5/day you get unlimited use.

When traveling by car to Lake Tahoe in the winter, always carry chains for your tires. Without them you won't be allowed to proceed. Severe snow conditions may temporarily close some Interstate 80 and Highway 50 passes, but highway crews will soon open them. For road conditions, crucial information if you drive here in winter, call the **Caltrans Highway Information Network** *(☎ 800-427-7623). For weather information, ☎ 510-562-8573.*

Yosemite

The gateway to Yosemite is **Merced**, a town in the Central Valley of California. From Merced, take Highway 140 east into Yosemite Valley, which is open all year. Merced is about three hours by car from San Francisco or five hours from Los Angeles. Allow another hour for the drive in along narrow, winding roads to the park. Train and bus connections can also be made from Merced into the park. Fresno, a larger city near Merced, has a commuter airport and several regularly scheduled carriers. From Fresno, Highway 41 proceeds to the southern entrance of the park, 36 miles from Yosemite Valley. The southern entrance is famous for the Wawona area, where giant sequoia trees are the main attraction.

Once in Yosemite you don't need a car because the well-organized shuttle buses take you about. Much effort now focuses on reducing the automobile impact in Yosemite. Tours can take you to distant areas of the park.

Mammoth

East from Yosemite, getting to Mammoth by car takes about six hours from Los Angeles or San Francisco.

The drive from Los Angeles crosses the Mojave Desert and then moves up Highway 395 on the east side of the Sierra.

The route from San Francisco is Highway 120 across the Tioga Pass in Yosemite, open only during summer, or Highway 50 to Tahoe and south on Highway 395, open all year. Visitors from San Francisco enjoy driving different routes coming and going to add scenic interest.

Both drives from Los Angeles and San Francisco rate high for traveler satisfaction. From San Francisco, for example, the crossing of Yosemite's high country is a mix of granite starkness and the lushness of Tuolumne Meadows. The Highway 395 route emphasizes the drier side of the mountains, the east side with its cattle-grazing flatlands, small wood-frame towns such as Markleeville, trout fishing along the East Carson River, alternate chaparral terrain and dense aspen groves, some rapid eight-percent-grade descents, and the smell of sage.

Air flights into Mammoth are through **Mountain Air Express** (☎ 800-788-4247) from Long Beach, San Jose and Reno during the winter ski season. Charter flights may be booked through **Mammoth Air Charter**; ☎ 760-934-4279.

Gold Country

To reach the Gold Country, you can start from San Francisco, 150 miles to the west, or Sacramento, which is closer. The most direct route to Columbia (a good starting point for a tour of Gold Rush towns) is east from Stockton on Highway 4. Highway 49 runs north and south through the heart of Gold Country. Without a car it is extremely difficult to see the Gold Country.

Getting there today is easier than it was for the miners, who had three alternatives. From the eastern US they could sail 15,000 miles around Cape Horn. Panama offered a shorter, but hotter and malaria-ridden crossing. The prospective miner could also push overland on wagon train paths, but these were poorly marked. Weather and Indians were equally hostile. The bravado of the mining era can be read in the motto, "The cowards never started, and the weaklings died on the way."

Information Sources

Lake Tahoe

For information and lodging prospects at the north end of the lake contact:

North Lake Tahoe Resort Association, ☎ 916-583-3494 or 800-824-6348, Box 5459, Tahoe City, CA 96145; Web site www.tahoeguide.com.

For the same information at the south end contact:

Lake Tahoe Visitors Authority, ☎ 916-544-5050 or 800-288-2463, 1156 Ski Run Boulevard, South Lake Tahoe, CA 96150; Web site www.virtualtahoe.com.

For hiking and wilderness backpacking in the area, especially in Desolation Wilderness, contact:

The Forest Supervisor, **US Forest Service**, ☎ 916-573-2600, Lake Tahoe Basin Management Unit, 870 Emerald Bay Road, Suite 1, South Lake Tahoe, CA 96150.

The Sierra/Gold Country

Reno, the fly-in gateway, is an hour northeast of Tahoe. Major lodgings in Reno offer shuttles to the slopes. For information, ☎ 800-367-7366 or write **Reno-Sparks Convention and Visitor Authority**, PO Box 837, Reno, NV 89504. Major airlines fly into the Reno Cannon International Airport.

If driving to or within the region, accurate road information, especially in times of heavy snowfall, comes from Caltrans (☎ 916-445-7623 or 800-427-7623). Always carry chains.

Yosemite

For Yosemite, contact **Yosemite Concession Services**-Reservations, ☎ 209-252-4848, 5410 East Home Avenue, Fresno, CA 93727; Web site www.yosemite-park.com.

The park service can be reached by writing to:

The Public Information Office Yosemite National Park, ☎ 209-372-0200, PO Box 577, Yosemite, CA 95389; Web site www.nps.gov/yose.

The park concessionaire manages most park information and all reservations. They distribute a brochure on the park and accommodations information. They can also send you information about activities, such as horseback riding or pack trips. Most campsites in the park can be reserved at ☎ 800-436-7275; and advance reservations are suggested. If you stay at a lodging in Yosemite, try to bring food for lunch or you may have to wait in a long cafeteria line while you could be out enjoying nature.

For reservations at Yosemite's five **High Sierra Camps**, contact the High Sierra Desk, Yosemite Reservations, 5410 E. Home Avenue, Fresno, CA 93727. Cost includes accommodations at tent cabins as well as breakfast and dinner. Due to high demand, applications are accepted mid-October through November and a lottery is held in mid-December. The camps are open late June through Labor Day, weather permitting.

A group active in publishing nature literature on the park and in leading hikes is the **Yosemite Natural History Association**, Box 545, Yosemite National Park, CA 95389. Write ahead for a list of literature.

Mammoth Lakes

For the Mammoth Lakes area, contact the **Mammoth Lakes Visitors Bureau**, ☎ 760-934-2712 or 800-367-6572, PO Box 48, Mammoth Lakes, CA 93546; Web site www.visitmammoth.com. One attraction there is Devils Postpile, a geologic phenomenon of tall basaltic columns. For a brochure on Devils Postpile at any time of the year, write: Superintendent, **Devils Postpile National Monument** (☎ 760-872-4881, 785 North Main Street, Suite E, Bishop, CA 93514). This is the only winter contact, November-May. The monument also has a summer office and phone at the monument itself: Devils Postpile National Monument, PO Box 501, Mammoth Lakes, CA 93546; ☎ 760-934-2289.

The Forest Service manages an interpretive center at Mono Lake for the **Mono Basin National Forest Scenic Area** (☎ 760-647-3044). For information on hiking and camping throughout the Forest Service area, contact **Mammoth Visitor Center Ranger Station**, ☎ 600-924-5500, PO Box 148, Mammoth Lakes, CA 93546.

Gold Country

Sacramento Convention and Visitors Bureau, ☎ 916-264-7777, 1421 K Street, Sacramento, CA 95814; Web site /www.sacto.org/cvb.

To request a copy of the *California Gold Discovery to Statehood Sesquicentennial Calendar*, ☎ 916-653-9599 or write to 914 Capitol Mall, Room 217, Sacramento, CA 95814.

For information on any California state park, such as the historic parks in the Gold Country, contact:

California State Parks Information, ☎ 916-653-6995, PO Box 942896, Sacramento, CA 94296-0001; Web site ceres.ca.gov/parks/travel. html.

For a California Visitors Guide, a state map, and a celebrations guide, contact:

California Tourism at ☎ 800-862-2543 or **California Division of Tourism**, 801 K Street, Suite 1600, Sacramento, CA 95812.

Within the Gold Country, each county and city has its own chamber of commerce/visitors bureau. They can

The Sierra/Gold Country

send detailed information on their area's lodging, restaurants, and attractions. Moving south to north, the resources are:

Yosemite-Mariposa County Chamber of Commerce, ☎ 209-966-2456 or 800-208-2434, 5158 Highway 140, Mariposa, CA 95338.

Tuolumne County Visitors Bureau, ☎ 209-533-4420 or 800-446-1333, 55 W. Stockton Road, Sonora, CA 95370.

Amador County Chamber of Commerce, ☎ 209-223-0350 or 800-649-4988, 125 Peek Street, Jackson, CA 95642.

El Dorado County Chamber of Commerce, ☎ 916-621-5885 or 800-457-6279, 542 Main Street, Placerville, CA 95667.

Placer County Visitor Information Center, ☎ 916-887-2111, 13464 Lincoln Way, Auburn, CA 95603.

Grass Valley/Nevada County Chamber of Commerce, ☎ 916-273-4667 or 800-655-4667, 248 Mill Street, Grass Valley, CA 95945.

Nevada City Chamber of Commerce, ☎ 916-265-2692, 132 Main Street, Nevada City, CA 95959.

■ Touring

Lake Tahoe

As early as 1870, Lake Tahoe flourished as a resort. Tycoon **Lucky Baldwin** built a sizable lodge and took guests around the lake in his 168-foot steamer. Early visitors caught legendary numbers of trout and kokanee salmon.

By the 1920s, skiing became popular in winter, especially when the federal government committed to keeping the major roads open over the high passes.

The Forest Service is a major information source for all kinds of year round touring information and adventure travel in the Tahoe region. Their summer headquarters is the **Forest Service Visitor**

Lake Tahoe Area

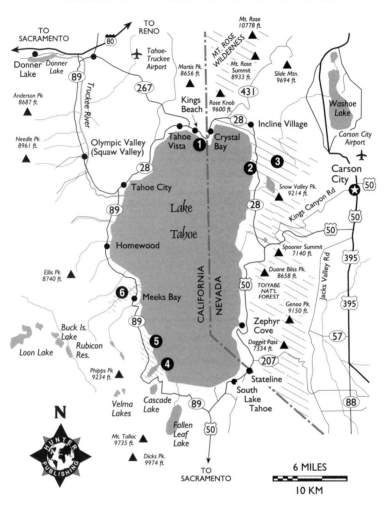

1. Kings Beach State Recreation Area
2. Sand Harbor Beach State Recreation Area
3. Lake Tahoe Nevada State Park
4. Emerald Bay State Park
5. D.L. Bliss State Park
6. Sugar Pine Point State Park

Center on Emerald Bay Road, ☎ 916-573-2674, not far from their all-year headquarters at 870 Emerald Bay Road, ☎ 916-573-2694. The summer Visitor Center typically opens Memorial Day and continues full-time through September, plus weekends-only in October. One interesting aspect of the Visitor Center is the **Stream Profile Chamber**, where you view fish swimming through a diverted section of the stream. This is especially intriguing in autumn as the Kokanee salmon in Lake Tahoe swim upstream to spawn. There is a quarter-mile loop trail, the **Rainbow Trail**, that shows a wetlands environment. At the Visitor Center, or the all-year headquarters, you can purchase maps of the region. The best one to begin with would be the *Lake Tahoe Basin Management Unit map*, showing the overall area. More specialized maps, such as one for hiking the **Desolation Wilderness**, can also be obtained. The Visitor Center interprets the human history of the region, circa 1890-1920, at the **Tallac Historic Site**, giving you a glimpse of the early tourism story in Lake Tahoe.

In summer, tour the lake by car and enjoy the outdoor activities of camping, hiking, and fishing. Because the lake never freezes, fishing continues through the winter. In winter the skiing is excellent throughout the area. In recent years cross-country has become popular at several locations, such as Kirkwood. Snow may fall in the region from October to June.

Touring Near Emerald Bay

The most celebrated scenic area, found at the southwest corner of the lake, is Emerald Bay. The contrast between the blue lake and the mountains rising 4,000 feet over the waterway has great appeal. Two attractive state parks, Bliss and Sugar Pine Point, stretch along the waterfront and offer excellent camping, hiking, and picnicking. **D.L. Bliss State Park** (☎ 916-525-7277) consists of 1,237 acres between Meeks and Emerald bays, with a sandy beach at Rubicon Point. The roadway along Emerald Bay often puts you high above the water, a perfect vantage point for sweeping vistas. If you park at Inspiration Point, you can also hike to an intriguing Norse-style structure called **Vikingsholm Castle**, a 38-room re-creation of a ninth-century Viking fortress. Eagle Falls and Sugar Pine Point State Park are other good places near Emerald Bay to hike, picnic, or view the lake. **Sugar Pine Point**

State Park is a dense 200-acre grove of large sugar pine trees, known for their long, slender cones. A historic Tahoe summer estate known as the **Ehrman Mansion** is worth a visit. The park is open all year and has become a favorite winter cross-country skiing site.

The Gaming Scene

The great indoor sport here is gambling, nurtured on the Nevada side at Reno and Crystal Bay on the North Shore and at Stateline on the South Shore. Nevada declared gambling legal in 1931. One-armed bandits, or a variety of gaming tables, nightclub acts, and fabulous buffets, such as the one at Harrah's, all invite the traveler. The gambling world flourishes around the clock, every day of the year, oblivious to mere diurnal or seasonal changes.

South Shore has a denser populace than the North Shore, including the major gambling establishments, such as Caesar's, Harvey's, Harrah's, and Horizon.

Yosemite

The history of major interest in Yosemite is not the human time frame but the **geological story**. Over eons the forces of glacial activity have scraped away at the granite rock, exposing the faces such as **El Capitan** and **Half Dome**, which stun the imagination with their size. The rushing Merced River has carried rock fragments and silt from higher mountain areas to the floor of the valley. Prior to the glacial periods, Yosemite was a sea with extensive sedimentary deposits. Gradually, geological forces of uplift thrust the sea bed to its present elevation.

Miwok and Mono Lake Paiute Native Americans established villages along the Merced River that runs through Yosemite Valley. The Native Americans called the Valley *Ahwahnee*, which apparently meant "gaping mouth." They gathered acorns and seeds, fished for trout, and hunted deer. Except for a period of years around 1800 when a disease known as "the fatal black sickness" forced them out of the area, the Native Americans lived peacefully within the Yosemite Valley. Not until much later, after the Gold Rush, did the white man stumble upon the area.

The Sierra/Gold Country

The first white men arrived in 1851. They were militiamen of the ragtag Mariposa Battalion, a group of miner-soldiers who attempted to establish order in the gold region. The first group included the militiaman whose thoughts approximated those of so many later visitors, nature lovers rather than soldiers. The Mariposa Battalion entered the Valley in pursuit of Ahwahneechee Native Americans who had retreated there after stealing mining supplies. It could be said that the battalion made a discovery in the realm of nature as astonishing as the discovery of gold in 1848.

Founding of Yosemite

The rapidity with which Yosemite was fenced, farmed, and logged by settlers alarmed the public, especially because the giant sequoias were at risk of being cut down. Public pressure on the California legislature created the **Yosemite Grant in 1864**. This was historically important because it was the first effort in the US to spare a forest area from commercial development and preserve it as public property. In 1864, President Lincoln signed legislation that gave Yosemite to California as a public trust. Yosemite was not the first National Park, an honor that fell to Yellowstone, but it was the first federally mandated park. Yosemite became a National Park in 1890.

John Muir's Legacy

Your best guide to Yosemite is the Scotsman John Muir, who came to California via Wisconsin and devoted himself to writing persuasive articles and books about conserving California's Sierra Nevada, or snowy mountains. He was the founding father of the US environmental movement and of the Sierra Club, which he started in 1892. Wilderness forests throughout the country were in danger at the time. Muir's ability to coin a phrase is well known. To him Yosemite was a "vast celestial city, not clothed with light but wholly composed of it."

Muir combined an exuberant feeling for nature, thorough competence as a botanist, and an apostolic fervor about preserving the rapidly disappearing wilderness. On a famous 1903 campout in Yosemite Park with Theodore Roosevelt, he reinforced and nurtured the president's own conservation ethic. As president, Roosevelt set aside five national parks, 23 national monuments, and 148 million acres as national forests.

"Wilderness is a necessity," Muir wrote. "Mountain parks and forest reservations are useful not only as fountains of timber and irrigating rivers, but as fountains of life."

> Prior to exploring Yosemite, read Muir's book, *The Yosemite*. The book goes in and out of print, but a library or bookstore can locate a copy.

Exploring the Valley

Start at the **Visitor Center** and take advantage of its excellent selection of guidebooks and maps. Rangers will suggest outings. Behind the Visitor Center is a re-creation of a Miwok-Paiute Native American village, depicting how the Native Americans lived in the valley, harvesting the black oak acorns for food, hunting deer, and living in bark structures. During summer months, various living history programs on Native American life are conducted, sometimes by actual Miwok descendants.

Here are three of our favorite beginning outings:

- Drive or tram around the valley to get a view of all the different falls. **Yosemite Falls** is the most obvious and dominant. Upper Yosemite drops 1,430 feet in one abrupt fall, and Lower Yosemite Falls drops another 320 feet. If you add up the intermediate cascades, Yosemite Falls drops a total of 2,425 feet, making it one of the world's longest waterfalls. Other falls to see are **Vernal**, with a 317-foot drop, **Illilouette** at 370 feet, **Bridalveil** at 620 feet, and **Ribbon** at 1,612 feet. Each has its own character, with Bridalveil, for example, a subtle diaphanous counterpoint to the pounding force of Yosemite Falls or the thundering power of Vernal Falls. See the falls both during the day and at night when there is a full moon. The month is also important. Falls are at their greatest force from May to July and then decline until the autumn rains bring them renewed runoff.

- Walk up to **Mirror Lake**. The walk is lovely and the setting, an alpine lake quickly silting in due to natural succession, illustrates the geologic forces at work today. You can also take the tram up to Mirror Lake, but no cars are allowed. The tram system continues to expand and roads in the park have been made into a one-way loop. The Master Plan, adopted in 1980 to guide the development of the park, calls for fewer cars and the removal of as many structures as possible. However, this is a slow process.

- Walk up to **Nevada Falls**. Part of the pleasure of this walk is the ever-changing vistas presented of such familiar landmarks as Yosemite Falls or Half Dome. During this trek you begin to appreciate the way more ambitious walks in the high country can open up engaging vistas. Here you see the two rock formations of Yosemite that surpass all others in their dimensions. **El Capitan** rises 3,464 feet above the valley floor, and is one of the world's largest rocks. At the east end of the valley looms **Half Dome**, rising 8,800 feet above sea level.

Seasons in Yosemite

Each season brings its special rewards to a Yosemite visitor. Indeed, there are connoisseurs of Yosemite who spend a lifetime making trips here at different times of the year. Spring is a time of

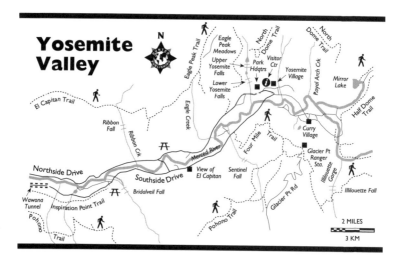

green foliage, wildflowers, and the roar of waterfalls. In summer the sun is highest, lighting the far reaches of the canyons, stimulating plant growth. Summer also brings the major crush of the four million annual visitors, straining the carrying capacity of the valley. In autumn you will encounter herds of deer passing through the valley on their way to winter foraging grounds at lower elevations. The oak tree leaves turn gold and the sumac attains a bright red. In winter the white mantle of the valley and the heavy snowpack at the upper elevations lend a crystalline aspect to the region.

Managing Yosemite

As a further move to reduce the need for your auto, the concessionaire and park service have organized an increasing number of paid tours through parts of the park. You can take free trams through Yosemite Valley at any time, with a tram passing the main check points every 10 minutes. You can also take a paid, guided tram tour of the valley with a naturalist. Other tours take you by bus to the magnificent overlook at Glacier Point, to Wawona to see the Big Trees, the sequoias, and to the high country of Tuolumne Meadows. An extensive number of free hikes, led by naturalists and rangers, occur each day on the floor of the valley. Tour schedules are published in the free *Yosemite Guide* that is available everywhere in the park. Artist trips, photography outings, bicycle rentals (for the nine paved miles of bike trails in the valley), rock climbing (with a knowledgeable guide), and horseback riding are just some of the summer activities. Ranger- or naturalist-led evening programs occur nightly at the lodgings and at the campgrounds in the valley.

If you are camping in Yosemite Valley, it's important not to tempt the bears with carelessly exposed food. At night be sure that all food is securely covered, stored in an ice chest or other solid container, and placed in the trunk of your vehicle. Failure to properly manage your food can lead to citations and fines. Careless campers and earlier garbage disposal practices have conditioned bears to seek human food.

The Sierra/Gold Country

Mammoth Lakes

Everywhere you look in the region, the pleasure of mountain scenery greets you. Mammoth Mountain dominates the eastern side of the Sierra. A gondola ride to the 11,053-foot summit, summer or winter, reveals a panoramic vista. Another favorite view, near Mammoth Mountain, is the overlook to the Minarets, spires to the west, which looked like Moslem churches to the early namers. This sawtooth effect was created by the freezing and thawing of water in the stone, gradually cracking off the sides of the rocks. From the Minaret Vista you get a sweeping view of the eastern Sierra, including the start of the San Joaquin River.

The choice scenic area is compact, taking in **Mammoth Mountain**, the **Minarets Vista**, and **Devils Postpile National Monument**. Early morning light offers the most satisfying time to see the Minarets from the vista turnout between Mammoth Mountain and the National Monument. A shuttle bus then takes you into the National Monument, where short and level hiking trails lead to the two principal features, Postpile and Rainbow Falls. Postpile amounts to geometric, blue-gray, basalt columns, 40-60 feet high, formed when a vertical lava flow cooled quickly. Geologists estimate this occurred about 100,000 years ago. **Rainbow Falls** is a sharp 101-foot drop into the San Joaquin River, where the sun creates a rainbow in the spray. The optimal time for viewing both Postpile and Rainbow Falls is early afternoon.

The town of **Mammoth Lakes** has an alpine lakes district on its edge, which is a pleasure to drive or walk around. The lakes are popular camping places. Campers tend to be fishermen eager to catch the stocked rainbow and brown trout.

The terrain north from Mammoth to June lakes contains one of the largest forest stands of Jeffrey Pine, noted for its vanilla-smelling bark. Walking through these stands on a warm summer afternoon is reminiscent of a bakery.

The morning sun on the mountains to the west and the evening light on the eastern peaks put a glow on each day at Mammoth.

Mono Lake

Mono Lake, just north of Mammoth, is the major natural history attraction in the region. The Forest Service, which has jurisdiction over the lake, maintains a major interpretive center at the south edge of the lake. Be sure to stop in to see the exhibits, get maps, and learn about the lake, especially the tufa spires, those other-worldly formations of minerals that now extend above the surface of the lake. The spires are visible due to the receding level of the water. The tufa towers are limestone deposits created from calcium-bearing freshwater springs bubbling up through the lake's carbon-rich, alkaline water.

The best place to see the tufa formations is at the **South Tufa** site. Rangers on duty lead periodic hikes there. You'll be amazed at the density of the non-biting insects, called brine flies, which make up the base of the animal food chain here, allowing for abundant bird life. More than 70 species of migratory birds feed on the flies. The populations of the migrating birds are huge, including about 150,000 phalaropes in July-August and 800,000 eared grebes from August to October.

Brine flies and brine shrimp attain explosive population levels at Mono Lake. The Native Americans of the area, called the Kuze-dika, enhanced their diet by eating the pupae of the flies.

Efforts to save Mono Lake from being drained by the Los Angeles Department of Water and Power, which had purchased the area water rights, eventually led to a Supreme Court-mandated settlement calling for restoration of inbound streams and stabilization of the surface level of the lake. A higher lake level provides more protection from predators to birds nesting on the islands and insures that the alkalinity of the water, which has already doubled, will not change further, affecting the ecosystem.

The main political controversy in the Mammoth Lakes region was, is, and always will be over water and the rights to control it.

Gold Country/Sacramento

The essence of the Gold Country during the sesquicentennial period can be seen at four special state historic parks.

The actual world of the Gold Rush was one of hardship. The miners were willing to endure hours of tedious work in icy Sierra streams to secure a few nuggets. For every lucky miner, a hundred failed. Costs were high, with a slice of bread going for a dollar, a

The Gold Country

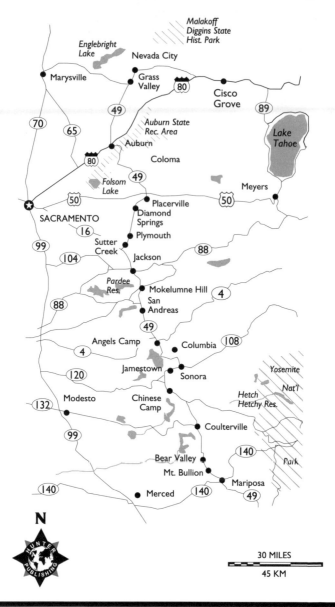

Malakoff
Diggins State
Hist. Park

Englebright
Lake

Nevada City

Marysville

Grass
Valley

80

Cisco
Grove

89

49

Auburn State
Rec. Area

Auburn

70

65

80

Coloma

49

Lake
Tahoe

Folsom
Lake

Meyers

50

Placerville

50

SACRAMENTO

Diamond
Springs

16

Plymouth

99

Sutter
Creek

Jackson

88

104

Pardee
Res.

Mokelumne Hill

4

88

San
Andreas

49

Angels Camp

Columbia

108

4

Jamestown

Sonora

Yosemite

120

Modesto

Chinese
Camp

Hetch
Hetchy Res.

Nat'l

132

Coulterville

99

Bear Valley

140

Park

Mt. Bullion

140

Mariposa

Merced

140

49

N

30 MILES

45 KM

shirt for $50, and a plain shovel for as much as $100. The enduring wealth of the mining era rested in the pockets of shopkeepers, who could charge what the market would bear for their goods. Illustrious California names, such as Mark Hopkins, started their fortunes here, selling hardware and vegetables.

The mining era turned brutal for those not certified as white Americans. Prejudice and avarice combined as the white Americans physically forced off or taxed off the Mexican, Chilean, and Chinese miners. Miners from other countries played major roles in the development of the Gold Country and the west in general.

Mexican miners from the state of Sonora, with their considerable experience in silver mining, were among the first to work the southern area of the Gold Country. The name Sonora on the map or the name Mariposa, Spanish for butterfly, suggest their presence. The numerous Chinese miners later became the work force that built the railroads over the Sierra. In 1856 the mining town of Chinese Camp was populated by about 5,000 Chinese miners.

Now the setting is tranquil, the small towns pride themselves on their underdeveloped status, and you can almost feel cares slough off as you drive around these foothills of the Sierra Nevada Mountains. The richness of the region today is measured by its natural beauty, its abundant fruit agriculture, rather than by its gold.

Coloma, Where Marshall Found Gold

The **Marshall Gold Discovery State Historic Park** (☎ 916-622-3470) celebrates how the Gold Rush began. The site at Coloma is where lumberman James Marshall slept and lived while he sawed logs for John Sutter's Sacramento settlement. At the site, the famous logging chute has been re-created. It was here that Marshall came running back to his workers with the news, on that fateful date, January 24, 1848. After finding some gold grains in the settled water he cried out, "Boys, I believe I've found gold."

Both Sutter and Marshall ran extensive tests on the metal and sought to suppress the news once they learned the truth. But the story of gold was too enthralling to keep secret. When the rush of miners arrived, wealth eluded Marshall, who died an impoverished and disappointed man, but others were luckier.

The Sierra/Gold Country

Near Columbia someone had the good fortune to find a solid gold nugget that weighed 195 pounds. The search for the Mother Lode, that vein of pure gold, was on.

What is impressive about the Marshall Gold Discovery State Historic Park is that the park preserves the entire town area. Most of the buildings are now mere memories, but a few remain, such as the Robert Bell Store. The Coloma Schoolhouse, a white wooden structure, shows what a thriving waterfront community once existed here. The Visitor Center has a museum with examples of large gold nuggets, such as miners dreamed of, and a restored Concord stagecoach, the plushest of the bone-jarring devices that brought some folks overland to California.

The sawmill has been re-created on the grounds near the river. Other gold-mining paraphernalia on display include stamp mills used to pulverize rock into more manageable sizes, from which the grains of gold could be extracted. Recreational gold panning occurs across the river, west of the bridge. On a hill above the site is a statue of James Marshall pointing down to where he discovered gold. Hikers enjoy the Monroe Ridge Trail leading away from the statue site. From high points on the ridge you are rewarded with a panoramic view of the valley.

The Gold Rush transformed the area within a few months. By the summer of 1848, over 2,000 miners were sifting gravel from the stream. By 1849 Coloma boasted a population of 10,000 souls.

Columbia, Where the Little Guy Found Nuggets

Columbia State Historic Park (☎ 209-532-0150), just north of Sonora off Highway 49, is an entire Gold Rush town preserved and restored. You can actually pan for gold today at the Matelot Mining Co. or watch a demonstration of how it was done. You can peer in through the iron shutters of the Wells Fargo Express Building and ride one of the stages that carried $87 million in gold dust back to San Francisco. Along your route a robber, similar to the legendary Black Bart, may relieve the stage of its fortune.

Strolling about Columbia, you get a sense of what life was like for the 15,000 miners who lived here during the period when a lucky miner could pan surface nuggets from streams. A museum in the brick Knapp Building exhibits the different mining techniques. At the Old Franco cabin you'll see what a typical miner's life was like. A walk through town will take you by a Mexican fandango dancing hall, a blacksmith shop, and the 1861 schoolhouse.

The Columbia Actors Repertory performs year-round at the Fallon House Theater. Columbia is a major festival site in the Gold Country, with the most prominent annual event, a **Fireman's Muster**, occurring in May. During the muster you can see old firefighting equipment. The passionate practitioners of old-time firefighting skills compete against each other in bucket brigades, water pumping contests, ladder raisings, and hose-cart relays. Fire was a major fear in the tinder-dry wooden Gold Rush towns. Other festivals here are the Columbia Diggins in June, a July 4 Celebration, and a Miner's Christmas.

The town had 5,000 inhabitants in 1854, making it California's second most populous community. Four banks, eight hotels, two fire companies, 53 stores, and 40 saloons flourished here.

The Empire Mine, Richest Gold Mine in California

The Empire Mine State Historic Park (☎ 916-273-8522), the richest gold mine in California, is intriguing both for what you see and don't see. Above ground at the Visitor Center in Grass Valley, you gaze upon some marvelous examples of gold in quartz rock. Outside, you stroll the landscaped grounds of mine owner William Bourn. The architectural gem is Bourn's **Empire Cottage**, a sumptuous stone building designed by noted architect Willis Polk. Adjacent to the cottage is a rose garden filled with blooms developed from ancient times to 1929. Above ground you can also glimpse the remains of the mining apparatus, the machine shops, and the stamp mill, used here for 106 years of operations. You can peer a few feet into the shaft of the mine, where the miners went down and the ore came out.

What you don't see (but can envision after you have viewed a scale model of the underground mine in the Visitor Center) are the 367 miles of tunnels, sometimes descending more than a mile and sprawling at all levels over a five-square-mile area. The underground is huge. The story of the Empire Mine is the later phase in the Gold Country saga, when the serious gold to be found lay in

The Sierra/Gold Country

deep rock veins, requiring massive capital to exploit. The secretly built model of all the underground tunnels was constructed by the mine engineers for the express purpose of identifying the veins of gold and plotting where to tunnel next. Color-coded wire indicates the relative richness of the ore in each tunnel. Once you've seen the model, you can appreciate the maze-like unseen world below ground. The mineshaft, beyond a glimpse of the first few feet, is now closed to the public. At the Empire Mine some 5.8 million ounces of gold were removed, worth $1.7 billion today.

Gold Country Personalities

Personalities have played a major role in the legends of the Gold Country. Aside from Twain, two of the most colorful were entertainer Lola Montez and robber Black Bart.

Lola Montez, who flourished in Grass Valley, arrived from Europe, where she had been the mistress of Ludwig of Bavaria among others. Lola intrigued miners with her noted Spider Dance, during which fake, cork spiders were shaken from her dress. She was famous as a beauty and as a singer.

Black Bart, otherwise respectable San Francisco citizen Charles E. Bolton, became a Robin Hood folk figure in California. Bart politely conducted 28 robberies before tripping up. His mode of operation was always the same. He waited alone, without even a getaway horse, along the road at an uphill spot where the horses slowed. His face was covered with a cloth flour sack that had holes cut for his eyes. He carried a blanket roll with an ax in it. With a shotgun (which he never fired and which was later found to be empty) Bart quietly asked the stage driver, "Would you throw down your treasure box, sir?" Bart never disturbed the passengers, except when he collected all their firearms; his argument was only with Wells Fargo, a company that he taunted with doggerel. With the ax, Bart would then cut open the box, remove the loot, and somehow disappear on foot into the woods. On his 29th robbery attempt a passenger, who had been let off the stage to do some hunting, surprised Bart as he was opening the treasure box. Bart disappeared, but dropped a handkerchief with his laundry mark that revealed his identity when it was traced to a San Francisco laundry.

Malakoff, The Environmental Sin

A final state historic park is the scar and eyesore of the Gold Country, both visually and historically. The site is the **Malakoff Diggins State Historic Park** (☎ 916-265-2740), 26 miles northeast of Nevada City. You can get there via Tyler-Foote Crossing Road from Highway 49.

Hydraulic mining was the technique used to seek gold at Malakoff, the world's largest hydraulic gold mine. Huge nozzles, called monitors, were connected with elaborate ditches and flumes that diverted mountain streams. The nozzles blasted away at the gravel hillsides, washing down the soil. The washed pit at Malakoff is fully 7,000 feet long and 3,000 feet wide. As the gravel washed through sluices, the heavier gold could be separated. The environmental disaster was due to all the silt that remained in the water and proceeded downstream. Farms were flooded by clogged rivers as the streambeds filled in with silt. Thirty-nine inches of mud accumulated at the bottom in parts of San Francisco Bay. The sight of a core sample of the Bay bottom, with the mud finally giving way to oyster shells, suggests the magnitude of the silting. Legal curbs on hydraulic mining began in 1884.

Today the park encompasses 3,000 acres of oak woodlands, pine forests, and meadows. The white wooden buildings of the North Bloomfield townsite, located in the park, have been restored and refurnished to show what life was like here in the 1870s.

Gold Country Museums

Aside from these major historical parks, there are dozens of small museums. Consider these on your itinerary:

The **Mariposa Museum and History Center** (☎ 209-966-2924, 12th and Jessie streets), in Mariposa, includes a stamp mill used to crush rock in search of gold, a monitor nozzle, and several horse-drawn vehicles from the mining era. While in town, be sure to see the stately Mariposa County Courthouse (☎ 209-966-2456) the oldest courthouse still in use in California. The white-frame structure was built in 1854 and cost $12,000. You can tour the inside, including the courtroom with its original furniture.

The Sierra/Gold Country

The **Tuolumne County Museum and History Center**, on West Bradford Avenue in Sonora, was once the county jail. Like many Gold Country structures, it was consumed in flames in the 1850s and then rebuilt. Fire was the scourge of the hastily built wooden mining towns, which explains why the fire company was such an important civil and social entity. The museum (☎ 209-532-1317) shows period clothing and historic photographs as well as the restored jail.

The **Amador County Museum** (☎ 209-223-6386), on Church Street in Jackson, resides in the historic Brown house, a brick structure from 1859. The museum's tour de force is an intricate working scale model of local mine structures. Among the museum holdings are clothing, household utensils, furniture, musical instruments, and literary evidence of mining era culture. The men who came to California to work in the mines were often the educated and prosperous sons of strong families. Sometimes the second son, who could not inherit the family land or business, was sent to seek his fortune in California.

The **El Dorado County Historical Museum**, at the county fairgrounds west of Placerville, boasts a restored Wells Fargo stagecoach, plus a re-creation of a turn-of-the-century store and kitchen. At the museum (☎ 916-621-5865) many of the holdings can be seen scattered around the surrounding grounds. The artifacts include a bark teepee structure such as the local Nisean Indians lived in, old and rusted mining equipment, aging stage coaches, and railroad cars in various stages of disintegration.

The **Placer County Historical Museum** in Auburn is housed in an architectural gem of the Gold Country, the Placer County Courthouse. This gold-domed structure stands forth regally, as befits the town through which the Central Pacific Railroad headed east into the mountains. Within the museum, be sure to see the gold nugget display in the gift shop and the elaborate Indian basketry in several display cases. If a docent is on duty, ask to be shown the historic Sheriff's Office. Inside you'll see the jail ledgers in which were kept the names of all those incarcerated, including a line describing their offense. Beyond the courthouse, stroll Auburn to see its antique stores and the statue to Claude Chama, the founding miner. The Placer County Visitor Information Center is east of town along Highway 80 at the Foresthill

Exit, 13460 Lincoln Way, Suite A, Auburn, CA 95603, ☎ 916-887-2111, or ☎ 800-427-6463. The Visitor Center is a thorough information source for adventure travel in the region, especially for hiking, rafting, and skiing. Placer County extends all the way from the Gold Country to Lake Tahoe.

The **Sierra County Museum** in Downieville (☎ 916-993-6900 or 800-200-4949) is a stone structure of mortarless schist, with heavy iron doors and shutters. Such buildings withstood the frequent fires of the mining era. Built in 1852, the structure was originally a Chinese store and gambling house.

Sacramento, En Route to the Gold Country

Sacramento is worth a stop for its **California State Railroad Museum** (see *Railroading*) in Old Sacramento and for a visit to Sutter's Fort (27th and L streets, ☎ 916-445-4422).

The Railroad Museum is in the restored **Old Sacramento** area along the waterfront, where most of the miners and supplies going to the mines landed from 1849 on. You could spend a half-day browsing in the Old Sacramento area.

Nearby is the California **State Capitol** building, a stately gold-domed structure at 10th Street and Capitol Avenue. From this building flow the laws that govern California, an entity with roughly the eighth largest gross national product on Earth, depending on how you're counting. The budget to govern the state ran to $67 billion dollars in 1997.

The most famous and historic building in Sacramento is **Sutter's Fort,** the restored adobe compound that was Swiss entrepreneur John Sutter's agricultural fiefdom in the decade before the Gold Rush. Costumed re-creators show how weaving or blacksmithing occurred there in the pioneer period. Adjacent to Sutter's Fort is the **California State Indian Museum**, preserving many artifacts from the first Californians. Sutter's Fort is at 27th and L streets.

The Sierra/Gold Country

■ Adventures

On Wheels

Scenic Driving: Lake Tahoe

 The spectacular drive here is the 72-mile circle of the lake, described in *Touring*. The drive will take a full day if you allow time for lookouts, a picnic, and some hikes.

One example of a stop on the lake is **Ponderosa Ranch**. Ponderosa, which is in Incline Village, was the ranch of the TV show *Bonanza*. The grounds are now a western-themed amusement park. This is one of the places in the Tahoe basin where you can go horseback riding.

Only a few miles north of Lake Tahoe lies **Donner Summit** and **Donner Lake**. Here the ill-fated Donner Party of 1846-47 passed a severe winter. Roughly half of the 89 persons in the emigrant group perished; those who survived did so partly by eating those who succumbed to cold and starvation. A monument at Donner Memorial State Park stands on the site of the Breen family shack. A stone base of the monument stretches up 22 feet, the height of the snow that winter. The **Emigrant Trail Museum** in the park displays Indian and Donner Party memorabilia, an excellent introduction to the early history of the area.

The Nevada mining towns, where silver was the prize, are also interesting to explore. The main destination is **Virginia City**, where the famous Comstock Lode of silver was discovered in 1859. After an intense decade of mining, the economic prosperity in the Tahoe region centered on lumber from 1870-1920. Tourism is the current major industry for Virginia City and the city of Reno, a thriving gambling and entertainment center. Carson City, the Nevada capital, is worth a visit for its elegant statehouse, history museum, and Victorian mansions.

Scenic Driving: Yosemite

Three scenic drives will complete your initial Yosemite experience. The excursions take you out of Yosemite Valley, but keep you within Yosemite National Park.

To Glacier Point

To see the entire valley from an elevated vista, drive or take the bus to the view turnoff on the road to Glacier Point and Wawona. This turnoff, just before the Wawona Tunnel, presents one of the most famous vistas in the park, rivaling the view from Glacier Point. From this elevated position you enjoy a sweeping panorama of all the major landforms in the valley. You have an excellent perspective here on the glacial geological forces that scoured out the upper part of the valley, peeling off the granite layers from the mountains and depositing a moraine of rocky debris at the western end. Three successive waves of glaciers slid across the granite face of Yosemite, polishing Half Dome and El Capitan to their present smoothness, with the most recent glacier retreating only 10,000 years ago.

The drive all the way to Glacier Point is possible only from June to October because of snow. A view from Glacier Point is well worth the 30-mile drive, however, because you can look straight down, over 3,000 feet, to the valley floor below, and see a sizable panorama of High Sierra real estate. Looking across the valley, Glacier Point offers the best close-up of the massive granite thumb known as Half Dome. From this height, the full drop of Yosemite Falls also becomes apparent. A mile stroll at Glacier Point can take you to the Sentinel Dome overlook. Because of the elevation, pace yourself and take the walk slowly.

During winter, the **Badger Pass Ski Area** opens for alpine skiing along this road. Badger Pass is noted for family, beginner, and intermediate skiing rather than challenging the expert. There is a Ski Tots Playhouse for young children. In summer, various hikes begin at Badger Pass. Summit Meadow, the large meadow above Badger Pass, is an excellent cross-country ski area, with long ski hikes possible through the woods, ending with spectacular overlooks of Yosemite Valley. If you have the will and the skills, this is also a favorite backpacking ski camping region in winter.

To Wawona

The *Sequoiadendron giganteums*, the Big Trees, can be seen at three groves in Yosemite. The most prominent grove lies 35 miles south of the valley along Highway 41 in Wawona, which means *big tree* in the original Native American language. The giant sequoias are the inland species of redwoods, the most massive living entities on earth. They are worth making a half-day trip to Wa-wona to see. At the Wawona area cluster of trees, called the Mari-posa Grove, the Grizzly Giant is the oldest tree, an estimated 2,800 years old, and has a base diameter of 30.7 feet. Nearby, the Massachusetts Tree, broken into chunks, shows the wood of the sequoia. There were two tunnel trees in Wawona, but one, the Wawona Tunnel Tree, fell over in the 1968-69 winter storms. The 232-foot California Tree remains an upright tunnel tree, but cars are no longer allowed to drive in the grove. A visitor now sees the trees on foot or by tram.

Ironically, one truth that the park service has learned in the last decades is the need for fires around the big trees. Fires clear out the undergrowth, allowing young sequoias, stimulated to germi-nate by the heat of fire, to grow in the newly available sunlight and in the mineral-rich ash soil. The park service now manages con-trolled burns here.

Other resources at Wawona include the venerable Wawona Ho-tel, with its weekend barbecues, and the Pioneer History Center that presents the life of early homesteaders.

To the High Country

Yosemite's high country offers an excursion through a rocky al-pine wilderness. The road is Highway 120, the **Tioga Pass Road**, which is closed in winter, meaning November-May. For informa-tion on road conditions, call ☎ 209-372-0200. While the valley floor is often crowded with visitors during peak summer months, the high country is less frequented. Wilderness permits are neces-sary for overnight camping. The high country acquaints you with the source of the **Merced River**, which flows through the valley, and also shows you an entirely independent watershed, that of the Tuolumne River, which lies to the north. Both rivers flow to the west from their snowy sources in the high country. The Tu-olumne was dammed early in this century to create the **Hetch Hetchy Reservoir**. To reach Hetch Hetchy, an eight-mile-long body of water, take the 38-mile drive from Big Oak Flat, passing attractive forests of sugar pines. The **Tuolumne Gorge** was thought by observers, such as John Muir, to equal Yosemite Val-ley in beauty, but San Francisco water interests succeeded in ar-ranging for the dam, despite a last-minute plea by Muir to

President Woodrow Wilson. You can view the Tuolumne Gorge and such phenomena as Waterwheel Falls, but hiking is required.

The season is short here, from June through October, with fields of wildflowers an enticement. At Tioga Pass, the road crosses the crest of the Sierra at 9,945 feet, the highest automobile pass in California. From the pass you see a divide with two worlds. Looking west, the moist rain-filled world of meadows and forests stretches before you. Looking east, you see the parched face of the high granite deserts. The spines of the high mountains halt the eastward movement of rain-filled clouds rolling in from the Pacific.

Scenic Driving: Mammoth Lakes

The scenic drive of choice here is the stretch of Highway 395 between Mono Lake and Mammoth, as described in *Touring*.

Scenic Driving: Gold Country/Sacramento

The best scenic drive in the Gold Country is up and down Highway 49, with many critical stops already discussed under *Touring*.

The pleasure of the Gold Country is partly that it rambles in an undefined manner, perfect for the explorer temperament of many travelers. Aside from the historic parks and museums, many dis-

Tufa formations at Mono Lake.

coveries, like hidden nuggets, await the visitor. Here are a few to keep in mind as you drive Highway 49:

At **Jackson** you can see two huge wooden wheels used to carry buckets of water and debris from the Kennedy Mine. Originally there were four such wheels in place, each 58 feet in diameter. Together they could carry 500 tons of water and debris from the mines each day. The wheels can be seen at a park north of Jackson on Jackson Gate Road. The Kennedy and Argonaut mines, among the richest and deepest in the Mother Lode, produced about $60 million in gold.

Architecturally, the **Chew Kee Store in Fiddletown** is unusual because it is made of rammed earth construction. The walls are 2½ feet thick. Built in 1850, the structure was a Chinese herb shop and home of Fiddletown's last Chinese resident, Jimmy Chow, until his death in 1965.

Placerville was a major supply site for the miners. Several famous captains of industry had humble beginnings here. Railroad magnate Mark Hopkins sold vegetables. Philip Armour ran a butcher shop. John Studebaker ran a wheelbarrow shop, amassing capital for larger ventures. Collis P. Huntington, later a rail tycoon, managed a store here.

Nevada City

Nevada City is another pleasant Gold Country town to poke around in. As a sample of the serendipity here, you'll stumble across the **Nevada City Winery**, known for its Zinfandel. Next door is the Miner's Foundry, a museum with foundry equipment, that also doubles as a performing arts venue. On Main Street, you'll happen on the Firehouse, a red brick building from 1861. So numerous and fearful were fires that fire prevention societies became a leading social force in the early Gold Country era. Down the street is **Nevada City Angler**, heaven for the trout fisher, where guide service, flies, and all sorts of fly fishing paraphernalia can be enjoyed. At the end of Main Street is the historic **National Hotel and Bar**, the longest continuously operating hotel in California. You might stop in for a drink at this dark wood bar and admire its collection of mixed drink shakers. One favorite local restaurant on Main Street is **Cirino's**. Nevada City is also known for its Victorian mansions, such as the **Ott House**, 450 Broad Street. The explorer will find many nuggets of pleasure wandering through the Gold Country. Nevada City prides itself on what its historic district lacks – no turn signals, no neon. The streetlamps are actual gas lamps.

Antique hunters will be delighted by the numerous stores selling varied wares. Jackson has several antiques stores. Because of the patronage from travelers, many artists have come here and sell direct to visitors.

Gold County Architecture

Victorian architecture in churches and residences could be another focus of a Gold Country excursion. The red **St. James Episcopal Church** (built in 1859) in Sonora and the **Bradford House**, across the street, are both fine examples of Gold Rush Victorian architecture. Grass Valley and Nevada City offer self-guided Victorian architecture walks. While walking Grass Valley, be sure to see the **Lola Montez House**, 248 Mill Street, which is now the Visitor Center for the region. As you stroll the town, stop in at the historic **Holbrooke Hotel**, 212 West Main Street; its wooden bar is inviting and the dining room is notable. One of the grandest Victorian houses is the **Frank Beatty residence**, 403 Neal Street. Autumn is a particularly lovely time to walk Nevada City because the sugar maples are aflame with color.

Annual Festivals

The most famous festival in these parts, aside from the Fireman's Muster in Columbia, is the annual **Calaveras County Fair and Jumping Frog Jubilee** held the third weekend in May. The Jumping Frog Jubilee honors Mark Twain and his story *The Celebrated Jumping Frog of Calaveras County*. You can visit the cabin in Angels Camp where he lived while gathering California material for his stories. A statue at Angels Camp recalls the author, who came west with his brother Orion, failed at mining, and took up the pen to earn his livelihood.

One pleasure of the Gold Country is how the terrain changes as you meander along Highway 49. Between Placerville and Coloma you're in orchard country, delightful at the spring blossom time. Mandarin oranges are a typical specialty crop. (A farm trails brochure listing local producers of fruits, vegetables, and herbs can be obtained from PlacerGROWN, 11477 East Avenue, Auburn, CA 95603; ☎ 916-889-7398.) Between Coloma and Auburn, the landscape becomes hilly and wild, punctuated by pastures overgrown with blackberries and woodlands dense with oak trees. From Auburn to Grass Valley/Nevada City stretches an urban corridor of businesses, ranging from automobile sellers to supermarkets. Beyond Nevada City the huge forests emerge again, with digger pines at the lower elevations, as you drive north to the cutoff into Malakoff Diggins State Historic Park.

Bicycling

The Gold Country

Every backroad of this treasured region is a potential bicycling adventure. The northern Gold Country is an especially hospitable backroads area for biking. One of the dependable organizers here is **Coyote Adventure Company**, 123 Nevada Street in Nevada City; ☎ 916-265-6909. They rent bikes and have good maps of Gold Country bike routes. Coyote offers two-hour and four-hour van-supported local trips, as well as more elaborate full-moon overnight bike outings. The Grass Valley Chamber of Commerce (☎ 916-273-4667) publishes a free brochure on its dozen favorite mountain bike outings in the northern Gold Country region, including a 10-mile loop possible around Empire Mine State Park.

Lake Tahoe

For a long, leisurely look at Lake Tahoe's scenic 72-mile shoreline, try the **Ring Around the Lake** route along the highways. You can still enjoy the view but cut the ride in half by cruising across Lake Tahoe on a tour boat, the *Tahoe Gal*, then tackling a 35-mile route that starts at Tahoe City. Call ☎ 702-588-9658 or 800-565-2704 for more information.

Paved shorter bike trails exist at the south end and on the west side of Lake Tahoe. The **Pope-Baldwin Bike Path** is maintained by the Forest Service for an enjoyable 3.4-mile, flat stretch along the south shore. Fifteen miles of paved pathway, known as the Tahoe Trailways, starts from Tahoe City.

At Tahoe, a scenic ride is **the Angora Lakes climb**, which combines the ease of a paved bike trail with some off-road extensions and a moderate 800-foot climb in elevation. Begin at the intersection of Tahoe Mountain Road and Angora Ridge Road, about a mile east of Fallen Leaf Lake. The ride provides stunning views of

Fallen Leaf Lake and Lake Tahoe, plus a glimpse of the aspen forests, which are ablaze with fall color in October. The best source for trail maps is the **Forest Service Visitor's Center on Emerald Bay Road** (☎ 916-573-2600; Highway 89, past Camp Richardson).

One bicycle rental provider in South Lake Tahoe is **Anderson's Bicycle Rental**, 645 Emerald Bay Road; ☎ 916-541-0500.

Biking the Ski Slopes

Around Lake Tahoe the major ski areas have become summer biking parks. You ride up the gondola with your bike and then ride down the mountain on dirt bike trails. Gravity replaces pedal power as the energy source in this down-the-mountain adventure, which extends the potential appeal even to a bicyclist who would otherwise be classified as a couch potato. Typically, the ski area will also rent bikes, which are sturdy models, as they have to be, to take the beating of rides down the bumpy, stony trails. The biker can choose a desired pace, ranging from a leisurely tour, with stops for enjoying the views, to hell-bent careening intent on setting a speed record in this rocky terrain. The latter style appeals especially to high-testosterone males under 30.

Squaw Valley and **Northstar** lead the way, offering bike rentals and lifts up the tram to elaborate bike trails that wind to the bottom. **Bear Valley** and **Kirkwood** are two other good options. (See thorough portraits of the ski areas and contact information, also good for summer biking, under *Downhill Skiing*.)

Yosemite

At Yosemite, the **Valley Floor loop** offers eight miles of scenic bike touring. The high country road is also a pleasure, but the traffic is considerable on the narrow roads.

Mammoth Mountain

Mammoth Mountain ski area, like the ski places at Tahoe, has gone heavily into summer biking. Mountain biking has exploded here in recent years due to the many miles of country roads, such as Scenic Drive Road north from Mammoth Lakes, and the leisurely ride through Shady Rest Park's dense forest. There are even rental units that advertise the ease with which their guests may bike in and bike out from their front doors. But the best reason

The Sierra/Gold Country

may be the opportunity to bike down Mammoth Mountain. At the base, Mammoth Mountain Bike Park will rent you a bike and the required helmet. A ride can be a two-hour jaunt, traversing switchback trails adroitly laid out for biking, with names like Over the Bars, Brake Through, and Paper Route. A cult of downhill racing has led Mammoth to organize several summer biking events. Mountain bike vacations in the area are organized by **Mammoth Adventure Connection** (☎ 760-934-0606).

Sacramento

At Sacramento, the abundant riverbank park lands provide not only a home for trees and wildlife but also a haven for its many cyclists. A paved, level bike path, known as the **Jedediah Smith Trail**, stretches for an enviable 31 miles from Old Sacramento all the way to Folsom Lake. City Bicycle Works will set you up with the right bike, a slimmer model for speed or a hardier fat-tired version, as you desire. In Sacramento, **City Bicycle** is at 2419 K Street, ☎ 916-447-2453. Detailed maps and information about bikeways is distributed by the Sacramento Metropolitan Air Quality Management District (Mobile Source Division, 8411 Jackson Road, Sacramento, CA 95826).

Railroading

Old Sacramento

Old Sacramento re-creates and preserves the Gold Rush and railroad era that flourished from 1850-1890. The **California State Railroad Museum** is one of the finest museums in the country, interpreting the influence that railroads had on the lifestyle of the West. Old Sacramento is the riverfront area that has been designated a 28-acre national historic landmark. The Gold Rush miners passed through this embarcadero, overrunning Captain John Sutter's nascent agricultural community in 1848.

Begin a tour at the **B.F. Hastings Building**, 2nd and J streets. The building was the first western office of the Pony Express and the home of the California Supreme Court from 1855 to 1869.

At I and L streets sits the **Big Four Building**, where the four merchants, Leland Stanford, C. P. Huntington, Charles Crocker, and Mark Hopkins, drew up plans to build the Central Pacific Railroad. The Big Four Building now is adjacent to the California

State Railroad Museum, which shows restored locomotives, simulated waiting rooms, films, and photographs.

While exploring in Old Sacramento, seek out the forlorn bronze face of Theodore Judah at the opposite end of the old Sacramento complex. It was Judah, the engineer, who had the original dream of the railroad and who persuaded the Big Four to build it. Judah, however, was squeezed out during the political struggle over control of the railroad. Also rendered irrelevant by the railroad was the **Pony Express**, which is memorialized in Old Sacramento with a bronze statue of a galloping rider and horse.

Gold Country

In the Gold Country, the town of Jamestown boasts a special rail attraction. **Railtown 1897** (☎ 209-984-3953) features steam locomotives and cars from the Sierra Railway, a Museum of Railroad History, and shops. You can board the train, called the Mother Lode Cannonball, for a 40-minute, six-mile round-trip scenic ride along an oak-laden terrain.

On Foot

Hiking & Backpacking

Each area of the Sierra and Gold Country has an ample number of day and overnight hikes, accessible locally with information from the Visitors Bureaus.

Tahoe

The **Desolation Wilderness** within the National Forest lands is sure to delight anyone interested in exploring even a small portion of its 300 miles of trails. Permits are required whether you are embarking on a day hike (permits should be available at the trailhead) or an overnight backpacking experience (obtain permits in person from the Forest Service office or the Visitor Center on Highway 89).

For stunning views of the main body of water, some high desert terrain, and the snowy peaks of the Sierra, try the **Tahoe Rim Trail**. Eventually the trail all the way around the lake will be completed as hikers gradually transform this dream into reality. Volunteers have cleared 132 miles of the trail and hope to complete the final 18 miles by the year 2001. Trailheads are accessible at various points around the lake. One taste of the trail would be a six-mile section that begins at the Nevada side of Heavenly atop Kingsbury Grade. This part of the trail teeters on the eastern slope of the Sierra, overlooking the green patchwork of the Carson Valley below. The trail then sweeps over a ridge and treats hikers to a view of Lake Tahoe before arriving at Star Lake, tucked against a granite outcropping.

To look at waterfalls and wildflowers in the Lake Tahoe area, try the **Half Moon Lake trail**, a 4½-mile moderate hike.

 *Maps and information on all possible Tahoe area hikes are available from the **Lake Tahoe Basin Management Unit** ☎ 916-573-2600 .*

One way to hike in the Tahoe area is to start at the top of the ski trams. Board the Heavenly Aerial Tram for a ride to the top and a hike on the Tahoe Vista Trail, a two-mile walk. Some guided nature walks are offered through Heavenly (see *Downhill Skiing, Heavenly*, for contact details). Squaw Valley also has hikes from the top of its tram.

Yosemite

Yosemite has delightful walks along the Valley floor, mentioned in *Touring*. If time allows only a single pleasure walk in the high country, the main attraction is the silky lawns of **Tuolumne Meadows**, one of the largest subalpine meadows in the Sierra. Tuolumne Meadows is a plateau at about 8,500 feet. The drive there is 56 miles from Yosemite Valley over winding roads, but well worth it for the views, lakes, forests, granite domes, and canyons. A ranger station at Tuolumne Meadows can help guide you to the hikes, horseback riding, and camping in the area. Tent-cabin lodging is available at **Tuolumne Meadows Lodge** and at **White Wolf Lodge** in the high country. Backpacking trips, trail riding excursions, and walking trips are possible. The walking trips, led by naturalists, are special because they make a circular route through the High Sierras, locating you on successive evenings at different primitive lodgings, spaced roughly 10 miles apart. The lodging provides you with shelter and meals, but reservations are required. Backpacking trips can also start from here and traverse sections of the **John Muir Trail**, which extends to

Mt. Whitney, 210 miles to the south. The John Muir Trail forms part of the serpentine Pacific Crest Trail, the 2,500-mile route from Canada to Mexico.

Mammoth Lakes

With an area map available from the Visitor Center in Mammoth Lakes, you can choose easy or more strenuous hikes. Keep in mind that the elevation is high, so allow a day to get adjusted, drink plenty of water when hiking, and be advised that underestimating your capacity is the mark of wisdom.

Enjoyable and easy hikes are available in the **Devils Postpile Monument** to see the principle features, as mentioned in *Touring*. The hike to the Postpile itself is only a quarter-mile. The hike to **Rainbow Falls** is a mile-and-half, but even young children do this level hike, taking their time. The National Monument has other hikes to be recommended, such as a wildflower walk at Agnews Meadow or a view of beaver dams at Sotcher Lake. You witness the effect of avalanches shearing off forests to create open space. You also see lakes, such as Starkweather, gradually progressing to become meadows.

Many hikes can be made from the lakes area at **Mammoth Lakes Basin** . Behind the town, tucked amidst the mountains, are Mary, Mamie, George, Horseshoe, and Twin lakes. The area is laced with hiking trails, which become the cross-country ski trails of winter, with headquarters at Tamarack Lodge on Twin Lakes. In summer, the alpine forests of lodgepole pine, the reflective waters of the lakes, and the granite mountains are the hiking impressions. This is also a jumping-off point for ambitious horsepacking or backpacking trips into the John Muir Wilderness.

Rock Climbing Yosemite/Sierra

The granite faces of Yosemite present some of the world's most fascinating climbs. A visitor to the valley floor will commonly linger for a few moments to gaze at the tiny figures scaling their way up the granite walls. All this climbing, which is extremely technical and dangerous, should be undertaken only with expert knowledge and instruction. Call the park service (☎ 209-372-8344) for information on climbing instruction.

The Sierra/Gold Country

The natural wonders of Mammoth are also a draw for rock climbers, offering opportunities to scale the Buttermilks or the Geothermal Boulders. **Mammoth Mountaineering School** (PO Box 7299, Mammoth Lakes, CA 93546; ☎ 760-924-9100 or 800-239-7642) is where you can learn to climb or have an experienced guide along as you tackle some challenging short climbs, such as Owens Gorge. **Kittredge Sports** in Mammoth (☎ 760-934-7566) and **Mammoth Adventure Connection** (☎ 760-934-0606) are other resources for your rock climbing passions.

On Horseback

Gold Country

The **Columbia Stage Line & Stable** (☎ 209-532-0663) helps to recreate the world of treasure boxes and those who struck it rich in California. They offer stagecoach and horseback outings in the area, showing you the back country streams filled with frenzied miners for a few years from 1849 on. The Columbia State Historic Park provides the perfect setting for this type of outing.

Horseback riding at Duck Lake in the back country behind Mammoth Lakes.

Yosemite

The favorite horseback activity is the several-day trip possible in the **High Country**. Advance planning and reservations are required. Contact the High Sierra Desk, Yosemite Reservations, 5420 E. Home Avenue, Fresno, CA 93727; ☎ 209-454-2002.

Mammoth

Nowhere in the Sierra is horseback riding or horsepacking into the mountains more extensive than at Mammoth. Each of the four main areas around Mammoth has its own pack outfit.

The oldest packing business here is **Roeser's Mammoth Lakes Pack Outfit**, started in 1915, making it also the oldest packer business in the eastern Sierra and one of the earliest businesses in Mammoth. Packers carried in mining supplies to the gold miners in the region before the pleasure traveler came onto the scene. The Summers family started the business. The Roeser family later bought them out.

A pack trip puts you in the capable hands of a wrangler, such as Larry Maurice, who knows the horses and the trail. Maurice understands well the mystique of the Eastern Sierra and happens also to be a cowboy poet. Maurice can lead your party on a four-hour trip into the back country, past Barney Lake, and on to Duck Lake and Pika Lake, crossing 10,750-foot Duck Pass. With a day on a horse you can see terrain that only a hiker in top condition could traverse.

Nothing surpasses an immersion in this wilderness as an antidote to citified malaise. A day of horseback riding in this back-country will leave you with memories of lodgepole and red fir forests, granite vistas still dotted with snow in summer, trout rising to take flies in remote lakes, clean air in a pristine setting, and the surefootedness of horses on the edges of precipices.

The horsepacking season runs June-September. All kinds of trips can be arranged, from a one-hour scenic loop along Mary Lake, suitable even for young children, to a week-long "spot" trip, meaning you are left out in the wilderness. One popular option is the "inclusive" trip, meaning the wrangler and horses stay with you, and the wrangler does the cooking.

To horsepack at Mammoth, contact **Mammoth Lakes Pack Outfit**, ☎ 760-934-2434; PO Box 61, Mammoth Lakes, CA 93546.

The Sierra/Gold Country

Another good information source is the **Eastern High Sierra Packers Association,** ☎ 760-873-8405.

On Water

Rafting/Kayaking/Canoeing

River Rafting

 The heart of the river rafting scene in Northern California is along Highway 49 at Coloma on the **South Fork of the American River** from April to September. In fact, statisticians of rafting claim that the South Fork of the American River is the most rafted river in the West, surpassed in the East only by the Youghenney in Pennsylvania. Rafting trips can start above Coloma with Coloma as the destination or depart from Coloma and end up where the river empties into Folsom Lake. All considered, there are 21 river miles to raft on the South Fork. Rafting companies organize day trips or set up overnight camps along the river.

Besides the moderate whitewater on the South Fork, there is more challenging rafting on the **Middle Fork** of the American River at Auburn along an 18-mile stretch. The **North Fork** of the American River also tempts rafters with a nine-mile run. The major rafting companies tend to run a few other rivers, such as the Kla-

Rafting the South Fork of the American River.

math near the Oregon border or the Salmon in the Marble Mountains.

One major provider is **Whitewater Connection** (PO Box 270, Coloma, CA 95613-0270; ☎ 916-622-6446 or 800-336-7238). Other rafting companies include **Earthtrek Expeditions** (PO Box 1010, Lotus, CA 95651; ☎ 916-642-1900) and **OARS** (PO Box 67, Angels Camp, CA 95222; ☎ 209-736-4677 or 800-346-6277).

Kayaking & Canoeing

Kayaking is also popular on the American River. One provider, offering lessons and outings from the San Francisco Bay area to the Gold Country or Tahoe, is **Current Adventures** (☎ 916-642-9755 or 888-452-9254).

Kayak or canoe trips in Mammoth may include peaceful paddles along Mono or Crowley lakes or more ambitious trips to the high alpine lakes. **Caldera Kayaks** (☎ 760-935-4942) is based at Crowley Lake Marina and provides lessons as well as equipment.

Boating Lake Tahoe

Boat cruising on Lake Tahoe is an exhilarating experience. Getting out on the water, summer or winter, provides a perspective on the lake and mountains that you can't get from shore. The view from the lake, especially as the urban skyline of South Tahoe recedes, transports you back to a pristine era, as if you are viewing the lake through the eyes of John Fremont or Kit Carson. Cruises sometimes combine dinner and entertainment, but at other times the outing is for the cruise itself, and in winter, one cruise converts to a ski shuttle from the south end of the lake to ski resorts on the north end.

The **Tahoe Queen** (☎ 800-238-2463) leaves for three excursions each day from Ski Run Marina in South Lake Tahoe to the choice setting of Emerald Bay. They also host an evening dinner and dance cruise.

The **MS Dixie II** (☎ 702-588-3508) cruises out from Zephyr Cover, Nevada, to Emerald Bay twice daily in summer. Evening cruises include cocktails, dinner, and dancing.

The Sierra/Gold Country

North Tahoe Cruises (916-583-0141) departs from 700 North Lake Boulevard on a two-hour trip emphasizing the history of the northwest side of the lake. Sunset cocktail cruises and champagne continental breakfast trips are among the offerings.

Fishing the Sierra & Gold Country

Several strains of trout, but mainly rainbow and brown, are the primary prize throughout the Sierra and Gold Country.

At Mammoth, **Crowley Lake**, actually a man-made reservoir, is in a class by itself because of its trophy trout. The mineral fertility of the lake produces an abundance of fly and shrimp growth that enables trout to gain weight fast. This reservoir, part of the Los Angeles Department of Water and Power operation, has a marina managed by Sierra Recreation Associates, where you can rent a boat or engage one of the expert guides, such as Ed Cereda. Anglers troll with Rapalas or Needlefish for the five strains of rainbows and browns in the lake. Still fishermen use nightcrawlers and "power bait," a synthetic bait, while bottomfishing. Crowley has many two-pound trout, some five-pound trophies, and did yield a record 18-pound brown trout. Ed Cereda remembers

Trout fishing in the Yosemite High Country.

fondly the seven-pound brown he caught in these waters. The season runs from the end of April through July. Crowley is stocked each autumn for the next season's fishing.

Mammoth Lakes, the cluster of small lakes near the town, provides good fishing from shore or small boats, which can be rented. The lakes are stocked weekly in summer.

A totally different approach to trout fishing in the Sierra is the search for wild trout in a sporting catch-and-release environment. **Hot Creek** at Mammoth provides such fishing. Hot Creek is a special scenic area where boiling fumaroles and heated springs enter a creek, reminding everyone of the volcanic presence beneath the Mammoth region. In certain areas of Hot Creek the public is invited to soak in the hot water. Hot Creek is also preserved as a special trout stream, considered world-class, sometimes rated by fishermen as one of the 10 best in the world. Anglers at Hot Creek must use dry or wet flies with barbless hooks. The style here is catch-and-release only. Hot Creek attracts the sport fisher, not the meat fisher.

Fly fishing fanatics focus on the **San Joaquin River** in the Red's Meadow/Devils Postpile area. The Mammoth Fish & Game office is a resource and may be reached at ☎ 760-934-2664.

On the road to Hot Creek, be sure to stop in at the **Hot Creek State Fish Hatchery**, one of three main hatcheries in the state. There you can see, in the raceways, thousands of the two-pound broodstock trout used to create the eggs for the state's fish-planting program. You can even feed the fish with the pellets they eat, creating a frenzy on the surface. The sight of lunkers at the Hot Creek Hatchery can excite the pulse of even a nascent fisherman. From this hatchery, more than 20 million trout eggs, four million fingerlings, and 800,000 catchables enter California fishing waters each year.

Both in the Gold Country and in the Sierra there are many opportunities to fish for trout and excellent support shops for the fisherman. One such establishment for the true fly fishing aficionado is **Nevada City Angler**, at 417 Broad Street in that city; ☎ 916-478-9301. It is an amazing coincidence that the people who own this shop happen to be named Michael and Sylvia Fisher. They can outfit you with any kind of fly rod and appropriate flies. They can also organize for you a trip to local streams, such as Yuba River, and guide you in catching salmon, steelhead trout, and the all-year rainbow and brown trout. The **Trout Fitter** in Mammoth Lakes is open year round, organizing trips, renting the right equipment, and offering advice. The Trout Fitter is at Highway 203 and Old Mammoth Road; ☎ 760-924-3676.

The **Lake Tahoe basin** presents opportunities to fish both in the huge lake and on many streams, such as the Upper Truckee. Tucked into the high country are trout-filled lakes, such as Echo and Fallen Leaf lakes. Typical of the Lake Tahoe sportfishing

The Sierra/Gold Country

Lake Tahoe Ski Areas

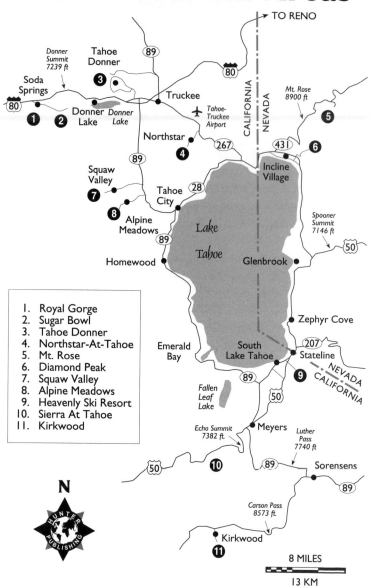

TO RENO

Donner Summit 7239 ft

Tahoe Donner

Soda Springs

Truckee

Donner Lake

Donner Lake

Tahoe-Truckee Airport

Northstar

CALIFORNIA

NEVADA

Mt. Rose 8900 ft

Squaw Valley

Tahoe City

Incline Village

Alpine Meadows

Lake

Tahoe

Spooner Summit 7146 ft

Homewood

Glenbrook

1. Royal Gorge
2. Sugar Bowl
3. Tahoe Donner
4. Northstar-At-Tahoe
5. Mt. Rose
6. Diamond Peak
7. Squaw Valley
8. Alpine Meadows
9. Heavenly Ski Resort
10. Sierra At Tahoe
11. Kirkwood

Zephyr Cove

Emerald Bay

South Lake Tahoe

Stateline

NEVADA

CALIFORNIA

Fallen Leaf Lake

Echo Summit 7382 ft

Meyers

Luther Pass 7740 ft

Sorensens

Carson Pass 8573 ft

Kirkwood

N

HUNTER PUBLISHING

8 MILES

13 KM

boats is the *Dory-L* (☎ 916-541-5448) departing from Ski Run Marina in South Lake Tahoe in pursuit of the lunker Mackinaw trout that lurk in the lake.

On Snow

Downhill Skiing: The Sierra

 California offers an itinerant skier some of the finest skiing in the world, especially at the major ski resorts in the Lake Tahoe basin.

All the ingredients necessary for an outstanding skiing experience are present.

The area averages 350-400 inches of snowfall per year. Major ski areas have also invested in snow-making equipment to give Mother Nature an assist in drought years. The ski season usually runs from mid-November to mid-March, even lasting a few weeks longer on occasion.

The sun usually shows a welcome presence in California skiing. You are not likely to experience here the long periods of bitter cold that characterize some inland skiing areas. Typically, a dazzling afternoon sun takes the chill off the early morning, creating a 25-45° afternoon temperature.

The lake can be seen readily from the ski slopes of three major resorts – Heavenly, Squaw Valley, and Sierra-at-Tahoe.

The Major Ski Sites

California skiing presents world-class runs at well-organized resorts. On the northwest side of the lake you'll find three of the stellar sites – **Squaw Valley, Northstar,** and **Alpine Meadows**. The fourth, **Heavenly**, sits at the south end of the lake. And the fifth and sixth, **Kirkwood** and **Sierra-at-Tahoe**, nestle in the mountains southwest of the lake. The Squaw Valley Winter Olympics in 1960 gave the world a taste for California skiing. There is some skiing in California from Mt. Shasta in the north to the mountains east of Los Angeles in the south, but the finest skiing is in the Lake Tahoe basin, and in the less accessible **Mammoth Mountain** in the eastern Sierra. The Lake Tahoe area has developed the largest concentration of ski resorts in the US. Nine-

Besides skiing, winter visitors at Yosemite enjoy hiking to see the giant sequoias.

teen ski resorts can be reached within a 45-minute drive of the lake.

Good access is a major plus for the Lake Tahoe region. The ski resorts and major lodgings are within an hour's shuttle or rental-car drive from the Reno-Cannon Airport. Most of the lodging takes place at the south end of the lake, where there are major casino hotels, such as Harrah's and Harvey's, and a chateau-like hostelry, the Embassy Suites. The main driving route is from San Francisco, about four hours by car to the north end of the lake, along Interstate 80, or to the south end of the lake, via Highway 50. Once you've arrived, the all-weather route around the lake is on the east side. The west side drive, past Emerald Bay, is closed in heavy snow, though take it if the road is open because the appearance of Emerald Bay from the vista turnouts on the road is the choicest view in the region.

Planning for Non-Skiers

If there's a non-skier in your group, the scenic tram rides at Heavenly and Squaw Valley to the tops of the mountains, with sweeping views of the lake, can be recommended. Both trams have restaurants at the top, pleasant places to pass some time, plus large sunny decks where a non-skier could curl up with a good book for a winter afternoon. A drive around the lake to see the views or an excursion ride on a tour boat, such as the *Tahoe Queen* or *MS Dixie II*, are other activities favored by non-skiers.

Skiers and non-skiers enjoy the diversion that the Nevada side of the border offers at the *gaming* tables and entertainment in the casinos. The casinos at Stateline also offer excellent buffet dinners at reasonable prices. Harrah's Forest Room is highly recommended. There are also gourmet restaurants, such as the Sage Room steakhouse at Harvey's or the California-cuisine offerings of Zackary's at the Embassy Suites. Evans Restaurant is the fine-dining pace setter in the region.

Planning a Ski Trip

A ski trip here requires some attention to planning, preferably with a map in front of you. Where will you ski? You can't go wrong with any of the top six ski resorts. Travelers often ski one per day, hitting all six in a week's trip. Where will you lodge? South Tahoe has plentiful lodging and three of the resorts – Northstar, Squaw Valley, and Kirkwood – have on-site condos and restaurants. You can be peripatetic and see the whole area or take a condo at one re-sort and ski back and forth to your front door for your whole vaca-tion period. If you want an alternative type of lodging, consider **Sorensen's**, a cluster of cabins run by hospitable John and Patty Brissenden, about 20 minutes from the south end of the lake. Sorensen's would be a good choice of lodging if you want to con-centrate your skiing at Heavenly and at Kirkwood. Some skiers also lodge in Reno to enjoy the nightlife and take day trips out to the slopes, though it's not a short commute if you do it repeatedly. And finally, how will you get around? A rental car gives you maxi-mum flexibility. Always carry chains and be prepared for storms, which can come up fast. Shuttles from the south end of the lake can take you back and forth to the ski areas.

All the major ski areas offer ski instruction programs, whether group or individual. Group lessons are usually two-hour to half-day affairs. Individual lessons can often be scheduled for one in-tense hour of instruction. Each resort also has a children's in-struction and daycare program, known as Starkids at Northstar, for example. Each ski area maintains an elaborate rental shop, so you don't need to bring skis if you don't wish to or don't have skis. The rental shops carry the new parabolic skis, giving you a chance to sample the evolving technology.

Prices for an all-day ski lift ticket are nudging upwards towards $50 per day, with Squaw Valley as the price leader.

Aside from alpine or downhill skiing, California also offers some of the country's most elaborate cross-country skiing. Northstar and Kirkwood have well-developed courses of cross-country track

The Sierra/Gold Country

and "skating" lanes, referring to the cross-country style of rapid skiing on short skis in the manner of a speed skater.

West of the lake along Interstate 80, at Soda Springs, you'll find **Royal Gorge**, the most developed cross-country site in the country, with over 200 miles of set track. Royal Gorge is the first of the destination cross-country resorts, complete with gourmet food and lodging setup, either mid-mountain or at its highway-side Rainbow Inn.

Let's look more closely at the six major alpine ski destinations and the country's premier cross-country resort. Each site has its own particular magic for skiers.

Heavenly

For a high intermediate or advanced skier, Heavenly offers enough runs to explore for days without repeating yourself.

Heavenly is heavenly both for its view of the lake and the diversity of its runs. The view of the lake from the top of the tram, plus even more rewarding views of the lake from the summit, make Heavenly special. The view can be savored while nursing a drink at the Top of the Tram Restaurant.

The size of Heavenly is amazing. Fully nine mountains and over 20 square miles of skiable surface delineate Heavenly, the largest ski area in North America. Twenty-six lifts carry skiers to the far reaches. The high-speed tram transports skiers quickly to mid-mountain, where they can disperse. Heavenly boasts 79 runs, including a seven-mile trail if you put several runs together. The vertical drop is a gargantuan 3,500 feet.

Access to the mountain is from locations in both states, Nevada and California. The Nevada side of the mountain, complete with its Boulder Base and Stagecoach lodges, is a good morning sun area. The California side, where the tram operates and the Main Lodge is sited, is a sunnier afternoon ski location.

Heavenly is an upside-down ski area, with one of its most challenging runs, a mogul-studded precipice called *Gunbarrel*, right at the bottom, in full view of a sweeping deck loaded with oohing and aahing appreciators of this nuanced alpine sport. Much of the base lodge has been rebuilt with reflective glass and a wood-shingle exterior.

Heavenly in Brief

Mailing Address: Heavenly, PO Box 2180, Stateline, NV 89449.

Information: ☎ 702-586-7000

Snow Conditions: ☎ 916-541-7544

Reservations: ☎ 916-541-1330

Terrain Percentage For: Beginner - 20%; Intermediate - 45%; Advanced - 35%

Summit Elevation: 10,040 feet

Base Elevation: 6,540 feet

Vertical Drop: 3,500 feet

Ski Area: 4,800 acres

Longest Run: 5½ miles

Lift Capacity Per Hour: 26,000

There are nine surface lifts, seven double chairs, eight triple chairs, three detachable hi-speed quads, and one tram.

Facilities: Five day lodges. Main lodge is on California side and the Stagecoach and Boulder Base Lodges are on Nevada side. All are full service. On the mountain, the Top of the Tram Restaurant provides food and drink, and the Sky Meadows Deck and East Peak Day Lodge provide picnic and barbecue sites, with some food and drink available.

Ski School: 100 instructors, including several bilingual

Rentals: Three rental shops

Cross-Country: In South Tahoe area

Season: Mid-November to April

Location: South Lake Tahoe, CA, 180 miles east of San Francisco, 70 miles southwest of Reno. California entrance is off Ski Run Blvd. Nevada entrance is at top of Kingsbury Grade.

The Sierra/Gold Country

Squaw Valley

Squaw Valley exudes a distinct world-class and Olympian feel. This aura is not merely an historic reflection of this site for the 1960 Winter Olympics, which celebrated some of the steepest runs in the nation. You feel it in the parking lot as you arrive and look around. Some of the patrons seem to be beautiful people who have just stepped out of advertisements. The women are wearing furs. In a shop next to the slope you can snap up a $500 skiing outfit. Squaw commands the highest lift ticket prices.

As you ascend the mountain, either in the speedy, six-person, modernistic gondola or in the huge 150-person tram-cable car, you get another impression. The mountain has ski runs spread out in wide bowls rather than narrow trails. Squaw maintains a 27-unit lift system, one of the most extensive in the country. Squaw is the only ski area in Tahoe that risks saying: If you have to wait in a lift line for more than 10 minutes, we'll refund your money and let you ski free.

The two day lodges at mid-mountain are elaborate affairs. Gold Coast complex at the top of the gondola includes large outdoor decks, a restaurant, bar, ski check area, and ski repair shop. High Camp complex at the top of the tram-cable car includes the rather posh Alexanders Restaurant, with white table cloths, glass wine glasses, and a view of Lake Tahoe.

Beginner and intermediate skiers feel comfortable at Squaw. The gradual slopes are near the top of the mountain, not in the path of a hotdogger's descent. An intermediate skier can roam over six peaks that receive an average of 450 inches of snow each year. An expert skier can trace the path of Olympians down renowned mountain KT-22 and the famous Red Dog run. A long end-of-the-day run sweeps the full distance of the mountain bowls down to the base of Squaw.

Squaw Valley in Brief

Mailing Address: Squaw Valley Ski Corporation, PO Box 2007, Olympic Valley, CA 96146.

Information: ☎ 916-583-6985

Snow Conditions: ☎ 916-583-6955

Reservations: ☎ 800-545-4350

Terrain Percentage For: Beginner - 25%; Intermediate - 45%; Advanced - 30%

2,000 vertical feet open for night skiing until 9 pm

Summit Elevation: 9,050

Base Elevation: 6,200 feet

Vertical Drop: 2,850 feet

Ski Area: 4,000 acres of open bowls

Longest Run: 3.6 miles

Lifts: 12 double chairs, seven triple chairs, one 150-passenger cable car, one six-passenger gondola, five surface lifts, four hi-speed quads

Lift capacity per hour: 49,000

Facilities: Base facilities include restaurants, shops, lockers, and lodging in the Squaw Valley area. Upper mountain includes two facilities, the Gold Coast complex at the top of the gondola and the High Camp complex at the top of the cable car. Both have a restaurant, bar, sun deck, and ski-shop.

Ski School: 150 instructors employing several methods of ski teaching

Rentals: Available at base

Cross-Country: Nordic center is adjacent to alpine area

Season: Mid-November to May

Northstar

Northstar is the most complete, residential ski area of the five major ski sites at Tahoe. Condominiums and a Village Mall of restaurants and shops give it a well-planned self-contained feel. The private, peace-and-quiet feel of Northstar is notable.

The mountain at Northstar, Mt. Pluto, has excellent intermediate runs and is well-patrolled by the Northstar staff, insuring safe skiing. Beginners and low-intermediate skiers find plenty of wide, meandering trails. Expert skiers rocket down steep chutes, such as the Schaffer Camp run. Ticket sales are limited by the carrying capacity of the mountain, insuring that lift lines will not be long.

The Sierra/Gold Country

The Starkids ski school guides children. Certified ski instructors assist adult learners. A six-person gondola takes skiers to the mid-mountain area, where most of the runs originate. Large decks at the mid-mountain Wine and Cheese House provide a rest area between runs.

From the ridge along the top of Mt. Pluto there are pleasing views of the lake, though they are obscured somewhat by trees. Northstar's northeast-facing direction protects it from the wind when the weather kicks up around the lake. A spa and hot tub in the communal Swim and Racquet Club take the chill off skiers.

Northstar also has developed an extensive cross-country system, complete with a Cross-Country and Telemark Center at mid-mountain. The Center is well-equipped with rental gear. Twenty-five miles of groomed paths await the nordic skier and the "skater" who prefers cross-country racing. Telemark or downhill skiing on cross-country skis is also allowed.

The food facilities, split between the base and the Day Lodge areas, range from Pedro's Pizza, a family pizza parlor, to the more elegant Schaffer's Mill Restaurant, which serves three meals a day. The Rendezvous Bar is a good drinking and meeting place.

Northstar in Brief

Mailing Address: Northstar-at-Tahoe, PO Box 129, Truckee, CA 96160.

Information: ☎ 530-562-1010

Snow Conditions: ☎ 530-562-1330

Reservations: ☎ 800-466-6784

Terrain Percentage For: Beginner - 25%; Intermediate - 50%; Advanced - 25%

Ski Area: 2,000 acres

Longest Run: 2.9 miles

Lifts: one gondola, four quad chairs, two triple chairs, two double chairs, two surface lists, one magic carpet

Lift Capacity: 19,400 skiers per hour

Facilities: On-site lodging in 200 handsome condominiums, with free bus shuttle in area. Village Mall contains restaurants, deli, ski shop, bar, general store, and child care center. Swim-Racquet Club with outdoor spa and hot tub. Wine and Cheese House at mid-mountain Day Lodge.

Ski School: Well-organized ski school for children and adults of all skill levels

Summit Elevation: 8,610 feet, Mt. Pluto

Base Elevation: 6,330 feet

Vertical Drop: 2,280 feet

Rentals: Available at ski shop

Cross-Country: The most elaborate cross-country system at Tahoe, with 25 miles of groomed trails and a mid-mountain Cross-Country and Telemark Center.

Season: Thanksgiving to end of April

Location: Off Highway 267, midway (about six miles) from Truckee to the north shore of Lake Tahoe; 40 miles southwest of Reno; 196 miles east of San Francisco.

Alpine Meadows

Though Alpine Meadows is only a mountain away from Squaw, the tone of the establishment differs markedly. Alpine Meadows is a family oriented day-visitor ski area, but it is not merely of family interest. Alpine includes grand slopes with runs second to none, including the notorious bump run called Scott's Chute. Over 2,000 skiing acres stretch across two large mountains.

However, the huge day lodge at the base, the most spacious such lodge in the region, epitomizes the matter of style. The main floor of the day lodge consists of a large cafeteria that plunges one into a massive party of families, teenagers, and college kids. Each year Alpine celebrates another season of friendly, family skiing.

The high base area and variety of sun exposures at Alpine combine to offer one of Tahoe's longest ski seasons and some of the most dependable snow conditions in the region, especially in late spring when other resorts falter. The terrain of the ski bowl is easily comprehended as you view it with a ski map in hand. Ski runs tend to converge at the base of the mountains near the central lodge.

The Sierra/Gold Country

Week-long ski clinics can turn the never-ever skier into an accomplished aficionado. Of the two mountains, Ward Peak offers good open-bowl skiing and Scott's Peak offers more tree skiing for the expert who wants to thread through the forest.

Alpine Meadows in Brief

Mailing Address: Alpine Meadows Ski Area, PO Box 5279, Tahoe City, CA 96145

Information: ☎ 530-583-4232, ☎ 800-441-4423

Snow Conditions: ☎ 530-581-8374

Reservations: ☎ 800-949-3296

Terrain Percentage For: Beginner - 25%; Intermediate - 40%; Expert - 35%

Summit Elevation: 8,637 feet

Base Elevation: 7,000 feet

Vertical Drop: 1,637 feet

Longest Run: 2½ miles

Size Of Skiing Area: 2,000 acres

Lifts: two triple chairs, seven double chairs, one surface lift, one hi-speed six-passenger chair

Lift Capacity Per Hour: 14,500

Facilities: Day lodge at base with large sundeck. Restaurant, bar, deli, cafeteria, ski shop, 24-hour check room. Free shuttle bus between skiing and lodging around North Tahoe. RV overnight parking, but without hookups.

Ski School: Daily instruction, group and private lessons. Specially priced lesson and lift tickets. Week-long ski clinics.

Rentals: Northern California's largest rental shop, with standard and premium equipment

Cross-Country: Nearby, with telemarkers welcome

Season: Tahoe's longest, mid-November to end of May

Location: On Alpine Meadows Road, six miles north of Tahoe City off Highway 89

Kirkwood

Kirkwood has the most wilderness feel of all the ski areas because it is set back in the mountains, far from the lake and from city development.

The ski area sprawls over a wide mountain, with plenty of beginner as well as expert runs. Kirkwood, whose base is at 7,800 feet, features snow of the highest quality all through its runs. A new lodge opened in 1997-98 at the base of the ski runs.

The cross-country program includes 80 miles of set track. The staff is highly professional, offering competent lessons. Conservation and environmental awareness are distinctive parts of the program. Posted signs show the wildlife often seen during winter in the meadows and at the lava cliffs above. Coyotes, golden eagles, weasels, martens, and chickadees are sometimes spotted by skiers. The Caples Creek trail takes you past beaver ponds. Scenic views show the western downslope of the Desolation Wilderness.

A large meadow at the cross-country trailhead allows beginning skiers to build their skills. Elaborate intermediate and expert trails can be found in the adjacent hills along the Schneider and Caples Lake trail systems.

Kirkwood offers condominiums you can ski to and the Cornice Restaurant for gourmet dining.

Kirkwood in Brief

Mailing address: PO Box 1, Kirkwood, CA 95646

Information: ☎ 209-258-6000

Snow Conditions: ☎ 209-258-3000

Reservations: ☎ 800-967-7500

Terrain Percentage For: Beginner - 15%; Intermediate - 50%; Advanced - 35%

Summit Elevation: 9,800

Base Elevation: 7,800

Vertical Drop: 2,000

Longest Run: 2½ miles

Size of Ski Area: 2300 acres, 68 runs

The Sierra/Gold Country

Lift capacity: 15,600

Lifts: 11 lifts, seven triples, three doubles, two surface lift

Facilities: Restaurants and decks at base, new lodgings also. Extensive condo lodging near base. Cornice is fine dining restaurant, Red Cliffs for Mexican food.

Ski School: Yes

Rentals: Yes

Cross-Country: Extensive system with separate lodge for cross-country. One of the more elaborate cross-country areas in the Sierra.

Season: November to May

Location: On State Route 88, 30 miles south of South Lake Tahoe

Sierra-at-Tahoe

A final major player in the Lake Tahoe skiing scene is the ski area known as Sierra-at-Tahoe, located on Highway 50 on the east side of Echo Summit, making it the closest snow-sports resort to Sacramento and San Francisco. Sierra-at-Tahoe has a number of positive features to recommend it. The view from the top of its highest lift at Grand View peak gives a stunning perspective on the Sierra, showing the ridge line of the Desolation Wilderness and a distant Lake Tahoe. Along the Desolation Wilderness ridge you see the peaks known as Pyramid, Ralston, and Tallac, the last of which is the highest peak in the Tahoe basin.

The Grand View lift lets even the beginning skier appreciate the spectacular view. Skiers relax at the top and enjoy the ridgetop restaurant, the Grand View Grill & Lake View BBQ, which offers a rare 360° view of the mountains from this lofty 8,852-foot deck. At this ethereal spot, a beginner skier can take the 2½-mile Sugar and Spice run to the bottom, making this one of the longer green runs anywhere. Indeed, fun, families, and beginner skiing are Sierra-at-Tahoe's strengths. For the youngsters, there is a Fun Zone area where costumed creatures lead the child into snow and ski fun. The specially designed Ski Tracks program takes a beginner skier, whether child or adult, literally by the hand and walks him or her up to a moderate level of proficiency. For someone who wants to learn to ski, this is one of the better programs.

Sierra-at-Tahoe boasts much good intermediate and some expert terrain, but does not compete with the elaborate downhill runs for experts at the other major ski sites. Tucked into the mountains, the resort is fairly well protected from winds. Snowboarders find Sierra-at-Tahoe a congenial place. Unlike the other major ski areas, Sierra-at-Tahoe closes down entirely in summer, so mountain bikers and hikers should go elsewhere.

Sierra-at-Tahoe in Brief

Mailing Address: 1111 Sierra-at-Tahoe Road, Twin Bridges, CA 95735

Information: ☎ 916-659-7453

Snow Conditions: ☎ 916-659-7475

Reservations: No lodging at ski area

Terrain Percentage For: Beginner - 25%; Intermediate - 50%; Advanced - 25%

Summit Elevation: 8,852 feet

Base Elevation: 6,640 feet

Vertical Drop: 2,212 feet

Longest Run: 2½ miles

Size of Ski Area: 2,000 acres

Lifts: 10 lifts, including three express quad chairlifts. One triple chair, five double chairs, one children's surface lift

Facilities: Restaurants and decks at base lodge and at top of mountain. Day care facilities.

Ski School: Full ski school program with First Track and Skill Improvement programs

Rentals: Full rental shop, with side-cut skis, snowboards

Cross-Country: Not on property

Season: Mid-November to April

Location: 12 miles west of South Lake Tahoe, off Highway 50 on the east side of Echo Summit. 83 miles east of Sacramento.

The Sierra/Gold Country

Yosemite

Yosemite has limited downhill skiing at **Badger Pass** (☎ 209-372-1000) good for beginners and low intermediates. More advanced skiers should stick with the Tahoe ski areas or Mammoth. California's first ski school opened at Badger Pass in 1928. The ski area is among the least crowded and most affordable in the Western States, Temperatures are mild, ranging from 30 to 40°.

Mammoth Mountain

Located on the east side of the Sierra, south from Yosemite, Mammoth Mountain has over 150 runs on 3,500 acres of ski area. Mammoth has many challenging runs and welcomes both skiers and snowboarders. The setting also presents the flinty, granite real estate special to the eastern Sierra, with its sharp, vertical peaks. The downside of Mammoth is that it is a fairly long drive to get there from San Francisco, about two hours longer than the Lake Tahoe ski areas. Take the all-weather route through the mountains at the south side of Lake Tahoe from Highway 50 to Highway 395. The Highway 120 pass to Mammoth through Yosemite is closed in winter. Highway 4 may also be closed.

Mammoth Mountain in Brief

Mailing address: PO Box 24, Mammoth Lakes, CA 93546

Information: ☎ 888-462-6668

Snow conditions: ☎ 888-766-9778

Reservations: ☎ 888-466-2666

Terrain Percentage For: Beginner - 30%; Intermediate - 40%, Advanced 30%

Summit Elevation: 11,053

Base Elevation: 7,953

Vertical Drop: 3,100

Size of Ski Area: 3,500 acres

Lifts: 29 lifts

Facilities: Child care, three day lodges, and food service at the base.

> **Ski School:** Yes
>
> **Rentals:** Yes
>
> **Cross-Country:** Extensive in Mammoth area, but not at the alpine ski area.
>
> **Season:** November to April
>
> **Location:** Off Highway 395 at Mammoth Lakes, 50 miles north of Bishop.

Cross-Country Skiing: The Sierra

Royal Gorge

Royal Gorge amounts to the largest and most elaborate cross-country ski resort in existence. The trends of the future in cross-country are being tested today at Royal Gorge. About 120,000 skiers glide across the trails at Royal Gorge each year.

The resort presents 88 trails, about 200 groomed miles in total, allowing you to ski for days without repeating a trail. Eight warming huts are scattered around the property. The resort boasts an eight-mile, gradually descending run as one amenity among many on its 7,000-acre site.

The Wilderness Lodge, in the heart of Royal Gorge, requires a several-day commitment, starting with a sleigh ride or a ski-in to get there. Once situated, you enjoy gourmet food, the relaxation of a hot tub, and expert guides taking you out on the trails.

The day skier at Royal Gorge benefits from a highly professional staff and a large north-facing mountain slope, located off Highway 80 at Soda Springs, four hours east of San Francisco.

Royal Gorge attracts three times more skiers than its closest competition in California. The California resorts also dwarf cross-country skiing in any other region, including New England or the Rockies. Only Anchorage, Alaska, with its Kincaid Park, rivals Royal Gorge in size.

Besides Wilderness Lodge, they have another facility on Interstate 80 known as Rainbow Lodge. This lodge can be a destination end-of-the day run from the upper slopes.

The Sierra/Gold Country

One scenic trail up to Snow Mountain Hut allows you to gaze out over the Royal Gorge on the North Fork of the American River.

For more information, contact **Royal Gorge Cross-Country Ski Resort,** ☎ 530-426-3871; PO Box 1100, Soda Springs, CA 95728.

Tahoe Donner

Tahoe Donner is a medium-size, high-quality resort off Highway 80, just west of Lake Tahoe at Truckee.

The guiding figure at Tahoe Donner was Glenn Jobe, who built up Tahoe-Donner with partner Kenny Stannard before moving on and putting Stannard in full charge. Earlier, Jobe also started the Kirkwood Cross-Country Resort. Glenn Jobe was 14th in the world at one time in the Olympic biathelete competition, an event requiring that you cross-country around a track, shoot a rifle, then repeat the process.

Tahoe Donner happens to offer night skiing Wednesdays and Saturdays on 2½ kilometers of lighted tracks, a special experience.

Tahoe Donner reflects some of Jobe's philosophic positions about the sport of cross-country. Jobe felt that cross-country should be a totally stress-free environment. Consequently, he and Stannard arranged the tracks so that most have skiers traveling in one direction only. You never need to watch for oncoming skiers.

Tahoe Donner now has 70 kilometers of tracks. Moreover, the tracks are laid out with the social element of the sport in mind. You ski directly alongside a companion to carry on a conversation, rather than on either side of a skating lane, used by fast skiers with their short skis.

Tahoe Donner extends out to a scenic region known as the Euer Valley, where the resort has a day lodge. Here you can enjoy gourmet food at the Cook House Café, as you can at the trailhead shop café, called the Donner Party Café. Euer Valley is a rustic cattle ranching area in summer, complete with old barns.

As with Royal Gorge, Tahoe Donner is a cross-country site only, though there is downhill nearby.

Tahoe Donner is four miles from Truckee on Alder Road. For more information, contact **Tahoe Donner Cross-Country,** ☎ 530-587-9484; PO Box 758, Truckee, CA 96160.

Northstar

Northstar is a full-service resort, where you can cross-country ski right to your condo. The cross-country trails are an adjunct to the large downhill program at this resort on the northwest side of Lake Tahoe, south of Truckee.

About 65 kilometers of groomed trails in all categories – beginner, intermediate, and expert – greet the skier at a mid-mountain location on the peak called Mt. Pluto.

At mid-mountain, if you turn right, there is the cross-country center, with views overlooking the Martis Valley. The operation offers both lessons and equipment. If you turn left, there are 20 kilometers of steeper, wooded trails, with a caboose warming hut and views of Lake Tahoe.

For more information, contact **Northstar-at-Tahoe Cross-Country Center**, ☎ 530-562-2475; Truckee, CA 96160.

Diamond Peak

Located on the northeast side of Lake Tahoe, Diamond Peak offers spectacular views of the lake from its Rim Trail. This newly developed cross-country area features pleasant wooded terrain of fir and pine trees, with plenty of ups and downs for variety.

Guided by Greg Mihevc, the enterprise has gradually organized parking along the highways and graduates each year to a more substantial warming hut/ski shop, offering limited equipment rentals, some lessons, and a modest restaurant.

Mihevc presents 40 kilometers of well-groomed trails. The parking is clearly marked on a pullout along Highway 431, on the hill proceeding from Lake Tahoe toward Reno. Diamond Peak also has downhill skiing, with a long ridge offering views of the lake. However, the cross-country is entirely separate from the downhill, insuring the quiet and solitude that so many cross-country enthusiasts seek.

The Rim of the Lake, Lover's Lane, and Vista loops are all for intermediate skiers. Black diamond areas for expert skiers are The Great Flume and Diamond Back. Each season, new trails are added.

The Sierra/Gold Country

For more information, contact **Diamond Peak Cross-Country and Snowshoe Center,** ☎ 702-832-1177; 1210 Ski Way, Incline Village, NV 89451.

Kirkwood

All of the cross-country areas flourish even with relatively little snow. Fortunately, cross-country requires only a fraction of the snow base needed for downhill skiing. Moreover, the grooming techniques in cross-country have improved in recent years, so the chippers resetting the track need only to carve up the top quarter inch of snow to make new track. Conserving snow can be a virtue in the California Sierra, especially in the cycle of drought experienced in the final years of the 1980s.

Snowshoe and cross-country exploring at Kirkwood, near Lake Tahoe. Even when skiing conditions are poor in other areas, Kirkwood enjoys good skiing, partly because the elevation is so high. Kirkwood's snow is also particularly dry and powdery.

The cross-country program is highly professional, organized by expert skier Debbi Waldear. Conservation and environmental awareness are distinctive parts of the program. Posted signs show the wildlife often seen during winter in the meadows and at the lava cliffs above. Coyotes, golden eagles, weasels, martens, and chickadees are sometimes spotted by skiers. The Caples Creek trail takes you past beaver ponds. Scenic views show the western downslope of the Sierra Nevada, plus the Desolation Wilderness.

A large meadow at the cross-country trailhead allows beginning skiers to build their skills. Elaborate intermediate and expert trails can be found in the adjacent hills along the Schneider and Caples Lake trail systems.

Kirkwood offers condominiums you can ski to and the Cornice Restaurant for gourmet dining.

The resort grooms over 80 kilometers of trails along 2,300 acres of hills.

Kirkwood is 35 miles south of Tahoe on Highway 88 near Carson Pass. For more information, contact **Kirkwood Cross-Country**, ☎ 209-258-7248; PO Box 1, Kirkwood, CA 95646.

Hope Valley

John and Patty Brissenden's Sorensen's Resort in Hope Valley presents yet another approach to cross-country. Sorensen's consists of 30 rustic cabins, gourmet dining (try the tomato tarragon soup) and plenty of cross-country trails leading right from the cabins. Indian Head Trail proceeds from the cabins into virgin terrain.

Hope Valley lies south of Lake Tahoe at the juncture of Highways 89-88. For the skier looking for a personalized alternative to the large resort, plus ample cross-country trails that are marked, but not groomed, Sorensen's is the place. Sorensen's does not charge for use of its trail system.

For more information, contact **Sorensen's**, ☎ 916-694-2203, 800-423-9949. 14255 Highway 88, Hope Valley, CA 96120, At Sorensen's Resort you'll find the Hope Valley Cross-Country Ski Center.

Bear Valley

Bear Valley offers a ski milieu as close as you will come to wilderness at a cross-country resort with groomed trails. The resort lies on Highway 4, east of the Gold Country Highway 49. The site is located south of the Mokelumne Wilderness, a wonderful backpacking region.

When the weather is stormy in the mountains, Bear Valley offers assured access because, though the resort area is high at 7,000 feet, you don't have to drive over higher passes to get there. However, always carry chains when going to any of these cross-country resorts.

The Sierra/Gold Country

Bear Valley is a small-scale resort where you can park your car and get all desired services, such as lodging, dining, and skiing, within walking distance. However, the kilometers of cross-country trails here are not small scale. Some 35 miles of groomed trails await the skier.

For further information, contact **Bear Valley Cross-Country**, ☎ 209-753-2834; PO Box 5120, Bear Valley, CA 95223.

Yosemite

Yosemite offers cross-country at several sites within the park, but the superlative experience is an overnight ski trip to Glacier Point. You ski out with a guide one day the 17 kilometers from Badger Pass to Glacier Point, stay overnight for one or two nights at the elegant stone lodge, and then ski back. Near Glacier Point, the highlight of the trip is a ski outing to Sentinel Dome, where a 360° panorama of the park opens up. From an elevated perspective you see El Capitan, Half Dome, the Clark Range, and many other features of the park.

Yosemite's most capable mountain guides manage the outings. You may find yourself led by Tim Messick, author of the volume *Cross-Country Skiing in Yosemite*. The guide cooks your food and assumes basic safety responsibility for the group. Intermediate skiing skills and good physical conditioning are advisable for this 7,000-8,000-foot altitude.

If you have the skiing skills and physical stamina to go out to Glacier Point and back on your own in one day, you don't need a guide. Moreover, if you possess snow-camping skills, you can camp out at Glacier Point on your own. However, most skiers will prefer the warm bunks, hot food, and even a few glasses of wine possible in the stone lodge at Glacier Point.

Another special Yosemite experience is a flight to the east side of the park at Lee Vining, followed by a trans-Sierra ski trip of five days across the high country and down to Yosemite Valley.

Yosemite has 45 kilometers of set track skiing in the park, but there are also 350 miles of ski-able roads, closed to cars by winter snow.

For more information, contact **Yosemite Cross-Country Ski School**, ☎ 209-372-8444; Yosemite National Park, CA 95389.

Mammoth

Mammoth has an engaging set of cross-country ski trails with set track around the small lakes in the area. You ski through the pine forests and enjoy the striking, clear skies of the eastern Sierra. The two cross-country trail systems are at **Tamarack** (☎ 760-934-2442) and **Sierra Meadows** (☎ 760-934-6161). Backcountry skiing is possible in Mammoth on the extensive Inyo National Forest Land public trail system.

Snowmobiling, Dog Sledding, Snowshoeing: The Sierra

Snowmobiling is popular in South Lake Tahoe at the golf course along Highway 50 that becomes a snowmobile park in winter. Contact **Lake Tahoe Adventures**, ☎ 702-916-3071; Highway 50, for details. They provide the snowmobiles for the golf course run and can also arrange shuttles and snowmobiles for remote rides in the Hope Valley, a half-hour south of Lake Tahoe. If you have your own snowmobile, the open lands in the Hope Valley are the area's most prominent snowmobile destination.

A similar snowmobile operation flourishes at the **Zephyr Cove Snowmobile Center** (☎ 702-588-3833) along the scenic west side of Lake Tahoe.

The extensive snowmobile trails throughout Mammoth take in the area's geological wonders and breathtaking vistas. Free trail maps are available at the Mammoth Visitor Center on Highway 203. For equipment, clothing and guides, contact **Mammoth Snowmobile Adven-Tours** at ☎ 760-934-9645.

Dogsledding is another intriguing but minor sport in

Dogsledding at Hope Valley, near Lake Tahoe.

California. The scene is unlike Alaska, where recreational dog-sledding wins numerous converts each year. In the Tahoe area the flat terrain of the Hope Valley is a favorite for dogsledding. One provider is Dottie Dennis, a 20-year veteran of the sport. Her lead dog Mazie and seven other canines can take you on a picnic ride or even a moonlight ride in the Hope Valley. Contact Dottie Dennis at ☎ 702-782-3047.

In Mammoth, you can ride behind a dog sled courtesy of **Dog Sled Adventures**, ☎ 760-934-6270.

Snowshoeing is making a comeback, using newer, smaller, lighter showshoes. Often the cross-country ski places are leading the sport. Typically, you can rent the new showshoes at **Kirkwood Cross-Country** (☎ 209-258-7248). The US Forest Service rangers conduct winter snowshoe tours on selected Saturdays in the Camp Richardson area (☎ 916-542-6584) along Lake Tahoe. Snowshoe trips, guided by rangers, are also popular in Yosemite.

■ Where to Stay & Eat

Accommodations at Lake Tahoe

 The most notable lodging on the California side of the border is **Embassy Suites** (☎ 916-544-5400; 4130 Lake Tahoe Boulevard, South Lake Tahoe, CA 96150. $$$) in South Lake Tahoe. Embassy Suites offers a living room separate from the bedroom, plus a cocktail hour in the evening and a full buffet breakfast in the morning. The scene is convivial in the huge atrium each evening as guests gather for a margarita or a glass of Chardonnay before dinner. Piano music wafts through the cavernous structure. In winter, skiers just in from the slopes may be hanging out in the heated pool or jacuzzi.

Inn by the Lake (☎ 916-542-0330, 3300 Lake Tahoe Boulevard, South Lake Tahoe, CA 96150. $$-$$$) is an attractively landscape inn/motel low-rise structure with large rooms and a quiet environment that is convenient to casinos and ski slopes alike.

Sorensen's (☎ 916-694-2203 or 800-423-9949; 14255 Highway 88, Hope Valley, CA 96120. $$-$$$) is a rustic yet modern cluster of cabins in a woodsy setting 20 miles from Lake Tahoe off Highways 50-89-88 in Hope Valley. It has a small, gourmet restaurant, personalized approach, and non-smoking environment. Hosts John and Patty Brissenden cater to hikers in summer and cross-country skiers in winter. Sorensen's is an excellent choice if you'd like to be away from the city.

Harrah's Hotel and Casino (☎ 702-588-6611; PO Box 8, Stateline, NV 89449. $$-$$$) is a five-star property with all amenities at the south edge of Lake Tahoe. Harrahs offers comfortable and large rooms, responsive service, and a lavish, gourmet buffet.

Harvey's Resort Hotel (☎ 702-588-2411; PO Box 128, Stateline, NV 89449. $$-$$$) is the largest of the gaming resorts at the south edge of Lake Tahoe. Harvey's has ample and comfortable rooms, plus a view of the lake from its tower rooms.

Some of the ski resorts also offer their own self-contained lodgings year round, such as **Northstar** (☎ 800-466-6784. $$-$$$) and **Kirkwood** (☎ 209- 258-6000. $$-$$$). See the complete descriptions of them under *Downhill Skiing.*

For lodging referrals at the South Shore, call the **Lake Tahoe Visitors Authority** (☎ 800-288-2463).

Accommodations at Yosemite

 Accommodations for Yosemite are diverse. All reservations are managed by **Yosemite Concession Services,**(☎ 209-252-4848). In Yosemite Valley you can bask in the first-class resort comforts at **The Ahwahnee**, take a rustic cabin at **Yosemite Lodge**, reside in an economical canvas cabin at **Curry Village**, stay at a drive-in campground, or pitch your tent and sleeping bag under the stars at a walk-in campground. You can even arrange a walking tour of the high country with lodging and meals awaiting you at the end of each day's hike. At the Wawona area, you can stay in the historic **Wawona Hotel**, near the Mariposa Grove of giant sequoia trees. Whatever your preference, it is necessary to make reservations in advance for the popular summer months.

Accommodations at Mammoth Lakes

 Once you arrive in Mammoth Lakes, the **Mammoth Lakes Visitors Center and Ranger Station** (☎ 888-466-2666) on Highway 203, three miles west of Highway 395, is a good first stop. You can obtain maps and all desired info on the region, either in person or mailed to you earlier if you call or write. There are several central reservations systems that can locate the right place, at the right price for you. Overall, the town has a clean, modern feel, rather than the old falsefront mining town one might expect.

Condos, such as **Snowcreek Resort**, make a good base of operation for a family trip. Snowcreek (☎ 619-934-3333. $$-$$$) has every amenity desired, including a jacuzzi a few steps away, good for an active family wishing to relax in the evening after a rigorous day of sporty outings. The condos are equipped for food preparation. Von's is a small supermarket in town.

A central lodging reservation service for many condos is **Mammoth Properties Reservations**, ☎ 760-934-4242 or 888-626-6684; PO Box 408, Mammoth Lakes, CA 93546.

Accommodations in the Gold Country/Sacramento

 Because of its many fine Victorian homes, the Gold Country has become a prime B&B territory for the California explorer. A good example in Grass Valley is **Murphy's Inn** (☎ 916-273-6873; 318 Neal Street, Grass Valley, CA 95945, $$-$$$). The house itself is architecturally interesting and dates from 1866, when one Edward Coleman flourished in the mining and logging business. The innkeepers, Nancy and Ted Daus, are knowledgeable and sociable people who can guide you with suggestions about exploring their area. The rooms, such as the West Suite, tend to have four-poster beds, floral wall paper and lace curtains, and a cruet of port for guests to sip. The establishment is of manageable size, eight rooms in two houses across the street from one another. Breakfast is memorable, with warm orange-flavored rolls and egg casseroles. Satisfying B&Bs like

Murphy's Inn have created a whole subculture of B&B lodging aficionados in Northern California.

Many of the early Gold Rush buildings have been turned into hotels. The general price ranges are moderate.

Thirteen of the historic bed and breakfast lodgings in El Dorado County have banded together and will be happy to send you a brochure. Contact **Historic Country Inns**, PO Box 106, Placerville, CA 95667.

The historic **City Hotel** (☎ 209-532-1479; One Main Street, Columbia, CA 95310. $$) is a premier Gold Country hostelry and dining room. Ten guest rooms in the 1856 building are furnished with antiques. Hospitality industry students from nearby Columbia College provide attentive service in the dining room.

Murphy's Hotel (☎ 209-728-3444; 457 Main Street, Murphy's, CA 95247. $$) dates from 1856 and devotes one room to each of several figures from the 19th century, such as Mark Twain or Ulysses S. Grant. The hotel's dining room is unpretentious. Try the prime rib or pot roast.

The **National Hotel** (☎ 209-223-0500; 2 Water Street, Jackson, CA 95642. $$) is large by Gold Country standards, with 44 rooms. The proprietors claim that every California governor has stayed here, plus a few presidents, such as Garfield and Hoover. The rooms are small, but the budget traveler will be delighted.

The **Jamestown Hotel** (☎ 209-984-3902; 18153 Main Street, Jamestown, CA 9532. $$) has been restored to its 1913 decor. Seven rooms are available in this small establishment. Like many of the other hotels, it has a restaurant on the premises.

The **Ryan House Bed & Breakfast Inn** (☎ 800-831-4897; 153 South Shepherd Street, Sonora, CA 95370. $$-$$$) is an 1855 homestead. Four rooms are available at this lawn-encircled abode. The garden area features rose bushes and wicker furniture.

The **National Hotel** (☎ 916-265-4551; 211 Broad Street, Nevada City, CA 95959. $$) illustrates just how popular the word National was for hotels in Gold Country. This 1856 establishment claims to be the oldest continuously operating hostelry west of the Rockies. A lavish bar, commodious dining room, and general Victorian air characterize this hotel.

The Sierra/Gold Country

Grandmere's Inn (☎ 916-265-4660; 449 Broad Street, Nevada City, CA 95959. $$-$$$) is on the National Registry of Historic Places. This 1856 Colonial Revival structure offers antique-filled rooms and a full breakfast.

In Sacramento, a spacious Victorian has been transformed into an international all-ages hostel offering shared and private sleeping quarters. Located at 900 H Street, the **Sacramento International Hostel** is within walking distance of the Old Sacramento Historic District. For information, call ☎ 916-443-1691. $.

Restaurants at Lake Tahoe

 Evans restaurant (☎ 916-542-1990; on Emerald Bay Road. $$$), a mile from the Highway 50 turnoff, is the fine dining leader of the Tahoe region. Evan and Candice Williams, with their able assistant, Jim Mann, and with chef Evan Smith in the kitchen, orchestrate the place, a Tahoe cottage setting. The inventive menu is described as American Gourmet, and it is tasty indeed. Guests are greeted with a glass of champagne and a special treat, such as chicken pate. In this pink-tablecloth ambiance, with soft lights, fresh flowers, and romantic music, you might start with the mushroom bisque streaked with spinach and proceed to the roast venison. Alternatively, the mesclun lettuce salad with grilled portabello mushrooms could precede a roast swordfish on polenta. Try the tarte tatin for dessert.

As a contrast to Evans, on the Nevada side, consider **Planet Hollywood** (☎ 702-588-7828; Caesars Tahoe casino in Stateline, NV. $$). This themed restaurant chain will appeal to those who enjoy movie-and-TV-world memorabilia and a high-decibel environment while eating. Videos of favorite movies play continuously. Merchandise and food are offered for sale. Try a margarita to get in the mood, followed by the St. Louis ribs or the Santa Fe chicken pasta.

For breakfasts, the **Red Hut Café** (☎ 702-588-7488; 229 Kingsbury Grade. $-$$) is a classic diner, where the waitress never allows your coffee cup to become even half-empty. Eggs, bacon, pancakes, and hashbrowns overflow from the plates.

The casino buffet dining rooms give good value for price, hoping to attract the gambler . The best of these buffets is the groaning board at **Harrah's** (☎ 702-588-6611. $$). The casinos each sponsor gourmet dining rooms, such as the **Sage Room** at Harvey's Casino (☎ 702-588-2411. $$), done in western motifs, with steak as the menu item of choice.

Zackary's, ☎ 916-544-5400, is the fine-dining restaurant at the Embassy Suites. $$.

Restaurants at Yosemite

 All food service in **Yosemite** is associated with the various lodgings.

Curry Village ($) has a cafeteria, good for fast food. The lines can be long, so you may want to do a picnic lunch.

Yosemite Lodge ($$) offers a comfortable and rustic dining room, with chicken and steak as good choices.

The Ahwahnee ($$-$$$) dining room, which requires that men wear a jacket for dinner, is the park's fine dining experience. Steak, lamb, and veal are good choices. This is the site of wine-and-food weekend celebrations in winter. Reservations are required for dinner.

Restaurants at Mammoth Lakes

 Mammoth hosts a range of interesting, small restaurants, where the owners are actively involved. Try the **Mountain Café** (☎ 760-934-9316; 437 Old Mammoth Road. $-$$) for a breakfast of huevos rancheros or a vegetarian omelette. After several years on a fishing boat out of San Diego, John Goforth, who felt he knew what fresh fish was all about, got the backing to open his **Ocean Harvest** (☎ 619-934-8539. $$) restaurant, where the sea bass, scallops, or orange ruffy would be good choices. **Berger's** (☎ 760-934-6622; 6118 Minaret Road. $-$$) is Gary Berger's eatery, where he will counsel that medium rare on the buffalo can keep this low-fat meat tender.

Restaurants in the Gold Country/Sacramento

 Several of the historic inns have their own restaurants. One of these is the **City Hotel** (☎ 209-532-1479; Columbia. $$). Try the continental specialties, such as grilled chicken breast in Champagne or the veal picatta.

Another is **Murphy's Hotel** (☎ 209-728-3444; Murphy's. $$). Try the prime rib or pot roast.

Try the gorgonzola pasta with prawns or the New York steak at the **Jamestown Hotel** (☎ 209-984-3902; Jamestown. $$).

At the **National Hotel** (☎ 916-265-4551; Nevada City. $$), sample the New Zealand rack of lamb or the roast pork.

Other restaurants here are independent of lodgings. A good example is the **Main Street Café** (☎ 916-477-6000; 213 West Main, Grass Valley. $$), an informal café with an inventive chef. The menu dances gracefully from buffalo burgers to gourmet Cajun.

Some of the better restaurants in the Gold Country are Italian. One good example is **Cirino's** (☎ 916-265-2246; 309 Broad Street, Nevada City. $$). In this unpretentious old bar, you glance up from your red-checkered oilcloth tablecloth at the stamped tin walls as you dine on Italian culinary specialties.

Another Italian place in Grass Valley is **Pasta Luigi's** (☎ 916-477-0455; 760 South Auburn Street. $$). The food is tasty, the atmosphere pleasant but unpretentious, and the prices offer good value. Try the linguini zingarella, a flat-noodle pasta with spicy sausage and sun-dried tomatoes, or the veal scallopine, thin strips of young beef sauteed with olive oil, marsala, and mushrooms.

A landmark in Old Sacramento is **The Firehouse** (☎ 916-442-4772; 1112 Second Street. $$-$$$), where former Governor Reagan held both of his inaugural dinners. It excels in entrées like honey and Szechuan peppercorn glazed duck breast or lamb noisette, and boasts an extensive list of mainly California wines.

 Amador County produces some of California's better Zinfandel wines. D'Agostini's is a brand to enjoy.

Camping & RV in the Sierra & Gold Country

 Throughout Northern California some campgrounds can be reserved for state parks (☎ 800-444-7275) and for national parks (☎ 800-436-7275).

At the southwest end of Lake Tahoe, **D. L. Bliss State Park** (☎ 916-525-7277) has 168 developed sites on the shore of Lake Tahoe. The park is 13 miles north of Highway 50 off Highway 89.

There are good campgrounds throughout the National Forest system, usually taking no reservations. One example would be **Woods Lake** in El Dorado National Forest, two miles west of Carson Pass off Highway 88. Call ☎ 916-644-6048 for information.

The hot water pools at **Grover Hot Springs State Park** have made this site a perennial Sierra camping favorite. Grover Hot Springs (☎ 916-694-2248) has 76 sites west of Markleeville off Highway 89.

In **Yosemite**, campers may choose from 15 campgrounds within the national park (☎ 209-372-0200), but during the popular summer months stays are limited to seven days in Yosemite Valley and Wawona and 14 days at sites outside of the Valley. Reservations require a minimum of two weeks to be processed, so be sure to plan ahead.

At the **Mammoth Lakes** basin area, try the **Lake Mary Campground** (☎ 619-924-5500), eight miles west of Mammoth Junction. There are 48 sites with picnic tables and fire rings. Lake Mary is another example of a choice Forest Service campground that does not take reservations. The Mammoth Ranger Station can provide information about the area's more than 700 campsites (☎ 619-924-5500).

In the Gold Country, **Malakoff Diggins State Historic Park** (☎ 916-265-2740) offers some of the most wilderness-like camps in the state parks system. At Malakoff you also learn about the final phase of the gold mining operations, placer mining.

Chaw Se Indian Grinding Rock State Historic Park (☎ 209-296-7488) near Pine Grove is a lovely camping area amidst large oak trees. You will see where the native Californians, over eons, ground acorns into meal using depressions in the rocks.

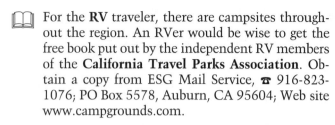 For the **RV** traveler, there are campsites through-
out the region. An RVer would be wise to get the
free book put out by the independent RV members
of the **California Travel Parks Association**. Obtain a copy from ESG Mail Service, ☎ 916-823-
1076; PO Box 5578, Auburn, CA 95604; Web site
www.campgrounds.com.

Near Sacramento, the Loomis Basin, 21 miles east of city, offers a
pleasing setting for the start of a Gold Country visit. The **Loomis
KOA**, ☎ 916-652-6737; 3945 Taylor Road in Loomis, offers complete hookups, tent sites, hot showers, a laundry and a pool to patrons. There are many other KOAs throughout Northern
California.

In the Gold Country, an RVer would be comfortable at the **49er
Trailer Village** (☎ 800-339-6981) in Plymouth, which comes
complete with cable TV and a jacuzzi, plus full hookups in its 329
sites.

Near Yosemite, **Yosemite Pines RV Park** (☎ 209-962-5042) in
Groveland would be a good location, only 22 miles from the park,
relatively close for daytrip excursions.

The largest and most complete RV campground in South Lake
Tahoe, especially good for family-style RV-ing, is **Tahoe Valley
Campground** (☎ 916-541-2222) at the end of C Street off High-
way 50.

■ The Mystique of Cross-Country Skiing

By Lee Foster

Soft, thick flakes of snow, falling at the rate of three inches an
hour, greeted me as I skied cross-country along the Aspen Forest
Trail at Bear Valley in California's Sierra. The aspen and pine
trees of the forest assumed a magical appearance, aspen branches
stark against the white and pine branches bent almost vertical
with the heavy snow. The gray sky of this major storm proved inviting, warm, and perfectly quiet, rather than ominous. Only the
crunch of my skis, gripping the snow in the touring track, broke

the complete stillness of the forest. In the good company of my two children, Karin and Paul, I savored the moment.

I was not alone in choosing this sport. Cross-country or nordic resorts flourish across America, while growth of downhill or alpine skiing has languished. Industry observers estimate that there are about 10.7 million downhill skiers, 3½ million cross-country skiers. What makes this sport so attractive?

Cross-country offers a pleasing mix of solitude and sociability. While skiing along, I've had wonderful talks with my children and other companions. One afternoon, Glenn Jobe, who then ran the Tahoe-Donner cross-country resort, regaled me with his cross-country exploits in the 1980 Olympics while we skied. Yet you can also ski alone or withdraw for a time into yourself while skiing with others. Encounters are purposeful, unlike the accidental meeting while waiting in line for a ski lift in downhill skiing. The people you meet when cross-country skiing, whether in lessons or on the trails, tend to be a friendly lot.

As a jogger who enjoys a couple miles of moderate running each evening, the prospect of skiing through the snow and forest environment is enticing. With cross-country I continue my fitness trajectory in a new mode. The dance-like elegance of a skilled cross-country expert is a pleasure to watch as the skier glides along the trails with relative ease, moving up hills with only a fraction of the effort required in walking. The fitness boom, such a part of modern American culture, will surely carry cross-country forward.

Cross-country delights me as a lifetime sport, safe for all ages. If you've ever been hit from behind by an out-of-control hot dogger in downhill, as I have, then cross-country suddenly looks more appealing. I want to ski forever, without injury, in a stress-free environment. Cross-country delivers on such a wish. You can ski with comrades across the generations in this sport. If you can walk, you can ski cross-country, though lessons on correct technique for an efficient gliding movement are highly recommended.

This is a gentle sport, allowing you to set the pace. There's plenty of excitement and speed, if you want it, in the version of cross-country called skating, using shorter skis. Moreover, each cross-country touring region has its "black," or steep, downhills, so thrills are possible. But for the touring skier, who enjoys an outing without the need for extensive vertiginous descents, flat "green" trails and intermediate "blue" trails suffice.

I also enjoy the dramatic winter landscapes that cross-country lets me experience. For example, I have skied out to Glacier Point and Sentinel Dome at Yosemite and stayed overnight in the lodge. Anyone can do this, but only if you cross-country ski 10.7 miles to the Point. The winter vistas in Yosemite from Sentinel Dome are panoramic and spectacular. Many other inviting areas of the California Sierra become accessible through cross-country. Potential places to explore are not limited by the sharp slopes required for downhill skiing. The wilderness region around Bear Valley, the back-of-the-mountain skiing at Royal Gorge, and the lovely National Forest land in the Hope Valley are among my favorite memories. I long to ski many new areas. On my future list is urban cross-country skiing around the lakes in Minneapolis. When will I have a chance to ski from B&B to B&B in the White Mountains of New Hampshire?

Cross-country in delicate, wild environments also pleases because it is such a minimum-impact sport. You ski along efficiently on top of the snow, causing no environmental damage. All trace of your tracks, in fact, will disappear with the spring melt.

Advances in the equipment for cross-country have lured me and others into the sport. The late 1970s invention of waxless skis, with the skis gripping the snow through scale-like ridges on the bottoms, has made the sport hassle-free. This advance is particularly relevant to California skiing, where snow conditions can change frequently, requiring a change of waxes. An expert will still enjoy the slightly higher performance of waxed skis, but the beginning and intermediate skier doesn't need to be troubled with this nuance. Boot bindings have also improved, allowing easier snap in and out, with more boot control over the slim skis. At the resort-operator level, machines that groom the trails have improved, cutting tracks that allow cross-country skiers to glide through the forest.

Cross-country ski resorts have also resolved a troublesome issue that ravaged the sport in the mid-1980s. The traditional touring skier was confronted with a new style of skating skier, fighting for the same narrow trail. Skating skiers use shorter skis and proceed with the motion of a speed-skater in ice skating. The solution has been to groom a 14-foot-wide trail with a skating lane of compacted snow and a double set of touring tracks.

Finally, cross-country offers major economies both in equipment and in trail fees. My equipment package at a sporting goods store, REI, cost $158 for skis, bindings, poles, and boots. Downhill would have cost substantially more, especially for the boots. Trail fees for downhill skiing now soar astronomically. A day at Squaw Valley downhill costs nearly $50, but a day at the most expensive and elaborate cross-country resort, Royal Gorge, costs about $15. Inherent economies in the cross-country concept will keep the price of the sport relatively low. Cross-country does not require a steep slope or any mechanized towing device to get participants up hills. Some publicly owned lands, such as Yosemite, have elaborate track systems and no trail fee charge.

Though I enjoy the track skiing of a resort (or Yosemite), the cross-country skier who prefers economies and no-track skiing can use National Forest roads and trails. California has organized a Snow Park permit system that allows parking in choice National Forest areas of the Sierra.

I have no wish to be apostolic about cross-country skiing. But someday perhaps you will cross-country through the forest, as I have, and watch a mound of snow cascade off a pine tree branch, near the top of the tree, and then proceed, like an avalanche, down the tree, cleaning off the snow from the entire tree. Or perhaps you will observe, as I have, the antics of a coyote hunting voles in the deep snow. Or maybe you will encounter the winter splendor of Yosemite's Half Dome and El Capitan from the elevated position of Sentinel Dome, accessible only to the cross-country skier. The sport offers many quiet and revealing moments, which tell a skier about the environment and about himself. After a few such moments you will understand why many outdoor enthusiasts enjoy this sport.

The Sierra/Gold Country

Chapter 7

Monterey, Santa Cruz & Big Sur

The varied waterfronts of the Monterey/Santa Cruz region, south of San Francisco, offer travel experiences that are visually rewarding and athletically exhilarating.

The dramatic sand dunes that initially announce the Monterey Coast reveal a dark blue body of water that is alive with frisky otters and playful sea lions.

The Santa Cruz Coast, with its high cliffs and water-carved rock bridges north of the city, is packed with wet-suited surfers patiently waiting for the perfect wave.

For the lover of more land-oriented nature, the redwood parks in the hills surrounding Santa Cruz and the ruggedness of the Big Sur coast beckon, as do gem-like state parks, such as Point Lobos.

The adventure traveler will find much appeal in the region, from the excellent scenic drives on the Big Sur and San Mateo Coasts to the superb bicycle path leading north from Santa Cruz to Wilder Ranch State Park. Four major redwood state parks have inviting trails and the inland Pinnacles National Monument is a rock climbing site awash with wildflowers in the spring.

On the sea, you can kayak the kelp beds at Monterey or surf the waves at Steamer Lane in Santa Cruz. Monterey also has a rare walk-in scuba site where novice divers get certified. North of Monterey, all the air sports can be enjoyed, from hang gliding at Marina Beach to skydiving at the Marina Airport.

The Monterey region of California encompasses lively, small cities and choice stretches of the California coast starting 1½ hours south of San Francisco. Any traveler who takes pleasure in history, nature, and the good life will welcome a chance to explore the area. Few regions offer as much to entice a visitor.

Monterey Peninsula

Geographically, the focus of the area is the Monterey Peninsula, which undulates gently into the Pacific Ocean, forming wide but little-protected Monterey Bay. Monterey was and is the major city on the Peninsula, with Pacific Grove and Carmel nearby. South from the Peninsula is the diverse wildlife habitat of **Point Lobos** and the spectacular scenic drive down the Big Sur Coast. Inland

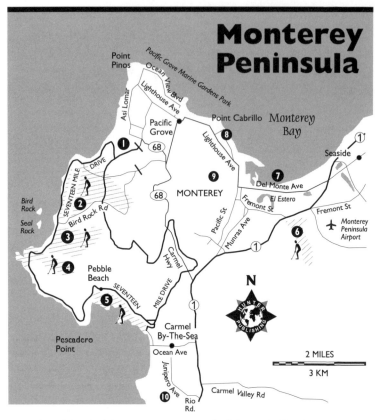

1. Spanish Bay Golf Course
2. Monterey Peninsula C.C.
3. Spyglass Hill Golf Course
4. Cypress Point C.C.
5. Pebble Beach Golf Course
6. Old Del Monte Golf Course
7. Fisherman's Wharf, Monterey State Beach
8. Monterey Bay Aquarium
9. Presidio of Monterey
10. Mission San Carlos Borromeo del Rio Carmelo

stretch some of the most productive agricultural lands in America, the fabled Salad Bowl of the Nation, around Salinas, which has been transformed in the last two decades into one of the largest premium wine producing areas in the state.

In **Monterey** and **Carmel** you can witness California's early Spanish-Mexican history, both the secular pueblo and the sacred mission where mission-founder Junipero Serra lies buried. Pacific Grove gives you an opportunity to stroll past Victorian houses that replaced an earlier Methodist seaside encampment. Monterey in the 20th century includes noted American novelist John Steinbeck's waterfront, where you can imagine his *Cannery Row* characters. Not far away, the galleries of Carmel have showcased the creations of local artists since the 1920s.

Nature at Monterey

The Monterey area also boasts the world-famous **Monterey Aquarium**, one of the most congenial introductions to nature that man has devised. On this raw coast you'll find a rugged landscape of contorted cypress and pine, fog-shrouded mountains, and mile-long sand beaches. Along this wondrous treasure of California seascape you can immerse yourself in the sea otter environment of Point Lobos, the Monarch butterfly town of Pacific Grove, the carriage excursion for nabobs along the 17-Mile Drive, and the rocky headlands of Big Sur.

The Good Life

Since fairly early times the settlers of the Monterey region have lived rather well. The tradition of the old and venerable Del Monte Hotel of the 19th century, with its upscale style, continues today, with many lodging and dining experiences worth celebrating on this "Riviera of the West Coast," as some residents characterize the area. The Monterey Plaza Hotel in Monterey or the Tickle Pink Inn above Point Lobos exemplify the finer destination lodgings. Creative chefs from the Sardine Factory in Monterey to the Grill on Ocean Avenue in Carmel offer culinary artistry at the forefront of the gastronomic scene. A traveler who returns home to recreate culinary specialties of the region may find himself or herself working with exciting new ingredients, from calamari to artichokes.

Residents here welcome the traveler and know that tourism is the mainstay of the economy. The resilience of the area, for a traveler, lies in its diversity, which prompts the visitor to return again and again. There is always another championship golf course like Pebble Beach to play, another fall migration of waterfowl at Point Lobos to witness, or a further adobe from Monterey's Spanish period to peruse.

Santa Cruz

Santa Cruz, which emerged like a phoenix from the Earthquake of 1989, lies on the sunny northern tip of Monterey Bay, 100 miles south of San Francisco. Weather here can total 300 sunny days a year with an average high temperature of 69°F. The population mix includes retirees, university students and faculty, craftspeople, artists, a cluster of professionals who have put lifestyle ahead of career advancement and moved here, and the ordinary people who keep the community rolling along.

Santa Cruz prides itself on a strong environmental ethic. Bike paths are everywhere. The downtown, after the earthquake, was rebuilt with stringent architectural guidelines that have re-created a small-town community feeling.

Climate and seaside location have made the Santa Cruz coast an appreciated resort region since 1865. Attractive beaches for swimming and sunning stretch along the coast for 29 miles. Some, such as New Brighton State Beach, have camping facilities.

The nearby **Santa Cruz Mountains** provide the lover of nature with a diverse, forested terrain, including California's first state park set aside to preserve redwoods, **Big Basin**.

■ Getting Here

The Monterey Peninsula can be reached from the north or south via **Highway 101** or the scenic **Highway 1**, which hugs the coast, offering intriguing views along the way. Driving time is 2½ hours via Highway 101 from San Francisco, with an added hour for Highway 1. Commuter air flights proceed to the Monterey Airport from San Francisco International.

Getting to Santa Cruz requires a choice. The region can be reached from the north or south via scenic **Highway 1**. The fastest route from the north to Santa Cruz is via **Highway 101** or **Interstate 280** to **Highway 17**, then across the mountains. The coast Highway 1 adds hours to the trip, but is well worth it for its scenic value.

Information Sources

For the Monterey area, contact the **Monterey Peninsula Visitors and Convention Bureau**, ☎ 408-649-1770; 380 Alvarado Street, Monterey, CA 93942-1770; Web site www.mpcc.com.

For the Santa Cruz area, contact the **Santa Cruz County Conference and Visitors Council**, ☎ 408-425-1234 or 800-833-3494; 701 Front Street, Santa Cruz, CA 95060; Web site www.scccvc.org.

■ Touring

Monterey

The historical story of Monterey is a major tourism draw. Monterey was the **Spanish-Mexican capital** on the Pacific coast, settled in 1770. The town flourished briefly as the American capital after roughly 1846. Eventually the Gold Rush shifted population growth slightly north, to San Francisco and Sacramento, the logical waystops to the mines.

Spanish and Mexican influences are felt strongly in downtown Monterey, both in the historic buildings and in the continuing architectural legacy that they nourish. You can trace the **Path of History** with a walking tour of 46 buildings constructed before the 1848 Gold Rush. Gold tiles set in the sidewalk mark the way for the two-mile, self-guided tour. In April, Monterey hosts a special open-house Adobe Tour of many of these structures.

Monterey is where much of the early historical drama of California played out, both at Junipero Serra's mission and at the trading docks along the waterfront. Merchant ships from Boston ex-

Monterey's Path of History

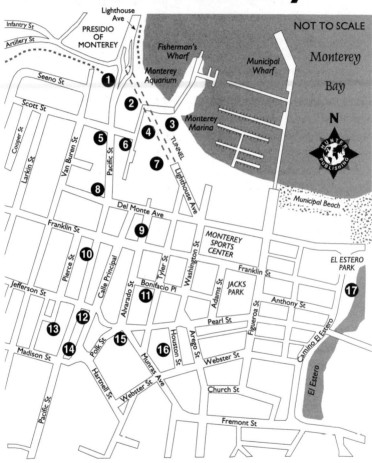

1. Vizcaino-Serra Landing Site
2. First Brick House
3. Custom House
4. Custom House Plaza
5. California's First Theatre
6. Boston Store (Casa del Oro)
7. Stanton Center (Maritime Museum of Monterey and Historic Center)
8. Casa Soberanes
9. Chamber of Commerce
10. Casa Serrano
11. Casa Estrada
12. Larkin House
13. Colton Hall
14. Monterey Peninsula Museum of Art; Civic Center
15. Cooper-Molera Adobe
16. Stevenson House
17. First French Consulate & Monterey Visitor Center

changed goods for cattle hides, also known as "California bankno-tes."

Juan Rodriguez Cabrillo discovered Monterey Bay in 1542 and claimed it for Spain, despite his failure to successfully dock his ship and set foot on land. Sebastian Vizcaino visited the bay in 1602 and became the first European to tread there. But no settlements occurred until Gaspar de Portola established, on the south shore of the bay, the first of Spain's four presidios in California. The main gate of the Presidio is at Pacific and Artillery streets, near where Vizcaino landed. Today the Presidio remains in military hands, with language studies one of its strengths.

Monterey Architecture

To sample the early architecture of Monterey, start near Fisherman's Wharf along the waterfront and look for the **Custom House**, 1 Custom House Plaza. Custom House is an 1830s adobe, the oldest government building on the Pacific coast. Here Commodore Drake Sloat raised the US flag for the first time in California, in 1846. The Custom House was where all goods shipped into the area were unloaded and the customs duties were collected. Today it is a museum exhibiting cargo items of the 19th-century trade. The Custom House Plaza echoes the design of early California settlements.

At Calle Principal and Scott Street, stop in at **Pacific House**, built in 1847. The two-story adobe has served as a storehouse for military supplies, a tavern, a courtroom, a newspaper office, and a church. Nowadays, Pacific House hosts a visitor center that interprets early California life, including the Native American culture.

On Pacific Street visit **Colton Hall**, built in 1847-49, where the famous constitutional convention of 1849 decided to align California with the free North rather than with the slave South. A museum displays early government documents.

The **Larkin House**, Calle Principale and Jefferson Street, dates to 1835 and is a good example of Monterey architecture, a style that combined adobe walls with second-floor balconies, wedding the architectural preferences of the Spanish to those of New England sea captains. The Larkin House contains many of its original furnishings and can be toured.

Legacy of the Larkins

If you have time to concentrate on only one of the historic buildings in the Path of History, the Larkin House would be a good choice. The house was the residence in the 1830s of Thomas Larkin, the American consul, and remained in family use until a descendant willed it to the state of California with all its furnishings intact. Take a guided tour if you want to enter the house. Otherwise, you can only observe the exterior and the gardens, ornamented with camellia flowers. Inside the house you'll see the locked tea set that Larkin is known to have owned. So precious was tea in the 1830s that it was kept under lock and key. Another object known to have been used by Larkin is a delicate ginger jar from China. Larkin's descendant, Alice Larkin Toulman, was the last resident of the house.

On the corner of Pacific and Scott streets, visit California's first theatre, built in 1846-47. Nineteenth-century plays are presented weekly.

The Missions

Several other buildings are interesting to visit, including the **Stevenson House**, where Robert Louis Stevenson stayed during his short sojourn here in 1879. The house, at 530 Houston Street, is open for tours and displays some Stevenson memorabilia.

At the same time Portola established the pueblo, Father Junipero Serra founded the second of what eventually became 21 California missions. He called it **Mission San Carlos Borromeo de Carmelo**. The mission started out near the pueblo, but was moved to a better water source and a more secure environment, away from presidio influence. The final mission site is close to the mouth of the Carmel River.

Fully restored, the mission is in Carmel at 3080 Rio Road. Partly because of the church's historical significance, Rome raised the Carmel Mission to basilica status in 1960. Momentum has been created to elevate Serra to sainthood, which will probably occur, but Rome proceeds at a Byzantine pace on these matters. The mission offers many interesting insights to the traveler. Serra's bedroom/writing room was spartan in the extreme. His library was quite amply stocked. From missions in Baja he brought silver chalices and adornments of great beauty. To be a mission father in the late 18th century required many skills, ranging from linguistic expertise to animal husbandry.

Spanish mission history can be further explored in the region at **Mission San Juan Bautista**, northeast of Monterey. Native Americans at this mission exhibited a high degree of musical skill in their choir and orchestra. In the Salinas Valley the **Soledad Mission** is now a mere adobe ruin, suggesting the solitude of its name. For the traveler who seeks out **Mission San Antonio de Padua**, further south along Highway 101 and west on Highway G14, both the setting, in an oak-filled grasslands, and the isolation of the restored mission are appealing.

John Steinbeck's Legacy

The final period of historical interest in Monterey is the heyday of John Steinbeck, whose novel, *Cannery Row*, happened to be published in the boom year of 1944. Sardine fishing and packing reached its peak, then quickly declined until the fish totally disappeared from these waters. A short walk from the Monterey Bay Aquarium, Cannery Row now flourishes as an area packing tourists, rather than sardines, into restaurants and shops. The marine biology lab of Steinbeck's pal, Ed "Doc" Ricketts, still stands at 800 Cannery Row.

Along with the Aquarium and the historic structures, the main experiences in the region are Monterey's Fisherman's Wharf, the cypress-strewn 17-Mile Drive, the butterfly town of Pacific Grove, the artsy town of Carmel, major annual events (such as the Monterey Jazz Festival in September and the AT&T Pro-Am golf tournament in late January/early February), inviting beaches such as the one at Carmel River, and the crown jewel of the state park system, Point Lobos.

Monterey Bay Aquarium

The Monterey Bay Aquarium (☎ 408-648-4888; 886 Cannery Row) honors the spectacular marine life that flourishes in upwelling currents of the deep sea canyons off Monterey. Unique currents and topography cause an abundance of mineral material to rise from the ocean floor, resulting in a bloom of small sea plants and animals that are the basis of the food chain.

The Aquarium's goal is to promote a greater knowledge and awareness of the dynamic and fragile world of the oceans. Opened in 1984 and funded by a $40 million grant from industrialist David Packard, the Aquarium is directed by Packard's daughter, Julie. The Aquarium is situated in the building once occupied by the Hovden Cannery, the largest of the now defunct canneries located here. It was a stroke of architectural genius that the aquarium directors chose to rehabilitate this existing building rather than create a monstrosity foreign to the site.

Twenty-three major indoor and outdoor exhibits await the visitor, the most spectacular being the **Kelp Forest**, a 66-foot-high tank with 335,000 gallons of sea water and numerous plants, fishes, and sea animals in residence. The forest of kelp, which grows as much as 10 inches per day, is the center of attention.

The Outer Bay

The Outer Bay wing focuses on the nearby ocean environment and the offshore reaches. It has a Plexiglas window that is said to be the largest window on Earth (90 x 54 feet), holding back a huge mass of water (35 feet from front to back). Advances in Plexiglas technology make this possible. Within this tank, viewable at eye level, one sees schools of tuna, giant turtles, and an occasional mammoth ocean sunfish. The Outer Bay tank is in a frenzy at the thrice-weekly feeding periods when the barracudas and other fish show how efficiently they can feed in the open ocean environment. As you walk into the Outer Bay area, you notice that the rooms are curved, rather than rectilinear, suggesting a different world, where spatial relationships will be novel. Launching the Outer Bay wing helped boost attendance at the Aquarium to roughly 2½ million visitors per year, the largest attendance of any US aquarium ever.

Exhibits at the Aquarium

A *Fishing for Solutions* exhibit focuses attention on the threats of worldwide pressure on fish, the last heavily harvested wild game, and how management of fisheries is critical if they are to avoid collapse.

Among longtime exhibits, the playful sea otters are extremely interesting to visitors. High metabolism rates require the otters to eat a quarter of their weight every day just to maintain their 100° body temperature in the frigid ocean water. They are constantly in motion, cracking abalone shells or scooping up fish for their sustenance. A drop of petroleum oil on a sea otter's coat can lead to excessive heat loss and hypothermia, which is one reason why conservationists in this area are so concerned about offshore oil drilling.

It is estimated that there are now about 1,500 wild sea otters along the California coast, with Point Lobos the most opportune viewing site. The market for beautiful sea otter furs is what first brought the Russians to California. It could be argued that the Spanish presence was largely an effort to counter this Russian expansion. Consequently, the sea otter might be seen as the most critical player in the development of California history.

Among the lesser, but still stunning, exhibits are displays of sharks and rays from the ocean floor or salmon and trout in the freshwater streams. Bubble-shaped viewing windows give a fish-eye view of some exhibits. Hands-on tanks afford visitors a tactile encounter with starfish and other tidepool creatures. The experience of the Aquarium is like moving from habitat to habitat rather than just tank to tank. Sea water is pumped directly through the exhibits, carrying the natural nutrients and life-forms that the plants and animals would encounter. The water is filtered for clarity during the day, but is pumped through in its natural cloudy state at night.

Cannery Row

The old Cannery Row and Wharf area along the Monterey waterfront is a pleasant place to stroll for its shops, restaurants, sea air, views of occasional sea otters, and its fishing fleet. In winter you can take a whale-watching boat out to see the gray whales making their way from Alaska to Baja. In the summer the fishing charter boats prosper here. All through the year an excursion boat with a tour of the harbor is a popular outing.

A welcome addition to the Cannery Row scene has been **A Taste of Monterey** (☎ 408-646-5446; 700 Cannery Row), where you can enjoy a striking view of the waves crashing onto rocks in the bay, with otters at play, while tasting the wines and produce of the region for a modest price. The wine tasting bar pours varietals of 20 local wineries. Your wine pourer can supply a map of the region with some suggested winery stops, perhaps Chateau Julien in Carmel Valley, then Smith & Hook or Paradiso Springs in the Salinas Valley for the views, and possibly Chalone on the east side of the valley for a barrel tasting. This is your one-stop shopping source for wine touring information and a bottle or two of the product to raise your enthusiasm level. Some wineries require an appointment; others simply allow you to walk in. The produce bar can prepare for you some Castroville artichokes or Watsonville strawberries, with any of the sautéed items laced with Gilroy garlic. It's a taste treat from a region with a cornucopia of specialty food production, which is part of the reason why area chefs create such works of art. Regional specialties, from flavored cheese to hot salsa, can be savored at A Taste of Monterey. If a few glasses of wine and some produce intrigue you, you might want to wander over to the weekly **Monterey Farmers Market** on Alvarado Street in Monterey. The market takes place each Tuesday from 4 pm onward.

The 17-Mile Drive

The 17-Mile Drive through the Del Monte Forest presents an appealing view of trees, coastline, and lavish private homes. Trees include prime stands of Monterey pine and cypress. The coastline presents ample places to walk or picnic, such as Spanish Bay, and good sites for observing sea life, especially at Seal and Bird Rock. The **Lone Cypress** stop salutes a singular tree whose gnarled appearance, growing out of the rocks and struggling constantly in the face of winds, stands as a symbol of tenacity and perseverance. Hundreds of sumptuous homes lend a fairytale aura to the woodsy 17-Mile Drive ambiance.

Pacific Grove

Pacific Grove, a town at the northwestern tip of the Peninsula, began as a Methodist camp in 1875. The celebrated natural phenomenon here is the gathering each year of monarch butterflies, who journey sometimes thousands of miles to overwinter in the eucalyptus and pine trees of Pacific Grove. The town celebrates with a Monarch Parade each October and a Victorian House Tour in April.

Carmel

Carmel is an appealing small village to stroll if you like to browse art galleries and shops. Look for the Gallery Tour brochure in the shops here. Ask for directions to poet Robinson Jeffers' house. Jeffers made his reputation celebrating the natural environment, but without seeing man as an improvement on the natural scene. Carmel goes to great lengths to maintain its high-tone village exclusivity through zoning rules designed to keep out the hoi polloi. At the south end of Carmel you'll find one of the loveliest beaches in California, little-used Carmel River Beach, which includes a parking lot, ample sand, and crashing surf – excellent ingredients for a beach walk. Close to downtown Carmel, an expansive beach stretches out on either side of Ocean Avenue.

The setting is enhanced by the view of Point Lobos offshore. Carmel River is safe for wading while the water flows in spring and early summer. Eventually the summer waves pile up a sand dam that traps the water, spreading it into a marsh that amounts to a major bird habitat.

Across Highway 1 from the Carmel River beach is a shopping center and entrance to the **Carmel Valley**, a sunny resort area. The Thunderbird Bookstore, at the entrance to Carmel Valley, is the main gathering place for bibliophiles.

Point Lobos

Point Lobos, immediately south of Carmel, is a noted 1,250-acre nature reserve. The presence of gnarled, green Monterey cypress and Gowan cypress trees was the original impulse for creating the reserve. Point Lobos is a naturalist's delight. More than 270 species of birds have been observed here. The tidepools teem with marine life and are easily explored at low tide. The name Point Lobos, Point of the Wolves, in Spanish, derives from the barking of sea lions and harbor seals, present here in great numbers. California gray whales pass close to land in their southward migration and can be spotted easily from the cliffs during December-

February. Divers explore the ample underwater state park immediately offshore, surfacing to exclaim about the sights. However, divers may also confide that an afternoon at the Monterey Aquarium can equal the best moments in a decade of diving.

Santa Cruz

Santa Cruz's main attractions include the Santa Cruz Boardwalk, the University of California Santa Cruz campus, the Long Marine Laboratory, Natural Bridges State Park, and the city's restored downtown, following the Quake of 1989.

The **Santa Cruz Beach Boardwalk** (☎ 408- 426-7433) located at 400 Beach Street, was built in 1904, burned down in 1906, and rebuilt in 1907. Its large roller coaster, the Giant Dipper, is a classic wooden structure from 1924 that has carried 25 million riders on white-knuckle trips. The Boardwalk has three arcades, a wide beach front, and the Coconut Grove Ballroom, featuring big bands. The centerpiece of the Boardwalk is the merry-go-round. A Danish woodcarver, Charles I. D. Looff, delivered the first 70 hand-carved horses in 1911. The carousel still operates today, along with its original 342-piece Ruth band organ, built in 1894.

West of the Boardwalk, the **Municipal Wharf** offers a pleasant stroll alongside fish markets, seafood restaurants, and pier fishing or deep-sea fishing excursions. If you walk out on the mile-long pier, the longest on the Pacific Coast, you get plenty of bracing sea air and a splendid view looking back at Santa Cruz.

The **University of California Santa Cruz campus** (☎ 408-459-0111, corner of Bay and High streets) is tucked among 2,000 acres of redwoods and rolling grasslands on the outskirts of town. The campus is interesting to visit for its architectural innovations and natural setting. From the university hills you see panoramic views of Santa Cruz and Monterey Bay. Self-guided tour maps are available at a kiosk a quarter mile into the grounds.

Pause by the side of the road as you enter the grounds to note the old Cowell Ranch building from the limestone-mining and cattle-ranching days. Of particular interest are the ambitious 17-acre farm and four-acre gardens, inspired by the late Alan Chadwick and his organic gardening technique, the French Intensive biodynamic method.

Santa Cruz Region

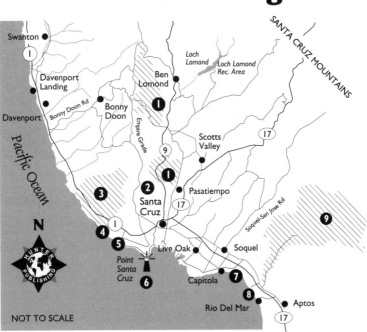

1. Henry Cowell Redwoods State Park
2. University of California at Santa Cruz
3. Wilder Ranch State Park
4. Univ. of California at Santa Cruz Marine Lab
5. Natural Bridges State Beach
6. Mark Abbott Memorial Lighthouse
7. New Brighton State Beach
8. Seacliff State Beach
9. The Forest of Nisene Marks State Park

Along the Ocean

The University's **Long Marine Laboratory** (☎ 408-459-4308 100 Shaffer Road) provides information and exhibits about the fauna and flora of tide pools and nearby ocean currents. Here you can see an 85-foot skeleton of a blue whale or touch starfish and sea anemones in a hands-on tank.

Natural Bridges State Park offers a special encounter in winter when the eucalyptus trees are filled with the migrating monarch butterflies. You can walk along the designated paths to see clusters of monarchs hanging on the trees. Walk also to the beach to see the "bridge" or sandstone arch that gave the park its name. Originally there were three bridges, as historical photos at the visitor center attest. One fell around the turn of the century. A second fell during a storm in 1980. Guided tours of the rich tide pools are conducted at low tide. Ask the ranger for the brochure, *Natural Bridges Tide Pools*, a succinct description of sea life.

Santa Cruz is now a gateway to the **Monterey Bay National Marine Sanctuary**, a huge protected ocean environment that extends from north of San Francisco to south of San Simeon. On the Wharf, at a Marine Sanctuary information booth, you can get a brochure on this massive resource, which will never see an oil rig upon it. This largest ocean reserve on the West Coast includes the very deep Monterey canyons, the deepest such canyons off the western US, a kind of invisible Grand Canyon on the ocean floor. A group active in promoting the sanctuary is known as Save Our Shores and operates an interpretive center (☎ 408-462-5660; Marine Sanctuary Center at the Santa Cruz harbor).

Downtown Santa Cruz

Stroll the re-created downtown area along **Pacific Avenue** to see what a special effort Santa Cruz made post-Quake. The downtown has been re-constructed using a varied, low-rise architecture. Landmark businesses, such as the Santa Cruz Book Store and the Santa Cruz Café and Coffee Roasting Company, have been re-located. Establishments such as Zoccoli's Pasta House lend a festive lunchtime aura as patrons grab a sandwich and a few minutes in the sun on the sidewalk.

One new structure of note is the **McPherson Center** (☎ 408-454-0697; 705 Front Street) home of the **Museum of Art and History of Santa Cruz County**. The new McPherson Center now unites these two previously separate institutions. Be sure to see the interpretation of Santa Cruz history, titled *Where the Redwoods Meet the Sea*, focusing on the area's complex economy, from redwood lumbering in the hills to the agriculture around Watsonville. The McPherson Center also hosts changing art exhibits and tends to be the venue for local cultural happenings. The adjacent Octagon Building, a noted historic structure that survived the Quake of 1989, is now the museum store.

Santa Cruz Serendipity

The **Santa Cruz City Museum of Natural History** (☎ 408-429-3773; 1305 East Cliff Drive) is an interesting establishment with displays on the local Ohlone Native Americans and how they survived by gathering acorns, fishing, and hunting. The museum exhibits the local flora and fauna as well as wildlife, from raptors to mountain lions.

One of the special aspects of Santa Cruz as an oceanside location is its excellent surfing. The surf area is also unusual because it can be viewed up close by the public. Simply walk or drive out West Cliff Drive to the Mark Abbott Lighthouse, which houses the **Santa Cruz Surfing Museum** (☎ 408-429-3429) celebrating the various decades that the sport has flourished. From the cliffs at Lighthouse Point you look out at Steamer Lane, the choice surfing area. You gaze right down on the surfers whizzing by, due to the unusual topography of Santa Cruz, which is actually facing south rather than west. In winter the hard-core surfing aficionados gather here for competitions.

One expression of the overall environmental consciousness of Santa Cruz are the **Farmers Markets**, held year round, but especially prominent in summer. The Monterey Bay Farmers Market occurs at 8 am each Saturday at Cabrillo College. A downtown version takes place at 2:30 pm each Wednesday in Santa Cruz at Cedar and Lincoln streets.

The area also supports many **U-pick farms** where locals and travelers enjoy getting seasonal berries and other foods. One of the more prominent such farms is the **Gizdich Ranch** (55 Peckham Road, ☎ 408-722-1056) in Watsonville. A brochure listing all the U-pick farms can be obtained from the Santa Cruz County Visitors Council.

The county also has over 30 vineyards united in a **Santa Cruz Mountains Winegrowers Association**, which puts out a handsome brochure on all the touring and tasting opportunities. The brochure also is available from the Visitors Council. A substantial and longterm player among these small-scale, quality wine producers is **Bargetto,** (☎ 408-475-2258; 3535 North Main Street, Soquel).

Monterey, Santa Cruz & Big Sur

■ Adventures

On Wheels

Scenic Driving Monterey

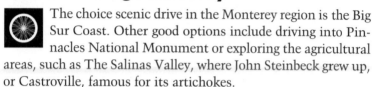 The choice scenic drive in the Monterey region is the Big Sur Coast. Other good options include driving into Pinnacles National Monument or exploring the agricultural areas, such as The Salinas Valley, where John Steinbeck grew up, or Castroville, famous for its artichokes.

Driving Big Sur

The Big Sur coastline is the most dramatic coast in California, winding 30 miles between Monterey and Big Sur. The road twists between cliffs, trees, and ocean, with occasional scenic turnouts. At **Pfeiffer Big Sur State Park** (☎ 408-667-2315) you'll find redwood forests, miles of trails, camping, and a two-mile beach. Pfeiffer offers access to 300,000 acres of backcountry in Los Padres National Forest and the Ventana Wilderness, appreciated by the hiker and backpacker. The campgrounds fill quickly, especially in summer and on weekends. The other major park here is the **Andrew Molera State Park** (☎ 408-667-2315) whose

The Lone Cypress, a symbol of tenacity in the face of adversity, along the 17-Mile Drive in Monterey.

boundaries encompass the Big Sur River. This is a walker's and camper's park.

Nepenthe (☎ 408-667-2345) is the restaurant to visit here, built of redwood and perched on a cliff 800 feet above the sea. Nepenthe serves as the gathering place for locals, among them many artists and writers drawn to the beauty of Big Sur. In the 1940s Orson Welles commissioned a student of Frank Lloyd Wright to build this structure as a honeymoon cottage for Rita Hayworth.

For a list of the small lodgings, restaurants, and shops along the rustic Big Sur route, contact the **Big Sur Chamber of Commerce**, ☎ 408-667-2100; Big Sur, CA 93920. Those who eschew the predict-

Big Sur Coast

1. Point Lobos State Reserve & Ecological Reserve
2. Garrapata State Park
3. Andrew Molera State Park
4. Pfeiffer Big Sur State Park
5. Julia Pfeiffer Burns State Park

able comforts of chain hotels in favor of rustic and romantic getaways might consider the artsy cottages at **Deetjens** (☎ 408-667-2377. $$) or the crashing surf at the **Lucia Lodge** (☎ 408-667-2391. $$).

The major destination, if you are traveling south, is William Randolph Hearst's fantasy castle, **San Simeon**, now a state park, 96 miles south of Monterey. San Simeon occupies 123 acres on a crest of the Santa Lucia Mountains above the sea. Allow a half-day to a full day, depending on your tastes, to make tours of La Casa Grande, the opulent edifice that Hearst financed and architect Julia Morgan built. Hearst's agents, with a fiscal carte blanche, scoured Europe for the trappings of history and brought back every Greek vase and monk's pew that was for sale. Hearst's Castle is a monument to the era when culture meant European antiques.

Inland from Monterey

Inland, **Pinnacles National Monument** (☎ 408- 389-4485) east of Soledad, makes a fascinating day or weekend trip from Monterey. The spires and crags tower 1,200 feet above the valley floor.They are a legacy of geologic shifts over eons. This activity shows the vitality of the San Andreas Fault. Trails take you to the top of these immense boulders, down into caves, and through the distinctive chaparral vegetation of the area. The monument offers a somewhat cramped park service camp on the west side and a more spacious private camp on the east side, accessible from Hollister. Spring, when the wildflowers are bountiful, and fall, after the heat and dryness of summer have passed, are the best seasons for a visit.

The **Salinas Valley** is one of the most productive agricultural areas in America. Fertile fields yield an abundant harvest of fruits and vegetables year round. The annual **California Rodeo** takes place here in July and amounts to a week-long celebration. For information, contact the California Rodeo Office, PO Box 1648, Salinas, CA 93902.

In Salinas, visit **John Steinbeck's birthplace** at 132 Central Avenue. The restored Victorian now houses a restaurant, the Steinbeck House (☎ 408-424-2735) open for lunch by reservation. The **Steinbeck Library** at 110 West San Luis Street exhibits first editions and letters by the author. The **Boronda Adobe** at West Laurel and Boronda Road can be toured, giving you a glimpse of early California rancho life.

Nearby, you can travel to the artichoke capital of the world, **Castroville**. These large thistle plants stretch over 10,000 acres around the small town. Stop in at **The Giant Artichoke** restaurant (☎ 408-633-3204), where you can eat an entire meal of artichokes. Artichoke soup, artichoke salad, and artichoke bread can accompany an entrée of either fried artichokes or artichoke hearts. The annual **Artichoke Festival** occurs each September.

Several wineries, large and small, are open for tastings in the region. Try the **Monterey Vineyard** (800 S. Alta Street, Gonzales, ☎ 408-675-4060), known for their Riesling. Among the select small producers to watch is **Jekel** (☎ 408-674-5522; 40155 Walnut Avenue, Greenfield). Try their Chardonnay.

Scenic Driving Santa Cruz

The most engaging drive in the Santa Cruz region is along the San Mateo Coast between Santa Cruz and San Francisco.

When making the drive, three stops at choice beaches are highly recommended. The stops, which epitomize the best the region offers, are at The James Fitzgerald Marine Preserve, Ano Nuevo Reserve, and Waddell Creek.

James V. Fitzgerald Marine Reserve Beaches, 12 Miles South

In the rush to reach beaches at Half Moon Bay, most travelers overlook this, the finest beach along this expanse of coast and one of the richest intertidal regions. You can meditate over tidepools with a variety of sea life here, either on your own or guided by the park naturalist.

The **Reserve** (☎ 415-728-3584), established in 1969, is south of Montara, in Moss Beach. Turn onto California Avenue and make a right on North Lake Street. Mass transit access is possible via Samtrans. Try to coincide your visit with a low tide, which you can discern by calling the Reserve ahead of time or by consulting a Tide Tables booklet available at all fishing tackle and bait shops.

There's plenty of parking, restrooms, stairs and paths to the beach, and a hiking trail along the bluffs to the south. Picnic tables in a sheltered cypress grove provide a protected lunch spot. You can enjoy a variety of terrain, including a sandy beach, a rocky shore, a stream corridor, and bluffs. Stop in at the naturalist's office for brochures and literature. Don't remove or disturb any of the marine life here, which is protected. The tidepool rocks can be slippery, so wear tennis shoes and plan to get your feet wet. Alternatively, wear high rubber boots.

Naturalist-led hikes focus on understanding animal relationships, adaptation techniques, habitats, and the food web of the reserve. Closest to shore, along the beach and protected inner reef, you'll find black turban snails in intense populations. Farther out, crabs populate the cobblestone lagoons. Red abalone, rockweed and nailbrush, chitons and urchins, green anemones and bull-whip kelp are some of the fauna and flora awaiting you here. You would have to journey to the South Pacific to find a richer ocean environment.

The best restaurant and bed and breakfast in Half Moon Bay is the **San Benito House** (☎ 415-726-3425; 356 Main Street. $$). The restaurant emphasizes the local produce of the Phipp's ranch, local seafood, and specialties such as veal grilled over mesquite.

Campsites are available at Half Moon Bay Beaches (☎ 415-726-8820). In windy weather, camp further south and inland at Butano State Park (☎ 415-879-2040).

Ano Nuevo State Reserve Beaches, 43 Miles South

In winter the **elephant seals** gather at Ano Nuevo. They were formerly hunted to the brink of extinction. Today, they have made a comeback and, guided by the ranger, you can walk out amidst these three-ton creatures. Reservations are required in winter for the guided walks (☎ 415-879-0227or 800-444-7275). Ano Nuevo is open for perusal on your own the rest of the year.

Summer is the off season for Ano Nuevo. Unlike the hectic winter, when you need a reservation to see the elephant seals, summer is a wonderfully quiet time. The size and diversity of this 4,000-acre holding are impressive.

Ano Nuevo State Reserve ranges from Franklin Point south to New Years Creek. The turnoff to the parking area is clearly marked. There's plenty of parking and a modest fee for day use.

Restrooms are located at thc parking lot.

Paths and trails lead to the beach, which offers good fishing for halibut, croaker, and perch. The easily accessible beach at the mouth of New Year's Creek, a short walk from the parking lot, is a good sunning and picnic area at low tide. The shoreline at Ano Nuevo includes sandy beaches, dunes, rocky areas, and bluffs. Get a map at the interpretive center, located in the old Dickerman Barn, where there are informative displays on nature and the human use of the area. Ano Nuevo is a particularly good area for sighting shore birds, upland birds, and hawks. You can also explore Native American middens and the legacy of the Steele Brothers dairy empire, which started here in the 1850s.

The 1½-mile walk out to the point is a favorite trek. A sensitive area with numerous harbor seals, there is restricted access in summer. For an ambitious, all-day outing, walk the beach north to Franklin Point.

The **Pigeon Point Light Station**, a few miles north, was built in 1871 to prevent a repeat of wrecks like that of the *Carrier Pigeon* in 1853. The lighthouse is an architectural monument, with brick walls seven feet thick. Pigeon Point functions as a rustic all-ages hostel (☎ 415-879-0633. $). You can view the outside of the lighthouse at any time. Tours take you inside on Sundays.

A good bed-and-breakfast in this rather remote coastal area is south at Davenport. The inn, called the **New Davenport Bed and Breakfast Inn** (☎ 408-425-1818; 31 Davenport Avenue and Highway 1. $$) also operates a restaurant, called the **Davenport Cash Store**.

Well-protected campsites in second-growth redwoods greet the visitor at **Butano State Park** (☎ 415-879-2040), a few miles north and inland.

Waddell State Beach, 46 Miles South

Waddell State Beach is interesting for several reasons. Wind surfers and hang gliders gather there in record numbers. An observer sees them airborne above the waves. The Waddell State Beach and bluffs have recently become a part of Big Basin State Park. A seal rookery flourishes offshore south of the beach. The **Theodore J. Hoover Natural Preserve**, which includes Waddell Marsh, is located at the mouth

Hiking at Pescadero Beach along the San Mateo Coast.

of Waddell Creek. Wherever a creek enters the ocean along the California coast there is interesting wildlife to observe.

Waddell State Beach (☎ 408-425-1218) is along Highway 1, a mile south of the San Mateo County line. There's plenty of parking, restrooms, and good fishing for lingcod, croaker, and perch. You'll find sandy beach and dunes, the stream and wetlands, plus low bluffs overlooking the ocean.

From Waddell Beach you can walk inland through **Big Basin Park**. In fact, you could walk all the way from the beach to the ridge of the Santa Cruz Mountains along a trail called the **Skyline-to-the-Sea Trail**, which became officially complete with the addition of the Rancho del Oso property along Waddell Creek and the beach. A bronze marker at the trailhead recalls that here Gaspar de Portola and his men rested for three days during their long walk from San Diego to San Francisco in 1769. Those ill in the party recovered their health so quickly that the Spanish called the area **Canada de la Salud**, Canyon of Health.

Backpackers can walk in to campsites upstream on Waddell Creek. Make prior arrangements for a space by calling Big Basin (☎ 408-338-8860). The first camp, **Alder Camp**, is a one-mile walk inland. **Butano State Park** (☎ 415-879-2040) north and inland, is the recommended car-camping site.

The best dining in this remote area is at **Duarte's** (☎ 415-879-0464. $$) in Pescadero, which is famous for its seafood and local produce specialties, such as artichoke soup.

Bicycling Monterey

The 18-mile **Monterey Peninsula Recreational Trail**, or Rec Trail, as it is called affectionately in Monterey, is a magnificent paved bicycle route. Starting in Pacific Grove, this wide path winds along the waterfront to the Monterey Aquarium and Wharf, then proceeds out along the shore and Highway 1 all the way to Marina State Beach. It passes through the decommissioned Fort Ord, where the sand dunes are gradually swallowing up the former rifle ranges. For the energetic biker who wants to stretch out on a dedicated paved trail, the Rec Trail ride to Marina State Beach is excellent.

The Rec Path for bicycling extends from Pacific Grove to Marina Beach on the Monterey Peninsula.

Bicycles, along with four-wheel surreys and inline skates, are available at **Bicycle Rentals** (☎ 408/646-9090; 640 Wave Street, Monterey). Another source is **Adventures by the Sea** (☎ 408-372-1807; 299 Cannery Row, Monterey) which rents bicycles and inline skates, as well as equipment for other sports, such as kayaking.

Bicycling Santa Cruz

Few destinations are so well laid out for bicycling as Santa Cruz. With ubiquitous bike lanes, it is easier to get around this small city on a bike than by car.

One of several good bike stores is **The Bicycle Rental and Tour Center** (☎ 408-426-8687; 131 Center Street) run by Rosemary and Michael Sarka. There you can rent bikes, helmets, and locks, and procure maps of all regional bicycle trails. They also lead bike outings if you want to explore in a group, whether to do serious mountain biking or experience an urban trip emphasizing Santa Cruz history. Local buses can take your bike, which extends your range. For example, a local bus can take you up to the Waddell Creek area, then pick you up later in the day.

The bike route to start on is the three-mile **West Cliff Trail** that leads out from the boardwalk towards the surfing area, Steamer

Lane. The route is marked and paved all the way to **Natural Bridges State Park**, an engaging place to look at monarch butterflies in winter and the sandstone arches all year round.

Beyond Natural Bridges, you can cycle with a mountain bike in **Wilder Ranch State Park** (☎ 408-426-0505), a working ranch from the 19th century. Be sure to get a good map. The area is rugged and not too populated with other bikers. New lands have been acquired by the city of Santa Cruz adjacent to Wilder Ranch Park, so anticipate that the 34 miles of hiking, biking and equestrian trails will expand. It's enjoyable to pack a picnic and spend a day exploring in Wilder Ranch Park.

Another favorite biking area is **Forest of Nisene Marks State Park**, east of Santa Cruz. Nisene Marks (☎ 408-763-7062) is an undeveloped area of second-growth redwoods. It has many miles of biking trails. Be sure to get a good map.

The **University of California Santa Cruz campus** also has good bike trails around it. A local bus can take you and your bike up to the campus if you want to avoid exerting yourself on the elevation gain.

A more extreme bike outing, driving north from Santa Cruz, would be a stop at the **Waddell Creek** parking lot for Big Basin State Park. From the Waddell Creek parking lot, you can bike 5½ miles into Big Basin, then leave your bike, and walk the final mile to Berry Creek Falls.

Railroading Santa Cruz

The prospect of a ride on an authentic steam-powered train, with the locomotive belching steam and sounding whistles, tends to excite explorers of all ages. Such a ride is possible near Santa Cruz, at Felton, on the **Roaring Camp and Big Trees Narrow-Gauge Railroad**, one of the last steam-powered passenger trains still operating. The entrance is off Graham Hill Road just south of Mt. Hermon Road, ☎ 408-335-4484. You can also enter from the nearby parking lot of Henry Cowell State Park. If you plan to visit the train and Henry Cowell Park, go directly to the park and walk to the train.

The tracks twist around a five-mile loop through redwood groves. Another set of tracks can take you all the way into Santa Cruz.

Back in the 1880s, lumberjacks and pioneers used the same train to make their livelihoods, hauling out lumber and shingles. During the hour-long trip you climb some of the steepest grades ever built for a railroad. Unfortunately, vandals burned the extraordinary corkscrew trestle that enabled the train to gain altitude rapidly. An ingenious system of rail switchbacks now allows the train to traverse the steep grades.

At **Bear Mountain** you can get off the train for a picnic or a hike in the redwoods and then catch a later train back to depot headquarters. The conductor gives a competent commentary on the flora of the region during the stop and as the train moves. At a pause in a cathedral of redwoods, he describes how new redwood trees sprout in a circle around the deceased mother tree.

Near the boarding platform, you can see the steam-powered sawmill. In the spirit of the setting, meals of barbecued beef are served. Local musicians sing ballads of the lumbering era.

Another popular ride is the **Moonlight Steam Train Party**, on Saturday nights in summer, with singing and dancing under the stars.

At **Roaring Camp** you can see a short, covered bridge and visit a reconstructed 1880s General Store selling items from western garb to a complete line of books for the rail buff. Legend asserts that the name Roaring Camp had its origin in the Mexican impression of the American settlers here. The Americans, who had a fondness for whiskey, had a roaring good time.

The railroad is rich in legend and history. Riding it today you relive the journey from the East Bay, boarding in Newark, down the East Bay shore, crossing the Santa Clara Valley, then over the mountains, to resorts in the redwoods or beaches at Santa Cruz. These Picnic Trains or Suntan Specials are now gone forever, but the present Roaring Camp Railroad arouses considerable nostalgia.

Five locomotives constitute the rail company's main holdings, ranging from the *Kahuku*, a 12-ton Baldwin locomotive from 1890, to the *Dixiana*, a 42-ton Shay locomotive from 1912.

On Foot

Hiking & Backpacking Monterey

The most popular Monterey area hike is on the **Rec Trail** that runs along the Pacific Grove and Monterey shoreline, passing through Cannery Row, and eventually snaking 18 miles north and east to the town of Marina. Hikers share the trail with bikers and inline skaters. Most of the hikers use the trail between Pacific Grove and the downtown Monterey plaza.

Another pleasing hike begins in Carmel at the **Carmel Beach**, which starts at the end of Ocean Avenue. This is a superb beach walk, especially as the light softens at sunset. Walk along the beach for a mile or so, then climb one of the many access steps, and walk back along Scenic Drive.

For a more ambitious walk, which shows you the special topography of the region, venture out to **Jacks Peak Regional Park** (☎ 408-755-4899), a county park two miles off Highway 68 at Olmsted Road. Highway 68 is a road that joins Monterey and Salinas. At the top of Jacks Peak Park, you can walk a mile-long scenic trail that offers breathtaking views of Monterey Harbor and the Carmel Valley. No other walk in the region gives you as clear a topologic perspective on this region, with Monterey pine tree forests on the wet ridges facing Monterey Bay and chaparral vegetation on the dry hills in the Carmel Valley. Beyond the nature trail, with its markers explaining the local flora and fauna, Jacks Peak Park has 11 more miles of trails for the hiker.

Strolling on the sand at Pebble Beach.

Backpacking is possible in the **Los Padres National Forest** in back of Big Sur. Permits are required. The forest service contact is ☎ 408-385-5434.

Hiking & Backpacking Santa Cruz

Santa Cruz offers four redwood state parks in the mountains. These are among the choicest hiking/backpacking areas in Northern California.

Most people think of California's "redwood country" as stretching north from San Francisco along Highway 101. However, there is another, appealing redwood country to the south in the Santa Cruz Mountains. Moreover, it was here that the idea of saving the redwoods began, with what was originally known as the California State Redwood Park. Known today as **Big Basin**, this was California's first redwood park.

The Santa Cruz Mountains redwood area provides a diverse, forested, hiking-and-camping terrain, and includes one of the state's least-used parks, **Forest of Nisene Marks**, now recovered from logging scars and emerging as a lush, second-growth forest.

A back road through the area, Highway 9 down the San Lorenzo River takes you through the arts and crafts center of Boulder Creek and several small villages with a Scots flair, such as Ben Lomond, to another major park, **Henry Cowell Redwoods State Park** (☎ 408-335-4598).

Once you begin to enjoy the trails of the Santa Cruz Mountains, an organization worth knowing about is the Santa Cruz Mountains Trails Association. Through the association you can meet fellow hikers and participate in the extensive volunteer work that helps maintain the trails. Over 100,000 volunteer hours have been contributed by this organization to maintaining trails since their first Trail Day in 1969. Trail Day is usually in April. For information, contact **Santa Cruz Mountains Trail Association**, ☎ 415-968-2412; PO Box 1141, Los Altos, CA 94022.

A group with a special interest in advancing the appreciation of natural history in the region is the **Mountain Parks Foundation**, ☎ 408-335-3174; 525 North Big Trees Park Road, Felton, CA 95018. This group enhances interpretive activities in the parks by sponsoring campfire programs, training volunteers who lead nature walks, arranging for the publication of nature literature, and maintaining the self-guided trails.

Monterey, Santa Cruz & Big Sur

Big Basin Redwoods State Park

Backpacking the Waddell Creek in Big Basin Redwoods State Park.

This was the first and is, in many ways, the most significant of all the California state parks. It was created in 1902 as a result of public outcry over the impending doom of virgin redwoods in this area. Much credit goes to Andrew Hill, a San Jose photographer who spurred the movement. The park lies on ocean-facing slopes about 20 miles north of Santa Cruz. You can reach it via Highways 9 and 236. Today, Big Basin (☎ 408-338-8860) encompasses 18,000 acres, with miles of trails that wind past streams, waterfalls and giant redwoods.

When you arrive at park headquarters, stop to visit the Nature Lodge, which celebrates the park's history, flora, and fauna.

The finest redwoods stand along the **Redwood Nature Trail** near park headquarters. This self-guided trail has the noblest redwood specimens in the region. You make the acquaintance of the massive Santa Clara Tree and the Chimney Tree, whose entire core has been hollowed out by fire. Growth continues in the Chimney Tree because the cambium layer next to the bark was not damaged.

Redwoods have a capacity to inspire wonder, partly because of their age. At park headquarters stands a cross-section of one tree that has been ring-dated as 2,200 years old. At the time of the Romans this was still a young tree. But it may in fact be countless eons older because most redwoods sprout clonally from the roots of their parent tree rather than from seeds. The same tree may continue to live in this way for thousands upon thousands of years.

The other main plants around the headquarters and camp-grounds are tan oak, Douglas fir, huckleberry, and western azalea. Huckleberries produce large amounts of food for mammals and birds in August. Azaleas perfume the air with their white blossoms.

At higher elevations and in more open terrain the vegetation becomes increasingly diverse, with much oak and madrone. The book, *Plants of Big Basin Redwoods State Park*, available at headquarters, has excellent photos and brief descriptions of plants found throughout the Santa Cruz Mountains.

Some of the choicest hiking among Big Basin's 60 miles of trails is the stretch from Berry Creek Falls to Silver Falls, which shows profuse wildflowers and lovely waterfalls in spring. Allow a half-day from headquarters for a loop trip to this area. The Skyline-to-the-Sea Trail threads through Big Basin to the ocean, allowing you to walk from the spine of the mountains to the sea. The trail ends at the most recent addition to Big Basin, the historic Rancho del Oso on Lower Waddell Creek.

Castle Rock State Park: Backpacker Rendezvous

High on the Santa Cruz mountain ridges above Big Basin rests **Castle Rock State Park**, a special place for the hiker, backpacker, and rock climber. Castle Rock's parking lot, on Skyline Boulevard (Highway 35) about 2½ miles south of the junction with Highway 9, is also a start of the **Skyline-to-the-Sea Trail**, one of the most inspiring hikes in the region. The official start of the trail is at the road junction. The phone for Castle Rock is ☎ 408-867-2952.

Rock climbers like to scale the large sandstone rock near the parking lot. This eminently climbable rock gave the area its name. All sorts of rock scrambling and climbing can be practiced here and throughout the park.

From the parking lot a 2.8-mile hike leads to the campground. You can hike in and out easily on a day trip if not staying overnight. Taking the Skyline-to-the-Sea Trail in and the Ridge Trail out makes a pleasant loop. You can also hike into the camp and continue, walking all the way to the sea.

The hike to the campground is one of the loveliest in the Santa Cruz Mountains. You pass several plant communities and see compelling vistas of the mountains in all their wildness. First you pass through a Douglas fir forest along a cool, moist stream, dark and peaceful, with some large madrone, tan oak, and bay trees. This jaunt ends with a view of Castle Rock Falls, slipping over sandstone in a sheer drop of over a hundred feet. However appealing, this scene is only a prelude of vistas to come.

Next you walk through a chaparral plant community, with its drier vegetation that is exposed to the sun. Chaparral comes from the Spanish, *chaparra*, for small scrub oaks. Manzanita, ceanothus, and chamise can be seen here. Red-tailed hawks wheel about in the sky, catching the thermal updraft from cliffs below you, looking for meals of mice and rabbits. In the spring there are wildflowers, such as Indian paintbrush. Panoramas of the mountains open up on the left as you hike along. You also pass many large sandstone outcroppings, including some carved by nature into caves, suitable shelter in a storm.

Finally you pass into an oak woodland plant community, where the trails are thick with leaf duff, soft to the feet. A range of oak species cluster here, including live, canyon, and black oaks. Buckeye trees make occasional appearances and some madrone thrive on these slopes.

Almost a Wilderness

Castle Rock State Park would qualify as a wilderness, except that some old access roads pass across it. Hiking through here may provide many private pleasures. While resting on the Ridge Trail, the plaintive yipping of coyotes may envelop you.

The elevations here are not those of the Sierra Nevada. Nevertheless, the 2,645- to 3,215-foot heights may affect your breathing pattern. Take things a little easier because of the thinner air at this altitude. With so much to see, consider it an enjoyable and educational stroll rather than an endurance test.

If you want to see lovely red-barked madrone in all their beauty, there is no finer place than the **Ridge Trail**. Actually, this growth has now become somewhat too thick, dominating the countryside, because fires here have been controlled for the last 50 years. A healthy burn will someday clean out this forest.

Once you reach the **campground**, you will realize how unusual it is. First, it is only accessible to hikers or backpackers, which thins the crowd considerably. But the camp itself is luxurious, with picnic tables, fire pits, and toilets. Excellent water is available from a tap that reaches into a spring. Though downed wood can't be gathered, bagged firewood can be bought. The camp fee itself is modest, but pack extra money for firewood and a map of the area if you don't already have one. There is also a pay phone here to alert the outside world of your progress, an unusual amenity in the wilderness. The fine self-guided nature trail at the campground, the **Danny Hanavan Trail**, acquaints you with the flora.

> *The map needed for Castle Rock State Park alone covers the first part of the Skyline-to-the-Sea Trail. The entire trail comes in two maps, with the second covering Big Basin. You can send ahead for the two maps with a stamped, self-addressed envelope to the ranger at Castle Rock State Park, ☎ 408-867-2952; 15000 Skyline Boulevard, Los Gatos, CA 95030. Phone for the current price and camp reservations.*

From Castle Rock to Waddell Beach

For a full-blown walk of 30 miles from the Castle Rock skyline to the sea at Waddell Beach, allow four days and three overnights. This gives you some time to look at nature as well as make the walk.

The next stop after the Castle Rock trail camp is **Saratoga Gap**, the junction of Highways 9 and 35. Saratoga Gap has a parking area that can be a starting or stopping point if you have two cars as shuttles. From Saratoga Gap you can walk toward Big Basin along a trail that closely parallels the highway, but the more scenic route is **Toll Road Trail**, which takes you away from the highway. These trails eventually join up eight miles later. You must back-track a mile along the trail by the highway to the camp at Waterman Gap if you take the Toll Road Trail.

The trail from Castle Rock to Big Basin will be improved eventually to eliminate one stretch through a subdivision. Call ahead to **Big Basin Redwoods State Park**, ☎ 408-338-8860, to register for the next camp along the trail, near Waterman Gap.

From Waterman Gap the next leg of the trail takes you to **China Grade** in Big Basin, where vast views of the forests and ridges of

Big Basin unfold. From China Grade you can glimpse the ocean that will wet your toes if you make the full walk through the Waddell Creek basin to the sea.

Much credit for the existence of the 30-mile Skyline to the Sea Trail must go to the Sempervirens Fund, an organization vital today and well worth supporting. An impressive turnout of 2,500 volunteers came together in one day to help build the trail. Now there is a network of more than 80 miles of trails between and within Castle Rock and Big Basin parks. Contributions of money and labor to build trails can be made to the Sempervirens Fund.

Henry Cowell Redwoods State Park: A Walk in the Forest Primeval

Henry Cowell is another of the majestic redwood parks in the Santa Cruz Mountains. A stately grove of the giant trees includes many first growth specimens with clusters of oxalis flowers around their bases. Fifteen miles of hiking trails await the traveler.

The main entrance to Henry Cowell Park (☎ 408-335-4598) is just south of Felton on Highway 9. This entrance puts you close to the **Redwood Grove** with its first-growth trees. The campground is on the east side of the park, accessible from Graham Hill Road. One hundred twelve roomy campsites lie partly in a unique forest of ponderosa pine, which usually thrives in drier environments. The camp boasts an amenity rare among state parks, hot showers.

Redwood Grove, with its 29 numbered interpretive stations along an 8/10ths-mile loop trail, offers one of the outstanding nature walks in the region. The walk begins near an attractive small Visitor Center devoted to nature exhibits and literature. Sword fern, oxalis, and ginger plants cover the forest floor. The first-growth redwoods are majestic and are named mainly after presidents and other dignitaries. The tallest here is 51 feet in circumference and 285 feet high. A strong wind broke off another 75-foot top section. Small specimens of the inland giant redwood and the so-called dawn redwood have been planted at the end of the trail. Though these young trees are overpowered in the battle for light by the indigenous *Sequoia sempervirens*, you can look closely at the leaves to note family similarities and differences among the three.

The dawn redwood is a tree with a special modern story. Fossil remains in California indicate that there had been three species of redwoods in earlier eons. Besides the coast redwood *Sequoia sempervirens*, and the inland giant redwood *Sequoia gigantea*, there was a third tree, which scientists named *Metasequoia* or dawn redwood. This tree was thought to be extinct, but in 1944 botanists cataloguing plants in China discovered dawn redwoods there. Many have been planted in California from seed or shoots brought from China since the late 1940s.

The San Lorenzo River passes through Redwood Grove. In winter there is a spawning run of salmon and steelhead.

Henry Cowell Park was formed in 1953 when Samuel Cowell donated 1,600 acres of land to the state in memory of his father, Henry Cowell. That donation included the superlative stand of first growth redwoods. The county later added another 120 acres.

In 1976, a new 2,335-acre section of Henry Cowell Park opened on Ben Lomond Mountain. This is the **Fall Creek Unit** of the park, west of Felton off Felton-Empire Road. The area was a busy limestone quarry from 1870 to 1925. Hiking trails open the Fall Creek unit to travelers. Reservations for backpackers to stay at the West Ridge Trail Camp can be made with rangers at Henry Cowell Redwoods State Park near Felton (☎ 408-335-4598).

Forest of Nisene Marks State Park

Marked *undeveloped* on some maps, the 10,200-acre **Forest of Nisene Marks State Park** (☎ 408-763-7062; Aptos Creek Road) offers a secluded hiking and backpacking experience, encompassing the complete drainage area of Aptos and Hinckley creeks. The generous Marks family of Monterey bought this property and deeded it to the state in 1963 with the proviso that it be named after their mother, Nisene Marks.

You can reach the park from Aptos Creek Road in Aptos, just off Soquel Drive. The park land was clear-cut of redwoods from 1893-1925 by the Loma Prieta Lumber Company, but by now attractive, second-growth forests have arisen. Production of lumber was sufficient for Southern Pacific to lay a broad-gauge spur track here in 1884. The top of the park is a ridge at 2,600 feet, south of Loma Prieta, which is one of the higher peninsula mountains, at 3,791 feet. You can walk about 30 miles of trails in Forest of

Nisene Marks Park, including one along the railroad track leading back to Hoffman's Historic Site, the original frenetic logging site. Buildings at Hoffman's are now being reclaimed by forest.

Nisene Marks Park has a special historical significance because near here, at Corralitos, the Portola expedition made European man's first recorded contact with redwood trees. The party was walking north past the Pajaro Valley in 1769 on their quest for what mapmakers had indicated was an excellent bay.

"The scouts came back from exploring what had seemed to be pine trees," wrote diarist Crespi, "which they were not; but very straight, very thick trees of no small height, with a very slight short leaf; some said they were savins (cedars) but in my opinion they are not, the wood is red, and they are not junipers; they may be savins, who knows, but if so, they are not like any others we have seen elsewhere."

Information Sources

Books about the region's flora and fauna can be found at local bookstores or Big Basin Redwoods State Park. The publisher is the Santa Cruz Mountain Parks Foundation, ☎ 408-335-3174; 525 North Big Trees Park Road, Felton 95018.

Hiking Companions: Contact them through the Santa Cruz Mountains Trail Association, ☎ 415-968-2412; PO Box 1141, Los Altos 94022.

Sempervirens Fund: The group active in acquiring land for the parks in the region is the Sempervirens Fund, ☎ 415-968-4509; Drawer BE, Los Altos, CA 94023.

Rock Climbing Monterey/Santa Cruz

At **Pinnacles National Monument** (☎ 408-389-4485), inland from Monterey, fans of rock climbing do technical scaling of the peaks. The more casual rock climber will find plenty of boulders to practice on.

Casual rock climbing can be done at the huge rocks in **Castle Rock State Park** (☎ 408-867-2952).

In Santa Cruz there is a huge artificial climbing wall at **Pacific Edge** (☎ 408-454-9254). Located in a former cannery, Pacific Edge is one of the larger rock gym facilities around, with ample artificial walls on which to practice climbing. If you want to take lessons and test yourself against a rock wall, Pacific Edge is the place to do it.

On Horseback

The **Pebble Beach Equestrian Center** (☎ 408-624-2756; Portola Road and Alva Lane, Pebble Beach) organizes rides through the exclusive Pebble Beach Forests on the Monterey peninsula.

Holman Ranch in the Carmel Valley (☎ 408-659-2640; 60 Holman Road) offers a more ranchy and western experience on its horseback rides.

Molera Horseback Tours (☎ 408-625-5486, 800-942-5486) in Andrew Molera State Park, 22 miles south of Carmel, offers rides in the rustic Big Sur region.

In the redwood forest mountains back of Santa Cruz, one dependable horseback riding provider is **Redwood Riding Adventures** (☎ 408-335-2156; 5423 Highway 9, Felton). They offer guided horseback riding on scenic trails for the novice and rental of quality horses for the experienced rider who wants to take off on his own.

On Water

Kayaking/Canoeing

Kayaking on **Monterey Bay** or into **Elkhorn Slough** is a major water sport in the region. Kayaks can be rented by the do-it-yourselfer; organized tours are also possible. Providers include **Otter Cove Ocean Sports** (☎ 408-647-0147; 32 Cannery Row #5, Monterey) and **Monterey Bay Kayaks** (☎ 408-373-5357 or 800-649-5357; 693 Del Monte Avenue, Monterey). Monterey Bay Kayaks is one of the leading providers of guided natural history trips into the Elkhorn Slough Reserve, offering good opportunities to see birds up-close. Kayaks can also be rented on the beach at **Lover's Point** in Pacific Grove. Kayaking in the kelp beds can often put you relatively close to sea otters.

Ocean kayaking is popular also in the **Santa Cruz Harbor**. Kayaking companies sometimes offer scuba, which requires a wetsuit year--round in these chilly waters.

Kayak providers in Santa Cruz include **Adventure Sports Unlimited** (☎ 408-458-3648 303; Portrero Street) and **Venture Quest** (☎ 408-427-2267; 125-A Beach Street). Venture Quest leads kayaking tours and holds safe-surfing lessons.

Boating

Excursion tours on the water are popular for fishing, sightseeing, and whale watching in winter. Whale watching is mainly December-February when the gray whales are moving south.

In Monterey the fishing/whale watching boats leave from the wharf. One provider is **Randy's Fishing Trips** (☎ 408-372-7440)

Carrera Sailing (☎ 408-375-0648; 66 Fisherman's Wharf in Monterey) offers boating and charters/cruises.

Providers for Monterey and Santa Cruz include **Chardonnay Charters** (☎ 408-423-1213; FF Dock, Santa Cruz Yacht Harbor) and **Shamrock Charters** (☎ 408-476-2648; 2210 East Cliff Drive).

Chardonnay is an upscale 70-foot sailing yacht, where your goal might be swilling a glass of wine at sunset. The Chardonnay operates between Monterey and Santa Cruz.

Shamrock has two traditional fishing boats, good for catching a salmon and cod or watching a migrating gray whale. Both operate out of Santa Cruz.

Another option in Santa Cruz is a 65-foot catamaran with public sailings, including the teaching of sailing fundamentals. Contact **O'Neill Yacht Charters** (☎ 408-476-5200; 2222 East Cliff Drive).

A main organizer of fishing trips in Santa Cruz is **Stagnaro's** on the Municipal Wharf (☎ 408-427-2334). The skipper, Ken Stagnaro, is a fourth-generation fisherman. They specialize in deep sea rock cod and salmon fishing trips.

Gateway Adventure Tours (☎ 408-479-4981) in Santa Cruz, operates from the Crow's Nest Restaurant in the harbor and offers Marine Sanctuary tours, whale watching, and private charters.

Pacific Yachting and Sailing in Santa Cruz (☎ 408-423-7245; 790 Mariner Park Way) has a fleet of sailing yachts from 27-43 feet. They have a sailing school, bareboat charters, and skippered charters.

W. H. Stark Schooner Sailing (☎ 408-462-2208; 1400 Wharf Road, Capitola) offers sailings on the 44-foot Stark for two- or five-hour Monterey Bay Sanctuary tours and fishing trips, operating on a regular schedule March-October.

Whale Watching

In this area the deep sea fishing and whale watching on the water occurs mainly from fishing boats that transform themselves to whale watching excursions. See *Boating* for more.

From shore, whale watching is possible at **Point Lobos** south of Monterey when the gray whales migrate south in winter.

Whale watching, in the winter season, December-February, is a major activity in Monterey. In fact, the city of Monterey celebrates with a month-long Whale Fest to mark the journey that the Pacific gray whales make each year from their summer feeding grounds off Alaska to their winter birthing lagoons in Baja, Mexico – especially Scammon's Lagoon. Hunted to the brink of extinction, the Pacific gray whales have now returned to healthy numbers. Fishing boats on the Wharf become whale watching boats in winter. **Monterey Bay Whale Watch & Nature Cruise** (☎ 408-375-4658) assures that each of its three-hour trips has a marine biologist aboard.

For fishing trips from Monterey, one more provider **is Chris' Fishing Trips** (☎ 408-375-5951; 48 Fisherman's Wharf). The boat goes out for salmon or cod, depending on the season and what's hitting.

Monterey Sport Fishing and Whale Watching (☎ 408-372-2203; 90 Fisherman's Wharf, offers the full panoply of fishing, cruising charters, and whalewatching, depending on the seasonal market.

In Moss Landing, north of Santa Cruz, another provider of fishing and charters/cruisers is **Tom's Sportfishing** (☎ 408-633-2564).

Observing eagles from a tour boat on **Lake San Antonio** is a special on-the-water nature trip available here. Lake San Antonio, inland from Big Sur at the town of Bradley, is one of the largest winter habitats for eagles in California. Eagle watch boat tours in this county park are available January and February, ☎ 408-385-8322.

Shore fishing occurs all along the coast for perch and other near-shore species. One place to start is the **Santa Cruz Wharf**, which extends a mile into the ocean. The Stagnaro operation can provide bait and fishing advice for shore/pier fishing. See **Stagnaro's Fishing Trips**.

Capitola Boat and Bait (☎ 408-462-2208; 1400 Wharf Road, Capitola) is a multi-faceted fishing resource. They offer skiff rentals for near-shore fishing, charter fishing trips, two-hour Marine Sanctuary sailing tours, equipment rental, bait and tackle, the full nitty gritty for the angler along the California coast.

Santa Cruz Sportfishing (☎ 408-426-4690; Upper Yacht Harbor, Dock H) offers charter boat fishing, Monterey Bay Sanctuary tours, and whale watching. One of their vessels is a 50-foot craft known as the *Makaira*.

Surfing/Windsurfing

Surfing is so popular in Santa Cruz and the layout of the surfing territory is so unusual and accessible to everyone that it is described in some detail under *Touring Santa Cruz*. The topography is such that the surfers zoom by right under the eyes of the hikers and bikers on the West Cliff Trail.

If you want to do it yourself, surfing, windsurfing, and kayaking lessons/equipment rentals are available on the beach in front of the **Westcoast Santa Cruz Hotel**, adjacent to the Boardwalk. This Cowell Beach scene is the hangout for a provider known as Club Ed (☎ 408-459-9283 or 800-287-7873). Surfboard rentals are also available on the beach at the Boardwalk from City of Santa Cruz Beach Rentals (☎ 408-429-3110). They offer boogie-boards, surfboards, wetsuits, and fins.

Windsurfing is popular at **Waddell Beach** on the San Mateo Coast. The combination of wind and good beach access make this public park setting a favorite for windsurfers.

Scuba Diving

Scuba diving is popular both in Monterey and at Monastery Beach near Point Lobos. In Monterey, along Cannery Row, scuba divers walk into the ocean at San Carlos Beach, utilizing a rare walk-in access site. This is a particularly congenial place for new divers to get their certifications. Showers are provided on the beach to rinse off the salt water after a dive. Some area hotels also provider lockers for scuba equipment. For details on the scuba scene in Monterey, contact the dive shop **Aquarius**, ☎ 408-375-1933; 2040 Del Monte Avenue.

In the Air

Ballooning

Ballooning takes off from the Marina Airport. The provider is Mike Eakins of **Balloons by the Sea** (☎ 800-464-6420). Balloons launch at dawn inland from Marina and drift down the Salinas Valley.

Scenic Flying-Skydiving

Marina State Beach and the **Marina Airport**, both north of Monterey, have become the major center for air sports in the region. Hanggliders launch at Marina State Beach. The novice can also take hang glider lessons here. Inland a few miles, off Reservation Road, the Marina Airport has outfitters for skydiving, ballooning, and tandem ultralight flying.

For hang gliding at the Marina State Beach, contact **Western Hanggliders** (☎ 408-384-2622). At the airport, the main organizer of air sports is Mike Eakins of the **Monterey Bay Aero Sportsplex** (☎ 408-384-3483 or 888-229-5867). For ultralight tandem flying, contact **Kamron Blevins** (☎ 408-883-9142). An hour-long flight with Blevins takes you out over the water to see dolphins and whales in season. Western Hanggliders can also take the fearless flyer on a tandem Big Sur glide off a 3,000-foot cliff.

Hang Gliding

Hang gliding takes place at Marina Beach. Lessons are available. On a busy day there may be 25 gliders in the air here. The organizer is **Western Hanggliders** (☎ 408-384-2622).

Parasailing

Parasailing at the Municipal Wharf in Santa Cruz is organized by **Pacific Parasail** (☎ 408-423-3545; 58 Municipal Wharf).

■ Where to Stay & Eat

Accommodations in Monterey

Among good lodging choices in downtown Monterey are the **Hotel Pacific** (☎ 800-554-5542; 300 Pacific Street, Monterey, CA 93940. $$$) and the **Monterey Marriott** (☎ 408-649-4234; 350 Calle Principale, Monterey, CA 93940. $$$). Both hotels are centrally located near the Monterey Fisherman's Wharf. The Pacific has a pleasing early-California architecture that blends in with the surroundings. The Marriott is elevated with a good view of the Wharf from its rooftop restaurant.

The **Doubletree Monterey** (☎ 408-649-4511; 2 Portola Plaza, Monterey, CA 93940. $$-$$$) occupies perhaps the choicest piece of property in the region. The Doubletree literally opens to the Custom House on the central plaza of old Monterey. You start the "Path of History" walking tour through the Doubletree environs. A statue of Portola identifies the area as Portola Plaza, lobby of the Doubletree. Adjacent to the Monterey Conference Center, the Doubletree has a large, open lobby and sumptuous rooms built in clusters around eucalyptus and cineraria gardens. Pool and tennis courts are available.

Monterey Plaza Hotel (☎ 408-646-1700; 400 Cannery Row, Monterey, CA 93940. $$$) provides an extraordinary view of Monterey Bay from an expanse of bayview windows and balconies, with Fisherman's Wharf just three blocks away. Sea otters, sea lions, and shorebirds cavort offshore. The decor of the hotel is pink Italian marble, with teak wood and brass accents, a theme that begins in expansive lobbies and hallways and extends to its 285 rooms.

The Victorian architecture of Pacific Grove is a carefully nurtured city amenity. Many Victorians have been turned into bed and breakfast inns. They are along Oceanview Boulevard or a couple of blocks inland.

Victorian B&Bs

Be sure to see the following:

Centrella Hotel (☎ 800-233-3372; 612 Central Avenue, Pacific Grove, CA 93950.$$-$$$) has 28 rooms, including attic suites and hot tubs.

Martine Inn (☎ 800-852-5588255; Ocean View Boulevard, Pacific Grove, CA 93950. $$$) has 19 antique-filled rooms, private baths, and views of the ocean from its front parlor.

Seven Gables Inn (☎ 408-372-4341; 555 Ocean View Boulevard, Pacific Grove, CA 93950. $$-$$$) is a photogenic Victorian B&B with 14 rooms, ocean views, and afternoon tea.

The **Gosby House Inn** (☎ 800-527-8828; 643 Lighthouse House Avenue, Pacific Grove, CA 93950. $$-$$$) in downtown Pacific Grove, offers a variety of accommodations either upstairs at the Victorian inn or next door.

The **Lodge at Pebble Beach** (☎ 408-624-381; PO Box 1128, Pebble Beach, CA 93953. $$$) and its sister facility, **Inn at Spanish Bay** (☎ 800-654-9300) are the choice places to stay along the 17-Mile Drive.

Carmel Lodgings

Among special Carmel lodgings is the **Mission Ranch** (☎ 408-624-6436; 26270 Dolores Street, Carmel, CA 93923. $$-$$$). Mission Ranch is a sprawling 20-acre property now owned by Clint Eastwood. The historic building here is the Martin Family farmhouse, associated with the lands around the Carmel Mission. You can lodge in rooms at the farmhouse or in outlying cottages, all overlooking the Carmel River drainage. **Mission Ranch Restaurant** (☎ 408-625-9040) offers dinners, Saturday lunch and Sunday brunch emphasizing local seafood.

Typical of Carmel's lodgings are cozy, small inns (never call them motels, a word forbidden here). One good example is the **Dolphin Inn** (☎ 408-624-5356 or 800-433-4732; PO Box 1900, 4th and San Carlos, Carmel, CA 93921. $$-$$$) run by Bob and Lorraine Luce. The Luces are knowledgeable observers of the region, able to guide you to anything from a hike to a restaurant. The inn has cozy rooms, with a picnic basket breakfast and morning paper, and a pool for swimming on sunny days.

Quail Lodge Resort (☎ 408-624-1581 or 800-538-9516; 8205 Valley Greens Drive, Carmel, CA 93923. $$$) in rustic and sunny Carmel Valley is one of the region's top resorts.

The **Tickle Pink Inn** (☎ 408-624-1244 or 800-635-4774; 155 Highland Drive, Carmel, CA 93923, four miles south of Carmel off Highway 1. $$$) has stunning ocean views from an elevated position. Perched high on a hillside overlooking the coast, the rooms are mainly large suites with private balconies. Fireplaces and minor courtesies such as washing your car windows early each morning suggest the level of service. This little-publicized lodging has depended on word-of-mouth to fill its rooms for two decades. Guests enjoy all expected amenities. The name requires some explanation. This property was once owned by a Senator and Mrs. Tickle, who liked pink flowers.

Big Sur Lodgings

In Big Sur the **Post Ranch Inn** (☎ 408-667-2200, Highway 1, PO Box 219, Big Sur, CA 93920. $$$) is the newest lodging. Post Ranch Inn places you high over the sea in a treehouse and cliff house environment. **Restaurant Sierra Mar** features contemporary cuisine, bar, and a warm basking pool on the cliff.

Another alternative in the Monterey/Santa Cruz region would be a condo or house on the sand dune beaches west of Watsonville. The lodging entity here is known as **Pajaro Dunes**, and features private beachfront homes and condos close to or on one of the loveliest sand beaches of the Golden State. This is a contemplative and quiet lodging choice, west of agricultural fields near Watsonville. If you savor sunsets, privacy, and the quiet of a beach

Monterey, Santa Cruz & Big Sur

environment away from it all, Pajaro Dunes (2661 Beach Road, Watsonville, $$-$$$) is an excellent option. The rental agency, **Holzman & Daw,** at ☎ 800-564-1771, handles many of the houses and condos.

Accommodations in Santa Cruz

Santa Cruz offers a range of lodgings for travelers with different styles.

For a cozy B&B, a good choice is **Babbling Brook Inn** (☎ 408-427-2437 or 800-866-1131; 1025 Laurel Street, Santa Cruz, CA 95060. $$-$$$). Owner Helen King has fashioned each room around the theme of an Impressionist painter. An actual brook runs through the property. Fresh-baked cookies are available in the afternoon, wine and cheese are served in the evening, and a breakfast of fruit and hot pastries is set out buffet-style in the morning. The inn offers plenty of local travel and restaurant information.

For a resort and condo-type setting overlooking the ocean, consider **Seascape Resort** in Aptos (☎ 408-688-6800 or 800-929-7727; One Seascape Resort Drive, Aptos, CA 95003. $$$). Seascape has swimming pools, its own beach access, and roomy condo units, plus one of the area's premier golf courses.

Within town, the classic hotel is the **Westcoast Santa Cruz Hotel** (☎ 408-426-4330; 175 W. Cliff Drive, Santa Cruz, CA 95060. $$$) above Cowell Beach. The hotel is located right on the beach and next to the Beach Boardwalk.

Still another option would be to rent a local house. One such house, **Black Pearl Cottage/Grey Tower Villa**, is superbly sited, overlooking the beach at 100 and 104 Second Avenue, Santa Cruz, CA 95062; ☎ 408-429-5377. $$$.

All ages of travelers are welcome at the **Santa Cruz Youth Hostel** (☎ 408-423-8304; 321 Main Street, Santa Cruz, CA 95060. $), which is located in the restored Camelita Cottages on Beach Hill, two blocks from the Boardwalk. Going north of Santa Cruz, there are similar Youth Hostel lodgings in the historic lighthouse at **Pigeon Point** (☎ 415-879-0633).

If driving north to San Francisco along Coast Highway 1, lodging options include the **Davenport Inn** (☎ 408-425-1818 or 800-870-1817; 31 Davenport Avenue, Davenport, CA 95017. $$) and Carol Mickelsen's **San Benito House** (☎ 415-726-3425; 356 Main Street, Half Moon Bay, CA 94019. $$). Another B&B in the Half Moon Bay area, close to the water and fishing boats, is **Pillar Point Inn** (☎ 415-728-7377; 380 Capistrano Road, El Granada, CA 94018. $$$).

Restaurants in Monterey

 With 350 white-tablecloth restaurants to choose from in the Monterey-Carmel region, prepare to have your taste buds delighted.

Some eateries are unpretentious places you might stumble upon, such as **Forge in the Forest** (☎ 408-624-2233; Corner of Junipero Street and Fifth Avenue. $$) in Carmel. Amidst a backdrop of historic blacksmith equipment, menu choices include the French onion or split pea soups, perhaps followed by a roast beef sandwich. Forge in the Forest is a cozy brick-and-ivy place for a drink or food, indoors or outside, around fireplaces in both locations, depending on the sunny or foggy outlook of the day. Like lodgings in Carmel, the restaurants have a dose of quaintness.

The parallel to Forge in the Forest on Cannery Row might be **Captain's Cove** (☎408-372-5411; 643 Cannery Row. $$), run by the De Oliveira family. Neither pretentious nor outrageous in price, the Captain's Cove serves a delicious oyster stew or the specialty of the region, squid, as a stuffed calamari. Squid surpasses salmon as a California commercial catch. When properly cooked, which is lightly, squid from Monterey Bay is a tasty regional specialty.

Moving on to the realm of fine dining, **Simpson's** in Carmel is a special place. A family affair run by the Littles and open for dinner only, Simpson's (☎ 408-624-5755; San Carlos Street and Fifth Avenue. $$-$$$) has Larry Little as your chef, Jeni Little doing the pastry, and Dana or Tara Little as maître d's. Patriarch Bob Little manages the fishing boat that brings in the fresh fish from Monterey Bay. Simpson's emphasizes dining rather than fast-food feeding, catering to the discriminating locals. The bright colors of the restaurant, especially the Maxfield Parrish-imitation murals, are meant to match the intense tastes. Simpson's has some comfort food, from iceberg lettuce wedge salads to angel food cake desserts, but mostly it's comfort food with innovation, such as mashed potatoes (only when Idaho potatoes are available) or a wild-rice pancake. The tastes explode with veal scaloppini or the seafood pasta, perhaps washed down with a Watsonville wine, River Run 1993 Zinfandel. Dessert might be an unusual liqueur, as Larry Little suggests, a River Run 1994 Zinfandel late harvest reserve that compares with a French Chateau Yquem or a German trockenberenauslese.

The **Grill on Ocean Avenue** (☎ 408-624-2569; Ocean near Dolores Street, Carmel. $$) emphasizes innovative European-style specialties with the freshest possible ingredients. Try the abalone, salmon, veal, or game-of-the-week, which may be deer. Delicious appetizers include escargot in French bread and mozzarella cheese pastries. Quiet atmosphere with a fireplace and warm decor accompanies exceptional service.

For breakfast or lunch in Carmel, try **Katy's Place** (☎ 408-624-0199; on Mission Street between Fifth and Sixth avenues. $-$$), a Carmel institution that opens daily at 7 am.

Hog's Breath Inn (☎ 408-625-1044; San Carlos between Fifth and Sixth avenues, Carmel. $-$$) is an English-pub style restaurant partly owned by former mayor, Clint Eastwood. Try the Dirty Harry sandwich. The setting is outdoors, next to an oak tree and in front of a bucolic mural.

Mission Ranch Restaurant (☎ 408-625-1044; 26270 Dolores Street, Carmel. $$) is situated on a large property along Carmel River. Ranch and restaurant are owned by Clint Eastwood. The restaurant, open for dinner, Saturday lunch and Sunday brunch only, features California seafood. Try the calamari omelet.

Old Monterey Café (☎ 408-646-1021; 489 Alvarado Street, Monterey. $-$$) is a friendly favorite of the locals, emphasizing informality, hearty food, and a convenient downtown Monterey locale. The specialty is tasty omelet breakfasts served until 3 pm. It's open for breakfast and lunch only.

Amarin Thai (☎ 408-373-8811; 807 Cannery Row, Monterey. $$) offers Thai food with the exceptional tastes and flavors of Bangkok court cuisine. The setting emphasizes relaxed Thai hospitality. Close to the Aquarium, this is a good choice for lunch after an Aquarium visit.

Fandango (☎ 408-372-3456; 223 17th Street, Pacific Grove. $$) combines European country-style cooking with a lively atmosphere. Try the paella, couscous, or Greek lamb shank.

Tarpy's (☎ 408-647-1444; 2999 Monterey/Salinas Highway, Del Ray Oaks. $$) is a gregarious restaurant in a historic roadhouse. Try the molasses bourbon pork chop or venison rib chop.

Domenico's (☎ 408- 372-3655; Fisherman's Wharf, Monterey. $$-$$$) is a respected Wharf restaurant, noted for its Italian specialties and its fish. The setting puts you close to the Wharf fleet, sea lions, and pelicans.

The **Sardine Factory** (☎ 408-373-3775; 701 Wave Street, Cannery Row, Monterey. $$-$$$) blends the nostalgia of Steinbeck's old Cannery Row with an elegant menu of seafood and steaks. Formerly a 24-hour cantina, the Sardine Factory has several dining rooms, the most popular of which is the glass-domed Conservatory.

Restaurants in Santa Cruz

 The overall trend toward ever finer dining in California finds ample expression in Santa Cruz. An abundance of local seafood and a growing number of area farmers specializing in small-scale agriculture, with the freshest vegetables and herbs, fuel the discriminating demands of local chefs.

The **Bittersweet Bistro** (☎ 408-662-9799; 787 Rio Del Mar Boulevard. $$-$$$) in Rio Del Mar, a town adjacent to Santa Cruz, epitomizes this trend. Chef Thomas Vinolus and his wife Elizabeth have raised the fine-dining standards of the region.

The Vinolus family has created an American bistro with a Mediterranean flare, fashioning all their food from scratch, emphasizing local ingredients, from Tomales Bay oysters to regional goat cheese from Davenport. Competing on quality rather than price, they serve sumptuous antipasto plates, venison entrées, and yellowtail fish dishes that keep the customers coming back. From an exceptional wine list, you might choose a California Merlot from Mt. Eden. Their triple-threat chocolate desserts are famous locally. Thomas Vinolus is a major fan of the local Farmers Markets, which unite specialty herb and vegetable growers directly with their patrons.

Bittersweet Bistro is a newcomer, complementing the established fine-dining restaurant of the area, **Shadowbrook**, (☎ 408-475-1511, 1750 Wharf Road, Capitola. $$-$$$). Shawdowbrook has long been recognized as one of the area's most romantic dining settings. Guests get to Shadowbrook via a quaint cable car.

For a romantic, cozy, candlelit environment within the city, choose the Northern Italian restaurant known as **Gabriella Café** (☎ 408-457-1677; 910 Cedar Street. $$), where the potato leek soup might precede the portabello mushroom entrée. Alternatively, the grilled octopus appetizer might be followed by a warm spinach salad. Gabriella Café is an intimate place with fresh flowers and charm.

India Joze (☎ 408-427-3554; 1001 Center Street. $-$$) offers intriguing Middle Eastern, Greek, and Mexican fare. This is inventive taste, strong on curries and coriander, in a casual setting. Try a curry dish or a Greek fisherman's soup, perhaps washed down by a local beer, Pacific Porter from the Santa Cruz Brewing Company. This is a particularly good and sunny lunch spot. India Joze is also a congenial place for dinner before the performance at the adjacent **Actors Theatre** (☎ 408-425-1003), the main theatre group in the region.

For tasty Mexican food in Santa Cruz, try **El Palomar** (☎ 408-425-7575; 1336 Pacific Avenue. $-$$), located downtown along Pacific Avenue in a handsome room with a high vaulted ceiling. Start with margaritas, then try their award-winning burrito de camarones, noted for its shrimp and whole beans in the tortilla wrap. Another good choice would be tacos de huachinango, which consists of charbroiled red snapper in a soft or crisp corn tortilla, topped with sour cream and guacamole.

If out on the Wharf, you might catch a fish dinner at **Sea Cloud** (☎ 408-458-9393; Municipal Wharf. $$), while watching the bay and shoreline scene.

Zoccoli's deli and pasta house (☎ 408-423-1717; 431 Front Street. $-$$) offers a full range of deli sandwiches and picnic fixings, plus a few tables on Pacific Avenue where you can enjoy a sandwich.

The **Santa Cruz Coffee Roasting Company** (☎ 408-459-0100; 1330 Pacific Avenue) is the place for your latte or cappuccino. From their tables in front you can watch the passing parade of locals.

The **Crow's Nest** (☎ 408-476-4560; Santa Cruz Yacht Harbor) is a romantic spot for a drink at sunset overlooking the harbor and sailboats.

Brew pubs are flourishing all over Northern California. In Santa Cruz, try the Pacific Porter or other hand-crafted brews at the **Santa Cruz Brewing Company** (☎ 408-429-8838; 516 Front Street). Another local brew pub with food is **The Seabright Brewery** (☎ 408-426-2739; 519 Seabright Avenue). Try their Pelican Pale Ale.

If traveling north from Santa Cruz to San Francisco, here are three good restaurant options.

Duarte's in Pescadero (☎ 415-879-0464. $$) is a classic destination dining stop in a small agricultural town. Try the green chili soup, perhaps followed by Dungeness crab, and don't overlook the olallieberry pie dessert. The local wine company, Obester in Half Moon Bay, might provide a Sauvignon Blanc for the occasion.

San Benito House (☎ 415-726-3425; 356 Main Street. $$), in Half Moon Bay, has an ever-changing menu of fresh regional specialties.

Moss Beach Distillery (☎ 415-728-5595; Moss Beach. $$) offers a tasty salmon, excellent sunset viewing, and tales of a resident ghost.

Camping & RV

South from Monterey, there are good campsites at the major state parks along the Big Sur coast.

The first major park you encounter south of Point Lobos is the **Andrew Molera State Park** (☎ 408-667-2315) located on Highway 1 almost 20 miles south of Carmel. Molera's boundaries encompass the Big Sur River watershed. This is a walkers' and campers' park. For the day tripper, the park offers a fine picnic area, with tables, in a grove of alders at the trailhead parking lot. Molera Beach awaits visitors who make a mile-long walk to the mouth of the Big Sur River. Appealing trails lead along the bluffs. You pass an old log cabin, once part of the Molera Ranch. Molera park encompasses four miles of ocean front and 16 miles of trails, including a River Trail and a Ridge Trail. First-come, first-served camping is available. You walk in with your gear a third of a mile to the campsites. Small rainbow trout are visible in the Big Sur River in summer. During the winter, salmon and sea-going steelhead trout fight their way upstream to spawn. A trail-riding concession, **Molera Horseback Tours** (☎ 408-625-5486) offers scenic horseback excursions.

Molera is a good place to view the songbirds and shorebirds of the region and to celebrate the **California Sea Otter Reserve**, which stretches all along this Big Sur Coast. The sea otters are an environmental success story, narrowly surviving a brush with extinction in the 19th century, when the Russians hunted them for their prized pelts. Now they have returned and even extended their range, decimating the abalone fishery (sea otters need to eat a third of their weight each day in shellfish just to maintain their $103°$ temperature in the $55°$ water).

The grand camping stop in Big Sur is 821-acre **Pfeiffer Big Sur State Park** (☎ 408-667-2315), where you'll find redwood forests, miles of trails, 218 campsites (no hookups), rangers to lead hikes and give talks, and a two-mile beach. The campgrounds fill quickly, especially in summer and on weekends, so make reservations early (☎ 800-444-7275).

Two miles north of Pfeiffer is a private campground, **Big Sur Campground** (☎ 408-667-2322). The private campgrounds complement the state park camps in the region. The private camps respond to camper demand for functioning hot showers and dependably clean restrooms with entrepreneurial energy. They cater to RV travelers, who want hookups, as well as tent campers. Generally, both the private and state park camps have scenic redwood environments, adjacent to streams. Big Sur Campgrounds has a few A-frame cottages for drive-in camping.

Camping Santa Cruz

Santa Cruz enjoys excellent beach access camping from cliffs east of the city. Choice campsites are at **New Brighton State Beach Park** (☎ 408-475-4850; 1500 Park Avenue, Capitola) and at **Manresa State Beach** (☎ 408-761-1795; 205 Manresa Road, La Selva Beach). All California state park camps can be booked by calling ☎ 800-444-7275. New Brighton has 115 sites and hot showers, but no RV hookups. Manresa has 63 walk-in campsites for tent campers only.

There is a full-service **KOA** about 20 minutes south of Santa Cruz along Highway 1 at 1186 San Andreas Road; ☎ 408-722-2377.

Several of the mountain redwood parks in the hills behind Santa Cruz offer good camping, sometimes in the redwoods. As with the beach state park camps, the reservations need to be made at ☎ 800-444-7275. The parks include **Big Basin** (☎ 408-338-8860; 21600 Big Basin Way, Boulder Creek), which has 36 tent cabins and 147 tent camping sites, with hot showers, a food store, and many miles of hiking trails. **Henry Cowell Redwoods State Park** (☎ 408-335-4598; 101 North Big Trees Park Road, Felton) has 4,000 acres of redwoods. There are 112 camping sites, available to tent campers and for trailers up to 24 feet and campers to 31 feet, but no RV hookups. Backpacking camping sites in the wilderness are available at **Forest of Nisene Marks State Park** (☎ 408-763-7062; Aptos Creek Road, Aptos). All the redwood parks of the area are discussed in detail under *Hiking & Backpacking Santa Cruz.*

■ Kayaking Elkhorn Slough

An Antidote to Environmental Pessimism

By Lee Foster

I am kayaking up California's Elkhorn Slough, north of Monterey, looking for the curlews, herons, and the snowy egrets. Thousands of birds rest on the banks and cluster in the waters.

The week before this kayaking trip I received a letter typical of what we all hear and see every day. The letter, from the World Wildlife Fund, said, "Without firing a shot, we may kill one-fifth of all species of life on this planet in the next 20 years." After outlining the rapacious activities of the most destructive species yet to evolve, my species, the letter closed with the admonition, "Extinction can come quickly. And extinction is forever."

The daily assault of bad news about everything from the wasteland pollution of Eastern Europe to the clearcut logging that wipes out endemic species in a pocket of a Brazilian rain forest makes me long for an immersion in something we are doing right, some small element in the good-news environmental story. Kayaking up Elkhorn Slough is a good place to start.

Fortunately, I am kayaking with Jeff Shrock, who has been perusing for years this seven-mile-long wetland, fully 2,500 acres of submerged and semi-submerged lands. He sees the same birds as I do, but knows their names and their calls intimately. Jeff alerts me to the magnificent bird resource that Elkhorn Slough represents.

"My greatest thrill as a kayaker comes when flocks of sandpipers are present," says Jeff. "There are thousands of birds in the flocks. They come flying at the kayak in dense numbers, directly, head on. When they reach the nose of the kayak, they split, veering off, half to each side, all guided by some seamless and beautiful intelligence, all directed by some special navigational skill. It's a wondrous experience to watch them up close."

Some birding records have been set at Elkhorn Slough. One skilled birder identified 116 species here at a single site. One Christmas day, the traditional Audubon bird-counting day around the country, 280 species of birds were counted here. These are records in birding circles. I can't help but realize that this estuary could have easily been built over and destroyed. Probably there would have been a modest but perceptible drop in bodyfat for millions of migrating birds as a result. What is remarkable is that Elkhorn has been saved, the largest remaining wetland between San Francisco Bay and Morro Bay.

I did not see some of the rarest and most endangered birds of Elkhorn, such as the snowy plovers, but Jeff assured me they were there. Moreover, their habitat was being monitored and controlled. For example, their nesting areas have been caged against foxes.

The present surge in kayaking interest around Monterey is, I realize, the second wave of kayaking in the region's history. Ironically, while the modern kayakers are ecotourists out to savor nature, the earlier ones were skilled Aleut Native Americans, in the employ of the Russians, systematically exterminating the sea otters for their pelts. So effective were the Aleut hunters that the sea otter was believed to be extinct. But, fortunately, a few wily individuals survived.

I paddle hard as we push through pickleweed vegetation in the slough. These estuarine marshes are some of the most productive acres on the earth, surpassing the productivity of a corn field in Kansas. One sobering fact that Jeff alerts me to is the geologic basis of all life here. After the Loma Prieta Earthquake of 1989, the slough dropped about one foot, radically changing the ability of plants and animals to survive in their specialized ecological niches.

On another occasion, I have approached Elkhorn Slough on foot. There is a fine visitor center located up the road from Moss Landing. An exceptional range of nature books, as expected, are on sale here. From the center, you can walk five miles of hiking trails around the Slough.

Elkhorn Slough is a destination for four seasons. Spring is for nesting birds and abundant wildflowers. Summer is a time of lush, green fecundity. Autumn is the showy migration period when bird populations soar. Winter is the harsh season when the survivors persist. Each season has its pleasures, which a lifetime can only begin to appreciate.

Elkhorn is a prominent example in the Watchable Wildlife movement. The movement suggests the advance of non-consumptive outdoor activities, watching the birds rather than shooting them. The constituency for Watchable Wildlife is much larger than for consumptive wildlife behavior, hunting and fishing, which have their place in certain rural environments.

Falcon Press, has come out with a book on each of the western states, indicating good places to watch for wildlife. Elkhorn Slough is one of the 150 celebrated places noted in their *California Wildlife Viewing Guide*. The books are lovely, filled with photos of birds, animals, and habitats.

The number of nature-appreciators at Elkhorn Slough is destined to surpass by manyfold the consumptive hunters. With cameras and footprints, these new-style tourists will eventually contribute to local economies in a burst of dollars. Globally, this is obvious in places such as Kenya, where viewing the wildlife is far more valuable than killing it. Preserving the wildlife is critical, in Kenya, to the survival of the human species, the Kenyan. Travelers will come to Kenya to enjoy the wildlife. Without wildlife, no travelers will come. The ecotourism at Elkhorn Slough is also more profitable for Monterey County than a farmed, paved-over, or duck-hunted Elkhorn Slough. Watching the wildlife is a sustainable activity, providing employment for the locals, such as Jeff Shrock, who devotes his life to kayak tourism. Ecotourism, like all tourism, must be profitable to be sustainable.

Recently, Elkhorn became slightly more protected as a peripheral part of a larger, new designation, the **Monterey Bay National Marine Sanctuary**. This is a 5,000-square-mile entity, including the offshore Monterey Bay Canyon, fully a third of the length of the Grand Canyon and twice as deep. Mining and dumping will be controlled in these waters, but fisheries will be continued and enhanced. The natural resources will be conserved. Some 20,000 gray whales pass through the sanctuary twice a year, going from the Arctic to Baja in January for the birthing of new whales and then returning to the Arctic in late spring for the explosion of krill, their food source, which occurs in the chilly, nutrient-rich, light-blessed waters of the Arctic. The new Marine Sanctuary includes 400 miles of coastline, such as Elkhorn Slough, and is the nation's largest protected marine region, one and a half times larger than any national park in the lower 48 states.

The place to see this Marine Wildlife Sanctuary, short of a kayaking trip or a wetsuit immersion, is, of course, at the Monterey Aquarium. The avowed purpose of the Monterey Bay Aquarium, simply stated, is to stimulate interest, increase knowledge, and promote stewardship of Monterey Bay and the world's ocean environment through innovative exhibits, public education, and scientific research. David Packard, the industrialist, had the means and exercised the daily direction to create an excitement about nature that is fundamental if we are to save the planet. About 2½ million visitors a year leave the aquarium with a renewed sense of the joy inherent in being one among 525 species in the aquarium. We are a species with a special responsibility to nurture the others in which we take delight. The new phase of aquarium development focuses on concerns over open ocean and deep sea environments, celebrating the deep canyons in the sea off Monterey.

Near the aquarium, the downtown Monterey Plaza has been completed with an element critical to understanding man's role in the local environmental story. The final element in the mix is the **Maritime Museum of Monterey**, recognizing that the ultimate success or failure of environmental efforts here is linked to the wise use of the sea. Monterey's ethnic harvesters of the sea are one focus of the exhibits. One becomes familiar with the Portuguese whalers, the Chinese squid fishermen, the Sicilian sardine catchers, and even the turn-of-the-century Japanese hard-hat divers seeking abalone.

As I kayak up Elkhorn Slough, passing the dozing harbor seals, I find my mental health improving. Elkhorn Slough is one of my personal antidotes to environmental pessimism. My hope is that you, too, will find such antidotes in your experience.

Index

Index

Index